CAMBRIDGE STUDIES IN
MEDIEVAL LIFE AND THOUGHT

Edited by M. D. Knowles, Litt.D., F.B.A.
*Honorary Fellow of Peterhouse and Emeritus Regius Professor of Modern History
in the University of Cambridge*

NEW SERIES VOL. XI

GILBERT FOLIOT AND
HIS LETTERS

GILBERT FOLIOT AND HIS LETTERS

DOM ADRIAN MOREY, 1904 –

Monk of Downside Abbey, Headmaster of
The Oratory School

AND

C . N . L . BROOKE

Professor of Mediaeval History
University of Liverpool

CAMBRIDGE

AT THE UNIVERSITY PRESS

1965

PUBLISHED BY
THE SYNDICS OF THE CAMBRIDGE UNIVERSITY PRESS

Bentley House, 200 Euston Road, London, N.W. 1
American Branch: 32 East 57th Street, New York, N.Y. 10022
West African Office: P.O. Box 33, Ibadan, Nigeria

©

CAMBRIDGE UNIVERSITY PRESS

1965

Printed in Great Britain at the University Printing House, Cambridge
(Brooke Crutchley, University Printer)

LIBRARY OF CONGRESS CATALOGUE
CARD NUMBER: 65–17204

MEMORIAE

VIRI DOCTISSIMI

ZACHARIAE NUGENT BROOKE

QUI NOS OLIM IN HAEC STUDIA

IPSE PRAELUDENS INSTIGAVIT

OPUS QUALITERCUMQUE CONFECTUM

DISCIPULUS MAGISTRO PATRI FILIUS

D.D.D.

CONTENTS

CHARTS

PREFACE

This book had its origin in a plan made some twenty-five years ago by Dom Adrian Morey and the late Dr Z. N. Brooke for an edition of Gilbert Foliot's letters. The edition is now complete, and an account of the collaboration which produced it will be given in the preface to *The Letters and Charters of Gilbert Foliot*, which is also to be published by the Cambridge University Press. It was originally proposed to give the edition an elaborate introduction: it was felt that the man and his letters provided the opportunity for a series of studies, but not for an independent biography. The present book is indeed no biography; but the studies outgrew the frame of an introduction, and came to have a life and being of their own. Close as the link must be between the two books, it seemed desirable to publish the studies separately; and the kindness of Professor Knowles in accepting the book for this Series finally settled the matter. Although the letters still remain the starting-point for our enquiry, investigation of an able man who played a conspicuous part in the affairs of his day, and who reflects (we think) with singular fidelity the habitual assumptions and modes of thought of the clerical world and of the society in which he lived, should provide the subject for a coherent study; that at least has been our aim.

We have had constant help in our work from many friends and institutions: a fuller list will be given in the Preface to *The Letters and Charters*. Here we must record first and foremost the founder of our collaboration, who lived to plan the edition but not the present book; the dedication is a small token of what we owe to him. Mrs Brooke, whose interest in both works was warm and constant, lived to read the dedication, but not, to our special regret, to see the book in print. To Professor David Knowles we owe help and kindness and encouragement over many years, valuable advice and criticism in the later stages, and the honour of a place in the present Series.

Dom Adrian Morey is indebted to the Abbot and Community of Downside Abbey for constant support and assistance, and to the

Leverhulme Trustees whose generous grant made some essential research possible. C. N. L. Brooke began serious work on the book at Gonville and Caius College, Cambridge, and finished it in the University of Liverpool: to both institutions he is deeply indebted for the generous help they have provided; a term's leave and grants from the University through its Joint Committee on Research made some of the work possible.

We are indebted to Dr R. W. Hunt and the Council of the Royal Historical Society for permission to reproduce a passage quoted on p. 71; and to the Honorary Secretary and Council of the Honourable Society of Cymmrodorion for similar permission for the passages on pp. 72, 103–4. For help in reading the manuscript and making improvements and corrections we are particularly indebted to Dr Rosalind Brooke and to Dr H. Mayr-Harting. We have also had generous help from Dr Helen Clover, Professor G. Constable, Dr D. Luscombe, Dr D. J. A. Matthew, Dr Eleanor Rathbone, and Professor P. Stein. To all those named here, to the Syndics and staff of the Cambridge University Press, and to very many others who have helped us, we offer our warmest thanks.

It may be convenient to note here that the closely related priories Llanthony (Mon) and Lanthony (in Gloucester) have been deliberately and (we hope) consistently spelt differently. When chapter x was written, we were unaware that Miss Marjorie Jones's Oxford Thesis 'The Estates of Hereford Cathedral, 1066–1317' (1958) covered our period, as well as the thirteenth century: we would like to take this opportunity to refer students of the subject to it.

R.A.M.

C.N.L.B.

LIST OF ABBREVIATIONS

A full bibliography of sources will be given in *The Letters and Charters of Gilbert Foliot* (forthcoming).

Ann.	Annals of.
Ann. Mon.	*Annales Monastici*, ed. H. R. Luard, 5 vols., RS, 1864–9.
BIHR	*Bulletin of the Institute of Historical Research.*
BM	British Museum.
Bodl.	Bodleian Library, Oxford.
Capes	*Charters and Records of Hereford Cathedral*, ed. W. W. Capes, Cantilupe Society, Hereford, 1908.
Cart.	Cartulary of (see full list in G. R. C. Davis, *Medieval Cartularies of Great Britain*, London, 1958). Abbreviated references are given to the following:
Cart. Colchester	*Cartularium monasterii S. Johannis Baptiste de Colecestria*, ed. S. A. Moore, 2 vols., Roxburghe Club, London, 1897.
Cart. Eynsham	*Eynsham Cartulary*, ed. H. E. Salter, 2 vols., Oxford Historical Society, 1907–8.
Cart. Gloucester	*Historia et cartularium monasterii sancti Petri Gloucestriae*, ed. W. H. Hart, 3 vols., RS, 1863–7.
Cart. Oseney	*Cartulary of Oseney Abbey*, ed. H. E. Salter, 6 vols., Oxford Historical Society, 1929–36.
Cart. Ramsey	*Cartularium monasterii de Rameseia*, ed. W. H. Hart and P. A. Lyons, 3 vols., RS, 1884–93.
Cart. Wardon	*Cartulary of the Abbey of Old Wardon*, ed. G. H. Fowler, Bedfordshire Historical Record Society, XIII, 1930.
CDF	*Calendar of Documents preserved in France*, I, ed. J. H. Round, PRO Texts and Calendars, 1899.
CHJ	*Cambridge Historical Journal.*

Chron.   Chronicle of: especially the following:
   Chron. Evesham *Chronicon abbatiae de Evesham, ad annum 1418,*
                 ed. W. D. Macray, RS, 1863.
   Chron. Ramsey   *Chronicon abbatiae Rameseiensis,* ed. W. D.
                 Macray, RS, 1886.
Code   *Codex Iuris Civilis.*
Conway Davies   *Episcopal Acts and Cognate Documents relating*
                 to Welsh Dioceses, 1066–1272, ed. J. Conway
                 Davies, I, II, Historical Society of the
                 Church in Wales, 1946–8.
CP   *Complete Peerage,* revised edition, ed. Vicary
                 Gibbs, G. H. White, *et alii,* London, 1910–
                 59.
CS   *Celt and Saxon: Studies in the early British Bor-*
                 der, ed. N. K. Chadwick, Cambridge, 1963.
Diceto   *Radulfi de Diceto decani Lundoniensis Opera*
                 Historica, ed. W. Stubbs, 2 vols., RS, 1876.
Duggan   C. Duggan, *Twelfth-century Decretal Collec-*
                 tions and their importance in English History,
                 London, 1963.
EHR   *English Historical Review.*
Ep.   *Epistola* (with number of letter in a letter
                 collection).
Extra   *Liber Extra,* i.e. *Decretales Gregorii IX,* ed.
                 E. Friedberg, *Corpus Iuris Canonici,* II,
                 Leipzig, 1881.
EYC   *Early Yorkshire Charters,* ed. W. Farrer (vols.
                 I–III, Edinburgh, 1914–16) and Sir Charles
                 Clay (vols. IV–XI, Yorkshire Archaeological
                 Society, Record Series, 1935–63).
Gervase   *The Historical Works of Gervase of Canterbury,*
                 ed. W. Stubbs, 2 vols., RS, 1879–80.
Gesta   *Gesta Stephani,* ed. and trans. K. R. Potter,
                 NMT, 1955.
GFL   *The Letters and Charters of Gilbert Foliot,* ed.
                 A. Morey and C. N. L. Brooke (forth-
                 coming).

Gibbs	*Early Charters of the Cathedral Church of St Paul, London*, ed. M. Gibbs, Camden third series, LVIII, 1939.
Gratian	*Gratiani Decretum*, ed. E. Friedberg, *Corpus Iuris Canonici*, I, Leipzig, 1879.
Hale	*The Domesday of St Paul's*, ed. W. H. Hale, Camden Soc., 1858.
HKF	W. Farrer, *Honors and Knights' Fees*, 3 vols., London, 1923–4, Manchester, 1925.
HMC	*Historical Manuscripts Commission.*
JL	P. Jaffé, *Regesta Pontificum Romanorum*, ed. W. Wattenbach, S. Löwenfeld, F. Kaltenbrunner and P. Ewald, 2 vols., Leipzig, 1885.
JS Epp.	*The Letters of John of Salisbury*, ed. W. J. Millor, H. E. Butler and C. N. L. Brooke, I, NMT, 1955.
JS HP (P) and (C)	John of Salisbury, *Historia Pontificalis*, ed. R. L. Poole, Oxford, 1927 (P); ed. and trans. M. Chibnall, NMT, 1956 (C).
Knowles, *EC*	David Knowles, *The Episcopal Colleagues of Archbishop Thomas Becket*, Cambridge, 1951.
Knowles, *Historian and Character*	Idem, *The Historian and Character and other Essays*, Cambridge, 1963.
Knowles, *MO*	Idem, *The Monastic Order in England* (cited from 1st edn, Cambridge, 1940; rev. edn, Cambridge, 1963).
Liverani	F. Liverani, *Spicilegium Liberianum*, Florence, 1863 (references are to items in 'Master David's register', on which see Z. N. Brooke in *Essays in History presented to Reginald Lane Poole*, ed. H. W. C. Davis, Oxford, 1927, pp. 227–45).
Lloyd	J. E. Lloyd, *A History of Wales from the Earliest Times to the Edwardian Conquest*, 2 vols., 3rd edn, London, 1939.

MB   *Materials for the History of Thomas Becket*, ed. J. C. Robertson and J. B. Sheppard, 7 vols., RS, 1875–85.

MB Epp.   References by number to the letters in *MB*, vols. V–VII.

MGH   *Monumenta Germaniae Historica.*

Misc. D. M. Stenton   *A Medieval Miscellany for Doris Mary Stenton*, ed. P. M. Barnes and C. F. Slade, Pipe Roll Society, 1962.

Mon.   W. Dugdale, *Monasticon Anglicanum*, ed. J. Caley, H. Ellis and B. Bandinel, 6 vols. in 8, London, 1817–30.

Morey   A. Morey, *Bartholomew of Exeter, Bishop and Canonist*, Cambridge, 1937.

Newcourt   R. Newcourt, *Repertorium ecclesiasticum parochiale Londinense*, 2 vols., London, 1708–10.

NMT   Nelson's Medieval Texts.

occ.   occurs.

PL   *Patrologiae cursus completus, series latina*, ed. J. P. Migne.

PR   *Pipe Roll*, cited by regnal year (*31 Henry I, 2–4 Henry II* and *1 Richard I*, ed. J. Hunter, Record Commission, 1833–41; the rest Pipe Roll Society, 1884–).

PRO   Public Record Office.

PUE   *Papsturkunden in England*, ed. W. Holtzmann, I, II, Berlin, 1930–6, III, Göttingen, 1952. (*Abhandlungen der Akad. der Wissenschaften in Göttingen*, Phil.-Hist. Klasse, Neue Folge, no. 25, 3 Folge, nos. 14–15, 33.)

Reg.   Register: especially the following:

Reg. Lincoln   *The Registrum Antiquissimum of Lincoln Cathedral*, ed. C. W. Foster and K. Major, 8 vols. (so far), Lincoln Record Society, 1935–58.

Reg. Osmund   *Vetus registrum Sarisberiense alias dictum registrum S. Osmundi Episcopi*, ed. W. H. R. Jones, 2 vols., RS, 1883–4.

Reg. Swinfield	*Registrum Ricardi Swinfield*, ed. W. W. Capes, Cantilupe and Canterbury and York Societies, 1909.
Rep.	HMC, *Ninth Report*, Appendix I, 1883–4.
Round, *GM*	J. H. Round, *Geoffrey de Mandeville*, London, 1892.
RS	Rolls Series.
Saltman	A. Saltman, *Theobald Archbishop of Canterbury*, London, 1956.
Sarum Charters	*Charters and Documents illustrating the History of...Salisbury...*, ed. W. R. Jones and W. D. Macray, RS, 1891.
SEBC	*Studies in the early British Church*, ed. N. K. Chadwick, Cambridge, 1958.
TRHS	*Transactions of the Royal Historical Society.*
VCH	*Victoria County History.*

CHAPTER I

INTRODUCTION: THE PROBLEM

A man may earn the attention of historians either because he was a personality of unusual interest or because they can see his age reflected in him with unusual clarity. The chief interest of Gilbert Foliot is as a mirror of his age. It is enhanced by the enigmas which surround him: he has been a figure of controversy among modern historians as he was among his contemporaries; and the explanation seems to be that he combined in himself to an exceptional degree the ideals, the prejudices and the paradoxes of his age. He was an ascetic monk and abbot, something of a scholar, a capable bishop, an inspiring preacher; he was also a harsh controversialist, was involved in forgery and practised unashamed nepotism. In the variety of his activities as well as of his character lies his interest to the historian. He was successively abbot of Gloucester (1139–48), bishop of Hereford (1148–63) and bishop of London (1163–87). As abbot he was an open defender of the claims of the Empress Matilda to the English throne; as bishop he was Thomas Becket's most forceful opponent among the clergy, and Henry II's loyal supporter. Both the anarchy and the Becket dispute gain a fresh perspective when seen in relation to his attitude to them; and for both his letters are a valuable source.

This book arose out of a study of the letters and charters issued in Gilbert's name. Revealing in different ways the society which produced their author and his work, the letters introduce us to the great personalities of the day, and above all reveal their author, a forceful, active man, lacking originality of mind, who helps us to understand the complex variety, the conventions, and paradoxes of his age. Gilbert's personality was not simple, and can only be made intelligible by a patient unravelling of every thread of evidence. The process does not make this book a biography in the ordinary sense; for that, the material does not exist, nor would a biography reflect Gilbert's real interest to the historian.

We have attempted first of all to interpret a major historical source; and through that source to see the personality which created it and the society it reveals. A series of studies of aspects of his life and work contribute, we hope, to a picture of Gilbert Foliot and his world.

THE PROBLEM OF GILBERT FOLIOT

And now we come at last and as it were unwillingly to the most enigmatic figure of all, to the man of probity whom even a pope reverenced for his austerity of life, the mirror of religion and glory of the age, the luminary who shed a lustre even on the great name of Cluny; the leader of the synagogue who raised the clamour for innocent blood; the Achitophel, who gave counsel as if one should consult God, against his master; the Judas, who made a pact upon the body of Christ, the church of Canterbury.[1]

Thus succinctly has Professor Knowles drawn into the frame of a single sentence the clashing colours in which the evidence portrays Gilbert Foliot. The problem is made all the more difficult because, in the same writer's view, the most powerful evidence against Gilbert comes from his own pen. Writing of his celebrated letter *Multiplicem*, in which he stated his case against Thomas Becket at the height of the conflict in which they were protagonists, he says: 'As a literary composition it must remain, with all its blemishes, a rhetorical masterpiece, but its cold and unrelenting hatred, which cannot pardon error or understand generosity, comes from the abundance of a heart in which humility and love had long ceased to harbour.'[2]

The problem of Gilbert Foliot would exist if none of his own letters had survived.[3] The son of a Norman family which, though not of the highest rank, was on the make in the twelfth century, Gilbert passed at a comparatively early age from a career of some promise in the academic world to the monastic life at Cluny. There he was remembered with respect and admiration—even at Cluny in the days of Peter the Venerable, still rich in young

---

[1] Knowles, *EC*, pp. 37–8.   [2] *Ibid.* p. 180.
[3] We owe the evidence of the abbot of Cluny and the pope, however, to the chief manuscript of Gilbert's letters.

noblemen of promise. And this is all the more striking, because Gilbert's stay there was short: he rose to be one of the priors of Cluny, then prior of Abbeville, abbot of Gloucester, bishop of Hereford and London. On his translation to London he received glowing congratulations from the abbot of Cluny.

Happy is the church of Cluny, which was found worthy to have such a son, who was to be a flower of the learned (*doctorum*), a mirror of the religious life, a glory of the present age; in whom God's grace, working before and after nature, made all things so praiseworthy that scarcely anything worth rebuke remained...; in whom a knowledge of many arts did not pile up, but annihilated vices; who thus converted a worldly philosopher to a true philosopher of Christ, that the truth and subtlety of the former was not lost; who put off the master of the schools[1] in such a way as devoutly to learn to be a disciple of Christ's simpletons; whom not necessity, but love alone, drew to Christ; not want, but solely a will to perfection, set apart from the world...; who, as a monk, kept nothing save his orders[2] from his clerkly life; as an abbot, did not abandon the life of a monk; raised to episcopal eminence, he lived as before.... This is the Lord's doing, and it is marvellous in our eyes. The whole church of Gaul knows this, almost indeed the whole Latin church, and they give praise to Cluny for such a son. Cluny knows this, and rejoices in the Lord therefor exceedingly.

The abbot was in a fix, and needed all the help he could get;[3] even so, we have no ground for dismissing his words as cynical flattery.

[1] 'magistrum scholarum...dimisit' has been taken to mean that Gilbert abandoned his master. But this is definitely contrary to the run of the sentence: '...qui mundanum philosophum uero Christi (*so* MS) philosopho sic mutauit, ut istius ueritatem retineret...: qui magistrum scholarum sic dimisit, ut discipulatum idiotarum Christi deuotus addisceret...'. 'Magistrum...dimisit' must be understood as balancing 'philosophum...mutauit'. There is no ambiguity about 'philosophum'; only Gilbert himself can be meant; and so we may be tolerably certain that he himself was the 'magistrum'. The abbot lays great emphasis on his learning, which certainly suggests that he is thinking of Gilbert as a master, not a pupil, in the schools. With this passage may be compared Reginald Foliot's flattery of his nephew (cited below, p. 36, n. 3). Cf. the dedicatory letter of his disciple Odo: 'Magistro scolarium, patri cenobitarum...' (below, p. 54, n. 1).

[2] There is no evidence what orders (if any, beyond the clerical tonsure) Gilbert had received before he became a monk.

[3] The papal schism presented the abbot of Cluny, in the borderland between France and Germany, with a problem. The abbot had made advances to

The steps in Gilbert's career reveal in different ways the esteem in which he was held, as we shall see; and in the same year, 1163, some of what the abbot of Cluny asserted was confirmed by the pope himself. The pope's letter opens with a hint that Gilbert is not without his detractors, but it is clear that Alexander III thought of him as a man of honourable and religious life. He makes two demands: that Gilbert shall give good and strict counsel to King Henry II, and that he shall take more care of his own health.

We have heard, and had it confirmed by true report of many folk, that you weaken and afflict your flesh beyond what is right and expedient, that you eat no meat, and do not restore your stomach with a glass of wine for its health. We are afraid that if the pack-horse is deprived of what it needs, it will fall from excessive weakness, and—Heaven forbid!—by your collapse God's Church will suffer heavy loss, since from your life and work it derives no mean benefits. We believe that you know how in the Old Testament it was not the custom to kill the turtle-dove, but one reads that its head was laid back along its feathers —signifying that a righteous man should not destroy his flesh by taking too little food, but by keeping from it anything excessive to cut back indulgence and vice....

And the pope warmly recommends his brother-bishop to follow the apostle's advice, take a little wine, and eat meat when under medical attention or ill, so that his body may not be weaker than need be, and he will be able to give more robust service to God and his Church 'to which you are exceedingly necessary'.[1]

Nor was the stream of golden opinions dammed by the conflict with Becket. At the height of the crisis a pile of testimonials was gathered and sent on his behalf to Rome; this, however, was evenly balanced by an ample pile of abuse collected from the

Victor IV, and was thus in trouble with Alexander III and the king of France. In 1161 Abbot Hugh was deposed, but he did not leave until 1163 (see GFL, Biog. Index, s.v. Cluny). In 1163 Abbot Hugh was thus desperately casting about for support. The letter is MB Epp. 20.

[1] 'Cui admodum necessarius es', MB Epp. 26. The pope refers to 1 Tim. v. 23 for the apostle's advice; and he recommends Gilbert to eat meat when ill or taking 'medicinam' (presumably at blood-letting time), and so avoids a breach of the monastic regulations to which Gilbert evidently adhered.

friends of the archbishop. Ten years later Walter Map, whose pen was not the most charitable of the age, described the bishop, now old and blind, but still active, as 'a treasure-house of goodness and wisdom'.[1] Map had had patronage from Gilbert, and held a prebend at St Paul's. This may have affected his judgement, but we may be sure that he would not have gone out of his way twice in *De nugis* to express his admiration of the bishop if it was not strongly and sincerely felt. These passages were written *c.* 1181-2. About this time, perhaps a few years later, Peter of Cornwall, canon of Holy Trinity, Aldgate, an Augustinian canon who owed Gilbert no financial benefits, described, in the preface of the first book of his massive *Pantheologus*, how he was inspired to write the book by a sermon Gilbert Foliot had delivered at one of his synods.[2] The canon, indeed, makes no reference to the bishop's character; but he speaks of the sermon in terms so glowing as strongly to suggest a general admiration of its author. The judgement is perhaps a little surprising. A number of Gilbert's sermons survive, and they do not strike us today as anything but devout (in a quite conventional way) and clever. It is, however, a common experience that sermons and speeches which inspired when they were delivered fail when committed to paper. Peter of Cornwall strongly suggests to us that he regarded Bishop Gilbert as a man of eloquence, and something more.

We shall in due course examine a great deal of evidence for and against Gilbert Foliot's integrity and good character. For the moment, enough has been said of the testimonials: what of the charges? Of these, perhaps three are the most serious, or at least the most revealing; that as abbot of Gloucester he connived at forgery; that when Becket went to Canterbury and Foliot to London, disappointed ambition drove the latter to chicanery in

---

[1] Translated M. R. James (Cymmrodorion Rec. Soc. 1923), p. 171; cf. pp. 19-20. For the context, see below, p. 103.

[2] See R. W. Hunt in *TRHS*, 4th series, XIX (1936), 33-4, 38 ff., esp. 40-1. The second and third books were dedicated to Ralph de Hauterive, who died in 1191 on crusade, and was last in England in 1189. The preface to Book I refers to Prior Stephen, who was elected in 1170. Since the whole work was not completed until after 1189, it seems likely that the first three books were written in the early or mid-1180's.

his dealings with the archbishop; that in his relations with Thomas Becket, he showed himself to be arrogant, cold and pharisaical.

It has long been known that Gloucester abbey, in common with many other religious houses, dabbled in forgery. It has recently been argued that forgery was perpetrated there precisely when Gilbert Foliot was abbot; in all probability in his last year of office, in or shortly before 1148.[1] If it is established that forgery was committed at Gloucester while he was abbot, as we think it is, one can hardly acquit Gilbert of being accessory to the crime; small wonder that he flared up when a charge of forgery was brought against Gloucester a few years later.[2] Forgery was common; it is a delicate matter to apportion guilt to the superiors of religious houses in which it was perpetrated, or to decide how much they really knew about it. But it was recognised to be a crime, and it is difficult to acquit Gilbert of complicity in a scheme which depended for its success on his good name with the bishop of Worcester and the archbishop of Canterbury. This incident perhaps requires rather special examination.

In 1162 Thomas Becket was elected archbishop at Henry II's behest. Against his election Gilbert's voice was strongly raised; and it was alleged at the time that his motive was ambition—he himself wished to be archbishop. This he strenuously denied.[3] But it is clear that for some reason he continued to object to being Becket's suffragan. When he was translated to London he refused to make a new profession of obedience to the archbishop. His refusal was upheld by the pope, on the technical ground that a profession once made need not be repeated. Gilbert, however, interpreted his own action to mean that he was not bound, as bishop of London, in allegiance to the archbishop of Canterbury; that he was free to raise the claim that London, and not Canterbury, should be the see of the archbishop. This was not a new idea: apart from ancient, or legendary, precedents, it had been raised by a bishop of London early in the century. It is difficult for us to take it seriously; and when all allowance is made

---

[1] CS, pp. 271 ff.   [2] See no. 128.

[3] See below, pp. 149–51; and for the claim to the independence of his see, pp. 151–62.

for the power which precedents and disputes had over the minds of twelfth-century churchmen, it is hard not to feel that the claim was a debating point, insurance against the likely event of Gilbert wishing to disobey the new archbishop. Insurance was certainly in his mind a few years later, when he organised the appeals of the bishops against Becket; and especially in the device of the appeal *ad cautelam*, the appeal against a sentence which had not yet been pronounced. Once again, the procedure seems a trifle absurd; and it is ironical that Henry II's chief supporter among the bishops should have let loose a flight of appeals almost beyond counting. But on this issue something less than justice has been done to Gilbert; he had at least one good precedent on his side. None the less, it seems clear that at least as soon as his translation to London was mooted, Gilbert began to plan legal devices of a highly ingenious character to avoid renewing obedience to his metropolitan.

And what of *Multiplicem*? It is the climax of the quarrel, a venomous reply to a pair of scorching letters of denunciation. It can only be understood in its context, as the peak of mounting anger on both sides. It is the sort of letter we should burn as soon as read, if not as soon as written. Even in the twelfth century, it is an extreme example of its kind; and it is clear that both its author and his enemies were torn between destroying it and publishing it in later years. This reveals that even Gilbert knew that all was not well with *Multiplicem*, and it prompts us to ask a number of questions.

CHAPTER II

THE LETTERS

The chief evidence to help us towards the solution of the problem of Gilbert Foliot's personality is his own letters; and this book is, in the first instance, an essay in interpretation. In the process, we hope to reveal something about the genre, about medieval letters in general, and also to show how Gilbert's can lighten many dark places in twelfth-century history. The eleventh and twelfth centuries were the golden age of medieval Latin letters. It is true that great collections were produced in late antiquity and again in the Renaissance; and occasional groups meet us in almost every century. But there is a concentration both of quantity and quality between 1050 and 1200 which is one of the chief reasons why this period is more easily brought alive to us, and so is comparatively better known, than the ages which immediately preceded it. But the interpretation of these letters is not always easy.

The collections are not evenly spread over the countries of Europe or the generations of this 150 years. They tend to cluster round a great man or a great event; and two great events in particular are illuminated by groups of letter collections: the contest of Henry IV and Gregory VII, and the contest of Henry II of England and Thomas Becket. The earlier group includes not only the *Register* of Gregory VII, but the various German collections that have been subjected to intensive and penetrating study in the fundamental book by Carl Erdmann.[1] These, and other surviving letters of the eleventh century, reveal that there was already a highly developed technique of letter writing which was widely known and widely used among learned men in different parts of western Europe. It was an artificial technique, based on the rules of rhetoric; but this did not prevent writers of letters from expressing their minds with quite remarkable freedom when they wished. That is to say, it was clearly recognised that different

[1] C. Erdmann, *Studien zur Briefliteratur Deutschlands im elften Jahrhundert* (Leipzig, 1938).

occasions demanded different types of letter; and as time passed, the rules for formal letters became increasingly formal, while the more skilled stylists devised more and more individual ways of expressing their own views.

These techniques were not new. The German letter writers studied by Erdmann were consciously imitating the letter-writers of the ancient world, especially Augustine and Jerome; and their range of techniques had already been shown in the letters of Gerbert, Pope Sylvester II (died 1003). Gerbert, like Jerome, particularly relished letters of invective. A splendid exchange between Charles, duke of Lower Lorraine, and the bishop of Metz, in which each accuses the other of treachery, is a particularly notable example. The duke's reply to the bishop was written for him by Gerbert; it is extremely withering; but it is accompanied by a friendly (or ironical) note from Gerbert explaining to the bishop that he had toned down what the duke actually said.[1] It is improbable, though not wholly impossible, that the whole correspondence was composed by Gerbert. He was certainly capable of it. Yet some of even Gerbert's letters were clearly meant to express his views and feelings in all sincerity.

The range of mood, then, was not new in the letters of the eleventh and twelfth centuries. What was new was the scale on which they were written: all over Europe there were folk who could, and did, compose them. Their degree of accomplishment varied enormously; but it was a common part of the civilisation of the age. Strangely enough, the technique did not long survive. In the late twelfth century the range rapidly narrowed. In the thirteenth the letter ceased to be a vehicle of personal expression: a wide variety of formal documents received new precision, but letters ceased to reveal personality or style. The technique of letter-writing, *dictamen*, had become almost a piece of verbal engineering. The formal swallowed the personal letter.

The supreme master of the art of letter-writing in the twelfth century was St Bernard; and if we wish to see in sharp focus what the letter-writers of this age hoped to achieve, we shall get our

---

[1] *Lettres de Gerbert*, ed. J. Havet (Paris, 1889), nos. 32–3 (trans. H. P. Lattin, Columbia Records of Civilisation, 1961, nos. 40–1).

clearest insight from him. Needless to say, he was far more ambitious and skilful than most of his contemporaries, and more daring; and his letters were mostly written at one end of the spectrum—the personal end. But this is all to the good, for it is essentially with letters as a means of self-expression, that peculiar gift with which the twelfth century was born, but which it lost, that we are concerned. Let us consider an example.

Your son, brother Walter [wrote Bernard to Peter the Venerable of Cluny], has become ours too, according to that rule: 'All mine are thine, and thine are mine.' Let him not be less intimate, because he is in common; and if it be that grace can do more—let him be more intimate, more acceptable, as he is to me because he is yours, so also to you because he is ours.[1]

The abbot of Clairvaux, not for the first time, had accepted a monk of Cluny at Clairvaux. In earlier days, he had employed some of his finest rhetoric in denouncing a monk of Clairvaux who had gone to Cluny. But now, he and the abbot of Cluny were friends, even, in some sense not easy to define, intimate friends. This letter's task was one of great delicacy. We can imagine how Peter the Venerable, if himself in such an embarrassing predicament, would have sent the words, in period upon period, rolling across the sands. But Bernard would not, could not admit shame or guilt in such a situation: the Cistercians had many such recruits. Characteristically, his solution was extremely bold: bold in its brevity, bold in its use of Our Lord's prayer, bold above all in his appeal to Peter's most characteristic quality, a charitableness which plastered over every kind of crack. To us the argument is somewhat as if a thief should say to his victim: 'we both have need, let us share your goods.' We may be sure nevertheless that Peter, however he may have felt his loss, accepted the letter, rejoiced in the felicitous expression of charity, relished the diplomatic skill, and rapidly forgave. The letter is, indeed, a brilliant example of Bernard's art: of how his letters are aimed at the human situation with which he is dealing, always brilliantly

---

[1] Bernard, ep. 267. The quotation is from John xvii, 10. The brother's name is variously given as Walter and Walcher.

tuned to the occasion, rhetorically perfect, in argument very commonly outrageous, acceptable only if the recipient accepted and submitted to the sanctity and prophetic authority of the sender.

The essential point is that the letters of Bernard are superb examples of what one might call the art of conversation, of mind speaking to mind; they are works of art, not spontaneous flourishes; but they express and meet human, personal situations. Recent studies have revealed with startling clarity the remoulding and polishing which Bernard and his secretaries applied to his works while preparing them for circulation.[1] The formal tricks of Latin rhetoric, as studied and practised, at least, in this age, tended to produce mountainous periods and monotonous rhythms. This was countered by many writers in the late eleventh and early twelfth centuries by a knowledge that the Latin language is much more flexible than the formal manuals suggest, and by constant searching after variety. The love of variety even entered the world of formal diplomatic: Gilbert Foliot's clerks, in the third quarter of the twelfth century, took evident pride in never saying the most banal things—that the bishop had affixed his seal, or granted his confirmation—twice in the same words. In Bernard's letters this fashion lies at the centre of his art. The Bolognese manuals of *dictamen* were already laying down rules: 'If these arrangements are not preserved, even if the composition is decent, the letter will be, from a rhetorical viewpoint, full of vice.'[2] Bernard had studied rhetoric but made it his servant. There are, indeed, some observable uniformities. He nearly always addresses his correspondents direct; he eschews in particular the fashionable arengas which rang the changes on the theme that it is the duty of a good man to do his duty. The recipient is made aware, in a flash, that the whole attention of Bernard's personality is upon him. If he addresses a king or a pope he will often start

[1] C. Mohrmann in *S. Bernardi Opera*, II, ed. J. Leclercq, C. H. Talbot and H. M. Rochais (Rome, 1958), pp. ix–xxxiii; J. Leclercq, *ibid.* I (1957), introd.; *Revue Mabillon*, XXXVII (1947), 1–16; *Revue Bénédictine*, LXI (1951), 208–29 (repr. in Leclercq, *Recueil d'Etudes sur S. Bernard et ses écrits*, I (Rome, 1962)).
[2] *Adalbertus Samaritanus Praecepta Dictaminum*, ed. F.-J. Schmale (*MGH*, Quellen zur Geistesgeschichte des Mittelalters, III, Weimar, 1961), p. 33.

more quietly, more respectfully than when addressing a colleague or a subordinate. It was a general rule that one should be slower off the mark with a superior, more abrupt with a subordinate.[1] Bernard obeys the spirit of the rule—a quiet opening is suitable on entering the presence of the great—but not the letter. The kind of model we meet frequently in Gilbert Foliot's letters containing congratulations or simply elaborate good wishes to a great man, followed by some petition or other, is rare in Bernard's files. If such were written, they were later polished away; as we know them, the letters, with few exceptions, have a unity of theme such as the younger Pliny would have approved. This is not to say that they have a unity of tone. Time and again, he wrote long letters of expostulation to the pope. Though there is much variety in them, a characteristic sample will open both largo and piano. After a while a note of perplexing irony, or a quiet roll on the timpani, warns us that a change is coming. The Latin language is peculiarly well adapted to subtle or sudden changes in tone; and Bernard loved to work his transitions now this way, now that. As the crescendo mounts, he draws in a large orchestra. His crescendoes make splendid reading still; one does not easily forget how he admonished the monks of Cluny—even if they were not ashamed of the impropriety of their ornaments—at least to count the cost; nor how the blandishments of the whore of Winchester (the eminent prince-bishop, Henry of Blois) are causing religion to lose its warmth in the diocese of York. But a fastidious modern reader will often feel that at the height of his passions, Bernard's art is less effective than in cooler moods. In part this is accidental: rhetorical flourishes were the fashion of his age; they are unfashionable today. In part, he was perhaps aware of it, for he toned down his flourishes in later years. But we must remember how often his appeals took effect. Sometimes when he froths and gurgles and blows bubbles at us we feel that the display of temperament is absurd. But it was not easy for kings and popes to laugh it off, for they knew that the letter expressed the indignation of the most powerful moral force in Christendom. There can be no doubt of Bernard's sincerity; nor that he in-

[1] Cf. *Adalbertus*, pp. 33–4.

variably calculated the effect of his words. That he sometimes miscalculated was scarcely the fault of his art.

It is plain that St Bernard achieved in full measure what a majority of self-conscious letter-writers of the age aimed at: rhetorical perfection, rhetorical variety, and above all appropriateness to their theme, to the office of themselves and their correspondents, and to the terms of friendship on which they stood. The most personal letters of this period, like Cecily Cardew's diary, were intimate and confidential, and intended for publication.

Friendship, like letter-writing, was fashionable among twelfth-century churchmen. The result is that it is extremely difficult for us to discriminate between the language of acquaintance and the language of intimacy. A kindly, diplomatic and charitable man like Peter the Venerable seems to be on terms of close friendship with everyone in Christendom.[1] In this situation the subjective judgement is often misleading; the authentic note of friendship, if it can still be caught in the twentieth century, can rarely be caught unless the author had real skill in writing. Formality of language does not prove formality of feeling. Personal expression was fashionable; but the real humanists, in this sense of the word, the men who could lay their hearts bare on paper, were few. The mingling of personal approach and formal rhetoric has some advantages: the rules of the game provide clues where subjective impressions may mislead us. These rules made fashionable a particular kind of letter which was appropriate between old or close friends: a pastiche of elaborate and allusive banter, whose meaning is usually at least two-thirds lost to us. In this manner John of Salisbury wrote on several occasions to Peter, abbot of Celle.[2] Close friends did not always write thus: if the occasion was appropriate to a more formal letter, they wrote more formally; one cannot prove men remote from one another because their surviving letters seem cold.

Where, in this milieu, does Gilbert Foliot stand? One cannot

---

[1] Cf., on St Anselm's personal letters, R. W. Southern, *St Anselm and His Biographer* (Cambridge, 1963), pp. 72 ff.

[2] See *JS Epp.* I, pp. xlvii–li, and no. 112; cf. e.g. no. 33.

claim him as a master of the art. Once or twice he touches the heights, though rarely without infringing modern taste. He aimed at variety, but was more the victim of the medium and its rules than the best letter-writers of the age, far more than Bernard. Certain phrases—'gratie debitorem', 'mores exuberant', 'uita comite', 'difficultas itineris'—recur again and again.[1] The petition preceded by *blandities* is so common as to be monotonous. Certain favourite quotations hide behind every bush as we are drawn mercilessly through each familiar shrubbery. Even when a superficial variety has been preserved, there is often a sameness of pattern which makes many a letter of Gilbert's as inevitable as a peroration by Macaulay. In both cases there are clear indications that the sensation is not produced by incapacity in the author; they did not care, or did not have the time, to polish and revise as did Bernard and his secretaries. The result is that there are warnings in Gilbert of the fate which was to overtake letter writing a generation later.

There are, however, quite substantial compensating virtues. He can be brief; and although he never rivals Herbert Losinga or Bernard himself for felicitous brevity,[2] his letters rarely run to length, and never to the prolixity of his first superior, Peter the Venerable. Flashes of humour are comparatively rare, but he can on occasion turn a point with real skill. Conventional phraseology is very common; but his letters to his subordinates, to those, that is, with whom he had personal contact, monks, archdeacons and canons, nearly always show real and sometimes anxious concern. From time to time he seems to take trouble in the composition of a piece of rhetoric; and on these occasions his success can be astonishing. *Multiplicem*, considered purely as rhetoric, is a masterpiece.

In Gilbert's time the formal treatises on *dictamen* were already laying down rules for the composition of letters; and we can see that some of the rules were followed by some letter-writers of

[1] E.g. nos. 19, 30, 38, 58, 62, etc. ('gratie debitores'); 4, 36, 38, 49, 62, etc. ('ad doctrinam scientia, ad honestatem mores exuberant'); 45, 46, 86 ('uita comite'); 25, 56, 58, etc. ('difficultas itineris').

[2] Herbert Losinga, ed. R. Anstruther (Brussels, 1846), *ep.* 4, holds the record with 20 words.

the period. But practice among those who regarded letter-writing as an art was considerably more flexible than the warring masters at Bologna really approved. One can observe in Gilbert's letters that he commonly works to certain patterns; he is not bound by them, but normally seems happy to use them. In addressing a subordinate, it was generally reckoned that one could go straight to the point; and, if necessary, be peremptory. In writing to superiors one should first beat about the bush, use *blandities*, congratulate them, if possible, expound one's devotion.[1] It was a part of Bernard's art to break these rules. Gilbert is not always bound by them, but frequently obeys them. A rule which was rarely broken was that if one replied to a letter, the reply should be attuned to the original; should take up phrases, ideas, echoes in it. In formal letters this becomes a formality, and may also disappear; the more informal the letter, the more intimate the correspondents, the more the reply will juggle with the original. This juggling is also a feature of rhetorical letters of controversy. The effect of this is that if one has the reply and not the original, one is often at sea. The principle is indeed vital for the understanding of these letters. It is central, for instance, to the interpretation of *Multiplicem*, which was addressed to a public enemy not a private friend, but in which Gilbert toys with, worries and gnaws the two letters to which it is a reply with exceptional care and skill.

One of the most interesting of his letters is no. 152, because it is a rare example of a letter in which he changes style half-way through. This is not a subjective impression: Gilbert says so himself. 'We turn to that mode of speech (*ad illum stilum*) which is [appropriate to] the occasion that makes a letter necessary just at the moment.' At first sight, this hardly seems tactful, since it marks the transition from congratulations to Abbot Froger of Saint-Florent, Saumur, on his election as abbot, to making certain specific demands of him. As Gilbert states quite specifically, he moves on to the *petitio*. We are, rather surprisingly, shown the mechanics of the letter. True, we are quite accustomed to these mechanics: if they seem crude to us, they were accepted at the

[1] Cf. e.g. *Adalbertus*, pp. 33–4.

time. But what was not accepted was to confess openly what one was at. Gilbert was not always tactful, but his errors of taste rarely took the form of saying plainly that he was sending his congratulations in order to accompany them by certain more urgent petitions. Our suspicions are aroused; and they are considerably deepened by observing that the change of style, which is clear enough, is the reverse of what one would expect. From the first half of this letter, one would scarcely know that Gilbert and Froger had ever met. In the address Froger is 'fratri karissimo', the greeting is 'salutem et sincere karitatis affectum'. All these words, however, can be used in a purely formal sense. It would be rare for Gilbert to use three words of 'affection' to a virtual stranger; there is certainly some hint of friendship here. On the other hand the greetings more commonly took the form of a pious ejaculation[1] when addressed to close friends; and the whole protocol was a formal expression of what was appropriate to the man and the occasion, so that it can never be interpreted in isolation. There is usually a hint in it of what is to follow, but nearly always too slight a hint to be pursued without further evidence. In the protocol to *Multiplicem* Gilbert addresses Becket without a word of affection or friendship; and the most elaborate of his letters has a greeting of rare simplicity: 'salutem'. To those who have steeped themselves in the letters of this period, it will be evident that both address and greeting were deliberate. There is a hint, too, in the protocol to Abbot Froger; but we cannot detect it till we have read the whole letter.

It opens with a paragraph of congratulations, very little different from many others which Gilbert wrote. Froger has made a good beginning; may the Lord lay his hand mercifully on him and complete his abbacy with a happy conclusion. Gilbert congratulates him in the happy expectation that God will bring good things to better. Froger's good life had been rewarded; the monks, 'we hear'—Gilbert uses the first person plural throughout—were unanimous; he prays that Froger will shine as a mirror of virtue and show the road of virtue to virtue's amateurs; God, he knows,

---

[1] Both types of greeting are normal in letter collections of the period. Gilbert's present no unusual features.

will see to it. Gilbert would like to say more, but trusts in the
divine unction which instructs Froger from within; and so he
commits the abbot's sails to God, who will navigate him out of
the tempest of this world into harbour, filling the gulfs of our
minds with the gentle breeze of the Holy Spirit. It is difficult to
imagine how a larger number of conventional metaphors could
be fitted into the space. From this, we could deduce little or
nothing about the relations of Gilbert and Froger.

Then comes the change. Gilbert announces a new style as he
enters the petitions. But he becomes more personal, more intimate, not less so. The first part of the petition is unremarkable.
The marcher lord Baderon of Monmouth was patron of Monmouth priory, a dependency of Saint-Florent.[1] Some quarrel had
arisen between Baderon and the abbot; Gilbert is trying to
smooth it out. He then passes to the prior, presumably of Monmouth; but this part of the letter is incomplete. As the text
stands he passes rapidly on to brother Robert de *Castro nouo*; and
with brother Robert, of whom Gilbert was evidently fond, we
pass indeed to a new style.

The plea for brother Robert is stated obscurely and allusively.
Robert was clearly a monk of Saint-Florent living in England,
most probably at Monmouth, who found the climate insufferable
and wished to return home. Exile in the cold north did not suit
him; like Ovid, his life was 'uita procul patria peragenda sub axe
Boreo'.[2] Gilbert may have this actual passage in mind; in any
case the association of northern stars and northern climates was
common in classical and sub-classical writers;[3] and Gildas had
specifically associated the *borialis axis* with Britain.[4] Brother
Robert was afflicted by the cold, by the undrinkable water
('coctione potabilis'), and by sickness; Gilbert suggests, perhaps
with exaggeration, that the climate will kill him. The association

---

[1] Monmouth priory was in the diocese of Hereford; other English cells of
Saint-Florent were Andover (Hants) and Sele (Sussex), in neither of which is
Gilbert known to have had an interest. For Saint-Florent and Monmouth, see
S. M. Harris in *Journal of the Hist. Soc. of the Church in Wales*, III (1953), 6 ff.

[2] *Tristia*, iv, 8, 41.

[3] *Thesaurus Linguae Latinae*, II, 1637, lines 20 ff.; and cf. coll. 1638 f.

[4] *De excidio*, iii, ed. Mommsen (*MGH, Auct. Antiquissimi*, XIII), p. 28.

of death and the northern stars seems to have suggested to the author's mind the Pythagorean doctrine that the mind or soul came from the region of the upper air, the world of the stars, and returned to its native place after death. The doctrine had been expressed in the elder Seneca's *Suasoriae*: on Cicero's death, 'the mind, drawn by its divine origin...will hurry back to its own home and its kindred stars'.[1] Gilbert's metaphorical use of a man's native air and stars for his birthplace may have been suggested by some passage like the question put to Polyneices in Statius' *Thebaid*: 'Where is your home, your land? From what stars has your mind been drawn?'[2] But the association 'originem ...hausit' may be a direct reminiscence of Seneca. He asks the abbot to allow brother Robert 'to enjoy his own stars and the air from which he took his origin'. 'Confidenter in amici castra migrauimus'—in effect, 'we have invaded your preserves.' The idea of the migration of souls[3] may be behind the use of the word 'migrauimus' (not recorded by the *Thesaurus Linguae Latinae* among the numerous words used with 'in castra'); and 'castra', though common in such metaphorical contexts as this, seems to be a play on brother Robert's name: the home of a man who came 'de Castro nouo' could not fail to be 'castra'.

This may or may not be an accurate description of the associations in Gilbert's mind. What matters is that the letter presupposes a mental process of this kind. In itself, this is not surprising. We could produce many analogies from this period; most striking, perhaps, are two letters of John of Salisbury to Peter of Celle written a few years earlier.[4] Both are variations on the theme of friendship; both appropriate to exchange between intimate friends. The second is largely unintelligible. It is un-

---

[1] *Suasoriae*, vi, 6: 'animus...diuina origine haustus...ad sedes suas et cognata sidera recurret' (for other references in Roman literature, cf. note by W. A. Edward, in *Suasoriae of Seneca the Elder*, Cambridge, 1928, p. 135).

[2] v, 24: 'Quae domus aut tellus, animam quibus hauseris astris?' The text in the manuscript of Gilbert's letter is very corrupt in this passage: we assume the emendations suggested in our edition.

[3] Which Gilbert, of course, would have regarded as a joke of the schools, not a serious doctrine.

[4] *JS Epp.* I, nos. 111–12.

intelligible precisely because the allusions are in part at least to a private world of fantasy. It reveals in an extreme form a highly developed literary fashion of the period. It was fashionable to charge one's Latin with every kind of echo; twelfth-century stylists are as full of the Bible, the fathers and the pagan classics as Pope is of the classical Latin poets. The more personal the letter, the more allusive it was expected to be. The sudden intrusion of this highly allusive style into a letter which otherwise does not depart from normal conventions is a clear indication that Gilbert and Froger were old friends; and we may take the reference to 'ancient friendship' which follows quite literally. The reference to style in the middle of the letter and to Seneca or whatever later on suggests that Gilbert and Froger had a literary training in common; one would be inclined to deduce that their friendship lay far back in their lives; and this may explain why the letter is both formal and personal: they were old friends who had not met much, if at all, in recent years. If their friendship belonged to Gilbert's schooldays, it lay at least thirty years back.

In no. 23 Gilbert congratulated Pope Celestine II on his accession. He performs the task with dignity, drawing in at least eight biblical echoes in the process, several of which feature commonly in his letters. Once again, it is the conventional expression of felicitations, to which he treated several eminent dignitaries. The words are never the same, the ideas are never much different. At the end, in a single sentence, Pope Celestine was treated to the petition: to be kind to Nigel, bishop of Ely. In the same way the letter to Abbot Froger (no. 152) starts as a conventional expression of congratulation and good wishes. The protocol sets the tone; it is formal, but hints at a friendship which is directly claimed at the end of the letter. It may be that Gilbert deliberately inverted the normal division of such a letter: if one writes to an old friend whom one has not seen for many years, it is natural for there to be an element of constraint at first, which may later melt. This arrangement would be subtly appropriate; and it would certainly conform with the conventions of the milieu for brother Robert, who was evidently a human link between Gilbert and Froger, to elicit the more personal style. But there is another and a simpler explanation. The letter as we have it is certainly corrupt, far more so than is common in the collection. It seems likely that the surviving copy was taken off a rough draft; that it was his original intention to write a somewhat formal letter, as was appropriate to a mixture of congratulation and petition; but that as he went on the vision of his old friend rose before him, and he dropped back into the style appropriate to close friends. He then left the draft as it was; we cannot tell what kind of letter was actually sent. But the draft, he may have felt, needed surgery too drastic to put it in proper form. It was an awkward mixture of two styles.

It matters little which is the true explanation. What is interesting is that the letter makes abundantly clear that the correspondents were old friends; and that one did not always have to write the same kind of letter to the same man. Gilbert, in fact, was perfectly capable of writing an entirely formal letter to an old and valued friend, if the occasion demanded it. Some of the letters of the late 1160's, quite apart from other evidence,[1] suggest close friendship between Gilbert and Jocelin, bishop of Salisbury; if one compared their tone with that of letters which Gilbert wrote to Jocelin in the 1140's, one would certainly deduce that it was a friendship which matured with the years; that they found one another in their common misfortune when both were drawing Becket's fire. It may be so; but no. 68 (?1146–8) contains the words 'pristina karitas' which remind one of those Gilbert used when writing to Abbot Froger. There is a distinct possibility that Gilbert and Jocelin were also old friends, perhaps fellow-students.

In no. 152 we observed a mingling of *blandities*, business and friendship. The same elements are mingled, though in different proportions, in an early letter, no. 6, which we take as a final example of Gilbert's capacity. At first sight it seems to say nothing at inordinate length; it has often been observed that the length of the letters of this period was in inverse proportion to their content. To put it another way, it was fashionable, when writing a letter of friendship, to take wings, and fly to the uttermost parts of the earth. When John of Salisbury thanked Peter of

---

[1] See below, p. 103.

Celle for the gift of his book *De panibus*, he treated his friend to an elaborate allegorical exercise, in which serious and frivolous were nicely mixed: serious gratitude for the gift, expostulation that the Frenchman had provided the Englishman with food but no wine.[1] In no. 6 Gilbert thanks Robert de Bethune, the saintly bishop of Hereford, for a gift of fish. 'To his father and lord Robert, by God's grace bishop of Hereford, brother Gilbert, called abbot of the church of St Peter of Gloucester—to haul ashore the net which was thrown into the sea, full of good fish.' Already the theme of the letter has been declared: St Peter's abbot has reminded the bishop of Peter's miraculous draught, and also of how Our Lord likened the kingdom of Heaven to a net which gathered fish both good and bad.[2] The abbot goes on at once to say that the bishop's present of fish has provided him both with food and with instruction. As we proceed it becomes evident that the bishop had sent two fish, one large, one small, of the same species; that he had also sent a message, but not, it seems, a letter. Gilbert handles the present as if it were a letter: he considers it in detail from every aspect and draws edification from it. It reminds him of the great fisherman, St Peter, who had fished Gilbert, tossed by the world's waves, and landed him in a great city of monks— presumably he refers to St Peter's, Cluny, although St Peter's Gloucester may also be in his mind. But this does not guarantee that Gilbert is of the elect, and Peter's fishing leads to a considera- tion of judgement. The two-ness of the fishes, reminiscent of the two fishing scenes in the Gospels, carried this thought a stage further: Gilbert feels that he is being impelled to *lectio divina* (as in St Benedict's *Rule*, cc. 48–9), for in the feeding of the five thousand the loaves signified the books of the law (the Pentateuch), the fishes the prophets and Psalms. Presently he passes on to con- sider the significance of the fact that the fishes were both of the same species: 'unity and peace you commend to me'. And on this note, after characteristic elaboration, Gilbert draws to a close. 'These points occur to me at the moment as to the ground for your gift; we look forward to seeing you and talking with you,

[1] *JS Epp.* I, no. 33.
[2] The echoes are from Matt. xiii. 47 and John xxi. 11.

and then, if you will, you will instruct me more fully.' Suddenly, without warning, Gilbert switches to business.

'You ordered me by the messenger who brought your gift not to be tortured by envy, not to faint and pine away, not to be tormented in my drought by the felicity granted to you, and by your wealth of fishes of such quality and quantity. You warn me against envy by your words, but entice me to envy by your deeds. Is it surprising if I am withered by envy, since the widespread influence of a rich neighbour forbids me to make a wretched little pool',[1] so that the poor man is tormented while the rich enjoys bliss? 'You order envy away; if you but grant permission to dig the pond, you yourself can uproot it. It will be no mean proof of friendship, but you will not allow a man to be tortured long, whose cure you know depends on you. Farewell.'

Thus, with a vision of Dives and Lazarus inverted, with phrases from Horace and (perhaps) from Ovid echoing in the distance, Gilbert at last reveals the point of his elaborate house of cards. The bishop and the abbot had had an argument about a fish-pond. One may presume that it was to lie on Gloucester's property in or near Hereford; very likely it was needed to provide fish for Gloucester's new dependency of St Guthlac and St Peter in Hereford itself, established in 1143—a suggestion which would add point to the emphasis on the great fisherman. The bishop, it seems, refused leave for the pond to be dug;[2] as a symbolic gesture of friendship, however, he sent a present of fish from his own pond. Gilbert picked up the present in the spirit in which it was intended, and turned the occasion with remarkable skill. The fish

---

[1] Taking 'iacentis' in the sense of 'being of no esteem'. There may be an echo in this passage of Horace, *Carm.* ii, 15, 1 ff.:

> Iam pauca aratro iugera regiae
> moles relinquent, undique latius
> extenta uisentur Lucrino
> stagna lacu. . . .

The bishop's ponds have cut everything else out.

[2] It is possible that it was not the bishop who refused permission: the echo from Horace's *Odes* might indeed suggest that it was the king who was responsible. But MS H's reading 'interdicitis', if correct, is quite specific; and the letter seems to lose most of its point if the bishop himself was not to grant the permission, but merely help in eliciting it; nor can one easily conceive that King Stephen would have been referred to by Gilbert in this period as a rich man of wide power.

reminded him of Peter...and of unity and peace. The *blandities*, spun out with all the elaboration suited to banter between friends, seems to be leading nowhere. Suddenly he turns in his tracks and brandishes a sword; a moment's inspection reveals that the weapon, though highly polished, is not sharp. The comic undertone of the conclusion is quite clear. But the point is made. We do not know if Gilbert was allowed his pond; he surely deserved it.

To evaluate the letters of Gilbert Foliot as historical evidence, then, requires a careful comparison with other letters of the period; and we need also to set the collection in its context if we wish to assure ourself of its authenticity, and to inquire to what extent Gilbert wrote or dictated the letters himself, to what extent they represent letters actually sent and delivered, to what extent he or his secretaries may have revised them after they were originally composed.

The massive dossier of letters concerning the quarrel between Becket and Henry II owes its survival to a variety of causes, which amply illustrate the reasons why the letters of this period were collected and preserved in such large numbers. At least four men among those involved in the quarrel had been in the habit of making collections of their letters for the use of posterity before the trouble began. The pope was in the habit of keeping a register of his more important or characteristic letters; none of the registers of Alexander III survive, but we have a dossier of his letters compiled for inclusion in it, and most of the papal letters dealing with the controversy are still to be found in this or other early collections.[1] Arnulf, bishop of Lisieux, issued the first edition of his collected letters while the trouble was on, about 1166.[2] John of Salisbury had already closed the first collection of his letters, which belong to the later years of his service of Archbishop Theobald, before the quarrel broke out;[3] his second collec-

---

[1] Cf. *MB Epp.* 695 for Becket's reference to this dossier. Presumably the collection of papal letters attached to Becket's own letters in MSS Vat. Lat. 6024, fos. 72–139 and BM Royal 13. A. xiii represents this collection (cf. below, p. 230, for a similar collection in B).

[2] See *Letters*, ed. Barlow, pp. lxxi, l.

[3] See *JS Epp.* I, pp. ix ff., corrected by R. W. Southern, *EHR*, LXXII (1957), 494–5; there will be further discussion in *JS Epp.* II.

tion belongs to the period of the crisis and its aftermath. Gilbert
Foliot had also made a collection of his letters, perhaps more than
one, before the 1160's, as we shall see. The papal register was the
formal record of a great office and a great official, not a comprehensive record, by any means, in this period, but evidently intended as a memory to the pope himself and his successors of his
more important acts and decisions. The register was taken off
copies made by the papal chancery when the letters were written.[1]
In the preface to the first edition of Arnulf of Lisieux's letters,
Arnulf tells his friend Giles, archdeacon of Rouen, later bishop of
Evreux, that he has obeyed his request and put the collection together; that he had himself no copies, so had had to approach the
recipients; that the earlier ones, 'studia...melioris etatis', had
been better, but had mostly disappeared; that the later ones reveal
the age and busy life of their author.[2] Almost identical sentiments
were expressed, somewhat more elegantly, by Herbert Losinga
half a century earlier. It is clear that Arnulf regarded his collection,
like the Roman collections of the ages of Pliny or Sidonius, as
essentially a literary affair. In revising a letter for the collection,
he was inclined to excise the petition, or other item of business;
and leave only the *blandities*.[3] Fortunately numerous letters
survive unexpurgated.

Thus the papal register and the letters of Arnulf represent the
opposite grounds for preserving letters, for their matter and their
manner. Most collections were valued in some degree for both.
The survival of John of Salisbury's early letters is something of a
mystery. Many of them were written on behalf of Theobald,
archbishop of Canterbury. But they are not an official record of
Theobald's affairs, a primitive register; and there are a number of
very personal letters interspersed. In general, the interest seems
to be a literary one, to show how letters can be written to deal
with a wide variety of situations. But it is not literature for polite

---

[1] Alexander III's registers are lost; but so much may be deduced by comparison with those of Gregory VII and Innocent III (we assume that Gregory
VII's is an original register, not a later composition. The latest study of this
problem will shortly be published by A. Murray).

[2] Arnulf, *Ep.* 1; cf. Herbert Losinga, *Ep.* 1.

[3] Cf. Arnulf, ed. Barlow, pp. lxii f.

entertainment so much as for instruction; and particularly, for instruction to those who handle an archbishop's correspondence. One manuscript seems to be copied from a sort of formulary preserved at Canterbury.

Becket's own letters, and the main dossier of the quarrel, owe their survival to a third kind of motive for recording letters. Like the famous letter of Abelard, the so-called *Historia calamitatum*, they are *pièces justificatives*, materials for an apologia. The precise nature and history of this apologia will be discussed elsewhere.[1] It seems that Becket deliberately chose to have his struggles and difficulties recorded by preserving the letters; and not his own only, but those of the pope and the other leading protagonists, not excluding Gilbert Foliot himself. How he would have handled them had he lived we cannot tell; but after the martyrdom the task of putting together the collection fell, it seems, to John of Salisbury. It may be that the delicacy of the issues raised by the letters gave him pause; for whatever reason, he seems not to have completed the work. When he went to be bishop of Chartres in 1176, he left behind his own brief life of Becket, and various assorted jumbles of letters. These the prior of Christ Church, Canterbury, Alan, later abbot of Tewkesbury, arranged as best he could; and Alan's collection, prefaced by John of Salisbury's *Life* and Alan's own addenda to it, was the form in which the letter collections of the crisis were most widely known in the late Middle Ages, and the form in which they were first published in the seventeenth century. This 'life and letters' is a remarkable achievement, and there can be little doubt that it reflects Becket's own determination to be remembered, and justified, by a plain unvarnished tale of the transactions. In the final collection all John of Salisbury's wit and fire were mobilised by Alan on the archbishop's behalf; but he made no effort to suppress John's criticisms, nor did he suppress *Multiplicem*. It is not an attempt to write objective history, which was unthinkable in the circumstances; but it is an attempt to state the case fairly.

[1] See *GFL*, introduction and *JS Epp.* II, introduction (forthcoming). A new study of the MSS of the Becket correspondence is being undertaken by Mrs Anne Duggan.

All of these elements went into the making of Gilbert Foliot's collections of letters: they are in turn literature and business, formulary and *apologia*.[1] Apart from the few which found their way into the larger Becket collections, there is no evidence that Gilbert's letters aroused much interest outside his own circle; but a surprising number of manuscripts survive. Two early fragments, now at Hereford and in the British Museum,[2] perhaps come from Hereford and Gloucester, and so originated in places closely connected with him. The letters in Bodl. Douce 287 (D) were very likely copied off a collection made under Gilbert's eye in or about the early 1170's. With Bodleian E Musaeo 249 (B) we come closest to Gilbert himself. Though written in a variety of hands, there can be no doubt that this manuscript was itself composed in Gilbert's *familia*. One of the hands can be identified as that of a scribe who wrote at least two of his charters; and this is the most interesting hand in the manuscript, that of a man who went through much of it when it was nearly complete, filling in blank spaces in the quires, adding a quire of his own. His interest lay in formal business and in formulas; it may be that he was the chief clerk of Gilbert's writing-office. The manuscript contains a large number of items which can be dated between 1140 and 1175; only two later than 1175, both *c.* 1177. It is reasonably certain that it was drawn up in the late 1170's.

When B was drawn up, Gilbert had been bishop of London for about fifteen years; none the less, it opens with the legend 'Epistole uenerabilis Gilleberti Herefordensis episcopi'. It seems clear that the legend was copied, at one or two removes, off a collection made while the author was still at Hereford, and this is confirmed by the Royal fragment, which has the same heading, and contains Gloucester and Hereford letters only.[3] It is also

---

[1] For the technical foundation of what follows, see *GFL*, introduction.

[2] Hereford, P. i. 15, fos. 147–154 v (H) and BM Royal 8. A. xxi, fos. 205–12 v (R). We leave out of account the Alessandrina MS (A), a later copy of Bodl. E Mus. 249.

[3] This, however, may simply be due to the fact that only a single quire survived. A calls Gilbert abbot of Gloucester; but this clearly represents a deduction from the letters with which the collection opens. H has no Hereford letters: it could be a collection made while Gilbert was still at Gloucester.

confirmed by a notable break in the chronological series of the letters: letters written between 1153 and 1161 are extraordinarily rare, and we may deduce that the first collection was made *c.* 1153. There is no clear indication how this collection was made. But there are several letters which seem to form duplicates.[1] It is highly improbable that all these letters were actually sent; and there are some letters of which two copies survive which seem to have been taken off different drafts. It is reasonable to suppose that, as with most letter collections of the period, the majority at least of the letters represent drafts and copies preserved by Gilbert and his clerks. Among the later letters there are some cases where one can prove that a draft was used by the compiler of the collection.[2]

Gilbert was no doubt proud of his style; the composition and survival of *Multiplicem*, to be discussed in a later chapter, would alone be sufficient to establish that. But it is not clear that the early collection or collections were made entirely on his initiative or with a purely literary purpose in mind. There is no great coherence evident in the selection of material, and we may suppose that the collection was put together to allow his immediate circle to study his method of letter-writing at leisure. But there is business or serious purpose in almost all the letters, even in such an effusion as no. 6, and the collection may have served partly to remind himself and to show others what essential business he had engaged in. The intrusion of a few charters even among the Hereford letters strongly suggests a practical concern; and we have already seen that Gilbert was a practical man who rarely (so far as the record goes) devoted excessive time or care to his letters.

It may even be that the early collection was put together by a clerk or clerks, although hardly without his knowledge and consent. The apologia of the early 1170's seems clearly to be the work of Gilbert himself. Twenty-one, at most, out of 94 letters were of his own composition; but it must have required considerable influence and initiative to put together all these letters so early. The

---

[1] E.g. nos. 17–18, 24–5, 36–7, 157–8.
[2] See especially no. 152 (above, pp. 15–20).

majority, however, of those not written by him were concerned with him, including a fuller collection of the testimonials elicited for him in 1169 even than in B. The condition of *Multiplicem* in D also suggests Gilbert's personal supervision.[1]

The final collection, however, was clearly the work of his clerks. Gilbert may well have played a part in the enterprise; and a few of the letters show signs of revision such as only he could have given to them. But there is very little revision of the manuscript itself, such as, for instance, Arnulf gave in person to Paris, Bibliothèque Nationale, MS lat. 14763. This may be due, in part at least, to the fact that Gilbert went blind in the late 1170's. But it is clear that the man whose hand we have identified as possibly that of his chief clerk felt that he was free to select what material he would. The book does not contain a self-conscious literary monument like the letters of St Bernard or the early letters of Arnulf of Lisieux. It is not simply a formulary, nor, in any straightforward sense, a register. It contains the earlier letter collections, altered and expanded, but not in any coherent order; it contains much miscellaneous matter concerning the quarrel with Becket. It includes a small decretal collection and the canons of the council of Westminster of 1175; it contains charters and bits of charters: an assortment of the contents of the bishop's files and pigeon-holes. Whatever part Gilbert played in it, what we have is a clerk's compilation out of diverse, ill-ordered materials. But once again, at the very end, appears *Multiplicem*. Its presence reflects in some way Gilbert's concern in the collection, although it is difficult to determine whether this second appearance, as it were, of Banquo's ghost, was Gilbert's final decision, or the work of a clerk who knew that he could safely ignore the instructions of his blind master.

The evidence indicates that H and possibly R came from circles where Gilbert had lived and moved; that D is a copy of a collection made under his eye; that B was itself written by his own familia. We know that St Bernard was cheated by at least one of his secretaries; that he had on one occasion to apologise to Peter the Venerable for an impolite letter in his name, which he had never

---

[1] See below, pp. 167–8.

seen.[1] But this incident casts no serious doubt on the authenticity of the main body of Bernard's letters; it only reminds us that we cannot assume even with Bernard that all letters written in his name—nor even in his style—were entirely his own work. The transmission of Gilbert Foliot's letters is a clear guarantee of their authenticity, in general terms. It does not prove that all were dictated by him, or that all represent letters actually sent. But we can dismiss any idea that the collection contains wholly spurious items.

We can also discount any notion that some of the letters were literary exercises, not intended to be real letters. Such literary exercises were written from time to time in this period; Becket's associates certainly wrote some to work off their feelings at key moments in the quarrel, and it has been alleged that a number of Peter of Blois's letters were exercises. Of Gilbert's letters the large majority give a clear and firm impression of being practical answers to particular problems or situations, and most of them would make nonsense as exercises. One might possibly interpret as exercises the two longest letters, no. 26 to Brian FitzCount on the empress's case against Stephen, and *Multiplicem*; but both have distinct indications that they are *œuvres d'occasion*, and the manuscripts seem to establish that Becket actually received *Multiplicem*.[2]

On the other hand, there are some letters which were evidently drafted, but not sent, and some which have clearly been somewhat revised.[3] In the absence of originals, it is impossible to check the extent of revision in detail. A comparison of the manuscripts of *Multiplicem* shows that no attempt was made to revise the body of its text after it had been sent. A comparison between B and the other manuscripts shows that a few letters were revised, but in all cases save no. 203 the revision is slight. Nos. 197 and 203 occur in two substantially different forms, but this is probably due to revision in the course of drafting, not to afterthoughts. The impression given by the bulk of the letters is

---

[1] See Leclercq, *Revue Bénédictine*, LXI (1951), 211–12.
[2] See below, pp. 167–8.
[3] See nos. 152, 203 and above, p. 27.

that they represent pretty faithfully what was sent out, or at least what was first drafted: the majority are not as carefully or as rhetorically written as the very best of the letters—many, one feels, could have been improved by their author had he devoted time to the task.

This is, to some degree, a subjective judgement; and it is theoretically possible that Gilbert was not himself capable of the higher flights, that his best letters were at least partially the work of his clerks and secretaries. Such a view cannot be wholly disproved. A detailed stylistic analysis might establish the homogeneity of the collection; but it could not possibly prove unity of authorship so decisively as style proves the authorship of St Bernard's major works. Yet there is no doubt that Bernard was assisted by his secretaries in their revision, and that those close to the saint had acquired the technique of writing with his highly individual style. To suppose that style alone can prove the authorship of a letter is a fantasy. In Foliot's case we may discount the possibility that any number of his letters were entirely the work of another. Archbishop Theobald was apparently content to leave many of his most important letters to John of Salisbury to compose; but Theobald seems to have had no personal interest in writing or in making any reputation for himself as a scholar. Gilbert was a *magister*, who regarded himself, and was evidently regarded, as a man of learning. It is possible that he left more to others in his later years. But at the end of his letter to Brian FitzCount he confesses that his prayers have been neglected somewhat for two whole days while he was composing: hints such as this can hardly have been faked. We can be confident that in general Gilbert took responsibility for the letters which passed in his name. His charters were clearly the work of his numerous clerks. The large penumbra of official correspondence on lawsuits and the like may partly have been dictated by him, partly by others—we have no means of deciding.

The view that Gilbert himself was an active dictator of letters was clearly that held at the time. In the summer of 1166 the English bishops in a body wrote a protest to the archbishop, which Thomas passed on to John of Salisbury for his comments.

I have read with great care [writes John] the letter which the children of the church of Canterbury, your brothers and fellow-bishops, recently sent you, their father, for your consolation and the support of the church after so long exile and proscription. My perusal suggested that nothing was more likely than that they were dictated by the counsel of Achitophel, who has evidently returned from hell to plague the faithful, and written by the hand of Doeg the Edomite, still thirsting for the blood of the priests, and insatiably searching out and persecuting the spirit of Christ which lives in the faith and charity of the elect.

Achitophel and Doeg are characteristic symbols behind which John hides some particular enemy; and later in the letter he reveals his identity.

Surely the bishop of London is he who first split the unity of the church in England—as is known to all—and gripped by the ambition to be archbishop—as is suspected by most—was the first inspiration and inciter of the whole dispute? Surely the very style of the letter reveals Achitophel and Doeg, of whose spirit it is full....For his speech betrayeth him.[1]

[1] *MB Epp.* 231; cf. below, p. 166.

CHAPTER III

THE FAMILY

It is in the nature of a letter collection that it should give us copious hints about the ramification of the author's family, without commonly providing information sufficiently solid to reconstruct his family tree. An eminent couple wished to marry in the early twelfth century, and consulted Ivo of Chartres; Bishop Ivo asserted that they were too closely related, and produced an elaborate family tree to prove it.[1] Gilbert's family seem never to have become involved in such difficulties, or if so, he has left us no record of them. But the information he gives is none the less interesting for that: it reveals the ramifications of a twelfth-century family to an exceptional extent; and shows how widely the sense of family ranged.

In the letter of the English bishops in which John of Salisbury detected the style of Achitophel and Doeg (alias the bishop of London), it had been pointed out to Thomas that Henry II had raised him from poverty (*ab exili*). This Thomas himself interpreted as a slur on his birth; he evidently felt that his own ancestors were not of such noble stock as the author or authors of the letter; when writing to Gilbert in person, the implication seems clear, though not explicit.[2] Thomas was sprung of citizens of London, his father was of knightly rank. We may infer that the Foliots were more than knights; but to say precisely who they were is exceedingly difficult.

The difficulty is enhanced by the terminology of relationship; above all, by the vagueness of *cognatus*, 'cousin' or 'relation', and the ambiguity of *nepos*, 'nephew', 'grandson', or 'cousin'.[3] In

---

[1] *Correspondance*, ed. J. Leclercq, 1 (Paris, 1949), no. 45.

[2] *MB Epp.* 123–4.

[3] *Cognatus* retained its classical sense, 'kinsman', and was almost as common and vague as 'cousin' (*consobrinus*) in Shakespearean English. *Nepos* seems most commonly to mean 'nephew' in medieval Latin. But it retained its original meaning of 'grandson' (as e.g. in *MB*, IV, 84), and Ducange records its use for 'niece' and 'cousin'.

spite of this, two important clues seem to be unambiguous. On one occasion Gilbert described the relationship to himself of William de Chesney, a baron and sheriff of Oxfordshire in Stephen's reign, as *nepoti auunculus*, which can only mean 'uncle to nephew'; this is confirmed by a letter to William's brother Robert, bishop of Lincoln, in which the son of one R. Brito is described as Gilbert's nephew and Robert's great-nephew (*nepos, abnepos*, again unambiguous).[1] Since there is no doubt that Foliot was Gilbert's family name,[2] the connexion with the Chesneys must be through his mother. We know that her name was Agnes, and we must assume that she was called Agnes de Chesney, that she was a daughter of Roger de Chesney and his wife Alice de Langetot, and so probably grand-daughter to Ralph de Langetot, a Domesday tenant under Walter Giffard.[3]

[1] Nos. 20, 173; cf. also no. 107 and *Gesta Abbatum S. Albani* (ed. H. T. Riley, RS), I, 139, which confirms that they were related. *Auunculus* in medieval Latin was used of a paternal or maternal uncle, and in classical usage also of an aunt's husband. In both the cases cited here, the use of one word describing the relationship (*nepos* or *auunculus*) would have left it ambiguous; the use of two leaves no reasonable doubt of the precise meaning; and *abnepos* can only mean 'great-nephew'. R. Brito is described as *affinis noster*: he was evidently Gilbert's brother-in-law.

[2] The meaning of the name Foliot cannot be certainly established. It was doubtless connected with *folium, feuille*, 'a leaf', and may be the same as OF *foliot*, a snare or trap, but the word is not vouched for in Godefroy's *Dictionnaire* before the fifteenth century (Jean Lefevre, *La Vieille*, ed. H. Cocheris, Paris, 1861, i, line 695; the derivation is accepted in E. Ekwall, *Concise Oxford Dict. of English Place-Names, s.v.* Chilton).

[3] In the Hereford cathedral obituary, the obit 'Agnetis matris Gileberti episcopi' is recorded on 1 May (R. Rawlinson, *History and Antiquities of...Hereford*, London, 1717, Appendix, p. (12)). It is possible that she was daughter of Roger de Chesney by another wife: but there is no evidence that he married anyone before Alice de Langetot; her sons seem to have been his heirs, and it would not be easy to fit two marriages into what is known of his career. In *Cart. Eynsham*, I, no. 124, Alice gives a comprehensive list of her children: all her sons, alive and dead, seem to be named, and her living daughters; but her dead daughters, who presumably included Agnes, are not named, although it is indicated that she had had some. It is probable, though not certain, that Alice de Langetot was a daughter of Ralph de Langetot. On this branch of the family, see H. E. Salter, *Cart. Eynsham*, I, 411–23; Farrer, *HKF*, III, 227 ff.; L. F. Salzman in *Sussex Archaeological Collections*, LXV, (1924), 29 ff. The pedigree is based on these studies. Cf. also *Cart. Dunstable*, ed. G. H. Fowler, pp. 49, 283 ff.

The heir of the elder William de Chesney was Matilda de Chesney, but her

The Chesneys were by no means a particularly distinguished family; but they held knights' fees in Oxfordshire and the east midlands, and Gilbert's uncle William de Chesney was a profiteer from the anarchy, who rose to be sheriff of Oxfordshire, for a time tenant-in-chief, and one of Stephen's leading supporters in the midlands. The anarchy nearly made the Chesneys into a first-class power, but after Henry II's accession they sank again into insignificance, and by the end of the century their male line was extinct.

If these inferences are correct they help us to settle a problem of great importance in understanding not only Gilbert's family, but his career: the question of when he was born. In 1169 he described himself as in the last age of man (*etas...ultima*);[1] he says, indeed, that it had caught up with him several years before. We may allow something for the circumstances: Gilbert, in the depths of his misery, was excusing himself for not visiting the pope. But in current analyses the last age of man was the sixth.[2] The penultimate, *senectus* or *grauitas*, ran from 50 to 70, the ultimate, *senium* or *senectus* (which could be used in one sense or the other), ran from 70 to death. If Gilbert was really over 70 in 1169, we have to face two serious difficulties: he must have been at least 87 when he died, and he must have been born in the 1090's, whereas his great-grandfather was apparently a Domesday tenant.

place in the pedigree is quite uncertain; Farrer's conjecture that she was a daughter of Hugh de Chesney by a hypothetical first wife is the most plausible so far made. She married Henry FitzGerald (died between 1173 and 1186), and through her sons Warin and Henry the estates of William de Chesney passed to the FitzGeralds (Salter, *op. cit.* 422–3); for further details, see Salzman's account, which must, however, be used with caution. For the Chesneys of Sussex and Norfolk, whose founder, Ralph de Chesney, may have been Roger de Chesney's father, see J. H. Round, in *Genealogist*, new series, XVIII (1901–2), 1–16 and *EHR*, XXXV (1920), 481 ff.; Salzman, *art. cit.* 20 ff.; *HKF*, III, 313 ff.

The family came from Le Quesnay (Seine-Maritime: L. C. Loyd, *The Origins of some Anglo-Norman Families*, Harleian Soc. 1951, pp. 27–8).

[1] No. 214.

[2] Cf. A. Hofmeister, 'Puer, iuvenis, senex...', *Papsttum und Kaisertum Paul Kehr...dargebracht* (Munich, 1926), pp. 287–316, esp. pp. 289–90, where the fundamental texts from St Isidore are quoted, and p. 316. Hofmeister's conclusion is that a man in the fifties was sometimes called 'old', a man in the sixties regularly so. This evidence is consistent with the view that Gilbert was about 60 in 1169.

Neither is wholly impossible; but combined they add up to a formidable difficulty, which is enhanced by the fact that if Gilbert was born in the 1090's, he was of the same generation as his uncles. The indications are that his grandmother was married c. 1085–90.[1] If this is correct, she could have had a grandson by c. 1105–10, but hardly earlier, and since Gilbert did not inherit his father's estates, he was presumably not an eldest son. It seems likely enough that Gilbert's phrase in 1169 did not refer to a specific age. Men and women in the twelfth century were often singularly vague about their precise ages, as the conflicting indications in the *Rotuli de dominabus* sufficiently indicate.[2] In no. 228 Gilbert himself was remarkably (and conveniently) vague about the age of one of Henry II's sons. In 1169 he may simply have meant that he was decrepit. He can hardly have been less than 50 in 1169; and the phrase is easier to understand if he was about 60. This suggests that he was born c. 1110. He can hardly have been born later. He was consecrated bishop in 1148, and must (by the canonical rule) have been over thirty. In 1139 he became abbot of Gloucester, and he had already had a scholastic career and been monk and one of the priors of Cluny and prior of Abbeville; and in spite of the tradition at Cluny of promoting young men rapidly, it is hard to believe that he was under thirty when he reached Gloucester, or under 21–25 when he entered Cluny.

Thus a date c. 1105–10 for Gilbert's birth is the only one which does no violence to the evidence, and it may be accepted with some confidence.[3]

The Chesney connexion is well-established; the Foliot line is more difficult to determine. It can be approached, however, from two points. First of all, there are clear indications that Gilbert was related, on the Foliot side, to the two earls of Hereford of his day, Milo of Gloucester and his son Roger. One chronicler makes Gilbert Milo's cousin (*cognatus*), another makes him

---

[1] See Salter, *Cart. Eynsham*, I, 411–12. This is a rough estimate, but cannot be far wrong. Her sons seem all to have died by 1170, but she was still active in the 1140's; her father and perhaps her husband were Domesday tenants.

[2] Ed. J. H. Round, Pipe Roll Soc. 1913, see p. xxxviii.

[3] See below, p. 73. (He is called *grandaevus* apropos events of 1162 in *MB*, IV, 17.)

consanguineus of Roger.[1] The Evesham chronicle, confirmed by a later source of little value, describes Reginald, abbot of Evesham (1130–49), as *nepos* of Milo.[2] A letter by Reginald addressed to Gilbert is preserved, a curiously involved piece of rhetoric, in the course of which Reginald describes himself as Gilbert's uncle (*auunculus*).[3] *Auunculus* could be used of an uncle on either side, but it is known that Alice de Langetot did not have a son called Reginald,[4] and it is clear that Reginald was a Foliot, even though no early source, so far as we can discover, gives him the surname. Gilbert's early letters show that his relations with Milo and his son Roger were not always easy; but he seems to have had a regard for Milo, and the connexion, the most aristocratic connexion of the Foliots, played a decisive part in his life. It was Milo who brought him from France to Gloucester, and it was doubtless Milo's influence which made him an Angevin.[5] Milo's influence in his election strongly confirms the other evidence that they were related, and that the relationship was not distant.

Roger de Pîtres, Milo's grandfather, had been a well-to-do Norman knight, but not particularly distinguished. He rose to be

---

[1] Gregory of Caerwent, Cotton MS Vesp. A. v, fo. 198 v; Gervase, I, 162. (In *CS*, pp. 260 ff. an attempt is made to reconstruct the chronicle of Gloucester as it was in the twelfth century. The thirteenth-century chronicle of Gregory of Caerwent, monk of Gloucester, of which a sixteenth-century copy survives in BM Cotton MS Vesp. A. v, fos. 195–203 v, is an important additional witness to this. It consists, down to the twelfth century at any rate, of extracts from the same source as the fifteenth-century chronicle, and although it contains some puzzling inaccuracies and raises some critical problems, it confirms most of the conclusions drawn in *CS*.)

[2] *Chron. Evesham*, p. 98; *Chron. Angliae Petriburgense* (ed. J. A. Giles, London, 1845), p. 84. On the latter, see F. Liebermann in *Neues Archiv* XVIII (1893), 235 ff.; A. Gransden, *The Chronicle of Bury* (NMT, 1964), p. xxviii and n. The Evesham chronicle survives in various versions: the printed text is in the main a faithful compilation of the early thirteenth century from earlier materials. With some reservations, it can be regarded as first-hand testimony on Abbot Reginald (cf. *CS*, p. 260 and n.). On Reginald, see *GFL*, Biog. Index.

[3] *Chron. Evesham*, pp. 112–13 n.

[4] See Salter, *Cart. Eynsham*, I, 411; cf. no. 124 (see above p. 33, n.).

[5] For the family of Milo of Gloucester, see *CP*, VI, 451 ff.; D. Walker, *Transactions of the Bristol and Gloucestershire Arch. Soc.* LXXVII (1958–9), 66 ff. (cf. Walker in *Transactions*, LXXIX (1960–1), 174 ff.; A. S. Ellis in *Transactions*, IV (1879–80), 161–4); *GFL*, Biog. Index, *s.v.* Hereford; R. H. C. Davis in *Misc. D. M. Stenton*, pp. 139 ff. esp. 143–4.

sheriff of Gloucester, an office inherited by his son, Walter of Gloucester, the Domesday tenant. Walter died in or after 1123, and he had already had the satisfaction of uniting his own inheritance to one of the most substantial fiefs in the southern March by marrying Milo, his son and heir, to Sybil, heiress of Bernard of Neufmarché. Milo carried the family to the peak of its influence by marrying his son Roger to the heiress of another marcher lord, Payne FitzJohn, and by winning his earldom from the empress in 1141. But Roger died childless, and although he had four brothers and at least three sisters, the male line failed; in the end the inheritance passed through the sisters and their children, and the chief legatees were the Bohuns, who revived the earldom in 1200.

Gilbert's uncle, then, was Milo's *nepos*, and Gilbert himself was Milo's *cognatus*. Both words were ambiguous, but *nepos* is unlikely to have been used of anyone more distant than a first cousin; and 'nephew' and 'grandson' were probably commoner usages. The cumulative evidence of relationship, and Milo's influence on Gilbert's election, strongly suggest that Gilbert was not more distantly related than first cousin or first cousin once removed. It is, however, inconceivable that Reginald was Milo's grandson, since Milo only married in 1121, and improbable that he was Milo's nephew. Walter of Gloucester, Milo's father, was alive in 1123, perhaps in 1126;[1] if Reginald was Milo's nephew, Walter was Gilbert's great-grandfather. This is not wholly impossible, but it strains credulity: it forces us to believe that Gilbert's great-grandfather was still alive when he was approaching twenty, which would be a rare situation in any age, exceedingly rare in the twelfth century. It is more probable that Reginald and Milo were first cousins, and Milo and Gilbert first cousins once removed. But there is no means of deciding whether Reginald's mother was a sister of Walter of Gloucester or of his wife, Bertha, whose origin is unknown.

Two further scraps of evidence link the Foliots with Gloucester

---

[1] Walter was alive in 1123; Milo was granted his lands before 1127 (Walker (1958–9), p. 68, suggests that he had succeeded by 1126, but the document he cites is of doubtful authenticity).

and the neighbouring counties. Reginald Foliot, before he became abbot of Evesham, had been a monk of Gloucester.[1]
Another relative was Richard of Ilchester, later a leading royal
clerk and exchequer official, archdeacon of Poitiers and ultimately
bishop of Winchester (1174–88).[2] Richard presumably came from
Ilchester in Somerset; all that is known of his early career is that
he was at one time a notary or clerk in the service of Robert, earl
of Gloucester, who died in 1147.[3]

The other main point from which the Foliots may be attacked
carries us to quite a different part of this island, and to the central
problem of Gilbert's family connexion. Who was his father?
The question cannot be solved with certainty. But there is one
piece of evidence to guide us, and it leads us straight to the most
important Foliot group in the country, which is where we should
expect to find the home of the man who patronised Thomas
Becket, and was cousin to Earl Milo.

Between 1163 and 1165 Gilbert wrote to the king of Scotland,
who was also earl of Huntingdon, asking him to confirm Elias,
proximo cognato nostro, in his inheritance, which he had lost on
account of his fidelity to King Malcolm's father.[4] *Cognatus* commonly meant 'cousin', and it is just possible that we should
render this, 'My first cousin'. But we have found no parallel to
this usage, and *cognatus* seems in fact to have retained its basic
meaning of 'kinsman', so that the natural interpretation of the
phrase is 'my next of kin': this would seem to have been the
classical use, and *proximus cognatus* was so employed in the *Digest*,
with which Gilbert was certainly familiar. Since Gilbert's father
would hardly have been chasing inheritances in the 1160's, if he
was alive at all, which is improbable, the 'next of kin' seems most
likely to be Gilbert's brother.[5]

---

[1] *Chron. Evesham*, p. 98.   [2] No. 197: 'cognato et amico suo'.
[3] *Miracula S. Nectani martyris*, ed. P. Grosjean in *Analecta Bollandiana*, LXXI
(1953), 411. Richard of Ilchester must have been a young man before 1147: it
is possible that Gilbert had a hand in finding him this early patronage.
[4] No. 151. On this see G. W. S. Barrow, *Regesta Regum Scottorum*, I
(Edinburgh, 1960), 101, and no. 320.
[5] Gilbert refers to his *canos*, his grey hairs, so he can hardly have been
Gilbert's nephew; nor is it likely that an uncle (however grey) would have been

An Elias Foliot held half a knight's fee from Earl Simon de Senlis in Lincolnshire in 1166, and also (himself or another of the same name) lands of the honour of Huntingdon in the 1170's and 1180's.[1] This provides us with the clue we need. In the mid-twelfth century the honour and earldom of Huntingdon passed to and fro between the family of the kings of Scotland and Simon II and Simon III de Senlis, earls of Northampton. King Malcolm was grandson to King David I; his father was Henry, earl of Northumberland and Huntingdon, who forfeited Huntingdon after the battle of the Standard in 1138; Malcolm himself recovered it in 1157.[2] If Elias had been too faithful to Earl Henry, he might well have been in trouble during the years of his forfeiture.

One of the stewards of David and Henry as earls of Huntingdon was a man called Robert Foliot, who makes several appearances among the charters of the Scottish kings.[3] We also meet him, in

pursuing an inheritance in the 1160's—though this is not impossible. For the phrase 'proximus cognatus' cf. *Thesaurus Linguae Latinae*, III, col. 1481, lines 17–21, and references there cited, esp. *Digest*, 38, 6, 8. In Roman Law it seems to have meant 'next of kin', and so we may presume that Gilbert intended it; but we cannot of course rule out the possibility that he simply meant 'very near relative'.

[1] On the Foliots of Hunts and Northants, see Barrow, *op. cit.* pp. 100–1; G. H. Fowler, *Cart. Wardon*, pp. 325 ff., which is the basis for what follows, unless otherwise stated. Elias occ. in BM Royal MS11. B. ix, fos. 7–8 (1148–53).

[2] G. H. Fowler in *Publications of the Beds. Hist. Rec. Soc.* IX (1925), 23–34; *CP*, VI, 641 ff.; Barrow, *op. cit.* pp. 98 ff.

[3] Barrow, *Regesta Regum Scottorum*, I, 100–1; and nos. 3, 7, 11–13, 15, 16, 20, 21, 34; A. C. Lawrie, *Early Scottish Charters* (Glasgow, 1905), pp. 48, 88, 88–9, 91–2, 100–1; *Cart. Huntingdon, Trans. of the Cambs. and Hunts. Arch. Soc.* IV (1930), 226–7. These documents cover the period [1114–21]–*c.* 1141. The Robert Foliot who witnessed charters of King Malcolm was presumably the younger Robert (Barrow, nos. 132–3, 148, 150–2). The younger Robert seems to have been steward to Earl Simon II (Barrow, p. 101 and n. 1; *HKF*, II, 357); but, as Professor Barrow says 'he and his family appear generally to have taken the Scottish side'. Precise evidence that Robert II was son to Robert I is lacking, apart from inferences drawn from Gilbert's letter. That they were connected can hardly be doubted, since both witnessed charters of the Scottish kings and of the Senlis earls (for the former, see above; for the latter, *Beds. Hist. Rec. Soc.* IX, 29, 32; B. A. Lees, *Records of the Templars in England* (London, 1935), pp. 185–6; *HKF*, II, 357. The first reference is probably to Robert I, the rest to Robert II). Tottenham (Herts) was in the hands of Robert II's heirs in the thirteenth century; Robert I and his descendants certainly had rights there (Lawrie, *op. cit.* p. 48; *Beds. Hist. Rec. Soc.* V (1920), 249—cf. *Cart. Wardon*,

Ramsey charters, with his brothers Payne and Elias, laying claim to various Huntingdonshire properties.[1] It would seem that the family rose to prominence as a result of its official position *vis-à-vis* the Scottish king; and it is reasonably certain that it was Robert's heir, presumably his son, another Robert Foliot, who raised the family into the class of tenants-in-chief by his marriage to Margery, heiress of Richard de Raimbeaucourt, the lord of West Wardon in Northamptonshire.[2]

Robert I had a brother called Elias and Robert II a son of the same name. But as Robert I was active from well before 1124 until *c.* 1150, or somewhat later, when he died, his brother would probably be too old to be the Elias of Gilbert's letter and the *carta* of 1166; and since Robert II married between 1155 and 1162, his son would be too young. Since the name occurs in two generations it is likely to have occurred in the third, which intervened; and in the period 1165–70 Robert and Elias Foliot witnessed a charter of William the Lion, king of Scotland.[3] This Elias is more likely to be Robert's brother than his son, who would in any case have been a small child at this time. Thus it is reasonably certain that Elias was the son of Robert Foliot I, steward of Earl Henry, and brother of Robert II, the tenant-in-chief. Earl Henry's

pp. 328, 370 n. 416). This evidence suggests that Robert II was Robert I's heir. A difficulty in our reconstruction is that if Robert II was Gilbert's elder brother, he must have been at least 45 when he won his heiress. This is not of course impossible, though perhaps a little surprising. But since Robert became a monk in the early 1170's, one would be inclined in any case to assume that he was in advancing years at that date. Gilbert was then probably in his early sixties.

[1] *Cart. Ramsey*, I, 143, cf. 106; *Chron. Ramsey*, pp. 306, 312 (ranging from 1124–30 to 1147–8).   [2] See the pedigree, chart 2 (p. 51).

[3] *Beds. Hist. Rec. Soc.* XVII (1935) (Harrold Cart.), p. 18. Fowler suggested Robert I died *c.* 1150. Since Robert II received his heiress and her inheritance between 1155 and 1162 and Elias (Robert I's younger son, if our reconstruction is correct) was chasing his property *c.* 1163, this seems likely enough, though perhaps rather on the early side. Robert and Gilbert's father would probably have been well over 60 in 1150. There is a reference to 'domus patris mei' in *Multiplicem*, in connexion with the events of 1161–2, which may imply that his father was still alive then; but it is probable that the phrase is an echo of Esther iv. 14 ('Tu, et domus patris tui, peribitis') and is not to be so literally understood. Other hints which might indicate that Robert I died *c.* 1163 are 'si patrem...aduersum uos' in no. 151, and his absence from the Hereford obituary in which his wife occurs. None of these points is of much cogency.

father, King David, was great-uncle to Henry II of England; and Henry II owed much to David. This connexion will help us to understand why Robert Foliot II won the noble prize of the Raimbeaucourt heiress, and if he was also brother of Gilbert Foliot, our understanding of his success becomes clearer still.

Robert Foliot II died clothed as a Cistercian monk. This may seem a strange ending for the brother of an eminent Cluniac; but Gilbert himself was no enemy of the Cistercians, and Robert had close links with Wardon abbey. It had been founded by his wife's family; he himself was a benefactor. It was a daughter house of Rievaulx abbey. When it was founded St Ailred was a monk at Rievaulx; when Robert Foliot married, Ailred was abbot of Rievaulx; and Ailred, as a very young man, had been steward of the kings of Scotland, at the same time that Robert Foliot I was their steward for their English honour. Soon after Robert II's marriage, to complete the links in the chain, St Ailred dedicated his *Sermons on Isaiah* to Gilbert Foliot.[1] This genealogical exercise provides a likely explanation of a somewhat surprising friendship. Gilbert and Ailred were almost exactly of an age, and it seems that they grew up in the same circle.

There is no record of Robert Foliot I before the period 1114–21, although if he was Gilbert's father, he must have married Agnes de Chesney well before 1110. Beyond him the family cannot be traced. There is little doubt that it was Norman in origin, and there are some hints that it had its roots in the Cotentin, more specifically in the neighbourhood of Cherbourg. A nephew of Gilbert who also bore the name Gilbert Foliot held property at Vauville in the Cotentin. He may be the same man who was Gilbert's steward in the diocese of London in the early 1170's, and was the unwilling witness of one of St Thomas Becket's miracles.[2]

---

[1] Cf. Sir Maurice Powicke, *Walter Daniel's Life of Ailred of Rievaulx*, pp. xlix, xciii, xxxix ff. Ailred was born in 1110.

[2] For all these details see Loyd, *The Origins of some Anglo-Norman Families*, pp. 43–4; *Sir Christopher Hatton's Book of Seals*, ed. L. C. Loyd and D. M. Stenton (Oxford, 1950), pp. 157–8; *MB*, II, 149 f.; Paris Bibl. Nat. MS Lat. 10087, p. 72 (a William Foliot witnesses a charter to Montebourg). In no. 261 Gilbert refers to a brother and a nephew, who had apparently been helped by a Norman justice living in or near Rouen.

In the twelfth and early thirteenth centuries Sampson, William and another Sampson Foliot were successively seigneurs of Montfarville, also near Cherbourg. These details lead us to suspect that the earliest recorded Foliot, the Rainald or Reginald Foliot (thus a namesake of the abbot of Evesham) who witnessed a charter of Neel, vicomte of the Cotentin, c. 1060, was not unconnected with Gilbert's family.

In 1086 a certain Rainald held various properties in Wiltshire and the neighbouring counties which were subsequently in the hands of various members of the Foliot family. The family tree cannot be traced at all exactly, but a throng of Foliots from these neighbourhoods—Bartholomews, Ralphs, Rogers, Richards, Sampsons and others—have been rounded up in a brief but crowded chapter of Farrer's *Honors and Knights' Fees*.[1] Farrer suggested that Robert Foliot, lord of Chilton Foliat in 1167, was Gilbert's brother. A link seems highly probable, but it is more likely that they were cousins. The family names Rainald (Reginald), Robert, Sampson suggest a connexion with Gilbert's family. Chilton was held of the honour of Wallingford, and Robert's predecessor seems to have been a certain Ralph Foliot, a knight of Brian FitzCount and Matilda of Wallingford, who occurs in the 1130's and 1140's. In nos. 29–30, written in the 1140's, Gilbert appeals to the bishop and prior of Winchester on behalf of his relative (*parens*),[2] Roger Foliot. Roger's father, he says, held only half a hide, and Roger himself held nothing but his arms; he was a knight of Brian FitzCount, evidently a domestic knight. The probability is very strong that Roger was a member of a cadet branch of the Foliots of Chilton.

This exhausts the direct evidence of Gilbert's lay relations bearing the surname Foliot. But the families of Foliot are by no means exhausted. There were the Foliots of Yorkshire, Henrys

---

[1] III, 234 ff. For the Foliots of Chilton, and the other branches of the family, see Appendix II.

[2] It seems reasonably certain that Gilbert uses *parens* in the broad sense of 'relative', not in the narrow sense of 'parent' (as in no. 162; cf. also no. 263). If Roger Foliot had been Gilbert's father, it seems strange that the son of a domestic knight should have felt able to patronise Thomas Becket; and the supposition runs counter to all the other indications we have of his parenthood.

and Jordans, the Foliots of Lincolnshire, William, Ralph, Gilbert and Alexander, and the Foliots of Devon.[1] We can trace a succession of Robert Foliots in Devon, royal serjeants and tenants of the Reviers earls, building up a sizeable fee as the years passed. About 1190 the current Robert Foliot died, leaving his estates to a quadrilateral of grandchildren, and so the property ran out into the sands. There is no evidence to link Gilbert with Yorkshire or Lincolnshire, but the Sampson Foliot who witnessed Earl Baldwin's foundation charter to Quarr was probably of the Devon family, and may be connected with the later Sampson Foliot of the Cotentin, who was a benefactor to Quarr and also witnessed a charter of an earl of Devon. These circumstantial details are all that there is to go on.[2]

If the Foliots are obscure and diffuse, they are clarity itself compared to the Britos and Banastres whom Gilbert's sisters married. Brito, the Breton, was one of the vaguest and commonest of twelfth-century surnames. Gilbert's Breton nephew married an heiress and succeeded to the barony of William Gulafre (or Gulliver); this we know from a characteristic letter, no. 173, in which Gilbert appeals to his uncle of Lincoln to provide ordination and a benefice for the younger brother.[3] Of the Banastres, we know only the churchmen; and to Gilbert's ecclesiastical relations we must now turn our attention.

Among the higher clergy Gilbert's relatives seem even more ubiquitous than among the nobility and the gentry of twelfth-century England. The family of Belmeis, from Beaumais-sur-Dive in Calvados, who provided two bishops of London and a multiplicity of lesser dignitaries to the chapter of St Paul's, were related to him; so was Richard of Ilchester, one of the leading administrators of Henry II's reign, and bishop of Winchester.[4]

---

[1] See Appendix II.
[2] Thomas Fuller (*Worthies of England*, London, 1662, p. 251) records a tradition that Gilbert was born at Tamerton Foliot in Devon. He cites a 'Manuscript of Baronet Northcott' which we have not identified. Since the connexion of Tamerton with the Foliots seems to have started in the thirteenth century the tradition is most unlikely to be correct.   [3] See above, p. 33.
[4] Nos. 4, 197. On Richard de Belmeis and Richard of Ilchester see *GFL*, Biog. Index.

Greater in numbers though not in power and wealth were the
nephews and cousins, the Foliots, Britos and Banastres, who received patronage from their distinguished relation in the chapters
of Hereford and London, and elsewhere.[1] In the sixty years
following Gilbert's departure from Hereford two Foliots were
elected bishops of that see; and this is hardly a coincidence,
although the first, Robert Foliot, is more likely to have owed
his early preferment, in the diocese of Lincoln, to Robert de
Chesney, and the second, Hugh Foliot, owed his own early
promotion in the diocese of Hereford to Robert. We do not
know how Robert Foliot was related to Gilbert; indeed, we
cannot prove decisively that he was.[2] But Robert's name, his
association with Hereford and Lincoln, their common interest in
family preferment, and the fact that Gilbert dedicated his Commentary on the Canticle to Robert, all suggest that they were
closely related. It is certain that they were friends; and here we
meet an interesting cross-current in ecclesiastical politics. In the
days of the anarchy, the Chesneys were supporters of Stephen,
Gilbert supported Matilda. In the Becket crisis, Gilbert was the
archbishop's most bitter opponent on the episcopal bench; but
Robert Foliot, 'English by nation, then archdeacon of Oxford'
appears among the list of the archbishop's learned supporters and
clerks, although with the archbishop's permission and blessing he
did not accompany his master into exile.[3]

The chapter of Hereford received at least three and probably
four Foliots under Gilbert, and at least one Brito, one Banastre
and four Foliots under Robert. London received eight of the
family, including two (one Foliot and one Banastre), who are
specified in the texts as Gilbert's nephews, and at least one
Belmeis.[4] Henry Banastre, treasurer of London, and Richard

[1] For what follows, see Appendix IV.
[2] But it is implied in no.231: '*nature* gratia superaddit affectum'; cf. *MB Epp.* 510.
[3] *MB*, III, 524 (Herbert of Bosham). Perhaps he was a nephew of Gilbert:
there seems to be no other Robert recorded in that generation of the main
branch of the family. On Robert Foliot, see *GFL*, Biog. Index. For the other
relatives, Appendix II.
[4] See Appendix IV and for other Foliots under Bishop Robert, *CHJ*, VIII, i
(1944), 8–18. Richard, dean of Hereford, *c.* 1186–*c.* 1200 was Richard Brito

Foliot, archdeacon of Colchester, were also canons of Hereford, and Ralph Foliot, archdeacon of Hereford and a royal justice, was also a canon of London. Three or four of the family had stalls in both chapters, so that the total number of the family's canons and dignitaries was thirteen or fourteen. Of these, ten or eleven owed their promotion to Gilbert. All these figures probably are, it must be stressed, minimum estimates. It is possible, though improbable, that Gilbert gave preferment to a Foliot here or a Banastre there who was not related to him; it is also possible, and not at all improbable, that others of his relations whom we do not know to be such received preferment in these chapters; the Belmeis family still had scions at St Paul's in his day, and among his young protégés we meet a man with the suggestive name of Ralph of Chilton.

Occasionally in the charters of the mid- and late-twelfth century we meet a group of Foliots together, a family party as it were. Occasionally we meet the bishop among his secular relations, as when he and two Foliot archdeacons, Walter of Shropshire and Richard of Colchester, witnessed a charter of Gilbert Foliot— possibly the bishop's seneschal—made 'with the consent of Walter Foliot and Geoffrey son of Serlo Foliot', and also witnessed by Robert Foliot of Cuxham and Robert Foliot of Evenley. More commonly one meets a mainly clerical gathering, as at St Paul's, in December 1178, when both Foliot of Hereford and Foliot of London were present with their trains.[1] Hugh de Marigny the dean was there, probably a relation of the Belmeis; also Richard Foliot, archdeacon of Colchester, Gilbert Foliot, canon of St Paul's, later archdeacon of Middlesex, Ralph Foliot, canon and later archdeacon of Hereford, and Ralph of Chilton.

(Oxford, Balliol MS 291, fos. 99 v–100 v). We assume that the Foliots and Banastres were all related to Gilbert. The decretal *JL* 14142 (*Extra*, ii, 22, 3) shows that Ralph de Hauterive, Master of the Schools of St Paul's and archdeacon of Colchester, was *nepos* to Gilbert.

[1] *Facsimiles of Early Charters in Oxford Muniment Rooms*, ed. H. E. Salter (Oxford, 1929), no. 49; *GFL*, no. 410. An earlier gathering (*c.* 1155: no. 312) included three Foliots of the Hereford chapter, four secular Foliots, William de Chesney, Henry, Early Roger's brother, 'Ralph Foliot nephew of the bishop', and four *pueri*—two Foliots and two Banastres.

But if we were to light on a really complete gathering of the clan
—of all the men whom Gilbert's sisters could not legally marry—
we should meet two bishops or more, possibly an abbot,[1] a posse
of archdeacons, dignitaries and canons; an earl, a sheriff, a tenant-
in-chief, innumerable sub-vassals and knights, even domestic
knights and two-virgate men. We should find prosperous men
who had risen as stewards and serjeants and by wealthy marriages,
and lean men who had sunk to the verge of villainy by being the
younger sons of younger sons in houses without the resources to
support them. We should meet five different men called Robert
Foliot,[2] to remind us that the study of twelfth-century genealogy
can degenerate into nightmare. But we should also meet a remarkable cross-section of English society, to remind us that the study
of genealogy can throw much light on the social scene.

The Foliots multiplied in the twelfth century, but they also
prospered. Gilbert's relations show above all how men rose to
prominence in the twelfth century. Milo of Gloucester was
hereditary royal constable: by service on the grand scale, and by
the calculated accidents of the anarchy, he rose to an earldom: the
Foliots owed their rise to the earls of Huntingdon and the earls of
Devon; two or three branches won through to receive patronage
from the king. The Belmeis had combined secular service on the
Welsh border to the Montgomerys, and after their fall to the
king, with ecclesiastical promotion. They belonged to the old
world, and did not only rely on their secular members to rear
children to carry on the family businesses. Gilbert Foliot belonged
to the new world, of Gregorian reform in action. He was celibate
and ascetic. He won the attention of the great while still quite
young: it was Stephen who appointed him to Gloucester, the
pope who moved him to Hereford, and a combination of king
and pope which translated him to London. But his move to
Gloucester he owed equally to his cousin Milo, and his move to

[1] In addition to Reginald, abbot of Evesham, it seems likely that Osbert
Foliot, prior of Gloucester and abbot of Malmesbury, 1176/7–1182, was related
to Gilbert in some way (on Osbert, see Dom Aelred Watkin in *VCH Wilts.* III,
218, 230).
[2] Cf. the innumerable Robert de Stutevilles who are sorted out with patient
and elaborate skill in *EYC*, IX.

London was no doubt made easier by the strong hold of his
Belmeis cousins there. In return for these services he provided
generously for his nephews and cousins. It would be premature
to place a cynical judgement on this: a bishop so widely connected
might well have had difficulty in filling the places in his gift without some nepotism. We cannot tell how characteristic Gilbert
was in this respect, since the ramifications of his family are better
documented than those of almost all his contemporaries on the
bench. But it is quite clear that he did not resist family pressure
with any vigour; that he took the conventional view that it was a
bishop's duty to provide for clerical relations, so long as he did so
without proceeding to absurd lengths.

Much of the evidence we have been using comes from chronicles and charters; yet without Gilbert's letters many links in the
chain would be missing. The letters have helped to reconstruct
the family tree: what do they tell us about Gilbert's attitude to
his family and theirs to him? The first thing they reveal, with
great clarity, is that kinship was not something to be disclosed on
every occasion, at all events in a letter. In writing to his ecclesiastical relatives, he rarely addresses them as uncle or cousin or
nephew: they are his brothers or sons in God, and it is this
relationship, and human friendship, which form the fitting subject
of a letter. The cumulative evidence makes it plain that Gilbert
was a good family man; that he was aware of the ramifications
of his family and proud of them.[1] But under normal circumstances the letter was not a medium in which this feeling should
be expressed. Sometimes one can discern another motive for its
suppression. When Gilbert described the case between the Lacys
and the earl of Hereford, his cousin, his relationship to Earl Roger
was never adverted to. On the other hand, when he needed the
judicial assistance of Richard of Ilchester, he addressed him as
cousin. When writing formally to appeal to the bishop of
Winchester on Roger Foliot's behalf, he does not mention that
he is his relative; when writing less formally to the prior of Winchester, he does. In this case, the difference is one purely of taste
and medium; the bishop was doubtless aware of the relationship.

[1] See below.

It is evident that Gilbert calculated whether the circumstances made a reference to kinship suitable or not. This calculation faithfully reflects the elements of formality in Gilbert's letter-writing. Other writers, whose humanism, or interest in describing human emotion, went deeper, expressed their feeling of family more freely than he. St Bernard, with characteristic boldness, poured out his human feelings in one of the most famous of his sermons. He made his brother's death the occasion, however, of something more than a mere lament: he carried his audience from the vale of misery to the heights of triumph over death, where human love is absorbed in God's love.[1] He thus expressed, vividly, almost violently, the depth of his family feeling and his sense that it was subordinated to spiritual relationship. This is the same idea which underlies Gilbert's failure to express what human kinship meant to him. A letter can express certain appropriate emotions, of which human friendship is one; or else it can express by its formality that business alone is its purpose. In the hands of a man of Bernard's imagination and daring it can express a far wider range of feelings or attitudes. Gilbert can be quite formal in addressing his relations; he can also use the language of close friendship. But it is clear that they meant much to him. It was a common practice to appoint young men to arch-deaconries in the twelfth century, and so they often held office for long periods of time. Thus it happened that Gilbert, in his thirty-nine years as a bishop, is only known to have appointed five archdeacons; all of these were certainly related to him. Two of them, Richard Foliot and Robert Banastre, were dispatched to Bologna to study canon law in the 1160's, but in 1168–9 Gilbert began to look for their return.[2] 'Note, I beg you, my dear, how long you have been away', he wrote to Banastre, 'how much labour and toil you have undergone by love of letters alone; take due care to carry back to us worthy fruits of your toil whenever you can.' To Richard he gave a more direct and instant summons:

I received your letter addressed to me with keen delight, but when I had glanced at it I read on with a sorrowful mind, beyond doubt. I was

---

[1] In Cant. serm. 26, *Bernardi Opera*, ed. J. Leclercq *et alii*, 1 (Rome, 1957), 169–81.   [2] Nos. 191–2.

hoping for happy news, and lo it brought me heavy sorrow. I am sad for the very noble young man who has paid the debt of fate so early. I am fearful that the like will happen to you; I hear that frequent sickness has attacked you. I command and enjoin you therefore, all excuses set aside, that if you feel Bologna in the least degree unsuitable or damaging to your health, for your soul's good you will leave it and fly away, and fail not to make a speedy return to us.

And he goes on to enjoin Richard to pass over his debts to Robert and hurry home so that he can free Robert to follow him. The bishop is in Normandy, 'and your return to me I expect and desire'. There is a manuscript of Gilbert's letters in the Biblioteca Alessandrina in Rome. The table of contents proudly boasts that Gilbert (as a letter-writer) was the equal of St Bernard. It is a bold claim. Bernard was the master of his medium, Gilbert its slave. But these letters to the archdeacons surely reveal genuine affection and concern. The witness lists of his charters and his letters alike show us a man with a powerful sense of family.

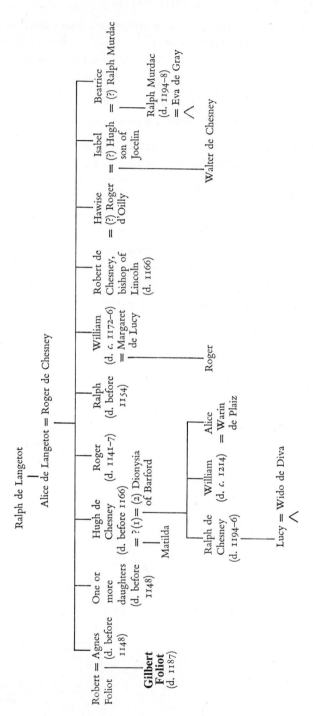

Chart 1. *The Chesneys*

Chart 2. *The Foliots and the earls of Hereford*

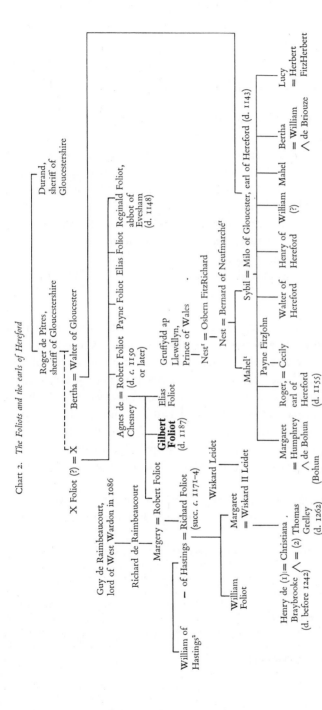

[1] See Lloyd, II, 397 and n., 438.   [2] Perhaps William son of Robert of Hastings, on whom see B. Dodwell in *Misc. D. M. Stenton*, pp. 150 ff.

CHAPTER IV

THE MASTER OF THE SCHOOLS

Gilbert Foliot's learning impressed some of his contemporaries more than it has impressed scholars today. The reason seems to be that he was a distinguished exponent of existing fashions, not an original or seminal thinker. There is evidence that he was a man quick to take up a new intellectual fashion which was congenial to his cast of mind; there is no evidence that he was ever in advance of the fashion. The interest of Gilbert's intellectual attainments, and of the study of his education and the formation of his ideas, lies in what is revealed of the way ideas were spread and used—of the part played by men of ordinary talents in the twelfth-century renaissance. The growth of the number of schools and scholars, the wide dissemination of ideas and fashions, was one of the most potent factors differentiating the intellectual revival of the late eleventh and twelfth centuries from the Carolingian and Ottonian revivals which went before. And the stages of this growth which lay before the mid-twelfth century are, on the whole, extremely ill-documented. A case-history such as Gilbert's has therefore a special interest. It is indeed not possible to pinpoint the places where he was educated; in the study of his scholastic career it is best to travel hopefully, for one will never arrive. But the course of the journey is in many ways exceedingly instructive.[1]

Gilbert was born about 1105–10; he entered Cluny well before 1139. We may therefore place his period of learning in the 1120's

---

[1] The literature on twelfth-century schools and scholars is vast. Much information and many references are usefully gathered in G. Paré, A. Brunet and P. Tremblay, *La Renaissance du XIIe siècle: les écoles et l'enseignement* (Paris-Ottawa, 1933); H. Rashdall, *The Universities of Europe in the Middle Ages* (3 vols., 2nd edn, ed. F. M. Powicke and A. B. Emden, Oxford, 1936); E. Lesne, *Histoire de la propriété ecclésiastique en France*, v (Lille, 1940); and the themes of this chapter will be more fully worked out in Dr Eleanor Rathbone's forthcoming book on English schools and scholars of the twelfth century. On legal studies, see below, pp. 59 ff.

and early 1130's. Gilbert's intellectual attainments and writings fall under three of the four headings into which the main studies of the late eleventh and early twelfth century were divided: liberal arts, biblical exegesis (*divina pagina*) and canon law (*lex ecclesiastica*). Only medicine is missing from the list. His theological works represent *divina pagina*, not doctrine (*fides catholica*);[1] and it is clear that his study of law included a thorough grounding in Roman Law as well as in canon law. Both facts are significant of the age and milieu in which he was educated.

In 1145 Gilbert wrote a letter to Robert Pullen, the eminent theologian and papal chancellor, in which he addressed Pullen as 'magistro suo karissimo'; since the phrase is repeated three times in a letter of no great length, it seems fairly clear that Gilbert had at some time been a pupil of Robert Pullen. Two letters in the Bodleian collection, not written by Gilbert but addressed to him, refer to one Master Adam as Gilbert's *magister* or *doctor*, *procurator* and *tutor*.[2] This seems to mean that Master Adam had been teacher and guardian, and looked after Gilbert's affairs. Gilbert was evidently not his only pupil and ward: one of the letters was written by a Ranulf de Turri, who claims to have stood to Adam in the same relation as Gilbert. The letters were addressed to Gilbert as bishop of London, and so cannot be earlier than 1163. Adam has recently died, leaving a load of debts and of children and other relations to be cared for; Gilbert is being appealed to to help Adam's son J., who is evidently trying to carry the burden.

Apart from quite general references—in no. 1 (1140) he tells us that he had heard long ago (*dudum*) in the schools diverse opinions propounded on true poverty of spirit—these are the only specific indications about his own early training; and the only additions made by other documents are stray references to his learning, the dedication of a theological work 'to G. Foliot, master of scholars and father of monks', and the abbot of Cluny's panegyric which

---

[1] Cf. B. Smalley, *The Study of the Bible in the Middle Ages* (2nd edn, Oxford, 1952), p. 76.
[2] No. 48 and *Epistolae*, ed. Giles, nos. 515, 517. No. 515 is from Ranulf de Turri, no. 517 anonymous; but the close verbal similarity between them indicates that both were written or dictated by the same author, though they may be petitions from two of Adam's son's friends.

indicates that Gilbert gave up a career as a master in the schools to become a monk at Cluny.[1] Master Adam is utterly obscure: his name was not uncommon, and was given to the children of any race. Ranulf de Turri ('of the tower') is equally unhelpful. Ranulf is unlikely to be a German name, and 'de Turri' is a surname met in England; but neither France nor Italy, nor even Spain, is utterly excluded for the country of his origin. We may suppose that Adam was a teacher who took in and brought up the children of comparatively well-to-do families who were intended for a clerical career. It is on the whole likely that Gilbert's father entrusted him to a tutor somewhere in England; more we cannot say.

Robert Pullen was anything but obscure. Born, it appears, in the neighbourhood of Sherborne in Dorset, he seems to have studied under the eminent theologian and exegete Anselm at Laon, about or soon after 1100; to have been teaching at Paris c. 1115–20; at Exeter in the next decade; at Oxford c. 1133. He was appointed archdeacon of Rochester c. 1138 and was again at Paris from c. 1138 until 1144, when he was promoted a cardinal and went to the papal Curia, where he stayed until his death, as papal chancellor, in 1146.[2] In the 1140's John of Salisbury, Simon de Poissy and the future

[1] E.g. *MB*, IV, 17; and see below, pp. 71–2, and above, p. 3 and n. The dedication is in Trinity Coll. Cambridge MS B. 14. 33 (see M. R. James's *Catalogue*, I, Cambridge, 1900, p. 432). There is some doubt whether the dedication, by an unknown 'Odo', belongs to the work to which it is now attached, an *Ysagoge* of the School of Abelard (ed. A. Landgraf, *Ecrits théologiques de l'école d'Abélard*, Louvain, 1934, pp. 61–298: the dedication is on pp. 287–9). The MS was at one time at Cerne and Belvoir—cf. MS B. It is one of the MSS, including MS B of the letters, presented by Prior William of Belvoir to Belvoir priory in the mid-fourteenth century (see *GFL*, introd.). We are much indebted to Dr D. Luscombe for help on this MS: he has convinced us that the dedication probably does belong to the *Ysagoge*, and that the work was dedicated to Gilbert when abbot of Gloucester. It shows that Gilbert had a reputation as a scholar and theologian, but is too obscurely worded to give any precision on his earlier career.

[2] F. Courtney, *Cardinal Robert Pullen* (Rome, 1954), chap. I, supplemented by C. N. L. Brooke in *Journal of Eccl. History*, VII (1956), 87–8. The link with Anselm of Laon seems likely, although the identification of Robert Pullen with Robert archdeacon of Exeter, connected with this in Fr. Courtney's reconstruction, does not seem very probable. The archdeacon seems to be the man whose year of death is given as 1123 in the Exeter Martyrology (Exeter Cathe-

archbishop of Canterbury, Baldwin of Forde, were among his pupils in Paris. But at this time Gilbert was already monk and abbot. He may have sat at Pullen's feet in his earlier sojourn in Paris, if it extended into the 1120's; or he may have been his pupil at Exeter. Pullen's move to Oxford in 1133 seems rather late for his connexion with Gilbert, so that the general probability is that Gilbert studied under him at Exeter. This may receive some support from a tantalising entry in the Exeter martyrology under 4 August: 'frater noster Robertus Foliot.'[1]

Evidence of Gilbert's friendships suggests that there was some variety in his early career.[2] Robert de Bethune, like Gilbert, had given up a promising scholastic life to enter the cloister; as a result of this the fervent but obscure house of Augustinian canons at Llanthony in Monmouthshire came to be noted as a centre of learning. Its chief patrons were Milo of Gloucester and his family; and in 1136 Lanthony *secunda* at Gloucester became its headquarters. By then Robert was bishop of Hereford (1131–48); and it is likely that it was through his grand relations that Gilbert first made contact with Llanthony and Robert de Bethune. If Froger of Saumur was a native of Anjou, we may be inclined to look in northern France for one of Gilbert's haunts. And what of his friendship with Jocelin de Bohun, bishop of Salisbury (1142–84)? Jocelin came of the family which ultimately captured the earldom of Hereford by marriage to one of Gilbert's cousins; we may therefore presume that Gilbert was not related to Jocelin. The Bohuns were descended from the *vicomtes* of Beaumont in Maine but derived their name from S. Georges-de-Bohon in Manche;[3] and Jocelin was related to the earl of Gloucester. Alexander III, Master Roland Bandinelli, claimed Jocelin as an old friend, which strongly suggests that Jocelin had studied in

---

dral MS 3518); and if Pullen had been archdeacon of Exeter, why did he relinquish the post, as he must have done, many years before he became a cardinal?

[1] Exeter Martyrology, 2 non. Aug. This Robert Foliot could be a layman, possibly one of the Devon Foliots (cf. above, p. 43).

[2] For what follows, see above, pp. 15–23.

[3] On the Bohun family, see Loyd, *The Origins of some Anglo-Norman Families*, p. 16; Knowles, *EC*, pp. 18, 19, 158–9. Earl Roger's sister married a Bohun, and the earldom was revived in 1200 for her grandson.

north Italy, perhaps at Bologna; and this is confirmed by the fact that his son Reginald, later bishop of Bath and archbishop-elect of Canterbury, was nicknamed the 'Lombard' and the 'Italian', because, so it was said, he had been brought up in Lombardy; but it is very likely that the name also implied that he was born there, perhaps even that he had a Lombard mother. He may have been born *c*. 1141,[1] more probably earlier, since when he was consecrated bishop in 1174 he had already been an archdeacon in his father's diocese for at least thirteen years, and had accompanied Becket into exile for a time in 1164. It seems that Jocelin became archdeacon of Winchester in the 1130's, and it may have been about this time or somewhat earlier that he went to Italy to study. But this does not help us to decide where he and Gilbert first met. It could have been in the household of the earl of Gloucester, or in the train of that other eminent Cluniac, Jocelin's patron, Henry of Winchester. Or it could have been in Bologna.[2]

RHETORIC

The style of Gilbert's letters does not help us to place with any precision the school where he had studied letters. By the early twelfth century the accomplishment of letter writing was one which could be learned in many different parts of Europe. Nor can one decide, by any simple test of language or *dictamen*, whether a particular letter or group of letters was written in Germany, Italy, France or England. There were schools noted for their skill in rhetoric or their humanist leanings such as Chartres; but any attempt to catalogue possible centres in this period meets its nemesis in Bernard of Clairvaux, the most brilliant stylist of the

---

[1] H. Wharton, *Anglia Sacra*, I (London, 1691), 561: a late medieval chronicle makes him 33 in 1174—with 24 as a marginal variant. The latter is incredible.

[2] On Jocelin, see *EC*, pp. 17 ff. He occurs as archdeacon of Winchester 1139–42 (Round, *CDF*, no. 157: cf. *Ann. Oseney, Ann. Mon.* IV, 23; John of Hexham in Symeon of Durham, ed. T. Arnold, RS, II, 302). On Reginald, see *EC*, p. 19. As archdeacon, he first occurs in 1161 (*Reg. Osmund*, I, 352: the date must be 1161, the only year when Alexander III was at Terracina on 8 December); he was in Becket's train, but later deserted the archbishop—*MB*, III, 524–5 (Herbert of Bosham): 'educatione et cognomento Lumbardus'; in *Cart. Bruton* (Somerset Rec. Soc. 1894), no. 381, he is called 'Ytalicus'.

age, the product of a teacher and a school which are wholly un-known. Nor can one state with any precision on what models Gilbert's letters were based. His manner of writing letters is a fair but conventional example of the pattern then universal among well-educated churchmen throughout western Europe. If we ask what earlier letter collections had Gilbert read and studied, we ask a question to which there is no clear answer. There is, for instance, a hidden echo of a letter of Sidonius Apollinaris in no. 103, although (happily for Gilbert's style) no other evidence of Sidonius's influence has been found. But a stray echo may come at second hand from some other writer or from a quotation in a glossary. It is highly probable that Gilbert had studied some of the well-known collections of earlier centuries, such as Augustine's and Jerome's. But they were not his models. Both in formal matters, such as the layout of the protocol and the arrangement of the letter, and in the attitude he shows to the medium, he was, as we have seen, a child of his own age. If we ask to which letter-writers of the early twelfth century he shows most affinity, the answer, so far as we have been able to discover, is to Hildebert, bishop of Le Mans and archbishop of Tours (1056–1133), and (more remotely) to Ivo, bishop of Chartres (c. 1040–c. 1116). It is probable that a detailed comparison would reveal numerous parallels to Hildebert and perhaps to Ivo in Gilbert's letters. But this would prove little, since both writers used freely the language of biblical echo and literary allusion which marked so many men's styles; and many of the same echoes figure in the composi-tions of almost any writer of the age. Through almost every letter that Ivo wrote one can feel the impact of his straightforward, blunt, forthright honesty. The personality and moral force be-hind Gilbert's letters are far less marked. But the medium is definitely similar: like Ivo, Gilbert is comparatively brief and practical; where they felt it to be appropriate, both are capable of elaborate allegorical flights. Hildebert was a more personal, more adept writer than either Ivo or Gilbert, although at bottom the medium and the language he used were similar. But it is striking that in one of Gilbert's early letters (no. 7) there is a quotation from Hildebert's famous letter to William of Champeaux.[1] The quotation was particularly apropos. Hamo, abbot of Bordesley, had asked Gilbert for a collection of his sermons; and among the arguments which Gilbert puts into Hamo's mouth is 'illud sapientis elogium' that a learned man ought not to be a miser of his learning. The eminent teacher William of Champeaux had become a canon regular at Saint-Victor, Paris; Hildebert congratulated him on this conversion, but argued strongly that he should not abandon teaching—and his argument seems to have played an important part in William's decision not to abandon his scholastic interests. It was a letter which would naturally interest Gilbert, who had 'cast off the mastership of the schools' to become a monk. The quotation is two full sentences; there can be no doubt that he is quoting. But it is odd that he should call Hildebert *sapiens*, a word normally (though not invariably) applied to Solomon in his letters. In Hildebert's letter the sentences are indeed wedged between two quotations from the sapiential books, and it may be that Gilbert had misunderstood or mis-remembered, and attributed to Solomon what (so far as we can tell) was really Hildebert's own coining.

There is, indeed, nothing surprising in this evidence that Gilbert knew Hildebert's letters, and may have known Ivo's; for of all the collections put together in Gilbert's childhood or early manhood, these two were the most popular, the most commonly to be found, indeed, in medieval and modern collections of manu-scripts of any twelfth-century collections apart from those of St Bernard and Peter of Blois. Of the two, Hildebert's seems to have been the commoner; his letters were a regular part of any medieval library which reflected more than a perfunctory interest in literature. No early catalogue of the Gloucester library sur-vives; but the manuscript at Hereford which contains a few of Gilbert's letters also contains some of Ivo's; and Lanthony had a collection of Hildebert's, at any rate in the early fourteenth century.[2]

---

[1] Hildebert, *Ep.* i, 1.

[2] For Lanthony, see *Centralblatt für Bibliothekswesen*, IX (1892), 208 ff. Library catalogues also reveal copies of Hildebert's letters at Canterbury (St Augustine's), Dover, Durham, Leicester, Meaux, Rievaulx and York (Austin Friars) (for references to library catalogues, see N. R. Ker, *Medieval Libraries of Great Britain*, 2nd edn, London, 1964).

It is possible that Gilbert had visited Le Mans or Tours and met Hildebert, who only died in 1133; it is possible that he had acquired his knowledge of letters in the famous school at Chartres, although most unlikely that he would have known Ivo, who died in or about 1116. If he spent some part of his years as a student in Maine or Anjou or Chartres, it might help to explain his friendship with Froger of Saumur. But all this is conjecture. The letters of Ivo and Hildebert were widely known, and Hildebert's letter to William of Champeaux, so appropriate to Gilbert's own conversion, might well have impressed itself on him in that period of his life.

ROMAN AND CANON LAW

Like those of Ivo of Chartres, Gilbert's letters reveal a deeper interest in law than in pagan learning; and the central problem of Gilbert's early life is the question where he had studied law. Once again, this is a question of more than antiquarian interest; for it is linked with the larger question of the development of legal studies in the first half of the twelfth century in western Europe as a whole. It is evident that law, and especially Roman Law, was Gilbert's chosen field of study. His letters show that he applied the authorities of Roman Law to problems of procedure in canon law courts without hesitation. This is all the more interesting because it is not easy to define the attitude to Roman Law of canonists trained in the late 1120's or 1130's. It is now generally accepted that when Gratian first compiled his *Decretum* he deliberately omitted all authorities from Roman Law; but that before his book began to circulate, in the early 1140's, a substantial number were added, especially in the sections on procedure.[1] It is clear that Gratian knew the authorities of Roman Law, knew

---

[1] See especially A. Vetulani in *Revue historique de droit français et étranger*, 4th series, xxiv–xxv (1946–7), 11–48; S. Kuttner, in *Seminar: An Annual Extraordinary Number of The Jurist*, xi (1953), 12–50. A. Vetulani's theory about the date of Gratian's *Decretum* has been made available to western readers in an article based on the study of the abbreviation of the *Decretum* in Gdansk (Danzig), Munic. Library, MS Mar. F. 275, in *Studia Gratiana*, vii (Bologna, 1959), 275–353.

the *Corpus iuris civilis* as it was known in Bologna in his day, but repudiated it as a source for canon law. The grounds for his repudiation are not known, but his attitude to Roman Law would appear quite naturally to be the private heresy of a great scholar; it seems gratuitous to attribute it to public policy.[1] It is, however, curiously difficult to be precise about the attitude of canonists to Roman Law in the period when Gilbert Foliot was being educated. In the nature of things we have no direct evidence of his views and attitude before 1140; but his letters written in the 1140's show us a man to whom it was natural to appeal to Roman Law when any legal issue was raised; there is no hint of doubt or hesitation.

The second point of interest is the problem of where Gilbert could have acquired his knowledge of Roman Law. Far and away the most famous Law School of the twelfth century was that of Bologna, famous not only for Roman Law, whose serious

---

[1] A. Vetulani, *art. cit.*, has recently argued that it was related to Pope Paschal II's attempt, in 1111, to resolve the tension between Empire and Papacy by surrendering the *regalia*, and that the separation of temporal and spiritual property was balanced by a separation of ecclesiastical and civil law; that Gratian did not repudiate Roman Law as such, but repudiated it as an authority for the spiritual courts. The experts have still to pronounce on this daring, and exceedingly interesting theory. To us it seems hardly convincing, because it seems to set Gratian in a false context, and involves the assumption that the decrees of the Lateran Councils of 1123 and 1139 (as well as the texts of Roman Law) are additions to the original *Decretum*. Professor Vetulani argues that the Danzig abbreviation was one of the sources of Paucapalea's *Summa* (before 1148); and, on this and other evidence, that decretist activity before 1148 was such that one can hardly believe that the *Decretum* was issued as late as 1140. But (*a*) all the evidence suggests that the *Decretum* had the decrees of 1139 attached before it *circulated*, whatever may have been its pre-history, and decretist activity can hardly have begun before the *Decretum* began to be known; (*b*) the evidence that the Danzig abbreviation preceded Paucapalea is very tenuous—depending e.g. on R. Gansiniec's suggestion, quoted by Vetulani, *art. cit.*, pp. 297–8, that fuller use of the *cursus* by Paucapalea shows it to be the later text. This argument has no force: if the other author understood and approved the use of the *cursus*, he would have used it anyway; if he did not, he might easily break Paucapalea's rhythms in ignorance or because they offended his taste. A similar argument has been used, and abandoned, in the study of Franciscan sources: see M. Bihl, *Archivum Franciscanum Historicum*, xxxix (1946–8), 14 ff. Some of the other arguments may carry a little more conviction than this; none seems really cogent.

study was revived there by Irnerius at the turn of the eleventh and twelfth centuries, but for canon law; the professors at Bologna took it upon themselves to sit in judgement upon the popes in the late twelfth century, to decide which papal decretals were good law; and they were not finally ousted from their self-appointed throne until the promulgation of the *Decretals* of Gregory IX. The brilliance of Bologna has notoriously put other schools in the shadow and in doing so obscured the true state of legal studies, anyway in the second half of the twelfth century.[1] It is no longer believed that Bologna had a monopoly of legal learning; flourishing schools of canon law, for instance, have been detected in Germany, France and England; and in the late twelfth century the study of canon law can never have been entirely divorced from that of Roman Law.

The true situation in the early twelfth century is much more obscure. The full text of Justinian's *Corpus* was rediscovered at Bologna in the second half of the eleventh century. Much of it was rapidly transmitted to other Italian cities, since Roman Law was practised in the courts of some Italian cities, and the newly discovered Bolognese text, the *littera Bononiensis*, only supplemented surviving extracts and manuals already well known. But the serious study of the texts of Justinian, which was at once academic and practical, the beginning of the age of the glossators, was the work of the school of Irnerius at Bologna. When Gilbert was a student, this school was already famous. Irnerius himself, the *lucerna iuris* whose lectures first raised Bologna to European distinction, died, it seems, in the late 1120's; in the 1130's the classical age of his pupils, the four doctors, was in full swing. The early glossators were mostly laymen and secular jurists, but there was no deliberate opposition between them and the Church's courts. By 1141, and possibly by 1125, the first text-book on the theory of procedure had appeared, the *Ordo iudiciorum* of Bulgarus, and this was dedicated to Cardinal Aimeric, chancellor of the Roman Church. This work has been called 'the oldest evidence of a scientific give-and-take...between the glossators of the Civil

---

[1] See especially S. Kuttner and E. Rathbone, 'Anglo-Norman Canonists of the Twelfth Century', *Traditio*, VII (1949–51), 279–358.

law and the Curia'.[1] A swarm of students had begun to flock to Bologna from abroad, and the new studies were attracting a new type of student, sons of nobles and beneficed clergy, men with a background not unlike that of Gilbert. It seems probable that it was in the early 1130's that Arnulf, later bishop of Lisieux, learned his law, very likely in Italy, very possibly in Bologna: about the same time, Jocelin, later bishop of Salisbury, may have been there.[2] It was certainly to Bologna that Thomas Becket went, for a year, in the 1140's, although he was able to continue his studies nearer home, at Auxerre. It was from Bologna that Archbishop Theobald fetched Master Vacarius, the Italian legal pundit who spread the knowledge of Roman and canon law from the curia of Theobald and a school in Oxford. [3] It was to Bologna that Gilbert sent his archidiaconal nephews and at least one other protégé, Master David of London, in the 1160's. At that date there can be no doubt that Gilbert regarded Bologna as the right school for his nephews and his archdeacons. It is probable that Gilbert had some acquaintance with the work of the glossators. In or about 1169 Master David wrote to him from Bologna, and referred to two of the four doctors, Bulgarus and Martinus, in such a way as to make clear that he assumed Gilbert would pick up the reference.[4] In nos. 96 and 295, (1150, 1152), Gilbert quoted tags from *Code* and *Digest* which are placed side by side in Bulgarus's *Excerpta*; and there is other evidence of Gilbert taking a line favoured by Bulgarus.[5] These are tenuous links, and illustrate the difficulty of being precise about the affinities of Gilbert's legal views. The same tag from the *Code*, indeed, was quoted soon after in a letter written in Archbishop Theobald's name by John of Salisbury; and since it is likely that John's knowledge of

---

[1] H. Kantorowicz and W. W. Buckland, *Studies in the Glossators of the Roman Law* (Cambridge, 1938), p. 71.

[2] F. Barlow, *The Letters of Arnulf of Lisieux* (Camden 3rd series, LXI, 1939), pp. xv–xvi; see above, pp. 55–6.

[3] On Vacarius, see F. de Zulueta, *The Liber Pauperum of Vacarius* (Selden Soc. 1927), esp. pp. xiii ff.; J. de Ghellinck in *Revue d'Hist. Ecclésiastique*, XLIV (1949), 173 ff.; Kuttner and Rathbone, *art. cit.* pp. 286–8; *JS Epp.* I, p. xxiii and n.

[4] Liverani, p. 626 = Vatican Lat. MS 6024, fo. 140 r–v.

[5] See p. 66.

such things came from Vacarius, it is perfectly possible that Gilbert, a frequent visitor to Theobald's curia in the late 1140's, owed his knowledge of it to Vacarius. But the basis of his legal learning must have been formed in the 1120's or early 1130's, and there is no reason to suppose that it was possible to study the *Corpus* in England so early. Gilbert's early education may have been gathered in England; but we have seen hints of foreign connexions in his early life, and the fact that he became a monk at Cluny rather than at one of the English houses dependent on Cluny, or resembling Cluny—like Reading, or his uncle's home at Gloucester—strongly suggests that he ended his scholastic career on the continent. The pointers so far considered, for what they are worth, indicate Bologna.

If we wish to make Gilbert's letters throw light on his early training, we must rely mainly on those written in the 1140's and early 1150's. In his later decisions, and in letters referring to his later cases, it is often difficult to know whether it is Gilbert's learning or that of the growing class of *causidici*, of trained legal experts, with which we are being presented. It can, however, be shown that in the 1160's and 1170's he himself freely quoted from Gratian's *Decretum*, and this illustrates the second difficulty: he did not cease to learn when he became abbot and bishop; like most of his contemporaries who were interested in canon law, he came to make regular use of the *Decretum*, even though it had not circulated when he was a student.

Gilbert, as we meet him in the letters, was an administrator rather than a scholar, a man with a practical rather than a speculative cast of mind. There is no evidence that he added anything to legal understanding, that he was an original glossator. This makes all the more striking the clear evidence in his early letters that he was at home in Justinian's *Corpus*, or at least in some parts of it. Over twenty of his letters contain quotations, or references, or reminiscences of the phraseology of the *Corpus iuris civilis*; about fourteen contain quotations or references to canon law.[1] The contrast

---

[1] Nos. 9, 16, 17, 26, 66, 93, 95–6, 106, 110, 113, 128, 133, 140 (?), 146, 158, 160, 176, 185, 212, 237 (?), 295, 342, 345, 347 (civil law); 9, 22, 157–8, 162, 170, 176, 200–1, 203, 212, 237, 243, 248 (canon law). (Some references are ambiguous.)

is striking. References to the *Institutes* occur only twice and then to its most familiar section: to Brian FitzCount in 1143 he quoted the definition of natural and human law which ultimately derived from Ulpian; he used the words of the *Institutes* again to Bishop Uhtred of Llandaff on the precepts of natural law, and he defined the phrase 'ius suum cuique tribuere', a favourite subject of the glossators, as the duty of treating the property of others as we would wish our own to be dealt with.[1] The familiar tag *ius suum* was a favourite with Gilbert and turns up in various contexts. His use of the *Code* covers the first ten books, although most of his references are to the seventh book. On the whole he seems to have made more use of the *Code* than of the *Digest*. When the practical purpose of the letters is considered it is not surprising to find that Gilbert does not seem to have been interested in general jurisprudence and that references to the last title of the *Digest* are rare. It is not possible to prove that he quoted the *Novels*, though at least one passage seems to indicate knowledge of them.[2]

The practical concern, however, must not be unduly stressed. It is noticeable that in one of his earliest letters, that to Brian FitzCount on the claims of the empress (no. 26), he uses *Institutes* and *Digest* to provide him with a doctrine of natural law; in this respect he was in marked contrast to Gratian, whose definitions were drawn from St Isidore.[3] Roman Law was a major part of the furniture of his mind.

Gilbert's study of procedure is clearly exhibited in a group of

---

[1] Nos. 26, 16.

[2] See note to no. 26. Gilbert had no consistent system of reference. He makes the customary distinction between *leges* and *ius*, referring to civil law, and the *canones* of canon law; he writes of the *decreta patrum* (cf. nos. 16, 95, 110, 128, 148, 212; and no. 248 for *canones et decretales epistolas* in a judge-delegate decision). He sometimes quotes the number of a book (*in primo Codicis*, etc.) or the name or author of a law, or both (*in eodem codicis Alexander Augustus*: cf. nos. 110, 158, 185). The quotations are sometimes exact, but minor errors are sufficiently numerous to suggest that, in the Bologna tradition, he knew by heart the sections of the *Corpus* he regularly used. It is noticeable that he never referred to secondary authorities by name, almost as though of set policy; in one instance where he refers to a conflict of opinions it is not clear whether he is alluding to the commentators or to a diversity of opinion among the legal experts present on the occasion in his own court (no. 185: cf. no. 96).

[3] On this letter, see below, chapter VII.

letters belonging to 1150 (nos. 93–6), which deal with two cases in which Roger, earl of Hereford, was involved: both of them were hampered by a variety of procedural difficulties, and in both Gilbert's own position was made more awkward by the fact—not revealed in any of the letters—that the earl was his cousin. In each case the earl (who was the defendant) appealed to Archbishop Theobald, who had become papal legate a few months before, and in each case Gilbert had to explain to a rather testy plaintiff that the appeal had terminated his jurisdiction over the case.[1] No. 96, to the archbishop, sets out the reasons for the judgement given in Gilbert's court. It had been necessary to reject the evidence offered by the plaintiffs, and Gilbert was at pains to explain why he did not allow the case to go in the earl's favour by default—in accordance with the maxim which he himself quoted: 'actore non probante reus etsi nichil prestiterit obtineat'. Gilbert states that the earl had already offered to give proof of his innocence; and that as the plaintiffs failed to bring satisfactory evidence he decided to accept the earl's offer. He was also moved to insist on proof by the notoriety of the earl's offences elsewhere, and by the secret confession of one of the earl's companions that the charge was true.

The commentators at Bologna disagreed as to whether the defendant should be admitted to take on the onus of proof instead of the plaintiff, and Gilbert actually followed a course which had the approval of Martinus and was based on the *Digest*.[2] He was also evidently acting with an eye to the general probabilities of the case, on justice, even, one might suspect, although he does not make this explicit, on equity. His procedure would doubtless have won the approval of Vacarius, Martinus's pupil. The commentators also disagreed as to the correct procedure when the judge had prior knowledge of the truth, and some held that he

---

[1] In no. 95 he explained to one of the parties the purpose of *apostoli*, letters to the judge of the higher court expounding the case, copies of which he will receive at latest on the day the appeal is heard (this is perhaps the earliest known use of the word in English sources; cf. no. 243).

[2] *Digest*, 22. 3. 14. For the commentators see V. Scialoja, 'Di una nuova collezione delle Dissensiones Dominorum', *Studi e documenti di Storia di Diritto*, IX (Rome, 1888), 269.

could dispense with the evidence and give sentence.[1] Gilbert pointed out that there were precedents among the *patres* for imposing an oath on the earl, and he may have had in mind either an opinion of Bulgarus or a canonical view which allowed the judge to order purgation when he had a strong suspicion against a defendant, a proceeding unknown to the civil law.[2]

Throughout his career as abbot and bishop, Gilbert was much concerned with the question of appeals; and in no. 95 he gave Gilbert de Lacy, one of the plaintiffs, a lesson on the law of appeal; in no. 93 to the plaintiff in the other case, Ralph of Worcester, he gave an even more elaborate account of the law of appeals— evidently Ralph, or his *causidicus*, had some knowledge of law. In both cases Gilbert's defence of his own procedure is based entirely on quotations from the seventh book of the *Code*, with no reference to canons or decretals. On the lawfulness of appeals, Gilbert held that they were permissible even in matters of small importance, a view which was in accord with that held by Bulgarus, although some canonists held a different view, based in part on the *Novels*.[3] Gilbert's opinion later became that accepted by the canonists.

The failure of King Stephen's attempt to proscribe the study of Roman Law and his order for the destruction of copies of the *Digest* is well known.[4] Gilbert's legal career in England underlines this failure; so does the request of Robert de Chesney, bishop of Lincoln, that Gilbert should correct and gloss his copy of the *Digest*.[5] A special interest attaches to this request. It seems fairly certain that Vacarius was teaching civil law at Oxford about this time, and so was very probably lecturing in Robert's own diocese

---

[1] Scialoja, *op. cit.* XI (1890), Fasc. 4.

[2] 'Inopia probationum per iusiurandum deciditur', Bulgarus, ed. Scialoja, *op. cit.* XI, Fasc. 4, p. 11; *Decretum*, C. 2, q. 5 *ad init.* Another tag is wrongly cited in *JS Epp.* I, 126 n., as from Bulgarus; it is from *Code*, 2, 1, 4, as Prof. P. Stein has pointed out to us.

[3] Cf. Bulgarus in L. Wahrmund, *Quellen zur Geschichte des römischkanonischen Processes im Mittelalter* (Innsbruck, 1905, etc.), pp. 154, 165; *Novels* 23, quoted in *Decretum*, C. 2, q. 6, c. 28; *JL* 13162 (cf. S. Kuttner, *Repertorium der Kanonistik*, I (Rome, 1937), 287).

[4] Cf. de Zulueta, *The Liber Pauperum of Vacarius*, pp. xiii ff.

[5] No. 106.

when the letter was written; yet it is to Gilbert that he turns. Copies of the *Digest* must indeed have been rare in England at this period, and it is significant to find one in the hands of a member of Gilbert's circle.[1] Gilbert evidently had a reputation among his colleagues as an expert on legal affairs, for the letters include a number of answers to consultations. In no. 95 Gilbert claimed a definite *magisterium* in legal matters, to talk with the authority of one who had wasted his life, so to speak, in law-suits. But he was not the only lawyer among the English bishops, and in the course of the 1150's a number of other expert *causidici* appear in the records.[2] Among his own contemporaries, it seems clear that Hilary of Chichester, who was skilled in both laws and had been a pleader in the papal Curia, was more highly rated as a lawyer by Archbishop Theobald and others than Gilbert.[3]

None of the qualifications one can make, however, to Gilbert's reputation as a lawyer, and especially as an exponent of Roman Law, reduce the force of the evidence that the books of Justinian had been woven into his consciousness, and that he was aware of the trend of argument on some issues at least among the Bolognese masters. The recovery of the *Digest* and its glossing was the supreme achievement of Irnerius and his pupils. Gilbert was a man to whom one turned for glosses on the *Digest*.

These hints point more strongly than the external evidence towards Bologna as the source of his knowledge of Roman Law. It would be easier, however, to assess their strength, if we were better informed on the state of legal studies elsewhere in the first

[1] The rarity of copies may be presumed from the fact that no English twelfth-century MSS of the *Corpus iuris* seem to be known (and cf. W. Senior, *Law Quarterly Rev.* XLVII (1931), 337 ff.). With all allowances made for the chances of loss and destruction, this is a striking fact.

[2] In the dispute between Battle abbey and Godfrey de Lucy the monks approached Gerard la Pucelle, Bartholomew of Exeter and John of Salisbury in their attempt to find an advocate: each refused, though Gerard spoke in the abbot's support (*Chron. Battle*, pp. 172 ff.: the passage also refers to other advocates of the day. On Gerard see Kuttner and Rathbone, 'Anglo-Norman Canonists of the Twelfth Century', pp. 296 ff.). Bartholomew was more of a civilian than a canonist: cf. Morey, p. 103. For *causidici*, see also the Anstey diary (ed. P. M. Barnes, in *Misc. D. M. Stenton*, pp. 17 ff., cf. p. 7).

[3] On Hilary see H. Mayr-Harting in *EHR*, LXXVIII (1963), 209–24; cf. *JS Epp.* I, p. xxxvi.

half of the twelfth century. The evidence is very scanty. Although there is little doubt that Gilbert could have picked up his knowledge of the *Corpus iuris* in other Italian cities, it seems rather unlikely that any of these had law schools at this time sufficiently famous to attract an ambitious student whose home was as far away as England. In the later decades of the eleventh century, in the various canonical collections emanating from the circles of the papal reformers, there were commonly included some extracts from Justinian's *Corpus* using the Bolognese text.[1] From a collection akin to the *Britannica*, Ivo of Chartres and his seminar derived the very numerous extracts which were incorporated in Ivo's *Decretum*. But there is no evidence of the systematic study of Roman Law in France in the early years of the twelfth century. There were men at Cluny in Gilbert's time acquainted with the law, but no evidence that Justinian was known there. The *Petri Exceptiones* and the *Brachylogus* bear witness to a knowledge of and study of Roman Law in provincial centres not as yet precisely determined.[2] Once again, such places could have provided Gilbert with his training; but there is no evidence that they were genuine centres of study, or would have competed in repute with Bologna.

The circumstantial evidence that Gilbert studied Roman Law at Bologna is thus tolerably strong; but it falls well short of demonstration. Of direct evidence there is none. And it would be rash indeed to argue from our ignorance that no centres other than Bologna could have given Gilbert his legal training. Wherever he received it, however, it was evidently inspired by the spirit of Bologna; and he is a valuable witness that, in spite of the personal idiosyncrasy of Gratian, the spirit which inspired

---

[1] Cf. M. Conrat, *Geschichte der Quellen und Literatur des Römischen Rechts ins früheren Mittelalter*, I (Leipzig, 1891), pp. 363–93; P. Fournier and G. Le Bras, *Histoire des collections canoniques en occident*, II (Paris, 1932), pp. 159–60, 175, also 30–1, 78, 126, 137, 154, 183–4, 190, 195, 200–1, 207, 220, 223–4; for earlier citations possibly or probably from other sources, see pp. 17–18, 45, 78, 117 n., 118, 120, 133, 143.

[2] See Conrat, *op. cit.* p. 79 n.; Kantorowicz and Buckland, *Studies in the Glossators of the Roman Law*, pp. 113 ff.; also Kantorowicz in *Revue hist. de droit français et étranger*, 4th series, XVI (1937), 588–640.

Gratian's disciples to fill his margins from the relevant portions of Justinian was being communicated to students from as far away as Britain in the late 1120's or early 1130's.

THEOLOGY

If Gilbert studied under Robert Pullen at Exeter in the 1120's, it is a reasonable presumption that he studied theology, for it was as a theologian that Pullen was always known. Yet it seems unlikely that Gilbert would have had time to proceed far in the study of theology at this stage in his career. At Pullen's feet he would have been instructed in a theology based on the biblical studies of the school of Laon, to which Pullen himself applied an austere but acute dialectic.[1] He was dialectician enough to make his mark in Paris in the days of Abelard and Gilbert de la Porrée, sufficiently conservative and spiritually minded to keep on good terms with St Bernard. But it is fruitless to search in detail for the influence of Pullen or of any other eminent theologian of the age in Gilbert's own studies and writings: they were essentially the fruit of his pastoral work, and although filled with ingenious exegesis and revealing some skill in dialectic, they avoid all issues of speculative theology. They show, furthermore, that Gilbert's theological interests (such as they were) did not constantly hark back to his schooldays: he strove to keep up to date, to refresh his own mind and that of his clergy with the latest fashions in biblical studies.

It may be that he learned from his own abbot, Peter the Venerable, that a man may be a busy administrator, and yet find time to write books for the edification of his flock and the good of the Church. It is clear that he put together a volume of his sermons while abbot of Gloucester, at the behest of the Cistercian Hamo, abbot of Bordesley, and that these were sent, with a covering letter, to the abbot; but the letter is all that survives.[2] Three works of Gilbert's are preserved *in toto*, all devotional works based

[1] Courtney, *Cardinal Robert Pullen, passim*, esp. chap. xv; on the school of Laon, see esp. Southern, *St Anselm and His Biographer*, pp. 82 ff.
[2] No. 7.

on scriptural exegesis and all written while he was bishop of London: his *Homilies*, his commentary on the *Pater noster*, and his commentary on the *Canticle*. None had a large circulation, and each survives in a single manuscript.[1] The first is preserved in a book which also contains Ailred's sermons on Isaiah, written in the period *c.* 1158–63 and dedicated to Gilbert in 1163 or 1164.[2] Since Gilbert's homilies were dedicated to an abbot, it is a reasonable conjecture that they were written for Ailred, and they can thus be dated *c.* 1163–7. The *Pater noster* was dedicated to Walter Foliot, formerly archdeacon of Shropshire, who was in office *c.* 1150–*c.* 1178,[3] and so belongs to the years *c.* 1178–87; the commentary on the *Canticle* was probably dedicated to Robert Foliot, bishop of Hereford from 1174 to 1186, and so was of about the same period.

These books, it must be admitted, are not of great interest today. They show reverence, conscientious workmanship, and dialectical ingenuity; but they cannot stand comparison with the meditations of St Anselm or the sermons of St Bernard. Yet the

[1] BM Royal MSS 2. E. vii (Commentary on the *Canticle*), from Rochester (listed among the books of Prior Robert of Walton in the Rochester library catalogue of 1202, *Arch. Cantiana*, III (1860), 61); Royal 2. D. xxxii (Ailred's Sermons and Gilbert's Homilies), from Christ Church, Canterbury (listed in catalogues of the early fourteenth century and later, M. R. James, *Ancient Libs. of Canterbury and Dover* (Cambridge, 1903), pp. 25, 162, cf. 506, 515); Worcester Cathedral Library, MS Q 48, fos. 60 v–69 (Commentary on the *Pater noster*). All these MSS are late-twelfth or early-thirteenth century. J. Leland, *Collectanea* (ed. T. Hearne), IV (III) (Oxford, 1715), 150, noted 'Omeliae Gileberti, episcopi Herefordensis' at Forde. The Homilies may in fact have been composed before Gilbert went to London: we only have the heading in the MS as evidence that he was bishop of London, and Ailred's sermons (see below) were composed over the years *c.* 1158–63. Forde was a Cistercian house, and would naturally acquire a book connected with Ailred. But it would equally naturally acquire a book connected with Hamo of Bordesley, and the volume which Leland saw is perhaps more likely to have been the lost homilies dedicated to Hamo. This exhausts references to Gilbert in known English medieval library catalogues. In some MSS there is confusion between Gilbert and Gilbert of Hoyland (Swineshead), the Cistercian, who also wrote on the *Canticle*, a much more popular work. Gilbert's commentary was printed by P. Junius, London, 1638, and reprinted by Migne (*PL*, CCII, 1147–1304).

[2] Ailred's book is in *PL*, CXCV, 361–500. Cf. *Walter Daniel's Life of Ailred*, ed. F. M. Powicke (NMT, 1950), p. xcvii.

[3] See below, p. 268.

evidence of Peter of Cornwall leaves no doubt that Gilbert was capable of inspiring his clergy, and of rousing in them an active interest in new fashions in exegesis.

Peter
was at a synod in attendance on Stephen, his prior, and Gilbert Foliot preached the sermon. When he heard it he could not restrain his admiration and praise. 'The whole sermon was varied by certain *distinctiones*, adorned with flowers of words and sentences and supported by a copious array of authorities. It ran backwards and forwards on its path from its starting-point back to the same starting point.' He then gives an example. When Gilbert spoke of Christ as a stone, he brought forward the stone which the builders rejected, which is become the head of the corner, he brought forward the stone which Jacob set up for a pillar and on top of which he poured oil, he brought forward the stone that was cut out of the mountain without hands. Peter was so much struck with this method that he determined to write a work in which the *lector studiosus* might find all such passages collected together and arranged. This is really important because it is an early example of the *distinctio* method, which in its simplest form consists in taking a word according to its senses and attaching a quotation of the Bible to each. The germ of it is old. But it was not developed as a systematic method of exegesis until after the death of Peter Lombard, when it arose and spread with great rapidity. It is unusual to get such a close view of the way in which a typical medieval form was transmitted.[1]

If we set Abbot Hamo and Canon Peter, and the witness of the written word together, we can deduce that Gilbert Foliot was a preacher of power and force, sufficiently instructed in theology and with sufficient flexibility of mind to pick up new trends and inspire others to follow them; but also entirely without originality or the power to fix on parchment the charm and persuasiveness which his audience appears to have felt. This is the common fate of successful preachers; but it would be wrong to ignore the evidence of his success, or to allow a comparison with Bernard and Anselm, immortals in the genre, to damn him. Nor have we the whole of his works by which to judge him. In 1181 or 1182 Walter Map described him at work on a new and large project;

[1] R. W. Hunt in *TRHS*, 4th series, XIX (1936), 33-4.

the commentary on the *Canticle* may be a part of what was produced, or the new work may be wholly lost. But the vision of
Gilbert Foliot, old and blind, launching on fresh ventures, is a
fitting close to this study of the formation of his mind.

The present bishop of London, Gilbert Foliot, a man thoroughly at
home in three tongues, Latin, French and English, in each of which he
speaks with the greatest clearness and eloquence, in this his old age,
when almost total blindness has come upon him, having already composed a few small but brilliant tractates, is now, as if atoning for a
wasted leisure, unmooring his boat from the shore; he is to venture on
the exploration of the open sea, and is hastening to redeem the time
he has lost by compiling with a swift pen (thumb!) a work on the Old
and New Testaments. Bartholomew, bishop of Exeter, again, an old
and eloquent man, is now engaged in writing; while Baldwin, bishop
of Worcester, a man of much learning, and wise in the things that
belong to the Lord, grows weary if his pen be idle. These men are the
philosophers of our day, who want for nothing, and have abodes filled
with all manner of supplies, and tranquillity outside: they have begun
well and will make a good ending.[1]

[1] *De nugis curialium*, i, 12, trans. M. R. James (Cymmrodorion Rec. Soc.
1923), pp. 19–20.

CHAPTER V

MONK AND ABBOT

In one of the most interesting of Gilbert Foliot's personal letters written, during the distractions of the dispute with Thomas Becket, to his friend the countess of Leicester, he looked back nostalgically to his life as a monk in the cloister. 'There is no end to our cares, and every day the world produces something to afflict our wretched souls and distract us from our devout resolution. How I remember the holy conferences which my soul had with its spouse while the silence of the cloister covered and held it: raised on high, it communed with the spirit.' He went on to describe his bitter repentance, with tears, of the excesses of his youth, and the joy of his striving in contemplation. Then his life was calm and regular, but later secular cares destroyed his devotion and the stability of the contemplative life. 'Now fear oppresses me, then hope returns; now good fortune raises my spirits, then ill casts them down.'[1] It is a moving contrast, though doubtless overdrawn and in part conventional, and we need not doubt that Gilbert genuinely regarded his years as a monk as a crucial period, and a happy one, in his life. He was born c. 1105–10; he studied law and probably theology. When he 'put off the master of the schools' he can hardly have been less than 21–25 years old. It is unlikely that he entered Cluny before 1130; more probable that he was clothed a year or two later. He can only have been a simple monk for a very few years at most, and then held two important offices among the Cluniacs. In 1139 he became abbot of Gloucester, in 1148 bishop of Hereford. At most, he was a monk for eighteen years, and the majority of this time was spent in office. At Gloucester he was head of a great community, and a great landowner, at a time of political strife and

---

[1] No. 195. This passage perhaps contains a distant echo of Gregory the Great (see note to the letter); but by using the imagery of the *Canticle* Gilbert has put the sentiment in a contemporary context. Cf. Ivo of Chartres, *Ep.* 38 (ed. J. Leclercq, I).

unrest; he was deeply involved in the affairs of Church and state. It may well be that the conditions of his life left him plenty of time even as abbot—perhaps even as bishop too, though he never lived in a cloister after 1148—for monastic pursuits. But the life of untrammelled care, of penitence and contemplation, if he had ever known it, was short.

For the ruling classes of Europe in the tenth and eleventh centuries the monastic communities inspired by Cluny, Gorze, Brogne or Glastonbury provided men with the life of peace; the vocation of their brothers in the world was to war. This is to simplify a complex picture, to forget the secular clergy, the city patriciates, the varied opportunities open to the privileged. Yet, compared with what the twelfth and thirteenth centuries were to see, the society of the tenth and early eleventh was comparatively simple in structure. The monasteries were not the homes, on the whole, of men with special vocations, but havens with doors wide open to those who preferred peace to war. Nor were the enormous monastic churches of the period closed to layfolk: throngs of laymen could worship in their naves, and witness the conventual mass at the end of a vista disturbed by only quite modest screens. It is probable too that the extent to which monks served parish churches has been commonly underestimated and the distinction between a monastic cell and a parish church served by monks overdrawn.[1] Cluny and its like were the homes of many fervent and holy men in this period, and there is much to suggest that they had earned their prestige. Cluny was a gathering place, however, of men of widely different talent and temperament; it was a haven of peace for the many—as even the Cistercian Ailred was to say of his Rievaulx[2]—with the communal worship of the church at the heart of its spirituality, accepting what came into its fellowship, not troubling (so far as one can tell) seriously to test the vocation of its recruits.

In the twelfth century the social opportunities open to men of talent rapidly became more complex, as did the pattern of monastic observance. The monastic orders multiplied; the secular

---

[1] See below, p. 85.
[2] *Walter Daniel's Life of Ailred*, ed. F. M. Powicke, p. 37.

clergy increased enormously, and so did their chances of education and of rewarding service to pope, bishops, kings and lords. The landholding and mercantile classes grew larger and more ramified; and the population of western Europe increased sufficiently to provide copious recruits for all the new orders of society. The reformed monastic orders offered a more specialised vocation; their churches were closed to layfolk; they lay hidden from the world. It is well known that although they lived out of the world the Cistercians influenced it profoundly—even to the point of being leaders in economic advance—and it has recently been shown that they were anticipated in some of their innovations by earlier movements. But this serves only to underline the variety of notions of the religious life which was conceived in the late eleventh and early twelfth centuries: from the hermit ideal of the Carthusians to the missionary purpose of St Norbert (before his Order was taken out of his hands and monasticised) or the military purpose of the knights.[1] This growth of new ideas has sometimes given historians the notion that the older monasticism lost face and recruits in the new world; and this has been enhanced by the notoriety of the conflicts between Cistercians and Cluniacs. The sensational growth in this period was among the new orders, especially the Cistercians; and the rapid expansion of opportunities in all directions must have prevented from reaching Cluny the variety of talent which it had drawn in earlier generations. Cluny itself suffered a severe crisis in the 1120's under Abbot Pons, and the recovery under Peter the Venerable (1122–56) must have proceeded slowly at first. It is clear, furthermore, that Abbot Peter himself, after defending Cluny against St Bernard's virulent attacks, accepted many of the Cistercian charges, and attempted some measure of reform.[2] But there are

---

[1] The literature on what several scholars have described as the monastic crisis of the twelfth century, and in particular on the problem of Cîteaux's origin and originality and the conflict of *vita contemplativa* and *vita apostolica*, is copious. The classical account is in Knowles, *MO*, chaps. XI–XIV; for recent controversies see esp. C. Dereine in *Cîteaux*, x (1959), 125–39 and refs. cited; Knowles, *Great Historical Enterprises; Problems in Monastic History* (London, 1963), pp. 197–222.

[2] See Knowles, *Historian and Character*, chap. 4; and on Cluny in this period

many indications that Cluny retained a fair measure of its prestige in the twelfth century; and Bernard himself, in his later years, more than once commended himself to the prayers of the holy church of Cluny.[1] The community seems to have been larger than ever; the number of its daughter houses grew substantially in this period; Cluniac monks were to be found as cardinals, bishops, and, very frequently, as abbots of independent Benedictine communities.[2] The traditional monasticism retained a fair measure of its glory; and whatever its weaknesses, it seems clear that Cluny under Peter the Venerable could still attract men of devotion, discernment and talent. The life of higher contemplation was one engaged in by comparatively few even among the Cistercians; the monastic ideal was still mainly a communal one. There are copious indications that many observers (unlike the young Bernard) did not regard the existence of Cîteaux as a condemnation of Cluny. Stephen of Blois was notably interested in Cluny, as his uncle King Henry I had been. His brother, Henry of Winchester, had been a monk of Cluny, and between them they placed Cluniacs as abbots in several independent houses. In 1148 Stephen founded Faversham abbey, as Henry I had founded Reading, on Cluniac lines, and colonised it with Cluniac monks. At about this time Stephen's most notable foundation, the great abbey of Furness, originally Savigniac, joined the Cistercian order.[3] There seems to have been no conflict between Cîteaux and Cluny in Stephen's mind, though it is likely he was well aware, if only from an external point of view, of the difference between the old and the new monasticism.

Among the Cluniacs made abbot by Stephen was Gilbert

and Peter himself, Knowles, *Bull. of the J. Rylands Library*, xxxix (1956), 132–45, and esp. *Petrus Venerabilis, 1156–1956*, ed. G. Constable and J. Kritzeck (Rome, 1956). We await the new edition of Peter's letters by Prof. G. Constable.

[1] *Epp.* 147, 228, 387, esp. the last: 'salutate nobis sanctam illam multitudinem uestram: et orate, ut orent pro puero suo.'

[2] For Cluniac bishops and abbots in England, see Knowles, *MO*, chap. xvi, esp. p. 284. Three cardinal bishops of this period, Matthew of Albano, Alberic of Ostia and Imar of Tusculum, were Cluniacs.

[3] On Stephen's foundations, see Knowles, *MO*, pp. 284, 227–8. Savigny merged with Cîteaux in 1147, but Furness only submitted after a protest and an appeal to the pope (*MO*, p. 251).

Foliot himself. In him likewise there is no trace of animus against Cîteaux. Among his early friends at Gloucester was Hamo, first abbot of Bordesley; and another of his friends was St Ailred himself. St Bernard's death was the occasion for a glowing panegyric from Gilbert's pen (no. 108), and he corresponded happily with other Cistercians.[1] Gilbert's asceticism and strength of character might lead one to expect that he would have been attracted by the Cistercians, or strongly aware of the contrast between his own communities and their's. Of this there is no indication. It is true that we know very little of his monastic life and monastic ideals.[2] But we may be tolerably sure that his ideal was the traditional ideal of an observant and regular communal life, not wholly cut off from the world, nor from its notions of social hierarchy; and we may conjecture that Cluny was intensely attractive to a young man of talent and good family, devout but ambitious, brought up before St Bernard's spell had been cast all over western Christendom. We may indeed wonder why Gilbert chose Cluny rather than one of its English imitators; it was certainly unusual for an English monk to open his career there. To this the most probable answer is that Gilbert was studying and teaching in a continental school, perhaps in Bologna, and was attracted by the great abbey lying (it may be) near the route to his home country.

It was not uncommon in this age for men to be appointed to high office in the Church comparatively young. But this practice was, at Cluny, established tradition in an exceptional degree. Since the tenth century the abbots of Cluny in their old age had trained up talented young noblemen to be their successors. Two abbots spanned the whole eleventh century: Odilo and Hugh remind us not only how good a risk the abbot of Cluny was for the actuary, but how exceptionally young they must have been

---

[1] In 1167 he dedicated the high altar of Coggeshall abbey (Ralph of Coggeshall, *Chronicon Anglicanum*, ed. J. Stevenson, RS, p. 16), and Walter Map (*De nugis*, i, 24) describes a visit to him of two Cistercian abbots.

[2] For testimonials, see above, pp. 3 ff.; echoes of the *Rule* occur in nos. 12 and perhaps 18; several of his early letters, e.g. on the Cerne affair, contain hints of his views on monastic observance. Professor Knowles has pointed out to us the similarity between Gilbert and the 'Cluniac die-hard' Cardinal Matthew of Albano (cf. *Historian and Character*, pp. 52, 67–8).

when they stepped into their inheritance. The failure of Abbot Pons did not bring this policy to an end: Abbot Peter himself was comparatively young at his elevation, and many of the men whom he sent out to be priors, abbots and bishops were young too. Henry of Blois was perhaps about 35 when he became abbot of Glastonbury, and still in his thirties when he was consecrated to Winchester.[1] Henry indeed was not only aristocratic and a Cluniac, he was a protégé of Henry I of England, who doted on his nephews. Although it is rare for us to be precisely informed about the date of birth of a twelfth-century ecclesiastic, there is no reason to suppose that the speed of Henry of Blois's promotion was exceptional. Hugh of Amiens, who was to die less than seven years before Henry, was promoted from Cluny to be prior of Limoges c. 1115; made prior of Lewes, the foremost Cluniac house in England, in 1120, made abbot of Henry I's new abbey at Reading in 1123; and was archbishop of Rouen from 1130 to 1164.[2] Hugh, like Gilbert—and St Odilo and St Hugh—had over fifty years in positions of authority.

On 8 February 1139 Walter de Lacy, abbot of Gloucester, was buried. Soon after, King Stephen nominated Gilbert Foliot to be his successor, and two monks of the house were dispatched to Cluny to obtain his release.[3] Since Gilbert's uncle Reginald, abbot of Evesham, had been a monk at Gloucester, it is clear that Gilbert already had links with the community, and the monks may have encouraged Milo the Constable, castellan of Gloucester, to inspire the king to appoint Milo's cousin abbot. In any case there can be

[1] On Henry, see L. Voss, *Heinrich von Blois* (Berlin, 1932). The date of his birth cannot be precisely determined, but it seems likely to have occurred about 1090 or slightly later. His parents had eight children, five sons, of whom Henry was the fourth, and three daughters, all of whom were probably conceived between c. 1080-1 (although there seems to be no precise evidence for the date of his parents' marriage: H. D'Arbois de Jubainville, *Hist. des ducs...de Champagne*, I (Paris, 1859), 397 and n.) and 1096, when Count Stephen set off on the First Crusade. The chances are that Henry was the fifth or sixth child and was born c. 1090-2; but he could have been born as early as 1084-5.

[2] See E. W. Williamson in *The Letters of Osbert de Clare* (Oxford, 1929), pp. 183-4.

[3] *Cart. Gloucester*, I, 17-18; Florence of Worcester, *Chronicon ex Chronicis*, ed. B. Thorpe (London, 1848-9), II, 114-15 (cf. *CS*, pp. 267, 277-9); cf. Ann. Worcester, *Ann. Mon.* IV, 378.

little doubt that Milo was the prime mover in the affair,[1] and the neighbourhood of this great baron, soon to be an adherent of the empress—though perhaps of doubtful loyalty—very rapidly placed Gilbert Foliot at the centre of a political situation of great complexity. On 11 June 1139, the feast of Pentecost, Gilbert was blessed at Worcester by the bishop of Hereford, Robert de Bethune.[2] On or about 30 September the empress landed at Arundel.[3] From 1139 until 1148 England was divided and Gloucester lay near the heart of the empress's domain.

Many of Gilbert's early letters describe the difficulties of the anarchy: disasters or threats of disaster to his abbey's properties, to its outlying dependent priories, to its neighbours and friends. But the abbey itself lay behind the strong walls of the city of Gloucester, whose castellan was the abbot's cousin, Milo, and later his son Roger. Within the precinct, most of the time, life could be comparatively undisturbed; and although the abbot of a great house had to be a traveller, there is no reason to doubt that the greater part of Gilbert's time was spent within his community; and these periods of comparative calm may well be included in his later memories of cloistered peace. Though much altered in subsequent centuries, an unusually large proportion of the abbey's buildings still survive. The Norman work in the choir of what is now Gloucester cathedral, the greater part of the nave and part (perhaps most) of the chapter-house were already built when Gilbert came to Gloucester. This was the age when abbots were building for themselves, for the first time, spacious apartments separate from the monks' dormitories and refectories; and the twelfth-century abbot's lodging, including a beautiful chapel, is still intact. It is not known whether this building was erected in Gilbert's time or later; nor indeed whether he carried on the building work of his predecessors in the nave of the abbey church.[4] It is likely, however, that he would have regarded an

---

[1] See pp. 35 ff.

[2] *Cart. Gloucester*, I, 18; Florence of Worcester, II, 115.

[3] Round, *GM*, p. 278.

[4] On the abbey church see A. W. Clapham, *English Romanesque Architecture after the Conquest* (Oxford, 1934), pp. 32–4; for the buildings in general, W. H. St J. Hope in *Archaeol. Journal*, LIV (1897), 77–119 (pp. 107 f. for twelfth-

abbot's lodging as primarily a place for receiving distinguished visitors and for the secular members of his household, and that he spent a greater part of his time than his successors in the late Middle Ages with the community:[1] and it is likely that the chapter house more or less as we know it was the scene of the conferences which Gilbert had with his monks, such as Abbot Hamo of Bordesley witnessed—and which inspired the Cistercian abbot to request his eminent Cluniac friend to put his interpretations of scripture on parchment for him (no. 7). This is a rare glimpse of the abbot within his cloister. The letters reveal a man concerned with every aspect of his work as abbot, able to inspire, then as later, by his preaching, but far from inclined (as St Anselm had been) to leave administrative chores to an underling. We know the names of some of the monks of his day: Osbert the scholar, Nicholas, future bishop of Llandaff (1148–83), Gilbert's successor Hamelin, Gregory, the old monk who was to impress Walter Map as a young man, above all Master Bernard, whom Gilbert sent to be abbot of Cerne, whose tribulations fill so many of his letters.[2] The respect in which Gilbert was held is revealed by the

century abbot's lodging, later prior's); D. Knowles and J. K. S. St Joseph, *Monastic Sites from the Air* (Cambridge, 1952), pp. 12–13.

[1] Abbots of large communities commonly already had a small staff of secular clerks and lay officials similar to those of a lay baron. Since none of Gilbert's charters as abbot has a witness list, we know nothing of his household as abbot.

[2] On Osbert, see G. F. Warner and J. P. Gilson, *Catalogue of MSS in the... Royal...Collections*, I (Brit. Museum, 1921), p. 149 (his precise dates are not known, but as one of his books was dedicated to Gilbert as bishop of Hereford, he was presumably a monk under Gilbert, certainly under his successor, and may be the prior of a Welsh dependency addressed in no. 10). On Bishop Nicholas, see Conway Davis, II, 655. On Hamelin, *Cart. Gloucester*, I, 19–22; on Gregory, Map, *De nugis curialium*, ii, I. Map had seen Gregory in Abbot Hamelin's time, but he was then an old man, and must certainly have been a monk under Gilbert. He died in 1157: Greg. Caerwent, Cotton MS Vesp. A. v, fo. 199 v, who notes that he had written many MSS. Under Hamelin Gloucester had a flourishing school, where Gerald of Wales, and perhaps Map too, received their early education (cf. Brooke, introd. to Map, ed. and trans. M. R. James, NMT, forthcoming). It is likely, though it cannot be proved, that the school already existed in Gilbert's time. For Master Bernard, see below, p. 81. To the 1130's and 1140's or a little later belong the interest in the legends of Llandaff, and in Geoffrey of Monmouth's *History*, revealed in Benedict of Gloucester's *Life of St Dubricius* and the collections in Cotton MS Vesp. A. xiv (see K. Hughes and C. Brooke in *SEBC*, chap. III, esp. p. 197, and

appointment of his protégé, in effect by the papal legate Imar (though apparently on the demand of the monks of Cerne, or of some of them), in 1145. Bernard may have tried to reform his unruly community in a somewhat high-handed way; in any case he was soon involved in difficulties, first with the bishop of Salisbury, then with his monks. The former abbot, who had been deposed, returned, supported (if we may believe Gilbert's account) by brigands, and Bernard's position became wholly untenable. It seems likely that the political situation in fact led laymen of the neighbourhood to join in what had originally been a matter of internal discipline. In 1148 Bernard resigned and returned to Gloucester; in 1150 we find him (still a monk of Gloucester) with Gilbert, now bishop of Hereford, by the bedside of the dying bishop of Worcester; later on he was prior of Gloucester; in 1160 he received another command as abbot of Burton; and at Burton he died in 1174/5.[1]

If Gilbert's letters to Bernard and others of his monks[2] reveal genuine concern for the welfare of some at least of his brothers, his letters to the monks of Cerne rebuking their contumacy and to Archbishop Theobald on the troubles in Worcester priory (nos. 47, 49) show an authoritarian attitude: 'I reckon one should give more credence to one truthful bishop than to an angry and disobedient gaggle of monks (*quam irate monachorum turbe et contumaci*)' he wrote to Theobald. But this was no doubt normal at the time among men (as were both Gilbert and Theobald) steeped in St Benedict's *Rule*, with its emphasis on the abbot's patriarchal authority; and in an age which knew nothing of democracy, before even the abbot's councils of the thirteenth century had been devised. And Gilbert was addressing an archbishop who was himself to fall out with his own monastic chapter not many years later.

p. 210 n.; cf. below, p. 159). The relics of the abbey library are listed in N. R. Ker, *Med. Libraries of Great Britain* (2nd edn, London, 1964), pp. 91–2. No. 39 also gives the names of two monks who were sent to help Bernard at Cerne.

[1] See Morey and Brooke, *EHR*, LXIII (1948), 523–6; Worcester, Dean and Chapter, Reg. A, fo. x; annals of Burton, *Ann. Mon.* I, 187 (1173 in Greg. Caerwent, fo. 199 v, q.v. for him as prior of Gloucester in 1160).

[2] Nos. 10, 21, 39, 46, 60, 64.

M & B

In a memorable passage of his *Gesta Pontificum* William of Malmesbury recalled the beauty of setting and rich fertility of the countryside in which Gloucester lay. Within a radius of less than thirty miles, intersected by Severn and Avon, lay a group of abbeys rivalled in number by those of Yorkshire and the Fenland alone.[1] One is reminded of Virgil's lines:

> Adde tot egregias urbes operumque laborem,...
> fluminaque antiquos subterlabentia muros.

Gilbert's links with them were close. Winchcombe received a Cluniac abbot in 1139, Malmesbury another in 1140; Evesham was his uncle's home. With his own bishop at Worcester Gilbert's relations were friendly, partly no doubt because Gloucester abbey was not plagued with the claims to exemption from episcopal control which poisoned the lives of so many Benedictine abbots and their relations with their bishops in this century. Robert de Bethune at Hereford and Jocelin de Bohun at Salisbury were possibly old friends, as we have seen, even though Gilbert fell out for a time with Jocelin over the affair of Cerne. Gloucester lay at the intersection of many roads which provided it with links with the churchmen and laymen of the West of England and of Wales; and the abbey into which Gilbert Foliot moved in 1139 represented much of what was most flourishing and most characteristic of the old monasticism.

Gilbert's abbey had traditions going back into the seventh century, but it was effectively the creation of the Norman Serlo, who was brought from Mont-Saint-Michel in 1072 to reestablish the ancient but decrepit foundation. Serlo was famed for his skill as superior: 'religionis discretio' was the mark of Gloucester noted by William of Malmesbury midway between Serlo's death (1104) and Gilbert's accession; and this 'sobriety and observance' (as Professor Knowles has interpreted William) were attributed to Serlo.[2] But the first Norman abbot was also a great builder and administrator. It was the Conqueror's habit to spend

---

[1] William of Malmesbury, *Gesta Pontificum*, ed. N. E. S. A. Hamilton (RS), pp. 291–3 (cf. *Georgics*, II, 155–7).
[2] *Gesta Pontificum*, p. 293; cf. Knowles, *MO*, p. 113.

the Christmas feast at Gloucester, and Serlo took advantage of
the gathering of the court to obtain grants of lands and other gifts
for his abbey from king and barons. The abbey's estates grew
steadily through his abbacy. In 1088 the city and abbey church
suffered disaster in the rebellion against William Rufus. This was
taken by Serlo as an opportunity to be grasped, and the next year,
on the feast of St Peter and St Paul, the new church of St Peter
was begun, the bishop of Hereford laying the first stone.[1] Serlo
built with great rapidity. By 1100 choir and transepts were
sufficiently advanced for the first consecration, and by then Serlo
had built up a community of 100 monks. In 1102 there came a
set-back, in the shape of a serious fire; and in 1104 Serlo died.
But his work was carried on by his successors, and in spite of
another fire in 1122[2] the nave was probably making steady progress. It remains one of the principal monuments of the massive
grandeur of Norman building in the first quarter of the twelfth
century; but the conception and scale of the building, as well as
the actual construction of the choir (most of it is still visible
behind the fourteenth-century stone scaffolding), were Serlo's.
The great nave made it what Serlo had clearly intended, the
monastic capital of the southern march and of Gloucestershire:
not only a splendid setting for conventual mass and monastic
offices, and for the monks' processions, but also (in its nave) a
place where the folk of Gloucester and its neighbourhood could
gather to pay their respects to the saint and make contributions to
his building fund; to witness the splendour of the monastic
liturgy; to join in High Mass; and last, but perhaps not least, to
see in stone and paint and glass and in the splendid ornaments of
a great abbey church the outward sign of God's favour (as they
understood it) to the Norman monks and the Norman conquerors.

In Gloucester at Christmas 1085 the Domesday Survey was
planned; and at Gloucester at Christmas 1092 the conquest of
Glamorgan. The would-be conquerors made offerings to the

---

[1] Cf. CS, p. 263.

[2] For these dates, see *Cart. Gloucester*, I, 12–13; Florence of Worcester, II, 77;
Greg. Caerwent, fo. 197 v.

abbey; with characteristic prudence they offered lands and churches in parts of Wales yet to be conquered.[1] In this even King William II took part, stirred by the dangerous illness which led him to make Anselm archbishop of Canterbury. The result of this and other groups of gifts from marcher lords was that Gloucester, along with several other English and Norman houses, acquired properties in Wales, and in particular properties belonging to the old Welsh monasteries, the *clas* churches.

It was thus a complex inheritance which Gilbert entered in 1139: a record of dignified observance which one can hardly doubt appealed to the Cluniac not insensitive to outward grandeur, though personally ascetic and severe in manner of life. But he also inherited a territorial power which gave the monks substantial resources, and obligations and administrative problems equally large. The outbreak of the anarchy enhanced these problems, and Gilbert had to use every resource to prevent St Peter's inheritance from being squandered. At one time or another in the twelfth century Gloucester had nine dependent priories, as well as controlling (from *c.* 1150) a hospital in the city.[2] Small dependencies were notoriously difficult to control, and conventual life was often most unsatisfactory in them. But they were regarded as an essential adjunct to a great Benedictine house in the twelfth century. This has been something of a puzzle to modern historians,

---

[1] For what follows, see *CS*, pp. 261 ff., 276–77.

[2] On the dependencies see D. Knowles and R. N. Hadcock, *Medieval Religious Houses, England and Wales* (London, 1953), pp. 61 ff. Bromfield (Salop), was a house of canons finally made into a dependency of Gloucester in 1155, but it seems that there were still canons at large making complaints of this in 1166 (*MB Epp.* 202). A similar story attached to Leonard Stanley, which became a dependency of Gloucester in 1146 (*CS*, pp. 280 ff.; nos. 97–8). It seems as if Stanley was a church in urgent need of reform, but the background was very complicated and is still obscure. On Cardigan and Llanbadarn Fawr see *CS*, p. 265 and n. Ewenny was founded in 1141 (*CS*, p. 266 and n.; cf. nos. 42–5). (Goldcliff priory, Mon., a dependency of Bec, has sometimes been attributed to Gloucester on account of Gilbert's interest in it, shown in nos. 58–60; but he was apparently acting simply as the archbishop's agent.) Ewyas Harold had been founded in 1100, Kilpeck in 1134, St Guthlac's Hereford became conventual in 1143 (see *CS*, pp. 264–5, 280 for Ewyas and St Guthlac's; cf. nos. 21, 83). On the hospital, see R. Graham in *VCH Gloucs.* II, 121; Knowles and Hadcock, *loc. cit.*

but it has recently been argued, with strong probability, that landlords who at this time granted churches to great abbeys liked to have them served by monks, to ensure the quality of the services and the efficacy of the prayers in them, and that this was regarded by the abbeys themselves as an essential part of the service they rendered to their patrons and to the lay world in which they lived. The practice of monks serving parish churches, and the notion that there should be links of this kind between layfolk and monastic churches, were a part of the old monasticism which was disputed by the new orders of the twelfth century. They were frowned on by reformers, and in the nature of things these practices have left little record behind them. The question of how common it was for monks to serve parish churches and how often monastic churches served local congregations must remain open; but the burden of proof can now be said to lie on those who deny that these links were a deliberate part of the economy of the old monasticism.[1] Gilbert himself took part in, or permitted, Gloucester to acquire three new dependencies: Leonard Stanley, Ewenny and St Guthlac's Hereford. The priory at Hereford at least may have been partly established before Gilbert's time. But conventual life seems to have been established in both by him; and the fact that he was prepared to allow these small cells to grow up under the shadow of castles deeply involved in the

---

[1] See D. J. A. Matthew, *The Norman Monasteries and their English Possessions* (Oxford, 1962), esp. pp. 51–65. In a well-known article (*Rev. Bénédictine*, XXXIX (1927), 227–50, 340–64) Dom U. Berlière implied that service by monks of parish churches is rarely recorded and must have been exceptional; and the view that monks served parishes was unpopular with Benedictine historians of the late-nineteenth century owing to its bearing on contemporary controversies. Dr Matthew admits the scarcity of direct evidence, but points out that any direct evidence on eleventh and early twelfth-century parishes is exceedingly rare, and that there is a great deal of indirect evidence—reforming decrees, interest of monasteries in parish churches, and the rapid increase in tiny 'priories'—which only makes sense if it was normal for monks to serve in one way or another as parochial clergy. D. Knowles in *Downside Review*, LI (1933), 501 ff., showed how slight the positive evidence for England was— though it does exist; but almost all the contrary evidence which he cited comes from the late-twelfth century or later, and it is clear that whatever was the normal attitude in 1050 or 1100, the notion that monks should be separated from the world had won the day by the time of St Bernard's death.

political troubles of the 1140's reveals that the notion of the monastic life as something divorced from the world, the Cistercian call of the desert, was alien from his mind.

The development of St Guthlac's very likely led Gilbert to wish to dig the fish-pond on which he and Robert de Bethune failed to agree.[1] This was a minor incident: but when building up this priory he can have had no illusions that Hereford was going to be a place free from trouble and violence. Two of his earliest letters describe the troubles in Hereford in 1140, when Geoffrey Talbot and Milo of Gloucester besieged it and turned the cathedral into a castle.[2] Although the fighting of the anarchy was sporadic, and the campaigning season never lasted more than a few months, Gilbert's letters give us other vivid glimpses of the troubles of the anarchy—of St Mary's church at Slaughter (Glos.) also turned into a castle, of fighting in the precincts of Malmesbury and Reading abbeys, pleas, sometimes for, sometimes against, barons and knights involved in the fighting, challenges to his powerful uncle William de Chesney, pleas on behalf of a poor cousin imprisoned in one of the bishop of Winchester's castles.[3] In 1145 Gilbert described to the pope how in Malmesbury abbey church, 'where God's praise reechoed from St Aldhelm's time, today a cohort of knights rages violently supported by a throng of attendants armed and ready for any impious act' (no. 35). After 1145 the anarchy quietened down; and the much later, but similar, plea to the pope for Reading abbey (no. 85), placed on the frontiers of the two warring factions, probably refers to the final stages of the civil war in 1152–3, when the middle Thames became once again the scene of fierce fighting, before the war was ended by the treaty between Stephen and Henry late in 1153. These letters help to clarify various aspects of the anarchy and to reveal a responsible churchman's attitude to them—most of all the account of the case for the empress which Gilbert sent

[1] See above, pp. 22–3.

[2] Nos. 1, 2; cf. Robert's *Vita* in H. Wharton, *Anglia Sacra*, II (London, 1691), 313–14 (a new edition has been prepared in an Oxford B.Litt. thesis by Miss B. J. Parkinson).

[3] Nos. 5; 35, 85 (as bishop of Hereford, 1148–53, prob. 1152–3); 3, 11, 22, 27, 32, 69, 77, 93–6; 20; 29–30.

to Brian FitzCount in no. 26. But this deserves a separate chapter.

Of Gloucester's dependencies, three lay in Wales, and these and its other Welsh properties were a constant source of anxiety to Gilbert. In the early days of the Norman invasions of Wales, Gloucester had acquired two of the most distinguished of the *clas* churches: Llanbadarn Fawr in Cardiganshire, the church of St Padarn and seat of bishops, and Llancarfan in Glamorgan, the church of St Cadoc;[1] and it also established priories in Cardigan itself early in the twelfth century and in Ewenny (Glam.) in Gilbert's own time, in 1141. For Cardigan there was a rival claimant in Chertsey abbey—it seems that in the political confusion of the invasions, the Clares had succeeded in granting it to both; in the end (after Gilbert's time) Chertsey established its claim. At Llanbadarn and Llancarfan, Gloucester had to reckon with the survivors of the Welsh *clas*. Shortly before Gilbert's accession, the Welsh revival, which was such a marked feature of this period, began, and in 1136 the Norman lords were swept out of the area and the old *clas* restored. In south Glamorgan the Norman lords, led by the earl of Gloucester, never lost their hold; but in Llancarfan Gloucester had to deal with a *clas* family of exceptional resource and ingenuity. The family which founded the diocese of Llandaff in the early twelfth century had previously been established at Llancarfan, and it seems clear that Gloucester early despaired of ousting them entirely; although it did succeed in overriding the claim of Llandaff cathedral to the church of St Cadoc. In the long run, an uneasy *modus vivendi* was established: Gloucester's claim was acknowledged and it received a substantial rent, while the family continued to squat in its old home.[2] The echoes of this dispute can be heard, dimly, in Gilbert's letter 70; no. 13, referring to raiders from Archenfield (now part of Herefordshire), and no. 65, referring to a Welsh raid on his properties which compels him to attend a meeting of Welsh princes, reveal some of the anxieties of the abbot of a great house near the march. They also explain his friendly encouragement, in no. 10, to the

[1] For what follows, see *CS*, pp. 265 f., 276 f., 315, and references there cited.
[2] Cf. *CS*, p. 288 and n.

prior of a lonely cell in Wales whom he commended for strength-
ening the lock on his gates and building a rampart and strong wall
round his house, lest all his good work be destroyed by the folk
whom Prior Osbern had himself described as shaggy and wild-
eyed. Gilbert, however, observes in effect that if the Welsh are
bad neighbours, the English are worse.

Although Gilbert himself was a fervent Angevin, and related
to some of the leading magnates of the area, he occasionally found
himself in difficulties with Milo or Roger,[1] or engaged in the
general effort of the more responsible churchmen to restore peace
in a divided country. When the empress left England in 1148 and
her cause seemed lost, Gilbert and his monks prepared to renew
their allegiance to Stephen; to safeguard what they had won in
the previous years, they resorted to forgery. This is the debit side
of Gilbert's account, and it will be treated at length in chapter VIII.
On the credit side belong his efforts to work in conjunction
with Archbishop Theobald to preserve the unity of the English
church in a divided England; with Theobald Gilbert's fortunes
and aims were closely united.

The personality of Theobald remains one of the enigmas of the
English church in this period; but it has become increasingly
clear in recent years how impressive was his record of patient
diplomatic achievement.[2] He was neither a prophet nor a time-
server. When he became archbishop of Canterbury he was compelled to submit to the authority of his suffragan of Winchester,
who was papal legate from 1139 to 1143. From 1144 to 1150 he
struggled with slow, but steady, success to revive the position of
Archbishop Lanfranc as effective head of the English church. No
doubt he had the interests of the church of Canterbury at heart;

---

[1] For Milo, see no. 24; it is unlikely that this was an isolated episode, and
nos. 77, 93–6 reveal some of the embarrassments his connexion with Roger,
Milo's son (however convenient in other ways) might bring.

[2] On Theobald see esp. Z. N. Brooke, *The English Church and the Papacy*
(Cambridge, 1931), chap. XII; Saltman, *passim*; *JS Epp.* I, pp. xxv–xxxviii.
In Prof. Saltman's very full and useful account he seems to underestimate
the friction between Theobald and Stephen, and also the significance of
the primacy dispute (cf. Brooke, *J. Theol. Studies*, VIII (1957), 187 ff.; *CS*,
p. 283 n.).

but his quest was not supported by narrow motives, for it is clear that he aimed also to unite the church in spite of the political divisions, and make it an instrument of peace. Henry of Blois had tried to resolve political conflict by throwing himself into it; but after he had changed sides twice without any significant success his methods were discredited. Theobald had the unusual advantage among the English magnates that he owed no allegiance to Matilda: he had been a monk in private station when the oaths were sworn to her in Henry I's time, and both as abbot and archbishop he had acknowledged Stephen as king; and shortly after his promotion to the archbishopric the appeal of the empress to the pope failed.[1] Stephen may have been partly attracted to Theobald as a man who owed nothing to Henry I and had sworn nothing to his daughter; and Theobald was able to avoid ever changing sides, anyway in a formal sense. Yet his relations with the king were not easy. In 1148 the king tried to prevent the archbishop from attending the general council at Rheims. The archbishop was even compelled to stage a little comedy: he conducted a solemn consecration of the bishops of Llandaff and Rochester at Canterbury, in the king's presence, a few days before the council was due to open; then he slipped away in 'a fishing smack which he had hired and hidden in a remote bay...that would carry no more than a dozen men' as John of Salisbury tells us, and so, as the pope is alleged to have said, 'swimming rather than sailing' he reached the council.[2] Theobald's disobedience roused the king's displeasure, and after his return he was promptly sent into exile again. After several months he landed in England under the protection of Hugh Bigod, earl of Norfolk. Not long after the king agreed to a reconciliation; but the archbishop's position remained precarious. Gilbert Foliot (now bishop of Hereford) wrote to the archbishop offering asylum in the west country, and in January 1149 Theobald is found at Worcester,

---

[1] See below, pp. 105 ff.

[2] JS HP, p. 7 (C), pp. 7–8 (P); Gervase, I, 134: Theobald consecrated the bishops of Rochester and Llandaff at Canterbury on 14 March (cf. Trans. St Paul's Ecclesiol. Soc. VII (1911–15), 168–9) in Stephen's presence; the formal sessions of the Council began on the 21st.

with Gilbert in his train.[1] The trouble subsided, and Theobald remained in England until 1152. Pope Eugenius III had recently frustrated Stephen's scheme to have his elder son Eustace anointed and crowned in his lifetime, and prohibited Theobald from performing the ceremony.[2] We can hardly doubt that the prohibition was inspired, and since Theobald was now high in papal favour it is a reasonable presumption that he was the pope's instigator. This seems to have been Stephen's suspicion; for when Theobald refused to anoint Eustace on account of the prohibition, the king chased the archbishop into exile.[3] Finally, in 1153, Theobald was able to show his hand: when the young Henry, now duke of Normandy, count of Anjou and husband of the duchess of Aquitaine,[4] invaded England, and Eustace conveniently died, Theobald was the leader of a group of bishops who negotiated peace between Henry and Stephen. Stephen was confirmed on his throne for his lifetime and Henry was assured of the succession. We may doubt if Theobald had this precise solution clearly in view for many years before; but the way in which the archbishop whose allegiance never openly wavered aroused royal suspicion, and the incidents of 1152, strongly suggest that Theobald had had a compromise in mind for some time as the only means of avoiding prolonged civil war. The succession of Henry II in 1154 was a victory, among other things, for Theobald's slow-moving diplomacy.

[1] No. 79; Dean and Chapter, Worcester, Reg. A 4, fos. x v–xi (extract in Saltman, p. 546 from printed text in W. Thomas, *Account of the Bishops of Worcester* (1725), p. 11; in the MS the document is dated 26 January 1148, but the years of king and bishop are given, and these prove that it was issued in January 1149 (i.e. 1148/9) as in Saltman). Cf. Gervase, I, 135–6; *Trans. St Paul's Eccles. Soc. ut sup.*

[2] Henry of Huntingdon, *Historia Anglorum*, ed. T. Arnold (RS), pp. 283–4; Gervase, I, 150–1; cf. Saltman, pp. 36–7. It seems that the archbishop of York, Henry Murdac, had agreed to ask the pope's leave for the coronation in 1151, but failed to obtain it. This is all the more striking since Murdac and Eugenius were fellow-Cistercians, and strengthens the supposition that Theobald's voice was against the coronation.

[3] Saltman, pp. 37–8.

[4] Henry did not assume the title duke of Aquitaine until late in 1153 (Z. N. and C. N. L. Brooke, *EHR*, LXI (1946), 86–8; cf. A. L. Poole in *Gesta Stephani*, ed. K. Potter, NMT, p. xxiv).

There was, however, another aspect to Stephen's displeasure. As the archbishop declined in royal favour, so he grew in strength and independence as head of the province of Canterbury. From 1139 to 1143 he had been subject to the legate of Winchester. After 1143 Henry of Blois's legateship was never renewed. But it was some years before the threat was lifted, and Henry and the bishop of St David's meanwhile were intriguing to be made archbishops in their own right. Theobald was abroad in 1143 and 1144, and the fruit of his visit to the pope was the confirmation of his 'primacy',[1] an event which called out a letter of effusive thanks from Gilbert Foliot to the papal chancellor, the English Cardinal Robert Pullen, and some verses of obscure rejoicing from Osbert of Clare. It soon appeared, however, that this was not the end of Theobald's difficulties. Primacy he had achieved, but primacy over whom? From now on he claimed to be primate of all England, and to be metropolitan over Wales. Yet the bishop of St David's continued to claim his independence, and Theobald had to argue with him in the pope's presence again in 1147. The claim died, for the time being, with Bishop Bernard early in 1148, but at the council of Rheims it was made clear to Theobald that his primacy did not extend over York. In his later years he altered his formal title to 'primate of the English', and the reflection of his disappointment can be seen in Becket's refusal to use the title 'primate'.[2] But Theobald received consolation in 1150: Henry of Winchester's case was finally repudiated, and Theobald

[1] See *GFL*, Appendix II, and refs. cited above, p. 88 n.; see no. 41 for Gilbert's response to the grant of primacy, and Osbert of Clare's no. 32 (ed. E. W. Williamson, Oxford, 1929) for a similar expression of pleasure.

The primacy was not granted immediately after Theobald's visit to the papal Curia. Pope Lucius II sent the Cluniac Imar, cardinal bishop of Tusculum, as legate to England; but Imar was recalled and Theobald's primacy confirmed in the opening months of the pontificate of Eugenius III in 1145. Gilbert Foliot attributed this to Robert Pullen; in addition, the affair of the York election had made St Bernard and his associates (of whom Eugenius was one) averse to Henry of Blois and therefore favourably disposed to Theobald (cf. Knowles, *Historian and Character*, chap. 5; St Bernard, *Ep.* 238).

[2] See below, p. 154 n.; for Theobald's titles, Saltman, pp. 190 ff.; for the failure of Theobald's claim over York in 1148, *JS HP*, p. 5 (C), pp. 5–6 (P)—the pope postponed the issue, but in effect he was clearly refusing Theobald's request.

was made legate for the English church, an office he continued to hold at least until 1159, perhaps until his death in 1161.[1]

Thus the decline of Stephen's favour went hand in hand with the growth of the pope's; and this was probably no coincidence. Theobald was trying to hold together the English Church in unity in a divided kingdom, and to do so effectively meant living on the edge between loyalty and disloyalty to Stephen. Gilbert Foliot's letters are striking testimony to the way Theobald tried to do this. Theobald was formally Stephen's man; Gilbert made no secret of being an Angevin. Yet in the mid-1140's (if not before) they became firm friends, and whenever Theobald went abroad he invited Gilbert to accompany him. In 1143–4 Gilbert refused; but in 1147 and 1148 he was with the archbishop. Although Theobald seems to have been on good terms with the bishops of Worcester and Hereford, Gilbert seems to have been the leading ecclesiastic in the empress's part of the country who was in closest touch with the archbishop. Theobald even used Gilbert as a post office, for forwarding letters to the more westerly bishops;[2] since

---

[1] Saltman, pp. 30–1, shows that Theobald became legate between October 1149 and the death of Bishop Simon of Worcester on 20 March 1150. Since Bishop Simon's deathbed repentance (Worcester Reg. A 4, fo. x) gives Theobald the precise title he used *before* he became legate, it seems likely that the appointment was not known in Worcester when this was written; and there is evidence that Henry of Blois was still hoping for the legateship himself between November 1149 and February 1150 (*JS Epp.* I, 254). Presumably, the grant was made in the opening months of 1150 (this would need revision if the date given in a fourteenth-century obit in the Worcester Antiphoner for Simon's death, 2 January, were to be accepted: cf. J. K. Floyer and S. G. Hamilton, *Cat. of MSS...of Worcester Cathedral* (Oxford, 1906), p. 92).

It is usually assumed that Theobald was legate until his death, but probably at this date the office lapsed at the end of each papal pontificate, and it is unlikely that Theobald was legate between the dual election of 1159 and the recognition of Alexander III late in 1160 (see *J. Theol. Stud.* VIII (1957), 189–90 n.). There is, however, some evidence that Theobald was legate again before his death: see H. Mayr-Harting, *Acta of the bishops of Chichester* (Canterbury and York Society, 1964), no. 36, note.

[2] See nos. 58–60, esp. 59, in which Gilbert passes messages and a letter between the archbishop of Canterbury on the one hand and the bishop of Llandaff and the monks of Goldcliff (Mon., dep. of Bec) on the other; and no. 76, in which Gilbert informs the bishop of Bath that Theobald has been empowered to release the bishops and abbots (suspended at Rheims in 1148) from their suspension, and asks him to inform the bishop of Exeter.

the occasions on which this is recorded were sometimes related to cases in which Gilbert was personally involved, this may have been part of a normal administrative routine. But it is clear that there was close trust between abbot and archbishop.

This relationship is one of many pieces of evidence to show that Theobald strove to act as primate of all England—both to preserve the rights of his see and to work for better order and peace in the land. In his later years Theobald issued a number of general confirmations to religious houses in different parts of the country of a kind normally issued by the king;[1] this is a witness to the confidence he inspired as a stable element in a fluid situation. Theobald lived surrounded by a glittering circle of clerks; and for all major business he seems to have liked to gather a group of bishops round him. Before 1148 there is no evidence that Gilbert joined in these gatherings,[2] and he never appears in the extant witness lists of Theobald's charters. Yet when Theobald went overseas in the 1140's, he always asked Gilbert to go with him. Various factors may have weighed with him: Gilbert's experience of the churches of the march may have made him a useful adviser in dealing with the Welsh bishops; his friendship with Robert Pullen may have given him influence in the papal Curia. It seems highly probable that it suited Theobald's plans to parade one of the most committed Angevins among the English higher clergy in his train to help convince the pope that Theobald's primacy was the key to unity and peace in England. It is ironical to recall that Gilbert abused his friendship and trust by foisting a forged charter of King Stephen on the archbishop, and by turning his experience in this primacy dispute against Theobald's successor.[3] But it is clear too that Gilbert's company was congenial to Theobald, and that he saw talent and promise in the young abbot. And the man who picked John of Canterbury and John of Salisbury, fetched Vacarius from Bologna, and saw in Thomas Becket

---

[1] See *CS*, p. 274 and n.

[2] Nor is there any proof that he did not; indeed the evidence about the gatherings is very scanty before the mid-1150's (when John of Salisbury's letters get under way; cf. *JS Epp.* I, p. xxxvi). Theobald's witness lists are not numerous enough for Gilbert's absence to be very significant.

[3] See below, pp. 127, 151 ff.

the makings both of royal chancellor and of archbishop, was no mean judge of talent.

When Gilbert became bishop of Hereford we are told that he wished to retain the abbacy of Gloucester, as Henry of Winchester retained Glastonbury.[1] To this the archbishop consented, but the monks, catching wind of it, hastily elected their subprior Hamelin, and had him blessed by the bishop of Worcester. Our informant is John of Salisbury, and he was writing c. 1164, when the dispute between Becket and Foliot had broken out: the whole passage is notably hostile to the latter. If partly or wholly true, the story may reflect the monks' fear of being treated as Roger of Salisbury had treated Malmesbury, or it may reflect their anxiety to be rid of Gilbert. If so, they did not succeed in poisoning his affection for his old home, and there is ample evidence that he retained his interest in Gloucester and was on good terms with his successor.[2] As for the scheme itself, Gilbert might have wished not only to imitate the brilliant Cluniac prince-bishop of Winchester, but more directly his own predecessor at Hereford, who had consoled himself for being head of a secular chapter by retaining the closest ties with his old community of Llanthony, whose headquarters now lay in Gloucester. If the story is to be believed at all, it seems probable that Gilbert's prime motive was not greed, but the wish to keep a *pied-à-terre* where he could resume the monastic life in those intervals of rest to which busy men are always fondly looking forward.

Gilbert Foliot was not without ambition; yet we need not doubt the sincerity of the nostalgia with which, as bishop, he looked back to his monastic days; and against John of Salisbury's later accusation that Gilbert was ambitious to become archbishop of Canterbury we can set an earlier anecdote. Writing c. 1159, before Gilbert's enmity to Becket had poisoned his pen,[3] John

---

[1] *JS HP*, p. 48 (C, P).

[2] See nos. 91, 128–30, etc.; and from no. 87 it seems that Gilbert may have intervened to help Hamelin over his election—if so, Gilbert hardly seems to have resented the event.

[3] See above, p. 31 and below, p. 166; the passage is in *Policraticus*, vii, 25, ed. C. C. J. Webb, II, 216–17. At the turn of 1163 and 1164 John of Salisbury was still hoping for Gilbert's help in his exile, and even as late as 1165

tells how the venerable Bishop Gilbert had told him, evidently in jest, that it was always the custom of monks to carp at their superiors. As a novice, in his ardour, Gilbert had charged his masters with worthlessness. Very soon he began to be promoted, and at every stage learned sympathy and respect for his colleagues, but still cavilled at those above him. As a prior he grumbled at abbots; as an abbot, better disposed towards abbots, he began to observe the vices of bishops; finally, as bishop, he spared his colleagues. 'Nor do I think he has laboured under the vice of envy; he is a wise man who has expressed with elegance what is somehow inborn in men.' When John observed his fellow men he rarely avoided irony, and perhaps we should not take him too literally. But the irony here seems slight—when compared, for instance, with John's famous account of St Bernard at the council of Rheims, which is very damaging to Bernard, whom John none the less fervently admired. The picture of the young man of talent absorbed in his work and station, carping at his superiors, is true to life; and the man who told it against himself was not wholly incapable of self-criticism.

he had still some hopes of Gilbert (*MB Epp.* 79, 226). No doubt when he wrote the *HP* he was already to some extent disillusioned with Gilbert; but in considering John's witness, it is well to remember his admission that he himself had repeatedly solicited Gilbert for help: 'Nunc autem eum [*sc.* Richard of Ilchester] et episcopum Londoniensem, qui regis gratiam dicitur habere pre ceteris, iterato sollicitaui scripto...' (*MB Epp.* 226). It is significant that John did not preserve any of his letters to Gilbert.

CHAPTER VI

BISHOP OF HEREFORD
AND LONDON

The most striking evidence of Theobald's trust in Gilbert came in
1148, when he arranged for his promotion to the bishopric of Hereford. 'Gilbert, abbot of Gloucester, was elected (*electus*) bishop of
Hereford by the advice and direction of the archbishop of Canterbury. He was personally acceptable to the duke of Normandy, now
king, who then controlled the election to this see.' Thus John of
Salisbury, who goes on to tell how the young Henry tried to insist
on an oath not to do fealty to Stephen, and how, after his consecration, Gilbert was instructed by Theobald to submit to the king
and swear fealty to him. This roused Henry's anger—the echoes of
his displeasure may explain the difficulties with Henry revealed by
some of Gilbert's letters written in 1153—'but the archbishop, partly
by threats, partly by promises, appeased the duke, and persuaded
him that a bishop had no right to cause schism within the Church
by refusing fealty to the prince approved by the papacy'.[1] By this
adroit manœuvre Theobald had secured as bishop in a crucial western see a man close to himself and acceptable to the Angevins, and
had won Stephen's recognition of his promotion.

There can be little doubt that it was Theobald who inspired the
choice of Gilbert. The precise stages in his 'election', however,
are not clear. Gilbert was acceptable to the canons of Hereford,

[1] *JS HP*, pp. 47–9 (C, P; from C, slightly adapted). John's narrative is
somewhat confused. He does not say directly that Gilbert took the oath to
Henry, and yet he implies it, and makes such an oath the ground of Henry's
anger; he tells us, furthermore, that the prognostic—taken by opening the
gospels at random—was 'Dormis? non potuisti una hora uigilare mecum?'
(*Mc.* xiv, 37) 'which many supposed was fulfilled later when, on his return to
England, he did fealty to king Stephen disregarding his obligation to the duke'.
If Gilbert entered any such obligation, under the circumstances of 1148, he was
extremely imprudent; nor is the oath needed to explain Henry's annoyance at
what he might well regard as a betrayal by a trusted supporter. It seems
probable that Gilbert, under Theobald's guidance, swore no oath to Henry.
For 1153, see nos. 101, 104–6.

whose dean was a friend of his (see no. 1). Gilbert's promotion was made possible in some measure by papal intervention. The pope made him vicar of the vacant see (no. 77), and it has been suggested that he provided him to the see. Since Robert de Bethune, his predecessor, died at the council of Rheims—that is, in the Curia—it is likely that some basis could have been found for a papal appointment in this case;[1] and if an election was held (as John's words seem to imply)[2] it was doubtless held under strong pressure from pope, archbishop and the young Henry. In any event, it was the pope who instructed the bishops of London, Salisbury and Chichester to assist the archbishop in performing the consecration, and when they refused to consecrate him outside England without royal consent, the pope instructed a group of French bishops, led by Milo of Thérouanne and Nicholas of Cambrai, to join the archbishop in the ceremony; and this was duly performed at St Omer on 5 September 1148.[3]

Gilbert's early years as bishop must have been extremely eventful. Although the anarchy had subsided, his first five years were punctuated by the invasions of the young Henry in 1149 and 1153, by wars and rumours of wars; and Gilbert Foliot was evidently much respected both by archbishop and king in the

[1] See below, pp. 204–6. In no. 80 Gilbert writes that it was by papal order that he was consecrated and had the church of Hereford committed to his care. But this, in a letter addressed to the pope, need mean no more than John's narrative proves, namely that the consecration was celebrated at the pope's order (so also *Cart. Gloucester*, I, 19). In no. 77 he describes himself as vicar of the diocese by papal mandate; Round (*GM*, p. 251) took this to mean that the pope had provided him to the see—and this seems to be the origin of the view that he was provided by Eugenius III. But the vicar was the spiritual caretaker of the diocese (see below, pp. 226–7), not the bishop-elect. If John's account implies that Eugenius ordered Gilbert's consecration while the English bishops were still in France for the council of Rheims, then there can hardly have been time for consultation with Hereford, and we may presume that the pope provided. But this cannot be established, and nearly six months passed between the former bishop's death and Gilbert's consecration. It is, however, possible that the right of the pope to fill offices which fell vacant in Curia, which had ancient roots, was invoked in this case. Other references are in ann. Tewkesbury, Winchester, Osney, Worcester (*Ann. Mon.* I, 48; II, 54; IV, 26, 379); Torigni, ed. R. Howlett (RS), p. 156.   [2] But *electus* was an ambiguous word.

[3] *JS HP*, p. 48 (C, P); *Cart. Gloucester*, I, 19; Gervase, I, 135 (also mentioning the bishop of Amiens).

opening years of Henry II's reign, between 1154 and 1161, when Theobald died. A few of Gilbert's letters treat of these events. One, at the very opening of his episcopate, describes how his predecessor had been too generous to Lanthony, and how Gilbert was compelled to recover some of the properties of his cathedral; another invited Theobald to take refuge with Gilbert in the west (nos. 80, 79). Several describe the promotion of his uncle Robert de Chesney to the see of Lincoln at the end of 1148; several more, the troubles of his cousin Richard de Belmeis in becoming bishop of London in 1152—and some describe Richard's difficulties later in his episcopate (nos. 80-1, 99-103, 109, 139-40). In 1153 he speaks more than once of his anxiety at the approach of the young Henry (no. 101, 104-6), who was not quick to forgive Gilbert, it seems, for swearing fealty to Stephen. Several reveal how strong his interest in Gloucester remained (nos. 87, 91, 128-30). But his relations with his canons, with the archbishop and with the king are largely hidden from us: some letters may be lost, but for the most part he dealt with these folk face to face, and no account of his dealings was committed to parchment.[1]

By c. 1161 his cousin the bishop of London had become incapable of managing his affairs, which were in considerable disorder, and Thomas Becket, as chancellor, asked Gilbert to administer the see. This Gilbert refused to do (no. 139), claiming in a letter to the king that it would be to the peril of his soul. But he continued to take a friendly interest in the dying bishop's concerns; and meanwhile a greater issue had arisen with the death of Archbishop Theobald in April 1161. The interpretation of the events which followed, and an estimate of Gilbert's work as bishop and ecclesiastical judge, must be worked out in detail in later chapters. For the moment let the events speak for themselves.

After considerable delay royal messengers came in May 1162 to Canterbury to arrange the election of Thomas Becket as archbishop.[2] First of all, at Canterbury, the monks elected him and

---

[1] What can be gleaned is discussed below, chaps. IX, X.

[2] For what follows, see in particular the lives of Thomas by FitzStephen (MB, III, 35-6); Grim (II, 366-7); Roger of Pontigny (the probable author of 'Anonymous I': IV, 17); William of Canterbury (I, 9); and Diceto, I, 306-7.

then in London his election was confirmed. Only one voice was raised, we are told, against Becket's election, and that was Gilbert Foliot's. He was overruled, and on Trinity Sunday the chancellor and archdeacon of Canterbury was consecrated by the precentor of the province, the bishop of Winchester, since the dean, the bishop of London, had died. After a further delay, the king, the new archbishop, the pope and the London chapter agreed to the translation of Gilbert Foliot from Hereford to London. The king (already beginning to be aware of coming trouble with the archbishop) wished to have Gilbert in regular attendance, and in the second see (in prestige) of the province; the archbishop was glad, it seems, to find some compensation for the man who was generally regarded as his rival for the primatial office; the pope, now and for some years to come, regarded Gilbert as a moderating influence in the affairs of Church and kingdom, a mediator in time of trouble; several of the canons of London welcomed in him their cousin and helper. The translation was authorised by the pope in March, and on 28 April Gilbert was enthroned, so Ralph de Diceto (then archdeacon of Middlesex, later dean) tells us, 'according to the desire of the whole chapter'.[1]

The clouds were gathering, and the first peals of thunder were heard in the council of Westminster the same October. In January 1164, at Clarendon, the bishops resisted the king's demand that they set their seals to his constitutions—to his open statement of the customs of Henry I in his dealings with Church and churchmen. Their resistance was unsteady, and Becket was

---

[1] Diceto, I, 309, confirmed by Becket in no. 142; the bull of translation is no. 141. Diceto dates the translation 6 March: this was clearly the formal election, or rather postulation in the presence of the king (since presumably Gilbert, as a bishop, was ineligible, and so had to be 'postulated', not elected—see no. 142). The pope confirmed and gave the necessary dispensation for the translation at Paris on 19 March (no. 141); Gilbert was enthroned on 28 April. Gervase, I, 173, dates the translation in January; as the king only landed in England on 25 January and certainly held a council in London early in March, we may accept Diceto's date, which fits that of the bull (see R. W. Eyton, *Court, Household and Itinerary of King Henry II*, London, 1878, pp. 58–9; *Misc. D. M. Stenton*, p. 21). Richard of Anstey came to court on 3 March, and waited in vain for an audience of the king for 4 days: the king was too busy. Diceto (II, 47) gives Gilbert an episcopate of 23 years, 10 months and 17 days, which, if correct, suggests that the bull was received at St Paul's c. 2–3 April.

well aware that he could not count on the bishops joining him in a united front; suddenly, without warning, he swung to the other extreme, and submitted to the king. So the constitutions were accepted. But Becket soon recovered his nerve and submitted the constitutions, and himself, to the pope; he also tried, unsuccessfully, to flee the country. The pope condemned most of the constitutions and pardoned the archbishop, and events rapidly moved towards an impasse. Henry had lost all trust in the archbishop whom he had created, and Foliot saw his fears fulfilled—though hardly, perhaps, in the manner he had expected. At Northampton in October 1164 Henry wished to put Becket on trial. The archbishop refused his jurisdiction, and eventually fled from the country. A strong embassy led by the archbishop of York and the bishops of London, Chichester, Exeter and Worcester went to the pope at Sens to demand the archbishop's canonical deprivation.[1] But the pope supported the archbishop, and the long years of crises and exile followed. At first, in spite of the language Gilbert used against Becket at Sens, he seems to have been trusted by the pope not only to keep the king from extreme measures but to act as a mediating force. In the former role Gilbert persisted, but his attitude to the archbishop became increasingly intransigent. He organised appeal after appeal against him to stave off the archbishop's censures; and in the early years, while the pope's position in Europe at large remained precarious, Thomas's hands were tied. The exchange of angry letters came to a climax in 1166—with *Multiplicem*; and finally, in 1169, Gilbert was excommunicated by Thomas for various offences, above all as the chief fomenter of the dispute among Henry II's ecclesiastical advisers.[2]

---

[1] Knowles, *EC*, p. 92. It is notable that the four bishops were the leading canonists on the bench, and somewhat surprising to find Exeter and Worcester, later to be supporters of Becket, in this galley. It seems clear that the bishops had agreed among themselves that Becket was to be removed (if at all) by canonical process, not by any act of the royal court. See below, pp. 180–1.

[2] For the appeal and exchange of letters in 1166, see below, pp. 162–87; on the events of 1169, Knowles, *EC*, pp. 99 ff.; *MB Epp.* 479–80, 488–90, 495–500, etc.; *MB*, III, 87 ff., 414 f. (FitzStephen, Herbert of Bosham), IV, 115 f. (Anon. II); Diceto, I, 333; Gervase, I, 211–12. *MB Epp.* 371 seems to show that Becket tried to excommunicate Gilbert in 1168; presumably the pope quashed this.

Gilbert claimed that his excommunication was invalid, since one of his numerous appeals to the pope was under way at the time; but he felt it prudent to act as if excommunicated. He was no longer the brilliant young abbot whom Theobald carried with him on his journeys to the Curia; he felt that he was entering the last age of man, broken by the circumstances of the crisis.[1] He set out again for Rome, avoiding Burgundy because of threats of violence; went south to Montpellier and S. Gilles, and so across the Alps to Milan. There he received a letter from the pope telling him that the archbishop of Rouen and the bishop of Exeter had already been commissioned to absolve him; and so he turned back. On Easter Day the commissioners duly absolved him at Rouen; but within two months a worse crisis was upon him. On 14 June he joined with the archbishop of York and other bishops in the coronation of the king's son, the younger Henry.[2]

[1] No. 212, written to the pope shortly after his absolution. For what follows, see Diceto, I, 337–8 and nos. 210–11; *MB Epp.* 627–8, 656, 658 ff. FitzStephen, Diceto and most of the letters say that the archbishop of Rouen and the bishop of Exeter were commissioned by the pope to absolve Gilbert. But some MSS of *Epp.* 655–6, 658 replace Exeter by Nevers (see *GFL*, note to no. 198): both bishops had the initial B., and Nevers was commissioned about this time to visit England with the archbishop of Rouen (*MB Epp.* 628 ff.): this is probably the source of the confusion.

[2] Diceto (I, 338) gives 18 June, but the other sources, notably the *Gesta Henrici* (ed. Stubbs, RS, I, 5), FitzStephen (*MB*, III, 103) and Gervase (I, 219) all give 14 June; and *MB Ep.* 676, written immediately after the event, confirms that it took place on a Sunday. It has been questioned whether the papal prohibition of February was known in England. It seems to us incredible that it was not, although the participants may not formally have received or admitted receiving it. And no English bishop could have been ignorant that coronation by York infringed the privileges claimed by Canterbury (on this see a forthcoming paper by Mrs A. Duggan in *Studies in Church History*, II). *MB Epp.* 700–1 imply that the pope was informed that York, Durham, London, Salisbury, Exeter, Coventry-Chester, Rochester, St Asaph, and Llandaff were the English bishops present. In *MB Epp.* 716 Becket specifically excused Exeter, but in terms which suggest that, though innocent, he may have been at Westminster at the time. Worcester was in Normandy (FitzStephen, *MB*, III, 103) and certainly objected; there is no evidence that Norwich or Winchester was involved (cf. Knowles, *EC*, pp. 136–7), nor St David's; the other sees were vacant. Full censure only fell on York, the officiant, and London and Salisbury, because they had only recently been released (on promise of good behaviour) from excommunication. It looks as if, *inter alia*, Henry II had found a test case on which he could carry the bishops with him. Why, is not clear. The privi-

The motives for this event are far from clear. No doubt Henry II wished to secure his succession; no doubt Roger of York was glad of a chance to flout the privileges of Canterbury; no doubt Henry II used it as a test case of his authority and brought every pressure to bear on the bishops. But the pope had expressly forbidden the coronation, and both he and Becket were exasperated by it. When it took place interdict on England was already threatened; under this pressure, and in fear (no doubt) of the consequences of the coronation, Henry II patched up an uneasy truce with Becket, and prepared to let him return. The pope was incensed by the coronation and issued anathemas on those who had taken part which he authorised Becket to publish; nor was Pope Alexander appeased by news of the reconciliation, which he regarded with scepticism.[1] The sequel is well known: Becket returned, but sending the anathemas before him; the young king, acting as regent, treated him as virtually a prisoner in Canterbury; tempers mounted; the archbishop preached his Christmas sermon, in which, using more tears than words, he denounced his enemies; and on 29 December the four knights came to Canterbury and murdered him.

Before the murder Gilbert had instructed his representative in the Curia, Master David, to make his case to the pope for absolution from the second excommunication. A letter of David's reveals graphically how his efforts were interrupted by the arrival of the shocking news from Canterbury; and in the event Gilbert had to wait till August 1171 for absolution. At first he seems to have felt inclined to defend the part he had played in the crisis, and to have prepared the collection of letters represented in the Douce MS[2] in his own defence. But Becket was being acclaimed on every hand a martyr, and Foliot's role became increasingly unhappy; about the time of his absolution he fell dangerously ill,

leges of Canterbury raised issues which are still not fully investigated; nor have the events which followed the coronation ever been clearly elucidated. The chief material is laid out, in some confusion, in *MB*, vii.

[1] *MB Epp.* 724 (cf. Knowles, *EC*, p. 138 and n.) makes it highly probable that Gilbert and Jocelin of Salisbury would have submitted to Becket in December 1170, but for the resistance of York.

[2] See p. 26.

and his old associate, the bishop of Salisbury, recommended him to ask for the intercession of the martyr.[1] In his extremity Gilbert permitted the intercession—his recovery, we are told, followed hard upon it—and this crowning indignity, coupled with Becket's canonisation, duly recorded in MS B, completed Gilbert's discomfiture.

We have little information, however, about his personal life in his later years. He continued to fulfil the duties of his office, appears frequently as judge-delegate still, and as dean of the province presided at the election of archbishops in 1173 and presumably in 1184. He was certainly not inactive. We have none of his personal letters later than c. 1177, but this is because the chief surviving manuscript (B) was compiled in or soon after that year. The formal record of his charters, cases, attendances at court goes on. We cannot tell how large a part he played in his own administration, but there is no reason to suppose that he retired. He must have been about eighty, perhaps over eighty, when he died on 18 February 1187.[2] Already, some years before, he had gone blind. His old protégé Walter Map, writing in 1181 or 1182, shows that to the end Gilbert had friends and enemies, and that even blindness did not keep him from work. Map is talking of detractors: as for his own, he says, he can safely ignore them, since his work is like a dry bone, which no dog will trouble to gnaw.

Were I moved, I should be still more surprised that Gilbert Foliot, now bishop of London, a man who is a treasure-house of goodness and wisdom, wealthy and distinguished, master of a most clear and lucid style, has been called a madman because he has written books, though nothing can be found more fit for its purpose than his work— I say I should be surprised at this, had I not read the words of the marvellous Cook (Martial):

'Rome, you read Ennius and leave Maro on the shelf.' And later he condoles with Homer and says: 'His own age laughed at Maeonides.'

[1] *MB*, I, 251–2.

[2] Diceto, II, 47, confirmed by St Paul's obituaries from the early thirteenth century onwards (St Paul's MS W.D. 12, fo. 10 v; cf. W.D. 4, fos. 92 v ff.; BM Harl. MS. 6956, fo. 107 v); also, it seems, by the *Gesta Henrici* (II, 5; cf. Eyton, p. 277 n.). The Hereford obituary (see p. 33 n.) has him under 17 February.

Now who is greater in his writings than Homer? Who more happy than Maro? Who, when he marks their abusers, will not be content to bear with his own? Who can be offended by the spite of his own time, knowing that it has been the same in every age? Write on, Gilbert, and care not; light up the dark places of God's law, and soften their pleasant hardnesses with your honeyed eloquence; with sweet serenity open up the wholesome difficulties, making the rough way smooth, and straightening the winding paths. Age and poring over books are now bringing blindness upon you, and are making your last years tuneful as of old were those of dim-eyed Homer. No longer with your bodily eyes, but with such as angels use to see the Lord, may you view and contemplate Him and His works, that through this darkness He may lead you into His marvellous light, who with God the Father and the Holy Spirit liveth and reigneth God, world without end. Amen.[1]

[1] *De nugis curialium*, IV, 5; trans. M. R. James, pp. 171–2.

CHAPTER VII

THE CASE FOR
THE EMPRESS MATILDA

Of Gilbert Foliot's early letters, the widest interest attaches, without question, to no. 26, his famous letter to Brian FitzCount on the right of the Empress Matilda to the English throne. The letter is well known; its witness has been heard by all recent students of the case, and it was used in particular by R. L. Poole to establish that the empress's appeal against Stephen went before the pope, not in 1136, as J. H. Round had argued, but at the second Lateran Council in 1139.[1] But the content of the arguments has received less attention, and it is the purpose of this chapter to suggest that the letter still has much to teach us on the tangled problem of the English throne and the law of succession, as well as on the personal situation of Gilbert, and of other leading churchmen, in the anarchy.

Brian FitzCount was a younger and possibly illegitimate son of Alan IV, duke of Brittany, who had been sent to the court of Henry I to be brought up; Henry, as Gilbert tells us, looked after him as a boy and a young man, made him a knight and gave him gifts and honours; in particular, he gave him the heiress of the

---

[1] Poole in *JS HP*, pp. 107 ff., correcting Round, *GM*, pp. 250 ff. The problem of the debate before the pope, its date, and the relation between Gilbert's account and that in John of Salisbury's *Historia Pontificalis* (P, pp. 85 ff.; C, pp. 83 ff.), are discussed in an appendix to Giles Constable's forthcoming edition of Peter the Venerable's *Letters*. We are much indebted to Prof. Constable for allowing us to see a draft of this. He confirms Poole's date for the debate (1139), and adduces other evidence that Peter the Venerable, abbot of Cluny, was present at the Lateran Council of 1139. But he points out that it is possible that there had been an earlier debate in 1136, and that John of Salisbury's account refers to this. While accepting this as a possibility, we feel that it is probable that John's and Gilbert's account refer to the same occasion: in both the central figure is Ulger, bishop of Angers (who may, however, also have visited the pope in 1136), and the arguments are similar; there are discrepancies, but they are easily explained. See further below.
On Brian FitzCount, see *GFL*, Biog. Index.

honour of Wallingford in marriage, and so endowed Brian as a tenant-in-chief. Along with the rest of the English barons, he swore in 1127 to accept Matilda as heir to England and Normandy; like the other barons he accepted the *fait accompli* of Stephen's accession; but when the empress came to assert her claim in 1139, he promptly joined her, and remained faithful to her until she left England in 1148—indeed, he continued to hold Wallingford against Stephen on behalf of the empress's son, the young Henry, until Henry came in person to his relief in 1153. Brian was not only one of the most faithful of the empress's supporters, he was capable of wielding a pen—or at least, of having his thoughts set on paper in coherent form. Gilbert congratulates him, in somewhat patronising fashion, for having written a 'book' on the empress's behalf; and then proceeds to show Brian what he ought to have said, to produce his own account of the empress's case.

Brian's 'book' is lost. There survives, however, an exchange of letters between him and Henry of Blois, bishop of Winchester, not unconnected with the issue.[1] The immediate occasion for those letters was a complaint by the bishop that Brian and his men had been molesting travellers to the bishop's fair. Brian's answer is that by following the bishop's order he has been deprived of the land which King Henry, the bishop's uncle, gave him, and is compelled to feed himself and his men as he can. Behind the immediate issue, very clearly, lurks a deeper one. In 1141, for a brief space, the empress's cause had triumphed, and among others who had joined her was the bishop of Winchester himself. The bishop, as papal legate, was the leading figure in the English church, and in the spring of 1141 the church declared formally for Matilda. Later in the year the empress's triumph proved abortive; the bishop changed sides again and was besieged by Matilda and Robert of Gloucester in Winchester; and they in their turn were besieged by Stephen's queen. Matilda's army was compelled to withdraw from Winchester, and in the confusion of the retreat Robert of Gloucester was captured by the queen's troops; he was soon after exchanged for Stephen, who was thus restored to his

[1] Printed, with commentary, by H. W. C. Davis in *EHR*, xxv (1910), 297–303.

kingdom, and in the recovery of Stephen's power which followed, it is evident that Brian FitzCount, established on an outpost far to the east of the main centres of Angevin power, suffered the loss of his lands.[1] On this account Brian can attribute his loss to the bishop's command: in the spring of 1141 Henry had instructed Brian to accept the empress as queen.

When Brian refers to the bishop's command, he deploys an impressive list of the English magnates who were witnesses to it. The list clearly belongs to the early summer of 1141, when the empress was at the height of her power: it includes the earl of Norfolk, created earl at the turn of 1140 and 1141, and Bishop Robert of London, appointed in June 1141; it includes some men like Archbishop Theobald who adhered to the empress only very briefly.[2] The letter itself is therefore unlikely to have been written much later than 1141. The fair was evidently the great fair of St Giles at Winchester, held in September—but hardly in September 1141, during the siege of Winchester; September 1142 therefore appears to be the earliest—and as we think, the most probable—date for the letters.

In the bishop's protocol he enjoins Brian to remember Lot's wife, and not to look back. The implication is that Brian had accepted Stephen as king in 1136; he must not cast backward glances at the empress. 'You treat with me concerning Lot and his wife' retorted the baron. 'I never saw them, nor knew them or their city, nor were we alive at the same time.' He brings the

---

[1] In 1141 and 1142, however, he had the support of the empress herself, who was stationed not far away in Oxford.

[2] The list is in *art. cit.* p. 302. It is noticeable that it refers to several men who received earldoms in the period 1141–3 without the title earl: William de Roumare (1141), Aubrey de Vere (1142) and Milo of Gloucester (1143). It also includes Geoffrey de Mandeville, who had received an earldom from Stephen in 1140 and had it confirmed by the empress in the summer of 1141, and yet does not name him earl. It was not, however, an invariable practice in the period for an earl to be given his title even in charters (cf. Clay, *EYC*, VIII, 46–7; J. F. A. Mason, *TRHS*, 5th series, XIII (1963), 3–4); Brian would not be used to giving it to men very recently created, and it is possible that he did not regard William de Roumare, who was of Stephen's creation (but seems to have been earl of Cambridge since 1139), as a genuine earl (on the earls, see *CP*, under titles; Round, *GM*, pp. 267 ff. and *passim*; R. H. C. Davis in *EHR*, LXXIX (1964), 299–307).

bishop sharply back to the present. 'You, who are a prelate of Holy Church, commanded me to adhere to the daughter of your uncle King Henry, and to aid her to obtain her right, which is taken from her by force, and to keep what she now has.' There is much more in the letter; but here lies its central interest: the reply of the blunt layman to the sophisticated arguments of the bishop.

Brian refers to an earlier exchange between himself and the bishop, which is also lost; and it may be to this that Gilbert refers in the opening of his letter. But it seems likely that over a year passed between the time of writing of Brian's extant letter and Gilbert's, which must have been written in December 1143 or early 1144. It is indeed possible that Gilbert saw Brian's extant letter, and the splendid roll-call of the empress's supporters in 1141 may have inspired Gilbert's roll-call of the bishops who stood firm at Clarendon in 1164, the list with which he taunted Becket in *Multiplicem*. But Gilbert's 'librum' implies a manifesto more elaborate than the letter, and more directed to the issue of the succession. It seems likely that Brian's troubles, and his controversy with Henry of Blois, inspired him to further efforts, to lay out more at length the grounds for his adherence to the empress. This manifesto, Gilbert tells us, was intended to prove perhaps the most contentious point in Matilda's case, 'you assert that by law (*iure*) those things which belonged to King Henry (*ea que regis Henrici fuerunt*) are due to his only daughter begotten in lawful matrimony'. It is evident that Brian had asked Gilbert to comment on this proposition, and this, in a general way, Gilbert proceeds to do. The context is essential for an understanding of the letter; for at first sight it seems to dwell in a rarefied world of argument, and to deal only with a corner of a highly complex dispute. The reason is plain: Gilbert was asked for his view on the issue of inheritance alone, and in giving it would obviously not cover again the ground which Brian had already traversed. It would be exceedingly interesting to know the grounds Brian himself had brought forward.

The law governing the succession to the English throne in the early twelfth century is imperfectly known, largely no doubt because there were many issues undecided and much diversity of opinion. What happened was governed by three things: by precedent, by the assumptions of the leaders mainly concerned, and by the circumstances of the moment. A glance at the history of the crown in the eleventh and twelfth centuries might suggest that a strict hereditary principle was not generally held: according to the rule of primogeniture, the next heir to the throne never succeeded between 1042 and 1189. Yet Gilbert's letter reminds us that this view is not wholly true: that for a variety of reasons the hereditary principle was gaining ground in the twelfth century.[1] And it suggests to us what some of those reasons were.

It seems a fair generalisation to say that in most kingdoms of western Europe in the early and central Middle Ages a man became king by inheritance, by the designation of his predecessor (or of some other interested party) or by election, and most commonly by a combination of all three.[2]

As for the third element, 'election', this played little part in eleventh-century king-making in England. In all kingdoms there was a formal process of 'election', that is, of acknowledgement and acclamation; and the formal process might be preceded by lobbying, and might be accompanied, as in Germany in 1002 and 1024, by some discussion. It was even possible for Ælfric the homilist to talk as if the people freely elected their king. But the 'election' itself seems normally to have been the formal acceptance of a *fait accompli*; this was certainly the case in 1066, when Harold was elected, anointed and crowned on the day after Edward the Confessor's death[3]—clearly the event was pre-determined—and William I's 'election' took the form of submission to the conqueror.

In 1077, under revolutionary circumstances, the German

---

[1] Cf. R. H. C. Davis, 'What happened in Stephen's reign, 1135–54', *History*, XLIX (1964), 1–12.

[2] For a recent general discussion, see Brooke, *The Saxon and Norman Kings* (London, 1963), chap. II. For Germany, H. Mitteis, *Die deutsche Königswahl* (2nd edn, Brunn, 1944); G. Barraclough, *Mediaeval Germany* (Oxford, 1938), I, 51 ff., and below, pp. 110–11, nn.; for France, F. Lot and R. Fawtier, *Histoire des institutions françaises au moyen âge*, II (Paris, 1958), 12 ff.

[3] Or two days after, if Edward died on 4 January (see F. E. Harmer, *Anglo-Saxon Writs*, Manchester, 1952, p. 560).

princes met at Forcheim and elected Rudolf of Rheinfelden to replace the 'deposed' Henry IV. This election was an act of revolution, and several generations passed before the idea which was implicit in it, that when the throne was vacant the princes could freely choose a successor, came to be accepted. It revealed that the idea of 'election' almost in the modern sense of free choice by a specified body of electors was conceivable in the eleventh century, but the circumstances which surrounded it showed how slight a hold such an idea had on most men's minds.[1] The confusion of the English rules of succession, and the constant breach of any strict hereditary principle, might have been expected to enhance the idea of election in England in the late eleventh and twelfth centuries. But curiously enough, the reverse was true: as election grew stronger in Germany, inheritance triumphed in England, and although designation continued to play its part, at least till 1603, and although events like those of 1327 and 1399 prevented the English from forgetting that the king was in some sort 'elected', primogeniture was so firmly established that in 1216 a small boy was successfully planted on the English throne in circumstances as dangerous as those of 1066.

The explanation of this paradox is complex; but a part of it, perhaps a large part of it, lies in the circumstances that any usurper, or anyone who could be considered a usurper, will be inclined to emphasise such elements of legitimacy as can be found in his title, and will attempt to prevent others from following his own example. William Rufus could claim that he had been designated by his father, and this claim was accepted by Archbishop Lanfranc, who, as archbishop of Canterbury, evidently had first voice in the 'election' once the king was dead.[2] Henry I could

---

[1] The other novelty in 1077—the attempt to extract promises from the newly elected king—even though only partially successful, had more immediate influence on the process of king-making in Germany. There was, however, some precedent for this, just as the English coronation oath was well established long before coronation promises were extracted from Henry I and Stephen. On the significance of Forcheim, see P. Joachimsen in G. Barraclough, *Mediaeval Germany*, II, 123 ff.

[2] In the Bayeux Tapestry Archbishop Stigand is shown presenting Harold to the people: this was presumably the act of 'collaudatio' at the opening of the coronation ceremony, at which the officiating archbishop presented the

not claim to have his brother's voice, since his brother had died suddenly, without any opportunity to name a successor;[1] and the archbishop of Canterbury was too far away to give him his voice if he had wished to. Henry won the crown by rapid action, by bribes and threats, and also in a measure, no doubt, because some of the English magnates regarded him as more suitable than his eldest brother, Robert. But his position was precarious until he had Robert safely locked in a British prison in 1106, and almost the whole of his reign, down to 1134, his brother was still alive; it can never have been far from Henry's mind that Robert might become the centre of a rebellion. There is much in his reign—his constant and successful efforts to overawe would-be rebels and the lavish patronage which surrounded him with loyal barons, like Brian FitzCount himself, of his own making—which suggests a man conscious of the need to guard against just this danger. And it helps to explain the curious claim which Henry seems to have made that his title was better than Robert's. The chronicles point out that Henry was born when his parents were king and queen, and that he was born in England.[2] His English birth may have commended him to his English subjects; it is likely indeed that it

king to the people for acknowledgement and acclamation. Whether or not Stigand crowned Harold in fact, the Tapestry is evidence that the archbishop would normally be expected to present the new king (on the interpretation of this scene, see Brooke, *The Saxon and Norman Kings*, pp. 10, 42; Stenton, *Bayeux Tapestry*, pp. 17–18). In 1135 the attitude of the archbishop of Canterbury was crucial to Stephen's success (see Brooke, *op. cit.* pp. 47 ff. esp. 52–4). The archbishop's precedence may have arisen from the custom that he anointed the king, a custom which had become a treasured privilege by the twelfth century; or he may have anointed him from Dunstan's time on because he had already the function of designating him. In any case the leading ecclesiastic of the realm would be the natural person to perform these functions: cf. the role of the archbishop of Mainz, who was able in 1125 to overrule the dying king's designation and arrange the 'election' of another king (see U. Stutz, *Der Erzbischof von Mainz und die deutsche Königswahl* (Weimar, 1910)).

[1] Unless, that is, Geoffrey Gaimar's account of Rufus's death is to be preferred to the other early narratives (cf. Brooke, *The Saxon and Norman Kings*, p. 218).

[2] See E. A. Freeman, *History of the Norman Conquest* (Oxford, 1867–79), IV, Appendix EE, where the texts are quoted. On Henry I and his patronage, see now R. W. Southern, 'The Place of Henry I in English History', *Proc. British Academy*, XLVIII (1963), 127–69.

did. His parents' status was more relevant to his title to the throne. It amounted to a claim that he was *porphyrogenitus*, born in the purple, and so had a better title to the throne than his elder brothers: that Robert could not claim the throne against him. If Henry was an accomplice to Rufus's murder—as was no doubt suspected by some then as it is by some today—it was not the removal of an overlord to whom one had sworn fealty, but the punishment of a blasphemous usurper.[1]

It is very hard to know how seriously we should take these claims; Henry, after all, like his brother and father, was *de facto* king, and ruled by strength more than by legal right, however good that may have been. But there is nothing incompatible in this with Henry taking seriously his strange claim; and we may be sure that there were important men about him—Archbishop Anselm for one—to whom right and law mattered immensely. No doubt the Church was prepared to accept a king who seemed in the situation *idoneus*, and we may doubt whether Henry needed much evidence of righteousness to win Gerard of Hereford or Ranulf Flambard of Durham or even Maurice of London who anointed him. But there were better men than these in the English hierarchy. There are strong reasons for thinking that Henry took his own claim seriously, whether from a desire to convince himself or to convince others; very likely from both. And to the reasons already indicated may be added another.

Gilbert Foliot's argument turns mainly on Matilda's hereditary right, and no question is raised about her father's right. To a modern reader it seems surprising that so much energy should be concentrated on this one aspect of the case. It is true that this was evidently the issue on which Brian had consulted him; but it is also true that John of Salisbury's independent testimony confirms Gilbert's evidence that when the case was tried on the issue of justice,[2] at the Lateran Council of 1139, two points only were

---

[1] Cf. Brooke, *The Saxon and Norman Kings*, p. 195.

[2] So much one may say, even if circumstances prevented the pope from making a judgement purely on the issue *quid liceat* (to adopt the language of Innocent III's famous *Deliberatio* on the imperial schism): expediency compelled him to forego judgement, i.e. to confirm his earlier decision in Stephen's favour, but tacitly, so as to provide the minimum of offence to Stephen's

raised: Matilda's legitimacy and hereditary right, and the oath which the English magnates had made to her in 1127. As we shall see, other issues counted, but inheritance was crucial to her, and, we may be sure, to her father likewise. Henry I had at least twenty illegitimate children; he made his eldest son Robert earl of Gloucester, and endowed him well. To his legitimate nephew Stephen he was equally generous, and the indications are that Stephen was his favourite relative. There is little indication of any affection between Henry and his daughter Matilda, who was shipped off as a small child to be empress, and who would probably have ended her days in Germany had Henry had any other legitimate children surviving when the Emperor Henry V died in 1125. By then Henry I was losing hope of having children by his second queen, and it is clear that he never seriously considered, as did some of the magnates, making Robert of Gloucester his heir. Suitability was set aside; Matilda, against her wish, was brought back from Germany; and against bitter opposition both from herself and the English barons, married to the count of Anjou. She was treated as a pawn.

At first sight this concentration on the legitimate heiress seems strange behaviour from the son of William the Bastard and from a man who had himself stolen his eldest brother's throne. But it is intelligible in a man who believed himself to be the legitimate heir to the Conqueror; and Matilda's title was in a way even better than Henry's, since her mother was the sister of Edgar the Ætheling, and sprung from the line of Cerdic and Alfred. We shall miss the significance of Henry's actions in 1127 and later if we forget that he had still to justify his title against that of the prisoner in Cardiff Castle.

Duke Robert's confinement has another lesson to teach us. In a recent and penetrating discussion of the issues in 1135, Professor Barlow has observed that there was precedent elsewhere in Europe for the consort of an heiress inheriting a kingdom. 'The

enemies. A decision for Matilda in 1139 would not only have raised the pope some enemies, but would have fomented civil war in England: the desire to avoid doing this seems to have been uppermost in the minds of Innocent II, in his later years at least, and of his successors.

one impossibility was for a woman to succeed as sole ruler in her own right and *expect to remain in that position*.[1] The italics are ours, and they are essential if one is to accept the truth of the statement. For not many years before 1127, when Matilda was a child, a lady had succeeded to the kingdom of León-Castile, and Urraca (1109–26) had lived and died sole ruler of her father's great kingdom. The career of Urraca and her father, indeed, provide many analogies to the situation in which Henry I found himself, and the diplomatic relations between England and Spain in Henry's early life at least were so important as to make it certain that he did not live in ignorance of some of these events.[2] The year before Hastings Ferdinand I had died and left three sons to dispute his inheritance. Sudden death removed one—and Alfonso was suspected of complicity in it—and imprisonment for life removed another, so that Alfonso was left in possession of the whole empire from 1073 until his death in 1109. In 1109 it passed intact to his daughter, but it was no easy matter for her to hold her inheritance together, and for a time she was unhappily yoked to the king of Aragon. When Urraca died in 1126 Henry I might well reflect that a lady could inherit an empire in her own right; but that if she did so it was wise for her to have a husband strong and able enough to help her to hold her throne, and to keep other men at bay. He failed to notice that the case of Urraca was a strong warning against marrying the lady off against her will to a man not *persona grata* with her subjects at large.

Thus Matilda became involved in Henry's designs to secure the throne which he had won, and in the grandiose dynastic ambition which suggested to him a union of Normandy and Anjou. In 1127 he had designated her, and the magnates had accepted her; later, it seems, he repeated the designation.[3] The barons had sworn to obey her. Every route to the throne—inheritance, 'election', designation—seemed to be well guarded. Yet when Henry died in December 1135 his favourite nephew engaged in the one

[1] F. Barlow, *The Feudal Kingdom of England* (London, 1955), p. 201.
[2] Cf. Brooke, *The Saxon and Norman Kings*, pp. 190–2, 218.
[3] See Freeman, *op. cit.* v, 205 and note, for the evidence; but cf. Round, *GM*, p. 31 and n.

wholly successful adventure of his life and stole his cousin's throne, and Matilda and her husband waited three years before taking any serious action. It is hard to know whether Stephen's action or Matilda's inaction is the more puzzling. It is clear that, at the time, the story was put out that on his death-bed Henry had changed his mind, and designated Stephen. It is even possible that the story was true; it is perhaps likely that whether true or not, Stephen, who was not present at his uncle's death, believed it. And Matilda and Geoffrey, her husband, were temporarily estranged from Henry, and apparently felt bound to accept the *fait accompli*, only returning to their design to vindicate the English throne for Matilda when it became clear that Stephen was not going to be a successful king.

As in 1066 and 1100, circumstances and the political realities of the situation may have been immediately decisive; but the ideas of the actors on the rights and wrongs of the situation, however eccentric, also played their part. It seems clear that the empress, for all her hesitation in 1135, still believed in her own hereditary right, and had by no means forgotten the oath which had been sworn to her in 1127; nor did she or those about her, so far as we can tell, seriously consider the idea either that Geoffrey should rule in his wife's name or that Matilda should rule in the name of her son, the future Henry II, who was already two years old when Henry I died. It seems likely that Matilda and Geoffrey's marriage was not sufficiently stable for the first plan to work, and the empress does not seem to have taken to the second until her own ambitions had failed and her half-brother of Gloucester was dead.

The earl of Gloucester was a figure of great importance in the story of Matilda's claim as well as in the political events to which it gave rise between 1139 and his death in 1147. When Geoffrey of Anjou invaded Normandy in 1138, Robert, who was then living on his Norman estates, formally renounced his allegiance to Stephen. In a sense, he then proceeded to use his sister for his own ends; for it was clearly to his interest to keep England and Normandy, in both of which he held large estates, under a common overlord. But it seems highly probable that Robert seriously believed in his sister's case. It was he who brought her to England in 1139, and it was his death which seems to have decided her to abdicate her claim in favour of her son; and if Robert had not been faithful to his sister, he might well have claimed the English throne for himself. It is true that legitimate birth was generally reckoned a necessary qualification for inheritance in twelfth-century Europe. But among the Normans this must have been a recent doctrine, and Robert was the grandson of the king universally known as William the Bastard.[1] It was no doubt partly due to the arguments raised in the circles of Stephen and Matilda that legitimacy came to hold a place in the principles of English law even loftier than that which it held in canon law.

This lends a special interest to the opening of Gilbert's argument. In the Gospels he finds evidence that the idea of inheritance has the sanction of Our Lord; but an objector could point out that this evidence concerns the relationship of Our Lord and his Father, that is to say, of father and son: a royal sceptre belongs to a son, not to a daughter. 'Let us hear what the divine law answers to this. In the Book of Numbers, the last chapter, you will find a passage which we have often heard the earl of Gloucester bring to our attention: Zelophehad was a Jew of the tribe of Manasseh, who had daughters but no son.' And it was ordained that everything which the father possessed should go to the daughters. The earl of Gloucester, like Brian himself, was a literate layman, or at least had literary interests; his admirers referred to him as a 'philosopher', and he was one of the most notable literary patrons of his day. William of Malmesbury and Geoffrey of Monmouth dedicated books to him; Geoffrey Gaimar was beholden to him; Serlo of Wilton wrote for him a splendid epitaph.[2] We catch in Gilbert's letter a glimpse into a lost world: the argument as it was conducted by the leading characters themselves. The hint that lies behind this fascinating reference to Earl Robert is reminiscent of

---

[1] On William's surnames, see Freeman, *op. cit.* II, Appendix M.

[2] On Robert as a patron, see J. S. P. Tatlock, *The Legendary History of Britain* (Berkeley and Los Angeles, 1950), pp. 429, 436–7; Geoffrey Gaimar, ed. A. Bell (Oxford, 1960), p. 204 (lines 6441 ff.); A. C. Friend in *Bulletin Du Cange*, XXIV (1954), 90 ff. (on Serlo of Wilton); cf. Walter Map, *De nugis curialium*, v. 4. The reference to Robert in Gilbert's letter is in MS H, but was omitted in B, and so was omitted in Giles's edition of the letter.

the impression created by the surviving letter of Brian FitzCount: we seem to see a half-literate layman not accustomed to the tortuous sophistries (as no doubt he thought them) of the schools; but holding firm to a small stock of unanswerable arguments. Brian's surviving letter turns entirely on one point, and a very telling one: he is doing what the bishop himself had instructed him to do. Earl Robert's favourite quotation, in the circumstances of the day, also carried weight. One would like to know, indeed, what he made of the sequel in the book of Numbers: the daughters of Zelophehad were instructed not to marry outside their tribe, and did in fact marry their first cousins. It is unlikely that he repeated this part of the story in his sister's presence, and one cannot be sure that he knew of it. He may have reflected in earlier days that even if one accepted Matilda's own claim, one did not have to approve her marriage into the tribe of the Angevins. Be that as it may, it is interesting to observe that Robert, the philosopher, for some reason seems to have preferred to use his sister as the figurehead rather than her son. But it is probable that his reason for this, at the theoretical level, was the oath which he—and Stephen —had sworn to the empress. It is possible, however, that Henry II was not so fond of his uncle's argument. The reference to the earl is not in the Bodleian manuscript of Foliot's letters, and this seems more likely to be due to revision than to a scribal slip. It may just be that Gilbert excised a reference whose significance would be lost on a younger generation; but it may also be that he removed a reminder which Henry II would have disliked. The study of letter-collections provides a host of minor problems of this kind; but as with so many, this leads rapidly into the world of speculation.

Gilbert passes from divine to natural law, by which he means the law of the order of nature, which, according to the tag of the Roman lawyers, gives his case a useful 'prop and stay'.[1] It establishes, in fact, that natural affection, in the animal as in the human kingdom, makes a daughter closer to a man than a nephew—an argument with which one may well doubt whether

---

[1] 'firmamentum et robur'; the phrase can be traced ultimately to Cicero, *Mur.*, xxviii, 58 ('fundamentum ac robur'); a recent use of it was in Lanfranc's letter to the pope on the primacy issue (*ep.* 5; cf. Southern in *EHR*, LXXIII (1958), 196).

Henry I would himself have agreed. Human law, he says, consists of 'ius ciuile', the law of individual states, and 'ius gentium', the common law of the nations. Both, Gilbert alleges, deny a man the right to disinherit either son or daughter except for certain specific reasons. Gilbert cites rebellion as a possible excuse for disinheritance, and this seems very odd when one considers that Matilda was effectively involved in her husband's war with Henry at the time of his death; and that this was the ground on which it could plausibly be argued that Henry I had changed his mind on his death-bed, and designated Stephen. Gilbert presumably believed that Matilda was not involved in open rebellion, and a little casuistry could no doubt have justified this view. Certainly he was on safer ground in listing the evidences of Matilda's faithful acquiescence in Henry's schemes in earlier years. Although 'ius civile' and 'ius gentium' were terms used in Roman law, Gilbert is certainly appealing to the law of his own day—to the law of England and of France in particular.[1] It is disappointing that he does not enter the question of English and Norman law more thoroughly; no doubt Brian was sufficiently informed about the custom of the kingdom of which he was a magnate. But what Gilbert implies is of great interest. He implies that the same rules of inheritance governed the descent of the kingdom as of any other inheritance. This may have been his conviction, and was no doubt a part of any man's thinking on the matter in the feudal world. But it may also have been a convenient way of excluding arguments against his case. The English law of succession to the kingdom was a nice tangle, and there was probably little in what was then known of earlier history to help Matilda's cause.[2] But an appeal to feudal law immediately simplified the issue; for in the feudal law of England and northern

[1] In both countries there was a powerful restraint on alienation in the twelfth century, which subsequently (and swiftly in England) broke down (see Pollock and Maitland, *History of English Law* (2nd edn, Cambridge, 1898), II, 254 ff., 308 ff.; and on French Law, II, 313). Roman Law gave the *paterfamilias* a clear right of *Exheredatio*.

[2] Pollock and Maitland, *op. cit.* II, 261, n. 2, cite the Mercian princess Quœnthryth as evidence that a king's daughter could be in some sense his heiress; but she did not succeed to the crown (she was in fact an abbess: on her see Levison, *England and the Continent*, pp. 251 f.).

France, a lady could inherit if she had no legitimate brothers. And did not the coronation charter of Henry I himself show that a lady could be heiress and could inherit?[1]

Thus law human, natural and divine, conspired, in Gilbert's view, to support the case for which Brian had fought and suffered grievous loss. One major difficulty remained; and after an aside in which he commends Brian for having turned back from the evil path of following Stephen (the turning back which reminded Henry of Winchester of Lot's wife), he deals with it. It is in some ways the most extraordinary part of the argument, but in this instance what is surprising is not that Gilbert should have controverted it, but that it should have been used by the supporters of the chivalrous Stephen. Twenty years later Richard of Anstey, the 'immortal plaintiff', won his inheritance by the unhappy expedient of proving his cousin Mabel illegitimate. Stephen, in the person of his advocates at Rome in 1139, argued likewise about his cousin the empress.

A few years before, Gilbert reminds Brian, Pope Innocent II had presided over the Roman council, and Gilbert himself was present with his master the abbot of Cluny—'I, the least of the Cluniacs'. There the case was argued; and the bishop of Angers, Matilda's advocate, raised two main points: her hereditary right and the oath which had been sworn to her. According to John of Salisbury,[2] Arnulf, later bishop of Lisieux, replied first that the empress was illegitimate, and secondly that the oath was conditional on Henry not changing his mind—and that he had changed his mind and designated Stephen on his death-bed, and so Stephen was formally accepted by the archbishop of Canterbury, who was also papal legate, with the will and consent of the bishops and other magnates. To this, according to John, the bishop of Angers made answer, defending the legitimacy of the empress and belabouring Arnulf. Gilbert, however, specifically says that no answer was made to the charge of illegitimacy, and proceeds to answer the point himself. Gilbert gives us to understand that the speech of Stephen's advocate ended in uproar; and he would

[1] Cited Pollock and Maitland, *History of English Law*, II, 262 n.
[2] C, pp. 83 ff. (and cf. p. xliii), P, pp. 85 ff.

hardly have said this if Matilda's case had in fact been defended further. It is likely enough that the pope was glad of an excuse to end a hearing which could only embarrass him; for whatever he may have thought of the merits of the case, he could not pronounce for Matilda without fomenting civil war in England—nor make any final pronouncement without embroiling himself with one potentate or another who had helped him to secure the papal throne during the recent schism. As the most recent editor of the *Historia Pontificalis*, Mrs Chibnall, has observed, John is probably mistaken in putting a reply into the bishop of Angers' mouth. Speeches in chronicles such as his were not expected to be verbatim reports, but were the opportunity for appropriate comment. It may at first sight seem strange that John should have embarked on a discussion of the case when Henry II was on the throne, since Henry owed his throne to a mixture of inheritance from Henry I and the empress and designation by Stephen. But John has laid the case out in such a way that he was able to indulge his spleen against Arnulf, his special enemy,[1] and also to answer his arguments.

If we place the two narratives side by side, it may clearly be seen that the main argument raised by Stephen's advocate was that the empress was illegitimate. Whether he really said that the oath ceased to count if she was not legitimate, as Gilbert alleges, or that Henry changed his mind and designated Stephen, we cannot tell: Gilbert had good reason not to dwell on any other arguments Stephen's advocate might have raised, and John was simply retailing the common form of Stephen's case. But both agreed that the question of legitimacy was crucial; and Gilbert reinforces this by saying that he himself had often canvassed the views of 'maiores natu, personas religiosas et sanctas'—evidently the question was under frequent discussion. To a modern reader, it seems as absurd, and distasteful, that Stephen's defenders should have raised this particular argument as it does that Richard III

---

[1] Arnulf was apparently responsible for some disaster which overtook John in 1156, and John may well have intended in this passage, as in his account of the Second Crusade, to blacken his enemy's name: for John's view of Arnulf, see *JS Epp.* i, nos. 18, 30; cf. G. Constable in *EHR*, LXIX (1954), 67–76.

dispossessed his nephew of his crown on a similar plea. But it is evident that in both cases there were men prepared to take the argument seriously. Gilbert, reasonably enough, treats it with scorn. But it is interesting to observe that his case for her legitimacy depended solely on the good name of St Anselm. No one questioned that Matilda was the daughter of Henry I and of his first queen, Edith or Matilda. But it was alleged, as it had been alleged in 1100 when they were married, that Matilda was a professed nun and so not free to marry, and that the marriage was therefore invalid. It is not clear that this argument had full force: that is to say, it may be that the marriage, as canon law then was, could in any case have been considered valid.[1] It is certain that Anselm was reluctant to allow anyone who had taken the veil to marry, but he was convinced (against his better judgement) that Matilda had not taken vows and was free to marry. Matilda had been sent as a child to be brought up under the wing of her aunt Christina at Wilton and Romsey abbeys.[2] Many people thought, so Eadmer tells us, that she had either been offered as a nun by her parents or had taken vows, but her own statement that this was not so, confirmed by the abbess of Romsey, convinced Anselm himself and the others who heard the case. It had evidently been the practice of eminent English ladies to assume the veil in convents to avoid the unwanted attentions of Norman suitors; and a picturesque story is told of how William Rufus came to Romsey to see Matilda, and of how Matilda wore the veil to put him off,

---

[1] Before 1123 it seems normally to have been held that the marriage of a monk was illegal but valid; the marriage of a widow who had taken the veil had been declared null by Pope Nicholas I, and it may have been held that a nun was in a different case from a monk. But Gratian, *Decretum*, D. 27, suggests that there was little clarity on the law on this issue: Gratian cites Nicholas, and also St Jerome's thunders against dedicated women who married; but he also cites Augustine against the annulment of a marriage between folk who have taken vows. On the later development of the law, see J. Dauvillier, *Le mariage dans le droit classique de l'Eglise* (Paris, 1933), pp. 170 ff. None of this was considered in 1100: for Anselm's perplexities see R. W. Southern, *St Anselm and His Biographer*, pp. 188 ff., who has shown that Anselm allowed Matilda's marriage with reluctance. But allow her he did, so he must have been convinced that it was at least defensible.

[2] Mrs H. Clover, *The Correspondence of Archbishop Lanfranc* (Cambridge Ph.D. thesis, 1961), pp. 115 ff.

and the abbess took the king to admire her roses. Matilda herself was alleged by Eadmer to have said that she had worn the veil at her aunt's behest, but torn it off and trampled on it when her aunt's back was turned.[1] We have no means of going behind Anselm's investigation; we can only say that Gilbert's dismissal of the charge seems not unreasonable.

Two intriguing hints, Earl Robert's favourite passage in the Book of Numbers, and Gilbert's canvassing holy and religious men of an earlier generation on Henry I's marriage, give us a glimpse of the Angevin party struggling to justify their cause. In a final assessment of Gilbert's letter, one would like to know how he came to be an Angevin, and how strong were his feelings and convictions of the rightness of the empress's cause. In the spring of 1139, at Milo of Gloucester's behest, Stephen appointed Gilbert to Gloucester; in the autumn the Empress Matilda landed in England, and soon after Gilbert's cousin and patron had been bought or enticed into the Angevin camp.[2] In the years which followed Milo added still further to his rank and to his lands by service to the empress, and even extracted the honour of Abergavenny out of Brian FitzCount for the help he gave him in the defence of the distant outpost at Wallingford. In Milo's wake the abbot of Gloucester declared for the empress. In a formal way he could hardly do otherwise; in the early 1140's the earls of Hereford and Gloucester were in a position to put the strongest pressure on him. But Gilbert's letter to Brian argues something deeper; it suggests a real conviction in the empress's cause. Once again, this is intelligible; for Gilbert had been brought up under the wing of the king of Scotland and his son; King David was the brother of the elder Matilda, and uncle of the empress; he was her most faithful supporter, and his subordinates in England, who included Gilbert's father and presumably his brothers, suffered for his loyalty to the empress.[3]

---

[1] E. A. Freeman, *The Reign of William Rufus* (Oxford, 1882), II, Appendix EE; Eadmer, *Hist. Novorum*, ed. M. Rule (RS), p. 122.

[2] Cf. R. H. C. Davis in *Misc. D. M. Stenton*, pp. 143-4.

[3] It has also been suggested that the sympathies of Cluny were for the Angevins, but this view rests on slender foundations (on this see Constable, *loc. cit.*, above, p. 105, n. 1).

In spite of Gilbert's loyalty to the Angevins, he remained in close touch with Archbishop Theobald, who was formally loyal to Stephen except during the short period of Stephen's imprisonment in 1141; and in 1148 Gilbert swore fealty to Stephen for the bishopric of Hereford, thereby incurring the wrath of the young Henry, the future Henry II. But it is clear that Theobald's allegiance to Stephen, though firm, was not unqualified.[1] Having learned from the mistakes of Henry of Blois, who had tried to settle the anarchy by involving himself in it, Theobald tried to lift the Church above the anarchy; and it was this attempt which led him to establish close relations with Gilbert. Gilbert could hardly refuse to collaborate with Theobald; there is indeed no reason to suppose that he wished to. Until 1148 this was not incompatible with his Angevin loyalties. In 1143-4, writing to Brian FitzCount, his zeal for the cause seems genuine enough. Innocent II had not helped them; but the new pope, Celestine II, was thought to favour the empress. Gilbert ends on a note of hope, and it is clear that the problem has filled him with real excitement. 'Farewell—and pray for me for at least two days, because for two days I have interrupted my prayers somewhat[2] to dictate this letter to you.' Within a few months Celestine was dead, and the hope was not fulfilled. The empress's hopes receded further; Theobald's growing influence worked in favour of the *status quo*. In 1147 the earl of Gloucester died. Early in 1148 the empress retired to Normandy. The cause seemed lost. Gilbert's relations with Theobald may have given him some embarrassment in earlier years. Now they gave him a chance to redeem a dangerous situation. As a conscientious churchman Gilbert might well feel that he should now follow in the archbishop's footsteps and submit to Stephen. As a landholder with much to lose he might well feel that he must make his peace with the king.

[1] See above, pp. 89–92, and for the events of 1141, when Theobald went over to the empress with Stephen's leave, Saltman, p. 16.

[2] 'somewhat'—'aliquantulum'—is omitted in MS B; as with the reference to Earl Robert, this may well be the result of later revision.

CHAPTER VIII

THE GLOUCESTER
FORGERIES

The later letters of Gilbert Foliot provide copious evidence that
he never forgot his affection for and interest in the community of
St Peter, Gloucester. This is revealed, perhaps, most strikingly in
the letters he exchanged with Roger of Pont l'Évêque, archbishop
of York (1154–81) in the mid-fifties on the long-standing dispute
between York and Gloucester. In the mid-eleventh century
Gloucester abbey had been in the hands of one of the Confessor's
ecclesiastical paladins, Ealdred, archbishop of York (d. 1069); and
the story was that he had alienated to York three of Gloucester's
manors.[1] This caused a running argument between Gloucester
and the archbishops of York, which was finally settled in a great
plea in 1157. The manors were restored to Gloucester in return
for a substantial concession of land. Shortly before the final settlement, Gilbert and Roger had been present at one of the many trials
of the case, and Gilbert had evidently become more than a little
heated in the argument. His letter 128 is an apology and defence
of his show of temper; 129 is Roger's reply, 130 Gilbert's winding
up of the exchange of letters. Peace was restored between the
prelates. But the first two letters help us to understand why
Gilbert was vexed. York had brought a charge 'de literis corruptis'
against Gloucester; and any ambiguity in the interpretation of
these words is cleared up by Roger's reference to 'accusatio falsi':
York had clearly charged Gloucester with forgery. This plea, says
Gilbert, was an invitation to say many hard things, for an advocate
to wax eloquent; but this we resisted. 'Although both [Glouces-
ter's] right and the disseisin were attributed to the letter(s), we did
not "set our mouth to heaven", and presume in the slightest
degree to raise a charge of *precum falsitas*, the falsehood of the

---

[1] On the dispute between Gloucester and York, see no. 128 and notes; *CS*,
pp. 271–2 and n. 3.

plea.' Then he quietly observes that he who brings a false charge
loses all he asks for, according to the law.[1] Such frivolities, says
Gilbert, we spared you, even if we did speak somewhat bom-
bastically, and make rather a fool of ourselves, out of love for the
brothers. The archbishop of York, though as determined as
Gilbert to make peace with a friend, did not allow him to get
away with this. If only he had raised the charge of a false plea!—
York could easily have proved the violence of the disseisin.
Whether York pressed its charge of forgery, we do not know.
But it is certain that the charge was justified, and probable that
Gilbert knew it to be justified. He had reason for his warmth.

In comparison with many other religious houses in England
and on the continent the number of forged documents which
Gloucester abbey held in its muniment room was modest. It is
doubtful if they mustered more than half a dozen. But it has
recently been argued that the most substantial of these were forged
at the end of Gilbert's time at Gloucester, and that a writ of the
Conqueror very skilfully forged by one of the leading experts of
the day was added shortly after. All these documents, especially
the last, had some bearing on the case against York. This is a
serious accusation, which cannot be laughed off as *frivola*, as he
would have liked. In any other period of the Middle Ages, it
would be very serious indeed. But in condoning forgery in the
mid-twelfth century Gilbert, one is bound to admit, was in good
company.[2]

Among the Cotton charters in the British Museum is a copy of
a charter of King Stephen for Gloucester abbey, dated 1138,

---

[1] 'Nam cum de literis corruptis ageretur, poterant in hoc articulo multa
durius obici, et per rethoricam auxesim, ut satis ipsi nostis, amplificari. Cumque
eisdem literis et ius et spoliatio innueretur, non in celum os nostrum posuimus
(cf. Ps. lxxii. 9) ut precum falsitatem uel in modico arguere presumeremus.
Cum iuris habeat formula, ut etsi sacrum oraculum huiusmodi precator
attulerit, careat penitus impetratis. Hec friuola sunt et his similia, in quibus
uobis pepercimus....' On the *iuris...formula*, cf. *Code*, 1. 23. 7.

[2] *CS*, pp. 270–83, on which what follows is based. The Cotton charter is
Cotton Ch. xvii, 3 (printed, from the Gloucester cartulary in the Public Record
Office, in *Cart. Gloucester*, 1, 222–5). T. A. M. Bishop (*Trans. Cambridge Bibliog.
Soc.* I, 439 (1953)) notes that it is in the same hand as Camb. Univ. Lib. MS
Kk. 3. 28, which was written at Gloucester.

accompanied by a covering letter from the bishop of Worcester written some years later, in which he asks the archbishop of Canterbury to provide the abbey with a confirmation of Stephen's charter. This is puzzling for two reasons. First, the royal charter is evidently a forgery. In form it does not resemble genuine charters issued by the royal chancery in that period, and it confirms certain grants to Gloucester abbey which were made several years after 1138, the date at which it pretends to have been made. The second difficulty is to understand why the abbot of Gloucester, whose name is given as Gilbert, and who was therefore certainly Gilbert Foliot, needed an intermediary in approaching the archbishop, since they were on terms of close friendship. In form Stephen's charter resembles some documents purporting to be confirmations by William I and William II to the monks of Gloucester, and there are reasons for supposing that these were in fact forged at the same time, or soon after, the charter attributed to Stephen, and by the same hand.[1] At some time in the mid-twelfth century the monks acquired the much more accomplished writ of the Conqueror, the 'original' of which still survives, now among the muniments of Hereford cathedral. There was a lingering doubt whether it might not be authentic until Mr Bishop and Dr Chaplais published their *Facsimiles of English Royal Writs to 1100*, in which they established that its handwriting, and the version of the Conqueror's seal attached to it, showed it to be the work of one of the Westminster forgers of the mid-twelfth century. One may interpret this writ as a later addition, for the last stages of the battle with York, to the home-made royal confirmations of which Stephen's is an example.

The fabrication of Stephen's charter and the confirmation by Theobald can be dated within the period 1146–8; and there can be little doubt that it is to be associated with the circumstances of 1147–8, with the death of Earl Robert of Gloucester and the departure of the empress. Gloucester had gathered new proper-

---

[1] No originals survive of these documents—indeed, one may doubt whether sealed 'originals' ever existed. On the original of the writ of William I forged by a member of the Westminster school, see T. A. M. Bishop and P. Chaplais, *Facsimiles of English Royal Writs to A.D. 1100* (Oxford, 1957), p. xxi, no. xi, and p. xxii, n. 1.

ties, and made various adjustments in its holdings, during the period of Angevin ascendancy in the west, without reference to the king. Some of these acquisitions were made possible by the circumstances of the anarchy; and although there is no proof that Gilbert had been a war profiteer, he had good reason to be anxious about the effects of the Angevin collapse and the revival of Stephen's power which was assumed to be imminent. How was the abbey to defend these acquisitions?

Stephen's charter was dated 1138, the last year when Gloucester could have extracted a confirmation from Stephen before the city and the abbey became involved in rebellion against him. Stephen himself would hardly have accepted the document or confirmed it without question. But in his later years a practice arose of turning to Archbishop Theobald for confirmations which would normally have come from the king—for general confirmations, that is, of temporal as well as of spiritual acquisitions. It is clear that this practice was due to Theobald's growing prestige as a man who had succeeded in holding the church together in a divided land: his position was more stable than the king's. The practice was just beginning in 1148, and Gilbert's charter is one of the earliest. The spurious charter of Stephen refers at one point to his 'brother-bishops', and was clearly drafted solely for the purpose of being confirmed by Theobald. Who devised the plot one cannot tell. There is no special reason to attribute either the scheme or the documents to Gilbert himself; but equally there is no reason to suppose him ignorant of what was done. The plot depended on the confidence which bishop and archbishop felt in the abbot of Gloucester, a confidence which cannot have been wholly justified. It is very hard to acquit Gilbert of acquiescing, at the very least, in this little conspiracy. By what procedure he squared it with his conscience we do not know. But it is worth relating this episode to its wider context, for it throws much light on contemporary attitudes to official documents, as well as on Gilbert himself.

Sensational forgeries were produced at many different periods of the Middle Ages. Perhaps no single later forgery can compare in scale or daring with the Forged Decretals, which were manufactured in France in the ninth century. But whatever claims can be made for that century, few would dispute that the eleventh and early twelfth were the golden age of medieval forgery. A significant proportion of the charters attributed to centuries down to the twelfth are forgeries: sufficient to make it necessary for a historian handling such documents always to consider their authenticity. In this respect the eleventh and twelfth centuries form a turning-point. From about 1160 onwards, not only were the chanceries of Europe growing wise to the danger and the problem, but for a variety of reasons the motives for forgery were in decline. In the eleventh and twelfth centuries social pressures were such that respectable men and respectable communities forged as they had not forged before and would never forge again. Forgery in this period was very widespread. One can find extreme examples as far apart as Monte Cassino, where in the early twelfth century Peter the Deacon was devising some extraordinary immemorial traditions, and Llandaff in South Wales, where in the same period the associates of Bishop Urban were, as has been said, forging a diocese.[1] In Britain, the *Book of Llandaff*, consisting of saints' lives and charters, represents a summit of achievement in the production of bogus documents. Equally, if not more remarkable, was the diffusion of forgery. In England it was commonest among the old-established Benedictine monasteries, among those which had been founded or refounded in the tenth-century reformation, and were well established before 1066. These numbered over forty in all; but only of about twenty-five can we say with any confidence that we possess sufficient of their pre-Conquest muniments, supposed or real, to have a secure check of their record as forgers. To these we may add the secular cathedrals, such as London and Wells, who have left us substantial records of their early muniments. From the records of these thirty odd communities come the enormous majority of surviving pre-Conquest charters. From these too come the enormous

---

[1] See H. Bloch in *Traditio*, VIII (1952), 159–264, esp. pp. 182 ff.; C. Brooke in *SEBC*, pp. 218 ff. Since this chapter was written, a general discussion of medieval forgery by H. Fuhrmann and others has appeared in *Hist. Zeit.* CXCVII (1963), 529–601.

majority of pre- and post-Conquest forgeries. Of the thirty one can say, in the present state of knowledge, that about seventeen committed or tolerated forgery on a fair scale—at least on as large a scale as Gloucester. Other forgeries may come to light, and other houses doubtless had individual spurious documents among their muniments; but if one is to consider forgery as a social phenomenon, rather than as an isolated misdemeanour, it is with substantial forgery that one must be concerned. To these seventeen we should add five or six more which, though founded after the Norman Conquest, none the less also thought it necessary to doctor their muniments. These included the great Benedictine houses of Battle, Colchester and Durham, which were founded so soon after the Norman Conquest that they became involved in many of the same problems and difficulties that their elder brothers experienced; Lewes priory, which devised a set of forgeries in the early thirteenth century to deal with a particular difficulty; the small convent of nuns at Wix in Essex, whose muniments were largely revised (it seems) by two professional forgers in the 1190's; and Llandaff, which had a story all its own.[1]

Needless to say, the figures given here are rough, and it would be entirely misleading to give statistics of the numbers of forged documents. A large number are still in dispute, and there is general agreement among scholars that most spurious documents are not wholly spurious. Many of the great series of forgeries contain some charters which had no basis in fact, in which everything granted is an anachronism, if not pure fantasy. But there is some basis for a large majority of inauthentic charters; and a puzzlingly large number of forgeries describe perfectly genuine transactions: all that has happened is that the original grant has had a face-lift or (in some cases) has been heavily disguised.

Many of the forgeries cannot be closely dated. But the bulk of

[1] See Appendix III. Forgery was doubtless not the prerogative of religious communities, although its frequency among respectable men in this age is partly explained by the force of group loyalties among such communities at this time. We know, however, far more about the muniments of religious houses than about those of lay families, owing to the chances of survival: if we had more lay documents, the balance of this discussion might be substantially altered.

these documents were concocted in the period 1000–1160, and a majority probably between 1066 and 1154. If it is true that there was safety in numbers, then forgery was comparatively safe in the eleventh and twelfth centuries. If one took account of the whole of Europe, one could go further, and say that it was common; even that it was normal for an established community sooner or later to revise and improve its muniments; that forgery was one of the elements in the common European culture of the twelfth-century renaissance. Some historians have said that it was hardly a crime. This cannot be accepted without qualification. A society which tolerated castration as a punishment for forging coins was not likely to treat forgery of any kind in a light-hearted way; and Pope Urban III in the late twelfth century had specifically to insist that un-frocking, degradation, branding and exile were more suitable punishments for clerks convicted of forgery than physical mutilation.[1] But it is clear that many forgers, when convicted, had nothing worse to fear than degradation; and it is also clear that many forgers were never convicted. The letters of Archbishop Theobald in John of Salisbury's early collection refer to several cases of forgery detected or suspected. Thus Eugenius III had removed Jordan, archdeacon of Brecon, from his office, but he was presently restored; and in spite of Theobald's protests he is known to have kept his archdeaconry until finally removed, and replaced, by Gerald of Wales in 1175. In this case, Theobald's plea for the restoration of Jordan's rival, Nicholas, was supported by Gilbert Foliot (no. 112); but although Gilbert had probably seen Theobald's letter, he made no reference to Jordan's crimes. Another of Theobald's letters, addressed to Gilbert's uncle, Robert de Chesney, is entirely concerned with the wickedness of forging papal bulls.

... The falsification of that seal is a peril to the universal Church, since by the marks of a single impress the mouths of all the pontiffs may be

---

[1] *Extra*, v, 20, 3: the culprit had forged the seal of Philip Augustus. In a decretal of 1174 copied in MS B, fo. 127 r–v (see below, p. 239 and n.), Alexander III instructed the bishop of Norwich to place a priest convicted of forgery in a monastery of strict observance, and imprison other offenders while awaiting further instructions.

opened or closed, and all forms of guilt may pass unpunished, and innocence be condemned. Those therefore who attempt such a crime must be punished as public enemies and as men who, so far as in them lies, would sink the whole Church in the deep. One such man is lurking in your diocese, to wit A. of Grimoldby, who having crowned with perjury the crime of forging papal letters, has now deserved to be fettered and bound by the sentence of excommunication. Wherefore we urge you to publish his sentence to all the world, and, if he can be caught, to cause him to be brought before us as a manifest forger and perjurer.

Another letter, concerning a notorious scion of the chapter of Llandaff, contains what might be a statement of the theme of Theobald's pontificate, 'with much zeal and effort we have often re-established peace between him and his adversaries, but every time peace has come back from the encounter torn and sadly changed', and concludes with this cri-de-cœur: 'we beg you [the pope] to give us a ruling on the punishment to be inflicted on those who forge your letters; it is difficult for us to wait for your advice on individual cases of this kind every time they arise.'[1]

In spite of this, it is clear that many forgers were never convicted. There were pressures which made forgery seem an urgent social necessity, and it had grown imperceptibly, as we shall see, in a world in which the status of and attitude to documents, were rapidly changing; and so forgery was widely condoned. The monks of St Augustine's, Canterbury, had their muniments embellished by a French monk called Guerno shortly after the Norman conquest. They brought Guerno's fabrications into court on numerous occasions: sometimes they passed muster, sometimes they were treated as forgeries. But we should never have heard of Guerno had he not confessed on his death-bed.[2] The master forgers were protected by the communities whom they

---

[1] *JS Epp.* I, nos. 86 (cf. note), 67, 57; cf. no. 73.

[2] The report of his confession is printed from a copy at Canterbury in *Literae Cantuarienses*, III (RS, 1889), pp. 365–7; on this document, and on Guerno's career and activities, see W. Levison, *England and the Continent in the Eighth Century* (Oxford, 1946), pp. 206 ff. To the documents attributed by Levison to Guerno, at least one for Christ Church, Canterbury, can probably be added (cf. Southern, *EHR*, LXXIII (1958), 194 n.).

served, and usually escaped punishment. It was the small men who paid the full penalty.

Charters were valuable documents. They provided title to land and to other property—churches, tithes, tolls, fisheries and so forth; and title to privileges, above all, for the privileged few among the great Benedictine houses, privileges of exemption from control by their diocesan bishops. Almost every monastic house in England which claimed exemption from the bishop forged to support its case; and the monks of Canterbury forged on the grand scale to support their claim to Canterbury's primacy over York. The reasons for this are not far to seek. Primacy, exemption and land-title all had a history going far back behind 1066; but the conditions under which they were exercised in the late eleventh and twelfth centuries differed widely from what had gone before. Neither supporters nor opponents of these privileges had sufficient historical understanding to realise why the historical records of earlier times were so deficient. The monks of Canterbury could produce no really valid testimony on the primacy, because the idea was entirely new in eleventh-century England; but to a masterful cosmopolitan scholar like Archbishop Lanfranc this was inconceivable—he came from a Europe buzzing with primacy disputes, and he assumed that England must have one too; and it was invented. But later on the York party counter-attacked, and showed how baseless, in terms of historical documents, was the Canterbury case; and so the monks of Canterbury, about 1121, forged a series of papal privileges to support their case.[1] The notion of exemption was indeed ancient, but it had a long and complicated history; and unfortunately for the English abbeys it had not been in favour with the bishops who refounded the English monasteries in the tenth century. But to the Norman monks who settled in the English abbeys after the Conquest it seemed inconceivable that the absence of written record represented the true facts of the situation; many an abbey had had a recent fire or its muniments had been neglected. It was obvious that the vital evidence had been lost; and in some cases very

[1] On these the literature is copious: see especially R. W. Southern, 'The Canterbury Forgeries', *EHR*, LXXIII, 193 ff.

ancient documents could be found which lent colour to the claim for exemption.[1] As so often, a specious antiquarianism was used to support a set of dubious claims—so specious, that many of the supporters were hardly conscious, no doubt, of what they were doing.

Yet perhaps the claims were not so very dubious; perhaps there was a sound case for exemption in some instances; and no one doubts that, as to land title, the bulk of the forging was in the interests of perfectly genuine rights. In earlier centuries much land had changed hands without any written instrument. It was only in the twelfth century that it became customary for all conveyances of land to be recorded in writing; and as late as the 1270's Edward I found numerous valuable rights based on oral witness which even he could not gainsay. All over Europe the eleventh and twelfth centuries witnessed the switch from oral to written testimony as the normal basis for a community's rights and privileges; and this transfer inevitably produced many difficult situations, threw many temptations in the forger's way.

A written instrument had not, before this, been held in such high esteem. A charter was often simply a narrative of a transaction, and it was regarded as authentic whether it was written on the same day as the transaction was agreed, or a week or a year or a decade later. What difference was there, one might ask, between the foundation charter of Quarr abbey, written down ten years or so after the event it records, and the foundation charter of Battle abbey, written down perhaps seventy or eighty years later than the event?[2] We do well to remember that the

---

[1] For the history of exemption in Normandy and England, see J. F. Lemarignier, *Étude sur les privilèges d'exemption et de juridiction ecclésiastique des abbayes normandes depuis les origines jusqu'en 1140* (Paris, 1937); D. Knowles, *Downside Review*, L (1932), 201–31, 396–436 (on the St Augustine's exemption dispute, see Levison, Appendix 1; E. John, *Bulletin of the John Rylands Library*, XXXIX (1956–7), 390–415).

[2] See V. H. Galbraith, 'Monastic Foundation charters', *CHJ*, IV, 205–22, 296–8 (1934) (with facsimile of the foundation charter of Quarr). The 'foundation charter' of Battle is B.M. Harl. charter 83. A. 12 (H. W. C. Davis, *Regesta Regum Anglo-Normannorum*, I (Oxford, 1913), no. 62). Other Battle documents were forged by one of the Westminster school (see Bishop and Chaplais, *Facsimiles of English Royal Writs*, pp. xxi–xxii and n.), and the Harl. charter, though not identical in handwriting, probably belongs to the same period.

written word had not acquired the sanctity which it has received since the invention of printing. Scribes copying charters embellished, abbreviated, expanded at times without anyone thinking much of it.

From this point of view, forgery is a phenomenon especially characteristic of the age in which the charter became a common legal instrument. Even in Henry II's day a high proportion of royal writs and charters were not written by his own chancery scribes.[1] Many of these must have been the work of the beneficiaries, who would always, however, have to take their charters to the royal chancery to have the great seal duly attached to them. The pre-Conquest diplomas were authenticated, in theory, by the crosses of the signatories. But none has survived with 'autograph' crosses upon it, and it is certain that copies made by a single scribe were regarded as fully authentic documents; there must be grave doubts whether originals ever existed in a great number of cases. It has been shown that in Athelstan's time diplomas for different beneficiaries were written in the same hands, and it is usually assumed that they were the work of royal scribes. But Dr Chaplais has recently suggested that they may have been written in religious houses near where the king was staying at the time of issue;[2] and there is no evidence of anything like a 'chancery' in the late tenth or early eleventh centuries. There is a pretty story in the *Liber Eliensis* that, between *c.* 970 and the Norman Conquest, the abbots of Ely, Glastonbury and St Augustine's, Canterbury acted in turn as 'chancellors'.[3] This may well reflect a situation in which monastic communities were in the habit of lending a hand in the composition of diplomas and the preservation of royal archives. It is much less likely that they had custody of the great seal. But the seal was only used to authenticate royal writs; and important as writs were becoming in late Saxon times, the diploma form was still used for documents of major consequence to religious houses. To men tenacious of

---

[1] T. A. M. Bishop, *Scriptores Regis* (Oxford, 1961), *passim*, esp. pp. 9–11.
[2] For what follows see P. Chaplais in *Misc. D. M. Stenton*, p. 89.
[3] *Liber Eliensis*, ed. E. Blake (Camden 3rd series, 92, 1962), pp. 146–7, cf. Chaplais, *loc. cit.*

early custom, especially to nostalgic Englishmen looking back to the good days before the Norman Conquest, it must have seemed that all the abbot of Ely, or of St Augustine's, had to do to secure a privilege or a confirmation from Ethelred II or Edward the Confessor was to write it out. But even if, by negligence, they failed to do this, their rights were not affected; for the memories of these communities were tenacious, and they did not forget that this or that king had made this or that grant. There was, to our way of thinking, a strange laxity about the way charters were produced in pre-Conquest times; this laxity doubtless grew in the memories of men of the next two generations—grew when the formality of legal instruments was also growing; and so, as in many other ways, this period of change produced the remarkable paradox that at a time when the authentic charter was firmly established as a formal, legal instrument, men who otherwise appear to be of high principles were condoning the most informal production, or reproduction, of documents new and old; in fine, were accessories to forgery.

One could go further, and say that the temptation to forge was greater, because the document, once written, was increasing in value, might even be an absolute necessity if one was to establish an ancient claim against a smart neighbour. We cannot tell to what extent it was public knowledge within a community that forgery was being committed; but it can rarely have been a close secret. There must have been many monks and many canons who connived at forgery, who would never have done it for private gain. But the loyalty of a group can on occasion be one of the most powerful, irrational and dangerous motives known to mankind. In this instance it was normally, perhaps, far from clear to its accessories that a crime was being committed; it was not, in the proper sense of the words, a sinister or a dangerous thing; and the community spirit of a medieval monastery was not checked or controlled by the other loyalties which commonly save members of a modern committee from proceeding quite so far.

In England these motives were enhanced by two factors: the chaos of land-tenure after the Norman Conquest, and the introduction of new ideas by the Norman monks. To a great extent the ideas would have come even if the Normans had stayed at home; and forgery in England, as on the continent, was in the main an incident in the changes and movements of the eleventh and twelfth centuries, movements and changes which made this age one of the great turning-points in medieval history. The papal reform brought new ideas of church government and church organisation, made the papal bull a specially valuable document. Legal change accounted for a high proportion of the pressures which led to forgery; and the intellectual revival not only provided more men with the necessary skill to forge, but led in the long run to the assumption that rights should be recorded in writing; it started the great shift from oral to literate government. At a higher level, the intellectual revival, the twelfth-century renaissance, threw up artists in crime as well as artists in letters and stone.

These things can be paralleled all over western Europe. The Norman Conquest itself was not unique to England; but it gave English monasteries the special problem of coping with a situation in which land rights were subjected to new ideas of land law. Domesday Book, so a twelfth-century writer implies, subjected England to a written law, *ius scriptum*;[1] and by this one presumes he meant that from then on it could be assumed that title to land would be supported by written evidence of some kind, even if only by the relevant entry in Domesday Book. It may be that this was not quite the truth of the matter, but Domesday Book is certainly the monument of a great period of change: of the chaos of the Norman settlement and of the growth of literate government. We must not attribute too much to the Norman Conquest; there was forgery before 1066, probably quite a lot of it in the early part of the eleventh century; but the Norman Conquest undoubtedly created new problems and new anxieties, and so enhanced the motives for forgery.

It took two or three generations after the Norman Conquest before the various factors we have been analysing ceased to

---

[1] *Dialogus de Scaccario*, ed. C. Johnson (NMT, 1950), p. 63. The author makes Domesday Book the coping stone in William I's supposed policy of subjecting the country 'iuri scripto legibusque'.

operate. Forgery did not decline in the early twelfth century; rather it grew. In England the climax came in the mid-twelfth century, in the reign of King Stephen. In the second half of the century forgery seems to have been a declining business. The forger had done his job; the muniments of the older religious houses had been tidied up, written title had been established for all and slightly more than all that they could reasonably claim. It was becoming much clearer what the law was on many points, and clearer how much could and could not be established in the courts of law. The church courts were becoming more effective, and passing some of their own sophistication and more mature techniques to the rapidly developing courts of king and baron. Bishops and kings gradually devised the technique of the *inspeximus*, a document which quoted and confirmed an earlier grant, so that even if damp spoiled it or mice gnawed it, no new copy would have to be forged.[1] The *inspeximus*, renewed for a price by every king on his accession, guaranteed the most vital items in a church's muniments, and also did something towards ensuring that the owners did not surreptitiously add to their documents, since a copy of the *inspeximus* would be preserved in the royal archives.[2] The monks of Durham produced most of their great series of forgeries in the 1180's; the nuns of Wix and the monks of Lewes theirs in the 1190's and the 1220's. The Crowland forgeries—the well-known productions of 'pseudo-Ingulf'— came in the fourteenth century; the University of Cambridge acquired venerable antiquity in the fifteenth.[3] But these adventures

[1] The *inspeximus* was in regular use in the royal chancery from the 1220's, but the principle underlying it had been perceived by Henry II, and is implied by the common clause 'sicut carta...testatur' in the twelfth century. English archbishops and bishops occasionally produced an *inspeximus* in the mid-twelfth century (see V. H. Galbraith in *EHR*, LII (1937), 67–73; C. R. Cheney, *English Bishops' Chanceries* (Manchester, 1950), pp. 90–6; Saltman, pp. 227–8).

[2] Though whether the earlier *inspeximus* was normally consulted is very doubtful (cf. the case of the Bristol charter of 1331, which copies an inspeximus of 15 Edward II but makes significant additions to the charter of John incorporated in it: this fact evidently escaped the notice of the clerks of the royal chancery: *Bristol Charters*, I, ed. N. D. Harding (Bristol Rec. Soc. 1930), p. 73 n., but see p. 78 n.).

[3] On 'Ingulf', see bibliography in C. Gross, *Sources and Literature of English History...to about 1485* (2nd edn, London, 1915), p. 247; the best study is still

belonged to a different world. Forgery had its place still after the mid-twelfth century; but it was the normal place of forgery among human misdemeanours. The golden age was past.

In 1138 Geoffrey of Monmouth issued his *History of the Kings of Britain*; in the same year Osbert of Clare produced his *Life of Edward the Confessor*. These books glorified Arthur and Edward, the men who played in English legend the part played by Charlemagne in the legends of the French and German monarchies. It may well be that Geoffrey's purpose was mainly literary; his principal achievement was to make Arthur respectable in Anglo-Norman, and European, circles, and so to inspire the late-twelfth-century cycles of romances.[1] But we do wrong to distinguish sharply between history, hagiography and documentary research in this period. William of Malmesbury, the most eminent historian of the age, had been interested in all three, and many other things besides. So was Osbert of Clare. He went to Rome in 1139 armed with his *Life*, and with a fine dossier of charters.

that by F. Liebermann in *Neues Archiv*, XVIII (1892–3), 225–67, esp. pp. 253 ff. For the forged papal bulls for Cambridge, see Cantelupe's *Historiola* (fifteenth century), ed. T. Hearne, in T. Sprott, *Chronica* (Oxford, 1719), pp. 253–80; and for later speculations of an even more improbable character, John Caius, *De antiquitate Cantabrigiensis Academiae* (London, 1568; 2nd edn, 1574). On late medieval forgery in general, see L. C. Hector, *Palaeography and Medieval Forgery* (London and York, 1959).

[1] The recent tendency among scholars has been to reduce Geoffrey of Monmouth's significance. It is clear that Arthur's fame was growing in many parts of Europe in the generation before Geoffrey wrote, and that the Arthurian cycles of the late twelfth and later centuries drew on many other sources. Geoffrey came in on the crest of a wave; the Arthurian revival would have been possible without him. Yet he remains a very important figure in it, for at least two reasons: he seems to have done more than any other man to make a specifically Celtic hero respectable in cosmopolitan circles, and his book, if we may judge from surviving manuscripts, was the most widely *read* of any Arthurian production of the period (though one must make allowances for the accidents of survival, and the fact that Arthur flourished in a partly oral milieu). In a similar way, recent scholars have tended to depreciate the importance of Chrétien of Troyes in the development of the Arthurian cycles. Yet Chrétien is the one twelfth-century author whose works were studied, so far as we can tell, by every would-be author of romances in his own and the immediately succeeding ages. The error springs from a confusion between 'source-material', which was copious and flowed through numerous channels, and powerful literary influences, which were few.

Both *Life* and charters were intended to show what a holy man Edward had been, how he had refounded and endowed Westminster abbey, and how he and the popes had granted it certain privileges. Osbert was deeply concerned with the glory of Westminster abbey: to crown it with King Edward's holy relics, to restore the properties which recent abbots had alienated, to unseat Abbot Gervase, King Stephen's illegitimate son, who had been intruded and not elected—and replace him, perhaps, with Osbert himself.[1] But it would certainly be wrong to exaggerate Osbert's personal ambition. Ambitious he doubtless was; but personal feelings were subordinated to the greatness of his house. One cannot help feeling that he would have been a happier and a better man if it had not been so. But Osbert was not a bad man. His letters and homilies and prayers reveal a person of deep and sincere devotion. He dedicated his energies to a variety of causes, among others to the cultivation of the festival of the Immaculate Conception and of the cult of St Anne. He showed the same single-minded fervour in pursuit of these aims as in pursuit of the canonisation of King Edward. But, as with Gerald of Wales at the end of the century, the cause of his church came first. The greatness of Westminster was never far from his thoughts; twice prior and twice at least an exile from Westminster, he sacrificed his career and his happiness by fighting each new abbot to secure the traditions and properties of the house. And in the end, one cannot but think, he sacrificed his conscience too, for the sake of the abbey.

It has long been known that the documents which Osbert took to Rome in 1139 were forgeries; and in recent years it has become clear that they were very recent forgeries. Dr Chaplais has argued, not only that Osbert must have known them to be such, but also that he had a hand in drafting them. The case against Osbert is cogent. The close parallels between the more substantial forgeries

---

[1] On Osbert, see esp. *The Letters of Osbert of Clare*, ed. E. W. Williamson, with a biographical 'Sketch' by J. Armitage Robinson; also Knowles, *MO*, pp. 511–13; on his *Life of St Edward*, which was edited by Marc Bloch (*Analecta Bollandiana*, XLI (1923), 5–131), see F. Barlow, *The Life of King Edward* (NMT, 1962), pp. xxx ff.

and Osbert's *Life* make it probable either that he was author of
both, or that he and the forger worked in unison.[1] If much special
pleading would be needed to acquit Gilbert Foliot of being
accessory to the Gloucester forgeries, even more would be needed
to acquit Osbert of being involved in the composition of those
of Westminster. Westminster was the headquarters of a factory
of forgeries in this period. It had made forged matrices of seals
of Edward the Confessor and William I, and scribes in the service
of the abbot of Westminster wrote and sealed writs and charters
for Coventry, Battle, Ramsey, Bury, St Peter's Ghent, and
Gloucester.[2] There is no serious reason to ascribe the seal matrices
or the composition of many of these numerous documents to
Osbert. The abbot's clerks were probably more deeply involved
in the fraud. The seal and the skilful reproduction of early documents by these clerks suggests that they were men trained to this
particular profession. It was in Osbert's fervent nature to lend a
hand in producing documents which Edward the Confessor
ought to have produced himself; or rather, which the monks of
Westminster must have produced for him to acknowledge, unless
they had been criminally negligent. He may well thus have inspired the clerks, whom we may believe to have been experts in
restoring monastic muniments; and he may have recommended
them to his friend Anselm, abbot of Bury, or to Gilbert Foliot[3] or
to others who profited from their skill. This is conjecture. What is
not conjecture is that out of such an alliance between zeal for a cause
and professional skill many of the forgeries of this age were born.

A high proportion of the surviving forgeries of St Augustine's
Canterbury were the work of Guerno, monk of St Medard at

[1] See Chaplais in *Misc. D. M. Stenton*, pp. 91 ff. The case rests not only on
similarity of style, but on verbal connexions of a complex kind between Osbert
and the forgeries.
[2] See the provisional list in Bishop and Chaplais, *Facsimiles of English Royal
Writs*, pp. xxi–xxii and n. (and xxii ff. for comments), supplemented by
Chaplais in *Misc. D. M. Stenton*, pp. 97 ff. The witness list to Davis, *Regesta*, I,
no. 137, for Bury, suggests that it comes from the same stable (cf. Brooke,
Downside Review, LXIX (1951), p. 230 n., drawing attention to this and other
documents with similar impossible lists from Westminster, Ramsey and
Ghent).
[3] See below, p. 144.

Soissons, and author of documents for his own home, for St Ouen at Rouen, for Peterborough abbey, and perhaps of one or two for Christ Church, Canterbury.[1] He seems to have helped the monks of Christ Church to take their first steps. They completed his work about 1121 by 'discovering' a splendid set of papal privileges, the famous 'Canterbury forgeries'; and the monk Eadmer, a man of fervent devotion to his own house and to all English traditions, as striking in its way as Osbert's, has provided us with a thrilling, and disingenuous, account of the discovery. Eadmer's share in the enterprise was probably less than Osbert's in the affair at Westminster; but Professor Southern does 'not think that, without a great deal of special pleading, he can be cleared from the charge of knowing that the privileges were forgeries and knowing that his account of their origin was false'.[2] Meanwhile the bishop of Llandaff and his associates were struggling to create the diocese of Llandaff out of the chaos which the decadence of the Welsh church in the century following the Danish raids, and the Norman Conquest of south Wales and the Welsh church, had caused.[3] His monument is the *Book of Llandaff*: lives of saints and charters, all equally fictitious, all tending to prove the antiquity and integrity and wealth of the see, and enshrining such genuine traditions as the men in his family and circle could gather. The final editor of the *Book of Llandaff* was a brilliant historical research student, a pupil, it has been guessed, of William of Malmesbury; and he has been tentatively identified with Caradoc of Llancarfan, a professional hagiographer from the same circle. It is indeed a little difficult for us to distinguish between forgery of charters and the embellishment of saints' lives, whose primary purpose was to establish the present possessions and privileges of their churches.[4] Caradoc was an extreme case of a hagiographer making bricks without straw; Goscelin of S. Bertin in an earlier generation, or Osbert of Clare himself, were

---

[1] See above, p. 131 n.
[2] Southern, *EHR*, LXXIII, 225–6.
[3] See above, p. 128; *CS*, pp. 315 ff.
[4] Since the saint was regarded as the living owner of his church or monastery, it was natural to support present privileges by reference to stories of grants made to the saint and by indications of his authority.

professional hagiographers who liked to have a solid foundation of earlier tradition on which to build. Granted this, they embellished freely. But this shocked nobody. Osbert added to the previous *Life of Edward the Confessor*; Ailred of Rievaulx added even more. None the less, there was an element of pure chicanery in the *Book of Llandaff*, and there are indications that Geoffrey of Monmouth knew more than he ought to have done about how the *Book* was composed.[1]

It was a small world in which these works of fiction, or partial fiction, were produced. The gift of Llancarfan to Gloucester abbey in the 1090's was one of the events which started, or spurred on, the interest of the Llancarfan family, first in discovering and inventing the traditions of Llancarfan, and later in building up the diocese of Llandaff. To this family belonged Bishop Urban and Caradoc, perhaps also Bishop Uhtred with whom Gilbert corresponded and Bishop Nicholas (1148–83), who was a young monk in Gilbert's community at Gloucester when he was promoted to Llandaff.[2] It was perhaps in the 1130's or 1140's—though it may have been later—that a collection of hagiographical material from Llandaff and elsewhere, incorporating much of Caradoc's materials, was carried to Gloucester where it subsequently became the nucleus of the hagiographical collection in Cotton MS Vespasian A. xiv (*c.* 1200).[3] At Gloucester, Llandaff material was combined with Geoffrey of Monmouth's *History* by Benedict of Gloucester in his *Life of St Dubricius*.[4] Geoffrey's chief patron in the 1130's seems to have been Robert, earl of Gloucester, who was looking after the temporalities of the see of Llandaff at the time when the *Book of Llandaff* was compiled (*c.* 1135), received the dedication of Geoffrey's *History*, and provided Geoffrey

[1] *SEBC*, pp. 201–11, esp. pp. 205–6, 209–11.
[2] Conway Davies, II, 506 ff.; cf. *SEBC*, pp. 223 ff.; *CS*, pp. 287 ff., 315 ff. On Bishop Nicholas, see *GFL*, Biog. Index; *SEBC*, pp. 227–8 n., corrected by I. Ll. Foster, *Antiquity*, XXXIV (1960), 236.
[3] K. Hughes in *SEBC*, pp. 183 ff., esp. p. 197.
[4] Printed from Vesp. A. xiv by Wharton in *Anglia Sacra*, II (London, 1691), 654 ff. The date of Benedict's work is not precisely known, but as he used Geoffrey of Monmouth it cannot be earlier than 1138 and is likely to be some time later; and the MS in which the work occurs is of *c.* 1200 (cf. *SEBC*, pp. 193, 210 n.).

Gaimar with a copy or a version of it as soon as it was completed.[1] From 1139 Gilbert Foliot frequented his court. Geoffrey of Monmouth's headquarters were at Oxford, where his colleague Walter was archdeacon, and where Gilbert's master Robert Pullen was teaching in the 1130's. In the period 1148–55, perhaps in 1150 or 1151, Geoffrey dedicated his *Life of Merlin* to Gilbert's uncle, the bishop of Lincoln. Finally, Geoffrey's *History* provided Gilbert with the ground, perhaps the inspiration, for his plea that London should be the seat of an archbishopric.[2]

Eadmer as a young monk may possibly have seen Guerno at work, or at least heard of his doings. But Eadmer's fame rests on his long and devoted service of Archbishop Anselm, whose *Life* he wrote.[3] In later life Eadmer was associated with Anselm's nephew, later abbot of Bury, in the effort to revive the earlier English custom of celebrating the Feast of the Immaculate Conception. Anselm the younger forms a link between Eadmer and Osbert of Clare: he was a close friend of both, and it may have been he who inspired Osbert to his imitation of Eadmer; one cannot prove that Osbert knew Eadmer personally, though it is not impossible. Eadmer and Osbert both had an intense love of old English traditions; a powerful devotion to certain saints and to certain institutions—a devotion to their monasteries which was so single-minded as to lead them astray. Anselm the younger is an enigmatic figure. He evidently had some of his uncle's charm and brilliance and curiosity. He was one of the authors of the early collections of 'Miracles of the Virgin', and in this work he was associated with Dominic, who was prior of Evesham in Reginald Foliot's time, with William of Malmesbury, Earl Robert's protégé, and Master Alberic, canon of St Paul's in the middle of the century.[4] Professor Southern describes Anselm as having 'a

[1] See above, p. 116 n.; Conway Davies, II, 634, no. L 87.
[2] See below, pp. 159 ff. For the *Vita Merlini*, see the edn by J. J. Parry, Univ. of Illinois Studies in Language and Literature, X, 1925, no. 3; see pp. 14–15 for the date.
[3] Ed. R. W. Southern, NMT, 1962 (1963); on Eadmer, see Southern, *St Anselm and his Biographer*.
[4] R. W. Southern in *Mediaeval and Renaissance Studies*, IV (1958), 176–216; on Anselm see Williamson, *Letters of Osbert of Clare*, pp. 191 ff.; on Alberic, below, p. 198.

strong practical sense in getting things done' and refers to a
charter describing how Anselm 'came into the chapter house at
Bury St Edmund's and gave the brethren' some properties so that
a mass of the Blessed Virgin should be said daily for the safety of
king and kingdom. 'It is of just such a practical and unstudious
spirit that the collection of miracle stories bears witness.'[1] The
story is also characteristic in revealing his interest in the king: he
was a personal friend of Henry I, whose court he frequented,
sometimes to the neglect of Bury. Even more ambiguous was
the high-handed way in which he took over the see of London
when he thought he had been elected bishop in 1137. The sequel
revealed that he was a man who made many friends and many
enemies, and the saintly Thurstan of York—a former canon of
St Paul's and so not unprejudiced—roundly asserted that he ought
rather to be deposed from his abbacy than elected to the bishopric.[2]

There is no evidence of direct contact between Anselm and
Gilbert Foliot, nor of any special interest on Gilbert's part in the
developing cult of the Blessed Virgin, and especially of the
Immaculate Conception, which was the common bond of interest
within this group. It is, however, probable that the festival was
celebrated at Gloucester in his time,[3] and certain that Gilbert and
Osbert were in touch in or soon after 1148, since Osbert wrote a
Life of St Ethelbert, the patron saint of Hereford cathedral, and
dedicated it to Gilbert.[4]

Some of the links in this chain are strong, some weak; but the
purpose of following it is not to show that Geoffrey of Monmouth, Caradoc, and Osbert, and the master forgers of twelfth-
century England were all friends, engaged in a common conspiracy
to hide the truth. Such a suggestion would be absurd. What is

---

[1] Southern in *Mediaeval and Renaissance Studies*, IV, 200.

[2] Diceto, I, 250.

[3] E. Bishop, *Liturgica Historica* (Oxford, 1918), p. 247 and note—the
Gloucester chronicle says 'apud nos', which, as Bishop observes, 'is not
absolutely cogent proof *for Gloucester*'. But it is highly probable that this has a
local reference, even though almost exactly the same words occur in the
Winchcombe annals (on the Gloucester chronicle, see *CS*, pp. 260 ff.).

[4] M. R. James in *EHR*, XXXII (1917), 215–16; cf. Williamson, *Letters of
Osbert of Clare*, pp. 23 f.

clear, however, is that the world in which the authors of historical fiction, of saints' lives of varying degrees of veracity, and of spurious charters moved was a small world, in which many of those involved must have known one another. It was clearly quite well known that muniments could be doctored and 'improved', and this inspired many respectable men to justify dubious means by unimpeachable ends. It inspired Geoffrey of Monmouth, who was perhaps not wholly respectable, to fiction on the grand scale, in the course of which he pilloried his chief rival, the *Book of Llandaff*. In 1148 it inspired the monks of Gloucester, perhaps led, perhaps followed by their abbot—who can say?—to plain forgery. Soon after, they learned that better work was being done at Westminster. It would be interesting to know how and why they lost confidence in their own powers after Gilbert's departure. It would be even more interesting to know whether it was connected with Osbert of Clare's visit to Hereford about this time.

Historical fiction, then, was entirely respectable in itself: St Ailred is sufficient guarantee for that. Fiction applied to documents was a crime; but it was a crime in which respectable men had been known to dabble for a supposedly good cause—for the good, not of themselves, but of the institution of which they were insignificant members. A man who respected the conventions of his age in the early twelfth century would find that it was conventional to be a monk, and also to be a monk of austere and zealous life; he would also find that it was conventional for monks and canons to condone forgery for the good of the cause. This is not to underestimate the difficulty of the former, or the admirable character of the monastic life led by many conventional men in this age; nor to forget that forgery was and is a crime. No doubt there were many unconventional men in the forgery business, and there were certainly numerous unconventional men in the cloisters. But it took a man who accepted the standards of his age with scarcely any question to combine these two roles. Such a man was Osbert of Clare; and such, in a rather different way, was Gilbert Foliot.

In Gilbert, one may suspect that the temptation to forge was not unconnected with his legal training. There was certainly an edge, a subtlety to his expedients in the Becket crisis which seems not incompatible with his record *c.* 1148. Yet if his career as a monk has hitherto appeared more righteous than it was, we cannot help feeling that less than justice has been done to Gilbert Foliot's activities between 1163 and 1170 in opposition to Thomas Becket.

CHAPTER IX

GILBERT FOLIOT
AND
THOMAS BECKET

Gilbert Foliot's career had many ups and downs; but at two points in particular he seems to have felt himself to be in the depths of the valley: in the months after his first excommunication in 1169, and in the months after the murder of Thomas Becket. In the summer of 1169 two elaborate attacks were mounted against Gilbert. Thomas gathered a dossier of invectives from many of the leading prelates of northern France to aid him in his denunciations at Rome;[1] and Herbert of Bosham wrote a letter to the pope in Thomas's name summing up the angry feelings of the archbishop's entourage.[2] Herbert listed seven 'objections': and to these we might add an eighth, which was perhaps in the author's mind, and was openly referred to in John of Salisbury's letters,[3] that Gilbert's spleen against the archbishop was due to his thwarted ambition: he craved his throne. From these documents we may put together the indictment against the bishop of London. The rake's progress was not the idle gossip of scandal-mongers, though it was the product of enemies in a bitter struggle. The witnesses are Thomas Becket and John of Salisbury, Herbert of Bosham—angular and eccentric, but a man of eminent scholarship and piety—William, bishop of Auxerre, the English Premonstratensian Milo, bishop of Thérouanne (successor of another Premonstratensian Milo who had been Gilbert's diocesan when he was prior of Abbeville and who had joined in his consecration), Baldwin, bishop of Nevers, Maurice de Sully, bishop of Paris and

---

[1] *MB Epp.* 542–8, 550–1.

[2] *MB Epp.* 537. Some of Herbert's letters were undoubtedly literary exercises: in this case, however, there is no surviving letter of Becket sent to the pope on the same occasion, and it is likely that this was actually sent.

[3] *MB Epp.* 231: cf. above, p. 31.

William, archbishop of Sens: a galaxy of detractors. Their story may be summarised as follows.[1]

In 1162 Gilbert Foliot had bitterly opposed Becket's election because, as was commonly thought, he wished to be archbishop himself. In 1163, on his own translation to London, he had refused to renew his profession to Canterbury.[2] This he later used as an excuse for disobedience to Becket, which he carried to the length of claiming that London should be the seat of the metropolitan see. In 1169 he was said to be suggesting that the primatial see be transferred from Canterbury to London, a threat cleverly used by John of Salisbury in an attempt to revive the loyalty of the monks of Canterbury to their archbishop.[3] When Becket fell out with Henry II, Foliot fomented the discord, and appealed to the pope against the archbishop even in the dark days of the council of Northampton, on the eve of Becket's exile. He then went to Sens as Henry's agent, and spoke venomously against Becket, until the pope was moved to halt the flow. In the early days of exile he was an accomplice of the king in despoiling the property of the exiled ecclesiastics. He ignored Becket's censures and associated with excommunicates; treated letters from archbishop and pope with contumely. The frequency of his appeals against every censure or rumour of censure was the common talk of the streets.

We may disentangle from this comprehensive list of offences four serious charges: that his venom against Becket arose from thwarted ambition; that he used legal cunning to build up a case to make London the seat of an archbishopric; that he acted as Henry's accomplice and fomented the dispute; and that he used the device of appeal, and especially of the appeal by anticipation, *ad cautelam*, in such a way as to bring derision on the jurisdiction

---

[1] There is no need to give a detailed narrative here: for the outline, see above, pp. 98–103, and for a full account, Knowles, *EC*.

[2] *MB Epp.* 35–6, 67; cf. 502, and *Causa inter Cantuariensem et Londoniensem*, *MB*, IV, 224–5; Herbert of Bosham, *MB*, III, 88; *EC*, p. 47 and n. 1. *MB Epp.* 36 suggests that Gilbert was to be forced to make profession; the rest of the series make it clear that this did not happen. But in *MB Epp.* 67 the pope assures Thomas that this is not to be to the prejudice of his see.

[3] *MB Epp.* 535, pp. 10–11.

of archbishop and pope, and to evade at every turn the consequences of his apparent readiness to submit to properly constituted authority. It will be convenient to take these charges in
order, melting the last into a general discussion of the famous, or
infamous, letter *Multiplicem*, on whose interpretation our view of
Gilbert Foliot's role in the dispute between king and archbishop
must ultimately rest.

CANTERBURY AND LONDON: GILBERT'S AMBITION
TO BE ARCHBISHOP

The charge of ambition he specifically denied, in an elaborate
disclaimer to Henry II written some years after Becket's death.[1]
It is hard to give this disclaimer an unqualified acceptance. There
is no doubt that he toyed with the idea of making London the
seat of the archbishopric, and he therefore presumably felt himself
equal to the office. In 1162 he clearly stated his objection to
Becket's election on the ground that Becket was an unsuitable
candidate, and he had good grounds for this objection. No one
could have foreseen the change which took place in the outlook
and manner of life of the worldly chancellor. But Gilbert's action
in 1163, and later, shows that he had something like a horror of
submitting to the authority of Thomas Becket. He refused profession to him; and he tried to keep the archbishop's authority in
more or less permanent suspension from 1164 onwards by his
constant appeals.[2] It may indeed be true that, at the conscious
level, Gilbert shrank from the idea of putting himself forward as
Theobald's successor in 1161–2. But it is possible to argue that
he reckoned himself, as a monk and an experienced pastor and
ecclesiastical administrator, a more worthy successor of Lanfranc
and Anselm and Theobald than the secular Thomas.

Yet the depth of his feeling against Thomas demands some

---

[1] No. 220; also in no. 170 (*MB Epp.* 225)—*Multiplicem* (see below, p. 171).
[2] It is interesting to compare with this the struggle of the bishops of Durham
to achieve independence of the archbishop of York (the *Gesta Henrici II et
Ricardi I*, II, 240–1, records the first round of this in a manner reminiscent of
Gilbert's defence in 1169).

more particular explanation than envy—we must return to it later—and it is difficult to believe that Gilbert had serious hopes of the primacy in 1161–2. The translation of a bishop was still a rare event, demanding special grounds and papal dispensation. It could happen: there was one precedent from each of the three Anglo-Norman archbishoprics in the previous hundred years. In 1069 John of Avranches had moved to Rouen; in 1100 Gerard of Hereford had gone to York, in 1114 Ralph of Rochester to Canterbury. Neither the precedent for moving a bishop from Hereford nor the precedent for transferring a monk-bishop to Canterbury was likely to inspire observers in 1161–2, or to give Gilbert (even supposing he wished to be translated) much hope. Still less encouraging was the precedent of his fellow-Cluniac, Henry of Winchester, who is said to have been elected to Canterbury in the 1130's, but failed to obtain his translation even though he was King Stephen's brother.[1] It is to John of Salisbury, writing in 1164, that we owe the not very probable story that Gilbert tried to hold on to Gloucester abbey when he became bishop of Hereford, as Henry held on to Glastonbury when he became bishop of Winchester; and John, writing in 1166, is our chief informant about the gossip that Gilbert had coveted the see of Canterbury. One cannot help suspecting that John and others in Becket's circle built up, in the mid-1160's, a picture of Gilbert opposing Becket with the same weapons and the same motives that Henry of Blois had deployed against Theobald.

One is bound to say that there is much about the election of 1162 which is obscure. The see of Canterbury was vacant for more than a year. This was nothing unusual, but we have no information about the lobbying and intrigue which doubtless filled the middle and later months of 1161; on this period Becket's biographers are silent.[2] The fact that Gilbert could make so formal a disclaimer to the king in the 1170's is strong evidence

---

[1] See Saltman, pp. 8 f.

[2] Although several of them indicate Becket's reluctance, which may have caused some delay. But there is no explanation of why it lasted twelve months. Grim (*MB*, II, 366) speaks as if the monks of Canterbury were reluctant to elect, but Roger of Pontigny (IV, 14–16) fits this into the events of May 1162.

that he had not openly canvassed for the position. But his anxiety not to serve Becket and his claim for metropolitan status for the see of London perhaps gave some excuse for a comparison with Henry of Winchester.

THE METROPOLITAN STATUS OF THE SEE OF LONDON

Gilbert was permitted to move to London without renewing his profession because the pope was bound to admit that his plea that a second profession was not necessary in such cases was canonically defensible.[1] Yet it is clear that legal rectitude was not Gilbert's sole motive for his refusal. His chief motive may not have been reluctance to make a personal profession to Becket. It is probable that he already had in mind the possibility that he might wish to raise the claims of London to be an archiepiscopal see. This claim had been made fifty years before by Gilbert's relative, Bishop Richard de Belmeis I,[2] on his accession to the see, and it is unlikely that Gilbert's relations in the London chapter in 1163 were ignorant of this. He would expect and be expected not to let down the tradition of his office and his family. It is true that there is no direct evidence of his interest in this particular claim before 1169, but it was not then a new idea in his mind.

John of Salisbury, writing to the monks of Canterbury in 1169, and wishing to raise panic in their minds, indicated that Gilbert wished to transfer the primacy from Canterbury to London. The earliest evidence of Gilbert's claim comes a few weeks before, from the vivid account written by a friend to Thomas Becket of the reception of the letters announcing that Thomas had excommunicated Gilbert of London and Jocelin of Salisbury.[3] The

---

[1] As is clear from *MB Epp.* 67 (cf. the *Causa*, *MB*, IV, 224–5).

[2] Anselm's letter 451 (ed. F. S. Schmitt, *Opera*, V, Edinburgh, 1951, pp. 398–9; old edns, bk III, no. 152). Anselm, writing to the pope in 1108, i.e. at Bishop Richard's accession, asks the pope not to give his assent if a petition comes from London for a pallium for its bishop 'quod nunquam habuit'. There seems to be no other evidence on this incident, save the implication in the Prophecies of Merlin (see below).

[3] *MB Epp.* 535, 502, 508; cf. 537, 545–7, 550; *MB*, IV, 225–6; R. Foreville, *L'église et la royauté en Angleterre sous Henri II...* (Paris, 1943), pp. 286–8; Knowles, *EC*, pp. 47–8, 160–2; C. R. Cheney, *BIHR*, XXXVI (1963), 7 and n.

letter was delivered formally in St Paul's, and although in the confusion it was not clear that it had been read, its contents were made known. The bishop was at Stepney. He immediately summoned a meeting of the London clergy to meet two days later; at this Becket's letter against him was read, and the bishop, 'bitterly angry and frowning deeply' listed his grounds for challenging the sentence. He then, as was his custom, renewed the particular appeal which happened to be pending at the time. Among Gilbert's pleas quoted on this occasion was the following:

(the archbishop) puts his scythe to another's corn, since he has power neither over my person nor my church—my person, since I never made profession nor promised obedience to him, nor to the church of Canterbury in the name of this church, that is, the church of London; my church, since the church of London claims back what was taken from it long since by the infiltration[1] of the pagans, to wit that the archbishopric ought to be at London, which we shall prove.[2]

It seems clear that in 1169 Gilbert was planning to transfer the primacy from Canterbury to London. It is very likely that this scheme first presented itself to his mind as a claim to independence. There was nothing new in a suffragan of Canterbury claiming metropolitan status in the twelfth century. As we have seen, an earlier bishop of London had made the claim; so had bishops of St Davids, perhaps a bishop of Llandaff, certainly a bishop of Winchester. Disputes about primacy and metropolitan status

[1] *irreptione*, 'by the creeping in'. Lupus (who published the first edition of the correspondence at Brussels in 1682) read *irruptione*, which Robertson thought 'seems preferable'. But it is likely that by design or inadvertence a play on the word has crept in here: Gilbert, or the man reporting him, has the idea of *raptio* in mind, although *rapio* and *repo* are etymologically quite distinct.

[2] *MB Epp.* 508 (VI, 605–6). The meaning could be 'there ought to be *an* archbishopric at London', but apart from no. 502 all the other sources are specific that Gilbert wished to *transfer* the see, not set up an additional metropolitancy. The *Causa* (*MB*, IV, 224–6) makes Gilbert argue that he is not bound to obey the archbishop, because he has not made profession to him, because London is the mother, not daughter of Canterbury—as it was in the days of 52 'apostolicorum', and as Gregory I intended it to be once again—and because Thomas cannot act as legate until he lands in England. The 52 'apostolici' were presumably the popes from Eleutherius (King Lucius's pope, according to the legend) to Gregory; the number is not noted in Geoffrey of Monmouth (see below), but could have been deduced from any list of popes.

were common in Europe in the century following the papal reform, during the revival of canon law, and especially of the Pseudo-Isidorian decretals, which accompanied it. In the French church these disputes went further back, but they rose to a climax in the late eleventh and early twelfth centuries. Following Pseudo-Isidore, the pattern of provinces and primacies in France was reckoned to be based on the Roman provincial organisation of Gaul. There was some good and some spurious history in this, for the pattern of early metropolitan arrangements owed a good deal to the Roman provincial boundaries. Thus Gregory the Great himself had planned to found archbishoprics in London and York, a scheme which presumably owed something both to memories of Roman rule in Britain[1] and perhaps to the historical fact that both London and York had been the seats of bishops in the fourth century.

The peculiar slant of disputes about primacy and metropolitan status in Britain after the Norman Conquest was due to the imperial ambitions of Lanfranc and the historical circumstance that a great part of the British Isles still at that date had no defined pattern of dioceses or provinces, was still in organisation 'Celtic'. Owing to the Danish and Norse onslaught of the ninth and tenth centuries, it seems that the Church in the Celtic lands had no clearly defined organisation at all.[2] Lanfranc made the claim that he was primate of all Britain, and attempted to extend his authority not only over the province of York but also over some Welsh, Irish and Scots bishops as well. This was regarded, not unreasonably, as Norman aggression, and the late eleventh and early twelfth centuries saw not only the spread of ecclesiastical

---

[1] Cf. Brooke in *SEBC*, pp. 211 ff. The geography of the Roman provinces of Britain is obscure, but London and York were certainly leading towns and the seats of bishoprics.

[2] See Lloyd, *History of Wales*, II, 447 ff.; Conway Davies, II, 443 ff.; and *CS*, pp. 315 ff., where it is argued that the Welsh church, like the Irish, had in early centuries a monastic organisation, with the monastic *parochia* as distinct from an episcopal diocese as the unit, and that the four Welsh dioceses of the twelfth century—even though St Davids and Bangor at least certainly had ancient roots—represented a radical simplification and rationalisation of older tradition after the decline of the eighth and ninth centuries and the Viking raids of the ninth, tenth and eleventh.

reform and Norman influence, but also a native revival in these lands. In the early twelfth century, in spite of some vicissitudes, York reclaimed its independence of Canterbury. At the same time the Welsh church was trying to claim independence of Canterbury, and most of the Scottish church was shaking itself free of York. The Scots were successful, the Welsh failed. This failure has sometimes led historians, to whom these disputes about primacy and metropolitan authority seem remote and even trivial, to underestimate the seriousness of the effort. There is copious evidence from almost every corner of Europe that this was one of the great issues in the life of the Church in the twelfth century. The dispute between Canterbury and York played a large part still in the quarrels of Thomas Becket; and although it is universally recognised that it was the breach of Canterbury's privileges in the coronation of the young king by Roger of York and Gilbert of London—aided and abetted by some of their colleagues—which led immediately to the final catastrophe, it has been less clearly recognised how the issue between Thomas and Roger was looming ominously in the background even before Thomas fell out with Henry.[1] But for an understanding of the twelfth-century Church, the other disputes are almost equally significant.

The onslaught of the Normans on the Welsh church found the native Welsh ill-prepared for resistance. But even in Lanfranc's

---

[1] This still awaits full elucidation. See no. 146 and *MB Epp.* 13, 27, 41–3, 47, 68, which show Thomas and Roger of York in dispute in 1163–4. The *casus belli* was Roger's claim to carry his cross in the southern province, but behind this lay Canterbury's claim, which seems to have been much in Thomas's mind at this period, to primacy over York. Although the title 'primate' was confirmed to Thomas by the pope (*MB Epp.* 170), there is very little evidence that he used it. It occurs in *Epp.* 502; but he never otherwise employed it in the protocol of letters or charters (see C. R. Cheney, *English Bishops' Chanceries, 1100–1250*, p. 65, and *BIHR*, xxxvi, 4 and n.), and with the exception of William of Canterbury, his biographers almost never called him primate. This omission is so striking that it can only mean that he refused to use the title —surely not because he was indifferent to it, but because (we must presume) he regarded it as a mockery till full primacy over York should be restored to him. This is of the greatest importance to an understanding of Roger of York's opposition; and is probably of greater significance than has been realised in explaining the alliance of Roger and Gilbert, which had such fatal consequences in 1170. The ringleaders in the coronation of the young king both claimed exemption from Becket's primacy.

time the cultured Welsh family which attempted to revive St Davids made it plain that it reckoned to have a tradition of independence of Canterbury: in the *Life of St David* written by Rhigyfarch David is depicted as an archbishop of terrifyingly potent authority; and this picture must certainly have been intended to edify contemporary opinion, since it is clear that the David of history was almost entirely forgotten.[1] Rhigyfarch's claim was not universally accepted even in Wales. He was answered a generation later by the authors of the *Book of Llandaff*, who made the counter-claim that their founders, Dubricius, Teilo and Oudoceus, were also archbishops; and there is no doubt that this was a defensive measure against the pretensions of St David's, not against Canterbury, with which, on the whole, the first bishops of Llandaff strove to be on good terms.[2] Ironically enough, it was the first Norman bishop of St Davids who made the first efforts to make these nostalgic claims effective. Between 1125 and 1130 the canons of his chapter wrote a letter to the pope in which they announced that their church had been metropolitan since Britain had first been Christian, since the time of Pope Eleutherius, who had sent missionaries to convert Lucius, king of Britain in the mid-second century. These papal emissaries had founded three archbishoprics and twenty-seven or twenty-eight bishoprics in the kingdom. Of the former, St David's had become one. It is clear that at some point, and to some degree, Bishop Bernard came to accept the independent aspirations of the Welsh princes; in his later years at least he came to terms with them, and they with him. It was normal in this period for an independent kingdom to wish to have, to claim to have its own ecclesiastical province or provinces and although the story which the chapter told was preposterous, in the circumstances of the time it was a reasonable answer to what they regarded as the aggression of the Normans in the church as well as in secular affairs. It was also thoroughly up-to-date, for the pattern of archbishoprics and bishoprics was clearly a somewhat fantastic gloss on what was known of the organisation of Roman Britain, which could

---

[1] See N. K. Chadwick in *SEBC*, pp. 134 ff., and Brooke, *ibid*. pp. 214 ff.
[2] *Op. cit.* pp. 214 f., cf. 136 ff., 144 ff., and *CS*, p. 319.

reasonably be supposed to have had three provinces and twenty-eight *civitates*.[1]

So long as Henry I was on the throne of England, it was not safe for a bishop whose headquarters lay in territory under Norman control to press these claims very hard. But the anarchy of Stephen's reign and the great revival of the Welsh princes gave Bernard an opportunity, or perhaps compelled him, to follow out the logical consequences of what may have been hitherto a mainly academic combination of Welsh tradition and contemporary continental church politics. In 1147 Archbishop Theobald, with Gilbert Foliot in his train, had to defend himself against a direct attack by Bernard in the papal Curia. The pope postponed the issue to the council of Rheims in March 1148. But Bernard never went to Rheims; apparently he was a dying man, and with his death the same year the claim went into abeyance. It was not forgotten. Late in the century it was revived, and pressed in earnest by the single-minded Gerald of Wales. Gerald failed as Bernard had done; but his failure was not due to the weakness of his cause. In the circumstances of the time there was little to choose between the case put up by Gerald and Canterbury's defence. But Canterbury appeared to have centuries of actual authority on its side, and this was a convenient excuse to confirm the *status quo*, a course which was politically desirable.[2]

The chief immediate consequence of the historical exercise of the chapter of St Davids in the 1120's was the picture of the early British church given by Geoffrey of Monmouth. He assigned to the British church three archbishops and twenty-eight bishops, adding the characteristic rider that they replaced pagan arch-flamens and flamens. He caused confusion in Wales by translating

---

[1] It was generally known to have had 28 *civitates*, from Gildas, who was quoted by other, more widely known authors. The only information we have today about the organisation of the church in Roman Britain is that three bishops, those of London and York and a third not securely identified, were present at the Council of Arles in 314. This information, if known, might well be taken by twelfth-century writers to imply three provinces. These deductions may appear far-fetched, but such deductions were undoubtedly made in the ninth and later centuries on the basis of Roman provincial lists.

[2] Cf. Lloyd, II, 623 ff.; Conway Davies, I, 210 ff. In the meantime Scotland was successfully vindicating its independence, though without an archbishopric.

St David's see to Caerleon-on-Usk, and it is highly probable that this was deliberately meant to confuse the rival claims of St Davids and Llandaff.[1] Since he knew his Bede, and so knew what Gregory the Great had planned, it was inevitable perhaps that he should place the other metropolitans in London and York; but there is nothing at all unlikely in the supposition that he knew perfectly well that Richard de Belmeis I had attempted to revive London's claim. Geoffrey's work was widely read, and it could not escape the attention of the canons of St Paul's; nor, since Geoffrey's principal patrons seem to have been Robert of Gloucester and Robert de Chesney, was it likely to pass unnoticed by Gilbert Foliot.

Not everyone in the twelfth century took Geoffrey seriously. William of Newburgh's attack is famous. There are also indications that Walter Map, a protégé of Gilbert Foliot and a canon of St Paul's in Gilbert's later years, knew what it was worth as history.[2] So, no doubt, did another Walter, archdeacon of Oxford when Geoffrey wrote, who was apparently his accomplice. But Walter's colleague Henry, archdeacon of Huntingdon, accepted the book without question within a few months of its publication; and there is no reason to suppose that their bishop, Robert de Chesney, or the bishop's nephew did not follow the opinion of most students of history in that age, that Geoffrey was to be taken at his word. John of Salisbury tells us that Geoffrey's *History* was the basis of Gilbert's claim: he refers both to the story of the arch-flamens and the flamens—and speculates whether Gilbert was proposing to reintroduce the worship of Jupiter—and the passage in the 'prophecies of Merlin' (book vii of Geoffrey's *History*) in which 'Merlin' foresees that 'the dignity of London shall adorn Canterbury'.[3] This occurs in the section of the prophecies in which Merlin is made to foretell events actually described later in the *History*: an obvious gambit designed to lend

---

[1] Cf. *SEBC*, pp. 201–11.

[2] See the forthcoming introduction to the reprint of M. R. James's text and translation of Walter Map's *De nugis curialium* in NMT.

[3] *MB Epp.* 535; Geoffrey of Monmouth, *Historia Regum Britanniae*, iv, 19, vii, 3, ed. E. Faral, *La légende arthurienne*, i, iii (Paris, 1929), 144–5, 191.

verisimilitude to the prophecies, before they embarked on the real future—the future in 1138—and descended into gibberish. But the double reference made Geoffrey's book seem emphatic evidence that London had once been the primatial see. In a Europe teeming with claims based on similar evidence, the authority of Gregory the Great and of Merlin, not to mention Gilbert's cousin and predecessor, might well seem overwhelming testimony not only to the veracity of London's claim, but to the duty of the bishop of London to press that claim. It could be argued that it was more substantial than the evidence which led Lanfranc to invent the primacy of Canterbury over York. We can appreciate the pressures on a man in Gilbert's position, if we study the career of Bernard of St David's or of Gerald of Wales, or of more than one archbishop of Canterbury, including Theobald and Becket, or of more than one archbishop of York, and especially of the hereditary canon of St Paul's, Thurstan of Bayeux, who became a dedicated archbishop of York and whose struggles are most vividly portrayed by Hugh the Chanter.[1] These pressures were all the stronger if the man was conscientious and wished to live up to the greatness of his office.

In reviving the claims of London, Gilbert may well have been conscious that he was imitating another eminent Cluniac of his day, though it is doubtful if Henry of Blois, bishop of Winchester, who was still alive in 1169, would have encouraged him in his courses. In 1126 Henry had been nominated by his uncle and namesake, King Henry I, to the abbey of Glastonbury; and when he was presented in 1129 to the wealthiest of the English sees, Henry of Blois was unwilling to surrender his rich and venerable abbey: he held it till his death. In the late 1130's, when his brother Stephen was king, Henry seems clearly to have expected the reversion of Canterbury; nor is it entirely clear why Stephen refused him this prize. In 1139 Henry was compensated for a time by the papal legateship, and when that was taken from him in 1143, he tried to establish a separate archbishopric out of the sees of Winchester and Chichester; and somewhat later, in pursuit of a different plan, 'he began to intrigue with' some of the cardinals

[1] Ed. C. Johnson (NMT, 1961).

(1149–50) 'to secure a pallium for himself and become archbishop of western England, or else to be granted legatine office' again 'in the kingdom, or at least to secure exemption for his see from the jurisdiction of Canterbury'.[1] This is John of Salisbury's account; as with Gilbert's effort at a pallium, we depend mainly on John of Salisbury, a devoted servant of successive archbishops of Canterbury, and a man content to let his wit play freely round these intrigues. We do not know what was the basis of Henry's plea that Winchester should become the seat of an archbishop. It may be that in 1149–50 he was so desperate to be free of Theobald's jurisdiction that any expedient was grist to his mill; the story may even be an invention. But it may have been a serious attempt, and it is likely that in this as in other ways, Gilbert paid him the compliment of imitation. Gilbert is said to have tried to hold on to his abbey when he was promoted bishop.[2] In the 1160's Gilbert was as desperate to evade Becket's jurisdiction as Henry had been to escape from that of Theobald, and with considerably more justification, as it seems to us. Gilbert's claim, like Henry's, is certainly not to be dismissed as frivolous, simply because it failed.

If we consider the substantial background to this plea, we may feel tolerably sure that it did not first enter Gilbert's head, nor indeed, into serious reckoning, between 29 and 31 May 1169. It was clearly something which had been pondered earlier, even if the reaction to his utterance on that occasion suggests that the claim was not widely known before.[3] But it seems likely that Gilbert knew the texts in Geoffrey of Monmouth and Bede—two of the most widely read historians of the Middle Ages—and the

[1] Ann. Winchester in *Ann. Mon.* II, 53. John of Salisbury, *HP* (C), p. 78 (Mrs Chibnall's translation); cf. Saltman, pp. 8–9 for a discussion of why Henry of Blois was not made archbishop.

[2] Though Henry was not his only precedent: Roger, bishop of Salisbury (d. 1139), though a secular, had held Malmesbury and Abbotsbury. Also, an abbot entering a secular chapter might well feel inclined to retain his *pied-à-terre* in the cloister, as Robert de Bethune had retained his close link with Lanthony.

[3] John of Salisbury and Gilbert's other detractors refer to the claim at this point, but not earlier. This suggests that there was some novelty in its becoming public property. It is noticeable too that in 1163 Gilbert defended Canterbury's primacy against York (no. 148).

claim of his cousin before he was translated to London; and it is difficult not to suspect that it was in his mind when he made his singularly obstinate refusal to renew his profession. We do not suggest that he refused profession to Becket solely on this account: but that the claims of his see, his skill and learning as a lawyer, his feelings against Becket and a feeling that he was the true leader of the English church were all elements in the situation when he stood out against the renewal of profession.

There is, however, one substantial argument against the view that he took this claim seriously, in its own right, and that is that he never himself openly referred to it in any extant letter, and never pressed it in public before or after 1169, and not even then to the point of making any formal proposal to pope or king. In 1169 it has all the appearances of an expedient in his dispute with Becket and it may be that it was never more than that. There were, however, very good reasons why he should not have pressed it, even if he did take it seriously. A claim to a pallium could only succeed if the claimant could hope to win the ear of the pope. If Gilbert had any such hope in 1163, he would obviously have to proceed with caution; and the dispute with Becket made it impolitic in the extreme to press any claim with Alexander III. While Becket was in exile there was no hope of interesting the pope in any idea of this kind: it could only be used, like Henry II's threat of seceding to the anti-pope, as a stick to beat the bishop's enemies. If Gilbert took the notion seriously, he had every reason to keep it in the background. After 1170 it seems likely that he abandoned it, and it was clearly not practical politics. It is difficult for us to conceive a situation in which the transfer of Canterbury's pallium to London—or the erection of an independent archbishopric at London[1]—could be taken

---

[1] If there was any such idea. This is not suggested by any of the sources: see above, p. 152n. But the plan to translate Canterbury to London seems to us so unlikely to succeed that one cannot help wondering if a notion of a separate province lay behind it. On the other hand, London lay too near Canterbury to make this satisfactory; and the later schemes of Archbishop Baldwin suggest that the idea of having the metropolitan headquarters within the orbit of the capital (such as, in a sense, Lambeth was later to become) seemed sensible to men without *parti pris*.

seriously. Yet it is clear that Henry II and Foliot reckoned in
Becket's early days that they might manoeuvre the archbishop
into a situation in which he was so heavy an embarrassment to
the pope that he would sacrifice Becket in order to recover the
undivided support of the English church. Becket's martyrdom
removed any such hope. The one surviving reference to London's
pretensions later than 1170 makes this abundantly clear.
This reference occurs in William FitzStephen's *Life of St Thomas
of Canterbury*, and there is more than a touch of irony in it. In his
famous rhapsody on the city of which both FitzStephen and Becket
were citizens by birth, the biographer wrote as follows:

...The bishop's see is in the church of St Paul. It was once a metropolitan see, and will be so again—so it is thought—if the citizens have
their way. But perchance the title of archbishop which Thomas the
blessed martyr held, and the presence of his body, may keep that
dignity for ever in Canterbury, where he lies. But since St Thomas
glorified both these cities—London by his rise and Canterbury by the
setting of his sun—by that same token the one might claim his merit
with greater justice than the other.[1]

Whatever FitzStephen himself really thought, the passage underlines how Becket's murder secured Canterbury from the loss of
its status, yet also reveals that there were still some who took the
claims of London seriously. The citizens of London were proud
folk. They claimed to have the right to join in the election of the
king; they were not unnaturally jealous of the status of Canterbury, which, if a man looked at the history of this island in the
long perspective of Geoffrey of Monmouth's *History*, might well
seem *parvenu*.

Was London's claim, in Gilbert's eyes, a cause to be fought for,
or was it just an expedient in the agonising conflict with Thomas
Becket? To this no certain answer can be given. There is nothing
to forbid the view that he felt the claim worth his serious con-
sideration, as something which might, after careful thought and
cautious sounding, be advanced in all seriousness; and that in the
event he felt compelled to use it as an expedient. This is the most

[1] *MB*, III, 2.

charitable view, and it is not the least probable. In his use of
appeals, especially of the appeal *ad cautelam*, one finds a similar
problem, to which, with rather more confidence, a similar
answer may be given.

THE APPEAL *AD CAUTELAM*

Herbert of Bosham asserted that the frequency and speciousness
of Gilbert's appeals was the talk of the streets. We can hardly
wonder. At Northampton in October 1164 he issued his first
appeal against Becket's charge to the bishops to support him and
excommunicate any who laid hands upon him.[1] From then until
1169 he was never, so to speak, out of quarantine for more than a
few months at a time. In his first appeal he was joined, as twice
later, by a group of his colleagues, but in each case he was the
ringleader, and perhaps the only one of the bishops who took
the appeals with full seriousness throughout their life. The appeal
of 1164 may well have been quashed by the pope at Sens: there is
no special record of its burial. In 1165–6 Gilbert was the victim
of mandates from Thomas and the pope to hand over the churches
sequestrated from the exiled clerks of the archbishop. He asked
the king to release him from this dangerous burden (no. 168),
and parried the mandates by a second appeal. At midsummer
1166 Becket issued his first long list of excommunications, and
the king, the bishops, and almost everyone in England not already
singled out reckoned that the sword hung over them. Gilbert
was able for once to rally substantial support for a series of appeals,
of which the appeal of the bishops was the most formal and
formidable. This was apparently the first appeal *ad cautelam*, an

---

[1] On the appeals, see *MB*, II, 337 ff.; III, 303, 308–9, 322 ff.; IV, 49, 60 ff.;
etc.; cf. Knowles, *EC*, p. 76 (October 1164); no. 166; cf. *EC*, p. 118 (1165–6);
nos. 165–8; *MB*, III, 94 (cf. 393); no. 169, *MB Epp.* 207, 221–2, 231; cf. *EC*, pp.
96–7 (1166); nos. 177, 180–3; *MB*, III, 94 (cf. 412–13); etc.; *MB Epp.* 339, cf.
341–3; cf. *EC*, p. 98 (1167); nos. 198–205, 210; *MB Epp.* 553; Diceto, I, 333 ff.;
Gervase, I, 212; cf. *EC*, pp. 99–100 (1169). (We assume that *MB Epp.* 408, in
which the pope restricts the interference of appeals with the archbishop's
powers, belongs to 1174, in spite of its presence in MSS of the Becket correspondence.)

anticipatory appeal, that is, against a sentence which had not been pronounced, but might fall on them at any moment. Henry backed the bishops so strongly that the pope was compelled to temporise, and the appeals were absorbed into a general investigation of the case by papal legates. The legates (no doubt deliberately) acted as slowly as they could; the final meeting of bishops and legates did not take place until 29 November 1167, when Gilbert, joined by Jocelin of Salisbury and perhaps by Henry of Winchester, renewed his appeal against all the unjust actions of Thomas, past, present and future. From this comprehensive gesture the pope released them in April 1168. But at the beginning of the following Lent rumours began to circulate that the archbishop, now papal legate, and free at last to show his full strength, was preparing to do so. At the beginning of Lent Gilbert issued once again an appeal *ad cautelam*. The archbishop treated it as invalid and excommunicated him on Palm Sunday. After some hesitation, and the conference already described which led the clergy of his diocese to join him in the renewal of his appeal, Gilbert decided to behave as one excommunicate. He submitted to the pope, but his submission was accompanied by a full defence of his appeals, a defence which was repeated at greater length in the literary debate between Canterbury and London devised by Gilbert or one of his supporters about the same time.[1] In his defence of the appeals, he reckoned them to start in 1166 and to number three. Although this left one out of the reckoning, it was perhaps not unjustified, since the appeal of 1166 seems to have been the first general appeal *ad cautelam* against the archbishop. Gilbert begins with two favourite quotations, one from Gratian forbidding the condemnation of a bishop without due warning, the other, the familiar tag *ius suum unicuique* from the *Institutes*; his main argument is concerned to justify the triple appeal. The

---

[1] No. 212; *MB*, IV, 213–43. The literary debate is preserved in MS B only, and although it raises quite frankly and freely the arguments against Gilbert, the latter has the last word, and the nature of the replies, combined with the MS tradition, makes it plain that it emanated from his circle. It has, indeed, quotations and arguments in common with his letters (see below), and shows the same familiarity with Justinian's *Corpus* and with Gratian. It must be the work either of Gilbert or of one of his clerks.

Code forbids a third appeal in the same case and Gratian appears to interpret this to mean that a third appeal is never lawful.[1] Gilbert argues that the ruling of the *Code* must be interpreted as condemning a third appeal only when a case has been lost after trial by three separate judges; it does not apply to an appeal by a bishop against his metropolitan. He points out that after appeal to the Holy See a sentence, if pronounced, is suspended; if given after the appeal it has no force at all. Gilbert has observed the sentence and ceased saying Mass in order to avoid giving scandal, since ordinary folk do not understand these legal distinctions. The legal authorities disagree, however, and so he has abandoned the dispute and received absolution in accordance with the pope's command. But he cannot resist a final thrust: he suggests that the pope should wait in future until a legal charge has been made against him by a plaintiff and suitable witnesses.

Herbert of Bosham and Gilbert both make it plain that it was the frequency of Gilbert's appeals which was chiefly called in question; but there is no hint in this letter that Gilbert felt called on to defend the principle of his appeal. It is true that this was subsequently condemned at the Fourth Lateran Council in 1215, and we can well understand the reason: there is copious evidence that frivolous appeals were a major stumbling block in the development of the papal courts, and the appeal *ad cautelam*, if it had caught on, could have played havoc with serious litigation. But down to the 1160's its use was a rare event, and the indications are that Becket regarded the appeals as frivolous, and so invalid, but not primarily because of the procedure; while Gilbert did not feel the need seriously to defend the latter: it looks very much as if he was not aware that the nature of his appeal was seriously controversial.[2] There is no attempt to defend it in this letter to the pope; and, even more significant, the literary debate of about the same period, which clearly represents Gilbert's case

---

[1] *Code*, 7. 70; *Decretum*, C. 2, q. 6, *dictum post* c. 39.
[2] Cf. *MB Epp*. 223, in which Becket argues against the validity of the appeal of 1166, but in doing so seems to imply that an appeal *ad cautelam* would be justified, but not under current circumstances: i.e. that it was the circumstances, not the procedure, which made the appeal frivolous.

and makes no attempt to skirt awkward arguments, does not refer
to this aspect of Gilbert's appeals. It could be argued that this was
a deliberate avoidance of a particularly difficult issue; but if so it
was a blatant failure, since Gilbert never gives any indication of
admitting a doubt about the validity of his appeals, and the literary
debate twice cites a text which could have been used to give
Gilbert weighty support on just this point.[1] 'As often as bishops
think themselves persecuted by fellow bishops or their metropolitan, *or hold them in suspicion,* let them quickly appeal to the
Roman see;...and meanwhile let no one presume to excommunicate them....If any should so presume, it will be void.' This
passage from Pseudo-Isidore was an unambiguous assertion of the
right of a suffragan to lodge an appeal if he viewed his metropolitan with suspicion. It was quoted in the debate as evidence
that if the metropolitan excommunicated after an appeal, his act
was invalid. We can be sure that if Gilbert had had serious doubts
about the principle of the anticipatory appeal, he would have used
this text to allay them.

This evidence strongly suggests that Gilbert regarded the appeal
ad cautelam as a perfectly correct procedure, even though it was
evidently rare. The text from Pseudo-Isidore suggests a reason
why the pope never apparently openly challenged Gilbert on this
issue: he may well have known that, as the law then stood, however undesirable the appeal *ad cautelam* might be, Gilbert had a
strong case. It is intriguing to consider why the dodge was so
little used, and why Gilbert should have hit on the idea. He was
no doubt a man well practised in searching out legal expedients
when in a difficulty. But there was at least one good precedent in
his own lifetime for a successful appeal *ad cautelam* of which he
was probably aware. In 1138, while Gilbert was still a Cluniac,
presumably at Abbeville, a monk of Cluny was consecrated
bishop of Langres. The case is famous, because Langres was the
diocese in which Clairvaux lay, and St Bernard could not be

---

[1] Gratian, *Decretum*, C. 2, q. 6, c. 16 (*MB*, IV, 218, 238). Here, as in nos. 201,
203, the canon is attributed to Pope Sixtus in error for Pope Felix. In Gratian
it immediately follows one of Pope Sixtus, and this was clearly the source of
the confusion. Both were in fact from Pseudo-Isidore.

indifferent to the choice of his own bishop. In the event, Bernard convinced the pope that the consecration had been illegal, and the pope deposed Gilbert's confrère. The technical ground on which the pope acted is not certainly known, but the only legal irregularity to which Bernard could point was that leading figures in the Langres chapter had appealed to the pope against the metropolitan's decision in the case before it was made. This was clearly an appeal *ad cautelam*, and it seems to have been upheld.[1] If this was so, Gilbert had reason to feel that since St Bernard had kept the archbishop of Lyons at bay, by the same token he could hold off the archbishop of Canterbury. Whatever we may think of the device, legal texts and precedent were probably on Gilbert's side in this matter. This helps us to understand why Gilbert was so confident of the legality of his own procedure.

MULTIPLICEM

In the summer of 1166 the English bishops appealed as a body against the archbishop's future acts, and launched letters to him explaining their point of view in measured, if not tactful, language. These Thomas passed to John of Salisbury, who in one of his most scathing letters (although advocating moderate courses) pointed to Gilbert as their author. This stirred the archbishop's exasperation still further, and he wrote a strongly worded reply to the bishops, accompanied by a fierce rap over the knuckles for Gilbert alone. But Thomas was not Gilbert's equal as a rhetorician, and he can hardly have bargained for the scorching rejoinder which Gilbert delivered. Never has the case against Becket been stated more elaborately, or with greater venom, than in the letter *Multiplicem nobis*. It represents the fullest statement of Gilbert's

[1] On the Langres election, see G. Constable in *Traditio*, XIII (1957), 119–52; on the legal issue, see esp. pp. 137–9. On p. 138 and nn. Prof. Constable cites Gratian, C. 2, q. 6, c. 25 (actually a Roman Law text) and St Bernard against appeals before sentence. A comparison of this and c. 16 in the same *quaestio* (see above) makes it clear that the issue at this time was not whether the appeal *ad cautelam* was legal, but the intention of the appellant. It is quite likely that the failure of Gilbert's friend at Arras in 1148 (no. 78) was due to the same procedure as at Langres.

grounds for opposing Becket, and has been regarded as the strongest ground for condemning Gilbert himself; as rhetoric it is his masterpiece. On all these grounds it demands our close attention.

Its authenticity has indeed been doubted; it has been suggested that it was a *jeu d'esprit* designed by Gilbert's enemies to discredit him. In view of Professor Knowles's full investigation of this question,[1] this argument needs no full answer here: it is inconceivable that any supporter of Becket could have given away so many hostages. There was much that could be said about the twists and turns of Becket's career, and *Multiplicem* says it. It is the work of an enemy; and although it is rhetorically superior to any other of Gilbert's effusions, there are copious indications of his mind and style. The special skill of the letter may indicate that he had helpers in it, or it may mean that he took even more than the two days needed to devise his letter to Brian FitzCount, that a great occasion stirred his latent talents to the full. However this may be, there can be no question that Gilbert inspired the letter and provided its main arguments.

It is perhaps surprising that it should have survived. Becket and his followers could hardly have been blamed if they had torn it up; Gilbert, converted to acknowledge Becket a martyr,[2] might well feel even more reluctant to preserve it. It is clear, however, that both author and recipient preserved it, and this is the most cogent evidence of all for its authenticity. It is preserved in three manuscripts, all of the twelfth century: in the magnificent Canterbury book in the Cotton collection which contains the earliest and best text of the collection of lives and letters of the archbishop put together by Alan of Tewkesbury;[3] in the Douce manuscript (D) which represents Gilbert's own effort to justify his

---

[1] *EC*, Appendix VII.

[2] See above, pp. 102–3.

[3] Cotton Claudius B. iv, fos. 93 (92) ff.; cf. *GFL*, introd. Alan, prior of Christ Church, Canterbury (1179–86), later abbot of Tewkesbury (1186–1202), seems to have edited materials left by John of Salisbury when he departed to become bishop of Chartres in 1176, to have added his own Life to John's and arranged and edited the letters with considerable skill and fidelity between 1176 and 1179 or 1180.

behaviour, and is probably a copy of a collection of the early 1170's; and in the Bodleian collection (B) of Gilbert's letters of the late 1170's. Alan made his definitive collection of the correspondence *c.* 1176–9, and it is clear that both his predecessors and successors viewed *Multiplicem* with suspicion. It appears in no earlier surviving collection, and later scribes of Alan's lives and letters refused to copy it, even though it appears from time to time in their indexes.[1] Some may have been put off by its length; but it is more probable that its vituperative contents led to its neglect.

The same reason seems to have given its author some disquiet. In the Douce manuscript *Multiplicem* appears in its proper place, but the author's name is suppressed; in B it appears at the very end, as a final afterthought, once again with the author's name suppressed.[2] It looks as if it had nearly been jettisoned altogether by Gilbert himself by the late 1170's.

In view of this, we may be reasonably certain that the copy in Alan's collection was derived from Becket's archive, not from Gilbert's. The text of one of Gilbert's letters in the same part of Alan's collection differs materially from that in B, and it seems probable that the difference is between a draft preserved in Gilbert's archive and the letter actually sent.[3] This may suggest that some of Gilbert's letters were kept by Becket and reproduced from his files; and it is in general unlikely that any of Becket's protégés would have asked Gilbert for copies of his letters in the 1170's. The unlikelihood virtually amounts to impossibility in the case of *Multiplicem*: it would indeed be extraordinary if Gilbert had furnished Alan with a copy complete with his own name, while he was carefully suppressing this in the copies preserved in his own office. Although the textual variants are slight, we may be reasonably certain that the Cotton copy derives from Becket's archives, the two others from Gilbert's. The suppression of the name in Gilbert's copies does not cast any doubt on the letter's authorship, rather the reverse: the letter itself reveals that it is an

---

[1] *Multiplicem* occurs twice in the index of Cod. Vatic. Lat. 1220 (fourteenth century), but not in the text (see note to letter).

[2] See above, p. 28.

[3] See *GFL*, notes to letter 197.

answer to Becket's attack on Gilbert,[1] and by placing his name last
in the roll-call of the bishops who 'stood firm' at Clarendon,
Gilbert proclaims his authorship. The textual evidence thus
demonstrates at the very least that the letter circulated in Gilbert's
and Thomas's circles in the latter's lifetime, and always purported
to be a letter from Gilbert to Thomas. It thus very strongly confirms the other evidence that it is genuine.

Multiplicem was preserved, but reluctantly: why was it preserved at all? It is clear that the great bulk of the correspondence
survived largely because Becket wished it to: he inspired the men
like John of Salisbury and Alan of Tewkesbury who gathered the
letters after his death. It is a reasonable conjecture that the letter
was kept on Becket's own instructions; and it is a striking testimony to the self-confidence of his later years and to his sense of
veracity. He wished none of the evidence to be suppressed.
Foliot's motives are something of a puzzle. The presence of the
letter in D suggests that he felt that its arguments still stood; the
removal of his name shows that he had doubts about its tone. Its
omission from its natural context in B suggests that Gilbert had
decided to suppress his masterpiece. The book was completed:
the chief clerk, if such he was, filled all the blank spaces and
rounded off his work.[2] Then, at the very end of the enterprise,
another scribe added a final quire, consisting solely of *Multiplicem*.
Did the ageing bishop relent?—or did one of his clerks insert it
without his knowledge? We shall never know.

Gilbert starts by raising his eyebrows: why has he been singled
out? Why has Thomas, a man of sober disposition and dignified
office, become so heated after reading a few innocent home truths
(*ad uerba ueritatis...innocentiam filii*)? Gilbert can hardly take this
in silence, or allow his contemporaries, or posterity, to take his
silence for a confession. Suavely Gilbert sets the tone of the letter,
a tone of shocked astonishment brilliantly sustained; and he makes
it plain that this is no private diatribe against his metropolitan,
but an open letter to justify himself in the eyes of contemporaries

---

[1] See notes to the letter in *GFL*: it contains many echoes of Becket's letter,
MB Epp. 224.
[2] See above, p. 26.

and of posterity. The letter which follows has many rhetorical twists, and debating points; but no attempt is made to win Becket over or make any concession to him. Every action of Becket's is set in its least favourable light. It is plain that Becket is only the audience in a purely formal sense: Gilbert is an advocate pleading in a court. It thus takes its place beside the controversial pamphlets of the twelfth century: St Bernard's appeal to a group of French bishops to support Innocent II, which may have been one of his models, and the invectives of Arnulf of Lisieux and John of Salisbury on the schism of 1159.[1] In tone it is very similar to these. Bernard's and Arnulf's jar on a modern audience more than Gilbert's. John of Salisbury's letter picked up the manifesto of the Council of Pavia and tore it to pieces. This is a version of the normal technique in answering a personal letter, whereby a writer charges his Latin and shapes his argument so that neither is intelligible unless the letter which is being answered is to hand. *Multiplicem* is charged with echoes of Becket's reprimand; but the answer is a debater's answer. The controversy had in any case reached a maximum of intensity, and both sides were heated. But *Multiplicem* is both more intelligible and more excusable considered as the manifesto of a cause than as a personal note from a suffragan to his archbishop. This helps to explain how Gilbert could be prepared to use it as an instrument of self-justification even after he had begun to have doubts about confessing its authorship.

The bishops, led by Gilbert, had commented severely on the way Becket became archbishop. In his letter to Gilbert Becket parried this, observing that there was no opposition at the time— save perhaps from those who coveted the post themselves; he also accused the English bishops of cowardice, and taunted Gilbert (whom John of Salisbury had likened to Doeg and Achitophel) with wishing to make him a Judas. These are the themes which provided Gilbert with his framework, and in subtler ways too numerous to mention he echoes the archbishop's taunts and accusations.

[1] St Bernard, *Ep.* 126; Arnulf, *Letters*, ed. F. Barlow, no. 28; *JS Epp.* I, no. 124.

Before God, he says, I did not aspire to the archbishopric.
Cupidity is indeed the root of our troubles, but I have offered no
gifts with a view to promotion. I made no complaint on my own
account, but on God's. I foresaw what was to come. Who is
ignorant that you paid many thousand marks for the chancellorship, and that this breeze—the pun on breeze and gold, *aura* and
aurum, cannot be rendered in English—has blown you into the
harbour of the church of Canterbury? In this way Gilbert throws
back the charge of cupidity, with slightly forced ingenuity.[1] He
then launches into a description of the path from Becket's election
as archbishop to his flight from Northampton. Becket had
accused Gilbert of ambition in 1162 and cowardice and treachery
in 1164. The charges are returned with interest: Becket was himself the ambitious candidate in 1162; it was he who showed
cowardice at Clarendon by giving way to the king and at Northampton by flight. It would be tedious to follow the argument in
all its rich and confusing detail, although the letter itself, with its
occasional sudden and dramatic changes of mood, and with the
ingenuity (sometimes perverse) with which Becket's charges are
turned inside out, makes fascinating reading. The evidence is
against Gilbert on several critical points. It is probable that
Becket resisted his own promotion and warned the king of the
consequences. It is only too apparent that Gilbert does not believe
in Becket's conversion. It was no doubt difficult to make out
then, as it is now, precisely what had happened to the worldly
chancellor when he became archbishop. Gilbert's view seems unfair
on any showing. In his account of Clarendon he reads a roll-call
of the English bishops who stood firm against the royal demands:
it is reminiscent of the roll-call of bishops loyal to Pope Innocent
in St Bernard's letter, or of the witnesses to Henry of Blois's
instruction to Brian FitzCount to support the empress in Brian's
surviving letter. It is less reminiscent of what we know about
Clarendon. It is true that Becket in the end suddenly collapsed

---

[1] It may well have been normal for the king to extract large sums from a
new chancellor, and it is quite likely that we can believe Foliot that Becket paid
heavily for the office, although there is no record in the Pipe Rolls and no
supporting evidence (cf. Knowles, *Historian and Character*, p. 106 and n.).

and gave way, and that he did it without consulting his colleagues. But it is reasonable to think that this was partly because he had so little cause to trust their support.[1] Becket behaved badly at Clarendon under difficult circumstances and vacillated thereafter: Foliot has blown the incidents up into as large a scandal as could be managed. It enables him to unveil little by little a very pretty picture of Becket as a vacillating coward who betrayed his colleagues. The climax comes at Northampton in October 1164, when the archbishop, finding his lands and properties threatened as well as the liberties of the Church, fled the country and left his colleagues defenceless.

The sword from which *you* fled hangs over *us*.... You have invited us perhaps to fly likewise; but the sea is closed to us. Since your flight all ships and all the ports are guarded against us. Islands are powerful bulwarks (*claustra*) of the lands of kings, from which a man may scarcely slip away. If we must fight, we shall fight at close quarters; if we must join battle with the king, where we smite with the sword, in the same spot will the sword of the enemy find us. If we deliver wounds, here stand we to receive them. And your annual revenues, my lord—do they mean so much to you that you would buy them with the blood of your brothers? The Jews repudiated the money which Judas returned to them, because they knew it was the price of blood.

With extraordinary ingenuity Gilbert switches from beating the drums to a venomous whisper.

Si cum rege pugna conseritur, unde percutiemus gladio, nos ibi gladius repercutientis inueniet; unde uulnus infligemus, uulnera declinare nequibimus. Et annui uestri redditus—nunquid uobis tanti sunt, ut fratrum uestrorum sanguine uobis hos uelitis acquiri? At Iuda reportante pecuniam, hanc Iudei respuerunt, quam sanguinis esse pretium agnouerunt.

The sudden change from *fortissimo* to *piano* was an old rhetorical trick used here with a skill worthy of a better argument. For Gilbert is in effect saying that Thomas has betrayed his colleagues

---

[1] On Becket's behaviour at Clarendon, see Knowles, *Historian and Character*, p. 111; *EC*, pp. 60 ff.

who had steadfastly resisted the royal onslaught; and he now goes on to say that Henry II is a good man of devout intentions who is bursting to set off on crusade. The right way to deal with him is not by violent attack, but by quiet remonstrance. No great issue is at stake: a few customs have been propounded which would best be altered by patience; Henry, indeed, would have surrendered them, save for his reverence for his ancestors and his fear of being accused of having the concession extorted from him by force. And finally, using the tone of patient sweet reasonableness which is affected most of the way through, Gilbert invites the archbishop to follow the example of Zacchaeus, and climb down. On this note the letter ends.

If the picture of the steadfast bishops at Clarendon is overdrawn, the pious and reasonable Henry II is fantasy.[1] Must we then conclude that it tells more against its author than against his enemy? —that 'its cold and unrelenting hatred, which cannot pardon error or understand generosity, comes from the abundance of a heart in which humility and love had long ceased to harbour'?[2] It may be said at once that *Multiplicem* is exceptional only in its

---

[1] Cf. *EC*, pp. 124–5. The most dubious passage is that in which Gilbert portrays the pious king preparing to leave his devoted family to go on crusade. The plan for a crusade is not otherwise recorded at this time, but *MB Epp.* 457 seems to show that such an idea was in the wind before *c*. Feb. 1169 (cf. no. 170 n.), and there is nothing improbable in its being adumbrated (or it may have been discussed between Becket and Henry in earlier days: cf. below, p. 179). In view of later family quarrels and infidelities, the picture of the happy family seems absurd. But we must beware of applying hindsight: no. 167 shows that the English bishops at large were prepared to put their names to a very similar statement, and *MB Epp.* 457 shows that John of Salisbury subscribed to a generally favourable view of Henry II's character in this period (he had reservations, naturally enough, but not on his family life). There is no clear evidence that Henry was unfaithful to Eleanor before the early 1170's (cf. V. B. Heltzel, *Fair Rosamond*, Evanston, 1947, chap. 1. The elder illegitimate children *may* have been conceived before their marriage); they were a good deal together in 1166–7, and in the latter year their youngest child, John, was born (R. W. Eyton, *Court, Household and Itinerary of Henry II*, pp. 98 ff.); the breach between father and sons was growing between 1170 and 1173, and came to a head in 1173. There is no reason to suppose that later events could have been foreseen in 1166. But the picture of Henry as a pious family man must have been quite unreal at any time.

[2] *EC*, p. 180, the conclusion of Professor Knowles's very penetrating discussion of the authenticity of the letter.

power: its author was evidently angry, as well he might be; but the language he uses was mainly from the stock-in-trade of medieval controversy. Yet one is bound to admit that the technical skill of the letter does not carry conviction. Gilbert has spoiled a good argument by constant and ingenious over-straining of his case. Yet it seems to us that this was rather the product of the exceptionally difficult position in which Gilbert found himself than of spiritual blindness. This can only be understood if we first reconstruct Gilbert's own attitude to the quarrel between king and archbishop.

In *Multiplicem* Gilbert deployed an elaborate argument which might be used, under certain circumstances, to justify the submission of an archbishop to the judgement of a royal court. The basis of the argument is that one must distinguish between the temporal and spiritual possessions of the Church: spiritual possessions, tithes, offerings and the like, are immune from lay jurisdiction; temporal possessions—lands granted by kings and other laymen, who have therefore the right to attach conditions to their gifts—are subject to royal jurisdiction. As spiritual lords the bishops are subject to the heavenly king, as earthly lords they are earls or barons. As such, Henry could summon Thomas to his court. Gilbert also deploys, even before this, two other arguments: first, he suggests that a king may be regarded as an ecclesiastical judge owing to the special character of his unction; and secondly he quotes the letter of Pope Leo IV (of doubtful authenticity) in which he invited the Emperor Louis II to correct any errors of judgement he might have committed.[1] It has been supposed that these represent the basis of Gilbert's own position, but this is not what he himself says, and the arguments are conflicting. Gilbert is trying to argue that Thomas has acted with absurd inconsistency: he first submitted to Henry's summons, then refused his jurisdiction. Gilbert accepts this refusal, and quotes three texts from canon law saying that no bishop or clerk may submit to judgement by a secular court. He then goes on to conjecture on Becket's grounds for answering the summons to

---

[1] Gratian, C. 2, q. 7, c. 41. On this curious text, see W. Ullmann in *Ephemerides Iuris Canonici*, IX (1953), num. 3–4.

Northampton, and puts the arguments outlined above into Becket's mouth. He specifically says at each point that perhaps Becket was guided by this argument: 'you reckon the king...not only a secular but an ecclesiastical judge....Perhaps you adduce in confirmation....If this is your view, then the opinion of those who hold that the king should deal with' some though not all ecclesiastical suits 'falls in with your wisdom'. Putting the arguments in Becket's mouth is an artificial twist, because no one would suppose that Becket accepted any such notions. It might therefore seem plausible to assume that they represent Foliot's own principles, were it not for the evident contradiction between the view that anointing with chrism makes a king an ecclesiastical judge and the view that a bishop can be judged, not as bishop but as baron. It is clear, in fact, that Gilbert is simply quoting current arguments on the subject.

The arguments are extremely interesting. It is indeed remarkable that this passage is the only substantial statement of theoretical grounds in support of what may, perhaps a little loosely, be called a moderate royalism as opposed to the consistent papalism of Becket. In the late eleventh century and the first quarter of the twelfth, a large pamphlet literature was composed representing a remarkably wide divergence of views on the relations of *regnum* and *sacerdotium*. The strength of the party opposed to strict Gregorian principles lay in the force of conservative opinion, which remembered the way in which a Charlemagne or a Henry III had governed the Church. In stating their principles they not surprisingly followed a variety of different lines of argument; by and large they did not match the papal apologists for coherence, though in part they make up for this in brilliance and ingenuity. Their strength lay, however, not in the statement of principles so much as in practice and tradition. As the twelfth century went on, the memory of the tenth and early eleventh centuries faded a little, and more and more leading churchmen were brought up to know and assume the principles of the revived canon law, which had the effective primacy of Rome at its centre. It became increasingly rare for anti-papal views to be stated in writing. The Becket dispute raised much argument, but almost no pamphlet literature.[1] This does not mean, however, that principles were forgotten, or the papal view tacitly accepted. The notion that chrism made an anointed king in some sense an ecclesiastic had been under fire for centuries.[2] The pope had forbidden the use of chrism at all in the imperial coronation in the ninth or tenth century: holy oil was employed throughout in the anointing. Chrism (oil and balsam) was especially associated with the ordination of priests and consecration of bishops, and this symbolic association made it suspect to the papal reformers, but all the more precious to the kings of Europe. The popes campaigned against the use of chrism, and eventually, a generation after *Multiplicem*, Innocent III condemned it. This campaign had some effect: in the anointing of Henry III in 1216, made under papal auspices, chrism was not used; it apparently went out for a century. Professor Schramm indeed believed that chrism had not been used as early as 1154. But the manuscripts on which he relied are considerably later, and there is no contemporary evidence to contradict the formal statement of Gilbert Foliot, who had been present in 1154, that chrism was used.[3] Gilbert's argu-

---

[1] Notable exceptions are the literary debate and the *Summa cause* between Henry and Thomas, printed in *MB*, IV, 201 ff. Both were preserved in Gilbert's archives, although the latter was apparently written by one of his enemies. To this one should add some letters of Bosham and others written as literary exercises, and make allowance for the fact that John of Salisbury and others relieved their feelings at length in their letters. But none of these covers the grounds of the controversy in the way in which numerous pamphlets had worked over the principles of lay investiture, etc., two or three generations earlier.

[2] Cf. W. Ullmann, *Growth of Papal Government* (London, 1955), pp. 225 ff.; for a somewhat later discussion, cf. F. M. Powicke, *Stephen Langton* (Oxford, 1928), p. 109.

[3] P. E. Schramm, *A History of the English Coronation* (Oxford, 1937), pp. 120–1, 126–7 and notes, assumed on the basis of the printed version of the Anselm *ordo* (L. G. Wickham Legg, *English Coronation Records*, Westminster, 1901), pp. 30–9, that chrism was not used in coronations of the second half of the twelfth century. But this text is taken from a thirteenth-century MS. So far as can be judged from the printed pontificals in the Henry Bradshaw Society (and the editors' notes) all the twelfth-century MSS indicate that chrism should be used on the head; and Diceto, II, 20, is explicit that it had been used in 1170. This supports Gilbert's statement about the coronation of 1154. The *Gesta Henrici II* (II, 82) only refers to holy oil in 1189 but Diceto (II, 69) says that he himself served it to the archbishop then. We may assume that chrism was not

ment not only clears up a difficulty in the records of the English coronation, but shows that papal condemnation of the use of chrism had some point: the significance of chrism did not pass unnoticed.

Even more interesting is the argument that temporalities and spiritualities should be distinguished; that bishops are also earls or barons. In this, as Professor Knowles pointed out, Gilbert was following an argument recently used by Gerhoh of Reichersberg.[1] It is improbable that Gilbert had read the relevant passages in Gerhoh. What Gerhoh had done was to find words for what had come to be accepted practice; and the same seems to be true of Gilbert's exposition. Lanfranc and William I and II had treated the bishop of Bayeux and the bishop of Durham as secular lords, and in the former case the king is reported to have said so unambiguously.[2] The rough-and-ready treatment meted out to these men would have seemed to some a trifle old-fashioned in the 1160's; but the distinction between spiritualities and temporalities on which it was based—and which implied that in some degree at least the bishops could be treated as lay lords—was generally

used in 1216, when the coronation was organised by the papal legate. (Cf. Ullmann, *op. cit.* p. 228 n. 2; Peter of Blois, *Ep.* 150, *PL*, CCVII, col. 440. For the use of chrism on the king's head, cf. Peter Lombard, *Sent.* iv, 23, *PL*, CXCII, col. 899, based on Hugh of St Victor, *De sacr.* xv, 1, *PL*, CLXXVI, col. 577.)

[1] *EC*, pp. 82–4, 153–4, citing Gerhoh, *Liber de novitatibus huius temporis*, *MGH, Libelli de Lite*, III, 296–8, 300–1; *De investigatione Antichristi*, pp. 333 ff., 343 ff.; cf. Ullmann, *Growth of Papal Government*, p. 411, n. 3. P. Classen, *Gerhoch von Reichersberg* (Wiesbaden, 1960), p. 314 and n. 33, points out that the similarity is one of argument, and that there is no evidence of verbal borrowing. In view of the slightness of Gerhoh's immediate influence, and the scarcity of MSS, Classen's view that direct influence on Gilbert is 'ganz unwahrscheinlich' seems not unreasonable. Classen, pp. 177 ff., shows that Gerhoh's doctrine (although not identical with the official doctrine of Frederick Barbarossa) fitted closely into the practice of his day in Germany; the same could be said of English practice. (For the dates of these works, see Classen, pp. 420 ff.) On the question of *regalia*, see I. Ott in *Zeitschr. der Savigny-Stiftung für Rechtsgeschichte, Kan. Abt.* XXXV (1948), 234–304; M. Howell, *Regalian Right in Medieval England* (London, 1962).

[2] Orderic, ed. A. Le Prevost and L. Delisle, III, 247; *De iniusta vexatione...* in Symeon of Durham, ed. T. Arnold, RS, I, 170–95 (whose authenticity has been impugned by H. S. Offler in *EHR*, LXVI, 1951, 321–41; but see Southern, *St Anselm and His Biographer*, p. 148 n.).

accepted. It had indeed been specifically condemned by Pope Paschal II, and although it had been suggested as a solution to the difficulties of the Investiture Disputes by more than one writer,[1] Gerhoh is one of the very few authors openly to defend it in the mid- or late-twelfth century. In practice, however, it had been tacitly accepted in England that the temporal possessions of a bishopric, or of an abbey which held directly from the king, were in the king's hands during a vacancy, and that the bishop or abbot owed services fully comparable to those of a lay baron.[2] In course of time the popes themselves retreated from Paschal II's position: by the thirteenth century the distinction between spiritualities and temporalities became the basis of assessments for papal taxation.[3]

But popes and canonists were extremely reluctant to accept the full implications of Gerhoh's doctrine; very largely, no doubt, because it was difficult to avoid the wholly unacceptable corollary that this might make the bishop subject to the judgement of the royal court. Gerhoh, indeed, had proposed a compromise to avoid the situation arising in which the king pronounced judgement on the bishop for anything save his temporalities. If a bishop broke his oath to the king, he could be deposed by his ecclesiastical superior, then relieved of his temporal fee by the king. This solution is not suggested by Gilbert in this passage, but there is some evidence that it represented his own view. Three of Becket's biographers indicate that at Northampton in 1164 Roger of York, Hilary of Chichester and Gilbert Foliot agreed to demand Becket's deposition from the pope if they could be excused from joining Henry in pronouncing judgement on him in the king's court. This would be consistent with Gilbert's apparently

---

[1] The distinction between 'secularia' and 'spiritualia' was advocated, or rather assumed, by Wido of Ferrara (c. 1086: MGH, Libelli de Lite, I, 564–5), and by Gregory of Catina (c. 1111, op. cit., Libelli, I, 538: for 'secularia' he uses the phrase 'secularium rerum seu temporalium atque corporalium possessionum') and countered by Placidus of Nonantula (1111, Libelli, II, 586–7). The distinction seems implicit in Const. of Clarendon, c. 11, which was not condemned by the pope.

[2] In practice, however, Henry II laid hands on 'spiritualities' as well as 'temporalities': see Howell, op. cit.

[3] Cf. W. E. Lunt, The Valuation of Norwich (Oxford, 1926), pp. 75–9.

sincere quotation in *Multiplicem* of the texts forbidding a clerk to be tried by a secular judge.[1]

Most of the arguments which Gilbert puts into Becket's mouth were not only anathema to Becket, but were only accepted with reservations by Gilbert himself. Why was he so reluctant to state plainly his own principles and the basis of his own actions that he developed this long and artificial debate with an imaginary Becket? Partly, it may be, because Becket himself had expressed some of these views as chancellor. The more one reads *Multiplicem*, the clearer it becomes that Gilbert is arguing, not with Becket the archbishop, but with Becket the chancellor. At first sight this seems a waste of time: the chancellor was no more. But in a document of this kind one must never forget the context out of which it came. It is an answer to a letter from Becket. One of the most serious charges made by Becket had been that Gilbert himself had coveted the office of archbishop, and Gilbert's well-known resistance to Becket's appointment was a plausible basis for this charge. It was therefore inevitable that Gilbert should harp on the chancellor's failings, should wish above all to justify his resistance in 1162 by the chancellor's behaviour. The letter appears to describe the events which followed 1162, but this is in part a subterfuge: Gilbert justifies his resistance in 1162 by trying to show that the old Adam was still governing Becket in 1164. And when Gilbert paints his fancy picture of the virtuous Henry II, it is a very reasonable guess that he was raising a ghost which Becket himself had raised in earlier days. We know too little of Becket as chancellor to be able to prove this; but there are twists and turns in *Multiplicem* which make better sense if Gilbert is reproducing arguments Thomas himself had enjoyed in his previous incarnation. This would explain why what is in effect an open letter should also be so deliberately addressed to Thomas himself, should take the form of a smooth discourse with Thomas. It may well be that it was an echo of the sort of smooth discourse with which Becket the chancellor had tormented the bishops in earlier days. If so, we can understand why Gilbert continued to

---

[1] See *MB*, II, 396; III, 308–9; IV, 49; above, p. 174: the three texts are all emphatic.

regard it as a fair defence until the canonisation of the martyr made it imperative to bury the chancellor.

There was, however, another and even stronger reason why Gilbert should be reluctant to show his hand. Whatever the theory might be, the bishops of any European kingdom in the twelfth century were bound to accept some compromise in practice if they were to combine obedience to pope and reviving canon law with service to their king.[1] This service was not only an obligation they could not easily evade—or they would tremble to evade, if the king had the strength of Henry II—but it was their traditional duty, and their conscientious duty: a kingdom's peace and good government largely depended on cooperation between the king and those magnates with the strongest stake in peaceful government, the bishops and abbots. Gilbert may or may not have believed that chrism made Henry II a kind of ecclesiastic, but he and his like certainly thought it represented the seal of divine authority on the monarch's brow. We need not doubt his sincerity when he described, almost lyrically, the happy cooperation of the two swords when Becket was chancellor.[2] This was the ideal arrangement. Everyone knew that conflicts could easily occur, but woe to the man through whom they occurred: Theobald had been a master at avoiding open conflict, Thomas, as chancellor, had ruled the king by diplomacy, while as archbishop he proved as tactless as could be. Gilbert no doubt appreciated some of the archbishop's difficulties, but we can sympathise with his exasperation; all the more because it is clear that up to Northampton all the bishops, even in a measure Becket himself, had assumed that some measure of compromise had to be accepted. Alan of Tewkesbury records in some detail a debate among the bishops at Northampton.[3] Each in turn gave his advice to the archbishop. Gilbert and Henry of Winchester, as dean and precentor of the province, opened. Gilbert advised resignation, using arguments very similar to those used in the bishops' letters of appeal: Alan may well have drawn on this in

---

[1] Cf. Cheney, *From Becket to Langton*, chaps. II–IV; Southern, *St Anselm and His Biographer*, pp. 142–50.   [2] No. 170, also printed *MB*, v, 526.
[3] *MB*, II, 326–8; cf. Knowles, *EC*, pp. 72–3.

making up the speech.[1] Henry of Winchester disagreed: it would be a dangerous precedent; if the archbishop and primate set such an example, what would happen to the rest of us? Hilary of Chichester accepted Henry's view in principle, but in times of crisis recommended some compromise: he suggested a temporary submission. The bishop of Lincoln, Gilbert's uncle ('a simple man of little wisdom' says Alan unkindly), reckoned that the king was after blood, and Thomas must surrender either his archbishopric or his life—'and I don't see what he will get out of the archbishopric if he's dead'. Bartholomew of Exeter also counselled compromise, since the times were evil, and the attack a personal, not a general one; only by a personal retreat could the Church at large be saved. Roger of Worcester refused to give advice: to counsel submission to the king was against his conscience; to counsel resistance would make him an outlaw. We need not suppose that these speeches are historical: in accordance with the convention of his age, Alan was recording the range of opinions which he reckoned to be appropriate to the occasion and the speakers. What is significant is that most of the bishops are made to accept in principle that the archbishop should resist the king, and that a majority also reckon that in practice compromise is necessary. Nor was the archbishop clear in his own mind: this discussion left him in that state of agonised doubt which prevailed from Friday till Tuesday, when, strengthened by the Mass *Etenim sederunt principes*, he had his cross carried before him into the king's presence, and wrung from an angry Foliot the famous taunt 'He always was a fool and always will be'.[2] The indecision, even at so late a stage, strongly confirms Alan's testimony that most of the bishops reckoned some degree of submission necessary.

They were simply putting into words what had in some measure inspired their actions and those of their predecessors since the time, not very long before, when the king's word had counted for more, the pope's for far less, than they did in 1164. On one vital point the Constitutions of Clarendon made no declaration: on how a decision was reached in a papal schism. The silence of

[1] Cf. II, 326 with nos. 166–7 (and notes to those letters in *GFL*).
[2] *MB*, III, 57 (FitzStephen); etc.; cf. Knowles, *EC*, p. 78, n. 1.

the Constitutions can best be explained by Henry's security—his grip on this issue was unchallenged—partly by the assumption that the issue was dead. The letters written by John of Salisbury for Archbishop Theobald reveal indeed that Theobald was far from powerless; but he exerted his power while allowing the king the illusion that he was making the decision. In the papal schism in 1159, Theobald made it perfectly clear that he accepted that Henry would decide to which pope the English church adhered, and he made it equally clear that Henry would, and must, decide for Alexander. A study of episcopal 'elections'[1] in Henry's early years would show likewise that Theobald ensured suitable appointments, not by pleading for canonical and free election, but by using all his influence to get the king to accept his candidates. The weakness of this diplomatic technique was that when the guiding hand was removed Henry felt free to act as he liked, and that after Becket's murder the king controlled episcopal elections more tightly, if possible, than before 1162. On both issues Theobald's practice—accepted, so far as we can tell, by his colleagues—was perfectly clear; yet nothing could be clearer than that under strict canon law the elections of popes and bishops were not matters for kings to decide.

In putting the Constitutions of Clarendon in writing, according to the view of Z. N. Brooke, which has won general acceptance, Henry II made it inevitable that what had been for the most part established custom should be condemned by the pope. A conscientious bishop was put into a position of extreme difficulty;

[1] The procedure laid down in the Constitutions of Clarendon, c. 12, was probably that commonly followed when Henry I sat on the throne. In Henry II's time the temporalities of vacant sees were in his hands, and homage and fealty were apparently exacted before consecration (cf. no. 220, which indicates that all the bishops had sworn fealty and/or done homage). But there is no evidence that elections were conducted in the royal chapel (as in Const. Clarendon); there is indeed almost no evidence of the procedure between 1154 and 1161 (see Saltman, pp. 126 ff.). Becket's election did not take place in the royal chapel but in England, and the form of the elections in 1173 seems to have been canonical (cf. nos. 220-1 and notes: Henry II was abroad, and the young king staged his protest, not at the elections, but when the bishops were gathered for the consecration). On this point Henry does not seem to have insisted; but he secured the election of his nominees no less effectively for that.

and while we may refuse to accept Gilbert's account of how all the bishops save Becket himself stood firm at Clarendon, we may reasonably accept the view that the bishops did everything they could to avoid agreeing to the promulgation of the Constitutions. Once the Constitutions were published, and most of them condemned by the pope, it became even more imperative than usual for a conscientious bishop who wished to prevent open conflict to avoid a public statement of his principles on a controversial topic. It can be argued that conflict was now necessary: Henry II had to be brought to his senses. If so, it was not immediately clear to Becket or his colleagues. He was still in doubt from January till October; and most of them remained in doubt long after that. But this doubt did not amount to surrender to the king.

Gilbert Foliot himself never gave up the idea—anyway until the 1170's—that Becket's appointment was a disaster which could only be rectified by his resignation. He therefore worked hard for the archbishop's removal; but clearly he reckoned that Becket must be removed by the pope, not by the king. Apart from his relations with Becket, Gilbert does not appear as a time-server or an ultra-royalist. If we may use the analogy of the reign of Charles I, he was not Strafford, who went over wholeheartedly to the king, but Hyde, who tried to save the situation by keeping the king within the bounds of tolerable custom. If we consider Gilbert's attitude to the Constitutions as revealed by his writings and his known actions, then we must say that Achitophel has no bad record. It is well known that he tried to avoid formal disobedience both to pope and king, and this has sometimes been viewed as showing obedience to the pope in the letter but not in spirit. Yet it is only fair to suppose that he walked the razor's edge in order to preserve the possibility of a reasonable peace. He was regarded as the effective ruler of the English church in Becket's absence; control of the affairs of the church was generally attributed to him.[1] He therefore deserves some credit for Henry's

---

[1] In *MB Epp.* 252 (late 1166) John of Salisbury reports that the king recently wrote to Gilbert 'quod se, totum regnum suum, et causam que inter ipsum et ecclesiam uertitur, ipsius tanquam patris et fidelissimi amici committat arbitrio. Et precipit ut officiales sui ei in omnibus usquequaque obediant.' Cf. Knowles, *EC*, pp. 115 ff.

comparative moderation in everything not directly connected with Becket; above all, for the fact, as it seems to be, that no serious attempt was made to go over to the anti-pope. This is one of the major puzzles of the crisis; it seems that the English bishops, like Theobald in 1159–60, left the king with the appearance of decision, but made it clear to him that he must not decide for secession.[1]

If one examines Gilbert Foliot's attitude to the Constitutions, it becomes evident that he strove very hard indeed to avoid the open acceptance of those which were obnoxious. Two crucial constitutions forbade appeals to the pope and the excommunication of tenants-in-chief without royal consent. It is true that Gilbert did everything he could to avoid being involved in the excommunication of a tenant-in-chief, that he presumably had the king's consent for most of his appeals to the pope, that there is no evidence for his attitude on some of the issues in the Constitutions. But the rapidity of some of his appeals seems to show that he reckoned he could if necessary appeal without royal consent, and there is no evidence that he accepted the king's view on criminous clerks.[2] In *Multiplicem* he quoted, as we have seen, the most

---

[1] There were indeed intrigues between Henry II and the emperor in 1165–6. In no. 155 Gilbert warned the pope of the danger of secession; in *MB Epp.* 213 Henry told Rainald of Dassel that he wished to secede; the threat and negotiations connected with it are referred to in *MB Epp.* 214, 194, 199, 151, 270 (all letters of John of Salisbury). But *MB Epp.* 213 is the only specific indication of Henry's wish, and the purpose of the letter was to obtain imperial escort for an embassy going to Pope Alexander in Rome! (Roger of Wendover and Matthew Paris attributed the letter to Gilbert, and associated it with the visit of the devil: see p. 245.) There is no indication that any English *bishop* was prepared to visit the anti-pope or that Henry himself made direct use of the threat in his negotiations with Alexander.

In 1166 (?) Henry II issued a further set of constitutions intended to cut off—or perhaps rather to threaten the severance—of Becket's and Alexander's jurisdiction in England. There is no reason to suppose that Gilbert was in favour of this move: very much the reverse, since he himself is charged in one of them with breaking the Constitutions of Clarendon by laying an interdict on the lands of the earl of Norfolk (in the Pentney case) (*MB Epp.* 598–600; etc. On date, see *GFL*). Henry II quickly withdrew; see p. 183 n.

[2] No. 197 shows Gilbert, c. 1168–9, tactfully but firmly attempting to remove two clerks from the royal to the church courts. In the Pentney case, in the end, he obeyed the pope rather than the king (cf. preceding note). It is difficult to be certain if Gilbert had Henry's approval before making most of

important texts on clerical immunity—though without embarking on the problem of double judgement on which Becket, supported by a sound canonical tradition, repudiated the Constitution.[1] Foliot's lavish promise to have the archbishop deposed in 1164 was evidently part of a determined effort to ensure that Becket was removed by the pope not by the king. The obscurity of his own position in *Multiplicem* was doubtless due to his consistent attempt to avoid being cornered. His aim was to keep Henry II and the English church respectable in papal eyes and to have Becket removed without the liberties of the English church being destroyed with him.

If Becket had been what Foliot supposed him, a royal plaything, a fake archbishop, then Foliot's position was sound: it was intolerable that the English church, whose unity and peacefulness had been so patiently restored by Archbishop Theobald, should

his appeals, though one presumes he did (cf. nos. 165, 171, 177, 203–4). That of 1167 was made when the king was temporarily absent from the conference, but it may have been prearranged. No. 201 suggests that the first appeal of 1169 was not made with Henry's previous consent: Gilbert describes it as if it will be news to the king. This falls short of proof. But the renewal of the appeal at the end of May 1169, in which a great number of the clergy of the London diocese joined (see *MB Epp.* 508), cannot have had Henry's specific approval, since he was in Gascony at the time. In any case the procedure of Const. Clarendon c. 8 certainly broke down in the late 1160's since it envisaged the archbishop's court as the normal terminus of appeals. In no. 204 Gilbert asks for a passport, according to Const. c. 4, but this was probably normal, and there was no difficulty in obeying the king *de facto* without committing oneself whether the pope was right or wrong in condemning the principle that royal leave was essential. Nos. 431, 435 describe one of several cases in which Gilbert was concerned in a suit involving advowsons, contrary to c. 1; but this case probably started after 1170 and the issue was one on which church and royal courts regularly disputed in the late-twelfth century (see J. W. Gray in *EHR*, LXVII (1952), 481–509; C. R. Cheney, *From Becket to Langton*, Manchester, 1956, pp. 108 ff.). No. 267 suggests that Gilbert was trying to keep a plea of debt out of the king's court, contrary to Const. c. 15; but the date of the letter is quite uncertain, and he was evidently hoping to save the face of the community of Rievaulx by settling the case out of court. We have no information on Gilbert's attitude to cc. 5, 9, 10, and the pope did not condemn cc. 2, 6, 11, 13, 14, 16 (see *MB Epp.* 45)—even though c. 11 made precisely the distinction between the temporal 'barony' and the spiritual office of bishop which Placidus of Nonantula condemned (see above, p. 178 n.). (On the aftermath, see below.)

[1] See C. Duggan, 'The Becket Dispute and the Criminous Clerks', *BIHR*, XXXV (1962), 1–28.

be torn to pieces by a clown. It is clear that a number of the English bishops felt sufficient sympathy with this point of view in 1164 to be prepared to support the king in seeking for Becket's deposition. The party which went to Sens to demand the deposition from the pope included not only the archbishop of York, Gilbert and Hilary, who were consistently in opposition to Becket, but Bartholomew of Exeter and Roger of Worcester, who later came to support the archbishop. The strength of his case and his steadfastness had not yet revealed themselves. There is nothing surprising in Gilbert's attitude in 1164. Nor did anything happen in the next two or three years to make Gilbert dislike or disapprove any the less of Thomas Becket. We may feel that Gilbert, like others round him, could have realised by 1166 that Becket was not still the chancellor in disguise; but in the intervening period during which Becket had lived among the Cistercians at Pontigny he had seen nothing of the archbishop, and the old Cluniac could hardly be expected to take the Cistercian novice very seriously. Gilbert's attitude is intelligible; whether it is excusable depends upon our judgement of Becket himself and of his cause. We have said as much for Gilbert as, in our view, can be said. We have no intention of acquitting him of a measure of blindness and obstinacy in his bitter opposition to Becket, and in his refusal to see any good in him, although no deep gulf separated the principles of Foliot from those of Becket.

The attitude to the relations of *regnum* and *sacerdotium* revealed under the surface of *Multiplicem* was one held, in all probability, by a number of the more conscientious bishops of the later Middle Ages: acceptance of papal claims in theory and principle, combined with such measure of compromise with royal authority as was needed to prevent needless and useless conflict. It is probable that most of the English bishops of the late twelfth century were considerably more 'royalist' than Gilbert shows himself.[1] Gilbert's attitude was not heroic, but it was eminently sensible; on this basis it may be defended or condemned.

If the arguments given above have foundation, the personal

---

[1] Cf. Cheney, *From Becket to Langton*, chaps. II, IV; Mayr-Harting, *EHR*, LXXVIII (1963), 209–24.

attitude revealed by the letter is more ambiguous than has been supposed. Gilbert worked within a tradition of merciless invective; he was trained in legal debate. His use of both rose above most of his contemporaries in technical skill, but rose above them not at all in charity of expression; the result jars on modern ears all the more for being cleverly written. It undoubtedly confirms the other evidence that he was angry and contemptuous in his dealings with Becket, and lends colour to John of Salisbury's accusation of pharisaism. But to read the depths of Gilbert's heart in it asks too much of the letter: it takes too little account of the artificiality of the medium and of Gilbert's limitations. We cannot judge Gilbert on *Multiplicem* alone; it must take its place in the museum of exhibits from which the man has finally to be reconstructed.

CHAPTER X

THE DIOCESAN BISHOP

No true estimate of Gilbert Foliot's complex personality is possible without some account of what should have been the supreme preoccupation of his active life, his work as a father in God responsible for the spiritual welfare of the people committed to his charge. As an ecclesiastical administrator Gilbert outlived the two great crises of his age, the anarchy and the Becket controversy, and, surviving into a less troubled time, appeared no doubt to the new episcopate of Henry II's last years as a reminder of outworn battles, and of passions spent and done. Towards the end of his long life Gilbert reminded Pope Urban III that he could look back, in the year 1186, on twenty-three years' experience as bishop of the London see.[1] When he died in 1187 he had completed thirty-nine years in the episcopate, fifteen at Hereford, twenty-four at London.

Gilbert's career covered a period of particular interest in the history of the English sees. Very roughly, one could summarise it as the age when, under the direction of Archbishop Theobald and his colleagues, the administrative framework introduced by Lanfranc was stabilised, and first steps were made towards a new quasi-bureaucratic regime within each diocese. One can observe these changes within the cathedral chapter and in the diocese at large. Many years ago Henry Bradshaw sought for the origins of the familiar constitution of the English cathedral chapters: the 'four-square' constitution, dominated by dean, precentor, treasurer and chancellor, and a variable group of archdeacons and lesser officials. Such a group of officials bears an obvious relation to the type of constitution normal in the cathedrals of northern France; but what is striking about the English model is its comparative uniformity. The closest parallel for this model Bradshaw thought he had found in Bayeux; and he assumed that it had been introduced into England from Bayeux by the first generation of

[1] No. 435.

Norman bishops. But recent study has shown that the model was not fully established either at Bayeux or in England in the late eleventh century; the story is now seen to be more complex. The model is the product of Norman and north French experience, clearly enough; and a blueprint for it existed already in 1091 in St Osmund's famous *Institutio* for Salisbury cathedral. But it was only slowly that the English cathedral chapters came to approximate to this model, only in the course of the mid- and late-twelfth century that it became fixed as the norm. It never became fixed at Bayeux itself, even in the late-twelfth century, when a former dean of Salisbury was bishop of Bayeux. The mid-twelfth century was the period when it was becoming established in many English cathedrals: when, for instance, Salisbury came into line with its own *Institutio*, when the same constitution was borrowed for the revived chapter at Wells, when Bishop Hilary was bringing Chichester up to date by establishing treasurer and chancellor. These formal developments clearly reflect a vital process of growth in chapter organisation whose nature is in considerable measure hidden from us; but it may be characterised as the age when the bishops were more fully in control of their chapters than ever again in the Middle Ages, and partly for this reason most active in reorganising them.[1]

In earlier centuries the cathedral chapter and the bishop's

---

[1] For this process in general, see K. Edwards, *The English Secular Cathedrals in the Middle Ages* (Manchester, 1949), pp. 1–22. The view expressed here about the 'four-square' chapter and its development was defended in a paper read by C. N. L. Brooke to the 11th International Historical Congress at Stockholm in 1960: see *Resumés des Communications* (Stockholm, 1960), pp. 120–1. In brief, the *Institutio Osmundi* is, we hold, genuine, and is based on the experience of Osmund and his colleagues in Normandy and northern France, but more specifically on the first recension of the *De officiis ecclesiasticis* of John of Avranches, archbishop of Rouen (1069–79). This and other Rouen uses provided the basis for the Rouen rites and customs invoked on several occasions in the twelfth century as the basic customs of some of the new Anglo-Norman cathedral chapters. For the development of the chapters at Salisbury, Wells and Chichester, see K. Edwards in *VCH, Wilts.* III, 156 ff.; J. Armitage Robinson, *Somerset Historical Essays* (London, 1921), chaps. III and IV, A. Watkin, *Dean Cosyn and Wells Cathedral Miscellanea* (Somerset Rec. Soc. 1941), pp. xxv f., 87–9; H. Mayr-Harting, *Acta of the Bishops of Chichester 1091–1207* (Canterbury and York Soc. 1964), pp. 41–8.

familia had been indistinguishable, but in the course of time, in a variety of ways and for a variety of reasons, the chapter became a formal institution, while the bishop still needed to have about him his personal clerks and secretaries, his lay officials, his attendants and domestic servants, and often his household warriors. The nature of the household of an Anglo-Saxon bishop is something almost entirely obscure. It seems clear, however, that in England as in many parts of the continent, the late eleventh and twelfth centuries, the period of the papal reform and its aftermath, saw a crystallisation both in the organisation of the chapters and in the diocesan bureaucracies which hardened the division between them and speeded the development of the bishop's household as an institution on its own. In Gilbert Foliot's time this movement was in mid-passage. The episcopal household was a marked feature of the age. It was particularly conspicuous where the chapter was monastic: even monk-archbishops, like Theobald himself, or secular archbishops of monastic cathedrals like Becket, were bound to gather round them substantial households; the circle of Archbishop Theobald and the *eruditi* of Archbishop Thomas were notable groups of scholars and administrators, including future archbishops and bishops, and even one future pope.[1] This was not wholly new, especially at Canterbury; but it is significant that it is precisely in this period that one observes, in every English diocese, the crystallisation of the bishop's *familia*. Dr Henry Mayr-Harting has recently shown this development in one of the smaller dioceses, that of Chichester, where it came late in the century, but when it came was particularly marked.[2] One must not exaggerate the division. On the day of Becket's martyrdom, he took lunch with his household, then went to join his chapter for vespers. Many of Gilbert Foliot's charters were drawn up in the chapter-house at St Paul's: it is characteristic of them to include witnesses from both *familia* and chapter. But the household was a clearly defined body of men; just as the documents produced by them had by the later years of Gilbert's career become specimens of a clearly defined diplomatic genre. The

[1] See Saltman, pp. 165 ff., 214 ff.; *JS Epp.* I, pp. xxvii ff.; *MB*, III, 523 ff.
[2] Mayr-Harting, *op. cit.*

Bodleian manuscript is a memorial, both of the diplomatic, and of the personnel and nature of Gilbert's household and staff. It is, indeed, the most substantial memorial that any bishop's *familia* of this period left of its activities. This is characteristic of Gilbert Foliot and his value to the modern student: it is the memorial, not the achievement, which was exceptional.

THE CATHEDRAL CHAPTER

The chapters of Hereford and London had been comparatively well established not long before Gilbert joined them, so that he had neither the scope nor the temptation for creative organisation which was presented to his contemporary Hilary at Chichester, nor the opportunity to influence the division of chapter incomes such as Bartholomew had at Exeter.[1] At the time of the Norman conquest all, or virtually all, the secular English cathedral chapters seem to have been subject to some kind of communal rule based on the *Institutio Canonica* of Amalarius of Metz promulgated in 816 or 817; in one or two cases this took the form of the so-called *Rule of Chrodegang*, which was in fact a conflation of Chrodegang's original rule with Amalarius. The bishops of the Norman settlement were used to a secular chapter in the more normal sense: to canons enjoying individual incomes, or prebends, and living in their own houses; to a chapter under a dean, in which the chief seats were allotted to a hierarchy of dignitaries and archdeacons; in which a proportion of the canons were already absentees, supporting a dignified position at the court of king or bishop, or even of the pope, by capitular and other sinecures. This was the kind of chapter which was organised by the first generations of Norman bishops.

The chapter of St Paul's is better documented for the eleventh and twelfth centuries than any other English chapter, and gives us a remarkable glimpse of what the history of a medieval chapter

---

[1] For Chichester, see Mayr-Harting, *op. cit.*; for Exeter, see Morey, pp. 81–2. For what follows see Brooke in *A History of St Paul's Cathedral*, ed. W. R. Matthews and W. M. Atkins (London, 1957), pp. 11 ff., 361 ff.; *CHJ*, x, 111–32 (1951) and the paper referred to above, p. 189 n.; M. Gibbs, introd. to *Early Charters of the Cathedral Church of St Paul, London* (Camden, 3rd series, LVIII, 1939).

could be. Briefly, one may say that it is far from clear that the communal rule of pre-conquest days was honoured; there may well have been some continuity between the pre-conquest chapter and that reorganised, but perhaps not radically reorganised, by Bishop Maurice about 1090. However that may be, Maurice's chapter contained Normans and English; it was, so far as we can tell, mainly a residential community, with a proportion, perhaps a large proportion, of married canons who reckoned to pass their prebends on to their sons. In a community of 30 there was room for some variety. The married canons of early days included Ranulf Flambard, who was probably an absentee dean in Bishop Maurice's time, and may have held on to the deanery for a few years after he became bishop of Durham; and the father of the celebrated Thurstan, himself a hereditary canon of St Paul's, later, as archbishop of York, to be the effective founder of Fountains abbey. Thurstan's career reminds us that the greatest of the English Cistercians, Gilbert's friend St Ailred, was himself the son of a married priest: his father was priest of Hexham, his grandfather treasurer of Durham.[1] But the campaign of the reformed papacy for clerical celibacy was taking its toll: the respectable married clergy were finding life more and more uncomfortable. By the time Gilbert was translated to London, the married canons were few. It is likely that they included one or two of his own relations, the Belmeis, who had flourished and multiplied in the chapter in the preceding generation. But in his day family patronage, as we have seen, passed from sons to nephews and cousins.[2] The chapter was still in substantial measure a resident community; but it was becoming increasingly difficult to regard residence as a normal part of the duty of every canon.

The statutes of St Paul's include a fascinating document attributed to Gilbert's protégé, Dean Ralph de Diceto (1180–1202), which underlines that the chapter is divided between resident and

---

[1] On Ailred's family, see *Walter Daniel's Life of Ailred of Rievaulx* (NMT, 1950), pp. xxxiii ff., and refs. cited, p. xxxiv, n. 4; on married clergy in general, Brooke in *CHJ*, XII (1956).

[2] Although at least one of his own protégés, Roger of Worcester, had a son (see p. 277).

non-resident canons, and lays down the process by which a canon may enter residence. Briefly, it provided a form of taxation which would ensure that the communal benefits accruing to resident canons were confined to a very few; and it has been argued elsewhere that it belongs, not to the twelfth century, but to the fourteenth.[1] The genuine statute of residence also survives,[2] and this makes it clear how different were the problems of the twelfth century and of the fourteenth. Ralph de Diceto's statute, issued a few years after Gilbert's death, appears at first reading a very lax affair. A man can call himself a resident canon if he is normally resident about one-quarter of the year. Ralph de Diceto was fighting a rearguard action: he was striving to preserve the old idea of a chapter, a body of canons normally resident, of whom a few might be absent on the king's service or the bishop's or in study, but the majority would normally be found in their stalls. He was fighting the absentee and the pluralist, at first sight, it may seem, somewhat half-heartedly. But it is clear that he aimed to preserve the resident community by accepting the principle that a canon could spend a substantial part of the year elsewhere; this might well have worked, since the higher clergy often engaged in a variety of occupations, none in itself wholly absorbing, and a canon frequently engaged in the king's or the bishop's service might reasonably hope to spend a substantial part of the year within reach of St Paul's.

It looks as if the decline of the hereditary, married canon made it difficult to fill the houses in the close. There was less difficulty in finding an absentee prepared to draw the income of a prebend. Twelfth-century pluralism was perhaps not so scandalous as that of the thirteenth, and not so often remarked upon; but Thomas Becket was not the only man to gather an archdeaconry here, a provostship there, a canonry in more than one place elsewhere, and a group of parish churches. He had held a stall in St Paul's itself; so did several other notable pluralists of the age. Gilbert's

---

[1] On the spurious statute of residence, see Brooke in *A History of St Paul's Cathedral*, pp. 86 ff., 363.

[2] On the genuine statute of Ralph de Diceto, see Brooke in *op. cit.* pp. 51, 363; below, pp. 271–2 n.

charters show that he had no hesitation in helping his own relations to add benefice to benefice.[1]

A twelfth-century bishop, if he was a strong personality and reasonably diplomatic, could dominate his chapter still: the thirteenth-century bishop, for all the close bonds which united him to it, was a visitor in chapter-house and cathedral, and many wise bishops were not very frequent visitors. This was partly due to the division between *familia* and chapter, partly to the process of legal crystallisation, not to say fossilisation, characteristic of the later Middle Ages; but it was also partly due to external factors. A twelfth-century bishop not only collated most of the dignitaries and canons to his chapters: he chose them; the patronage, in great measure, was his. Increasingly, as the thirteenth and fourteenth centuries wore on, the bishop found himself in competition with king and pope for patronage, and even, in some measure, with other magnates and with the chapter itself, which could, in the last analysis, refuse to let a new canon into his stall. One has only to read the names of the canons of St Paul's to see that Richard de Belmeis I (1108–27) or Gilbert Foliot had a strong hold over chapter patronage. The author of the *Magna Vita* of St Hugh describes how, as bishop of Lincoln, the saint took exceptional pains to ensure that his nominees were suitable; the author clearly implies that Hugh expected to have a free hand in his choice of the personnel of his chapter.[2] This is not to say that no later bishop was in control of his chapter or on good terms with it, still less that all twelfth-century bishops managed their chapters. But relations more formal and distant were the norm in the later Middle Ages; and the serious disputes in the twelfth century took place in the monastic not the secular cathedrals: between Nigel and the monks of Ely, and between Theobald, Baldwin and Hubert Walter and the monks of Canterbury.[3] In contrast,

---

[1] Cf. esp. nos. 259, 410–11, 402–3, 408 (Ralph de Hauterive, see p. 45 n.; William de Belmeis; Gilbert Banaster).

[2] iii, 8, ed. D. Douie and H. Farmer, I (NMT, 1961), 110 ff.

[3] *Liber Eliensis*, ed. Blake, pp. 294 ff.; E. Miller, *The Abbey and Bishopric of Ely* (Cambridge, 1951), pp. 166 ff.; *JS Epp.* I, pp. 71 ff. (Ely), I f. and notes (Canterbury); Saltman, pp. 56 ff.; *Epistolae Cantuarienses*, ed. Stubbs (RS) *passim*. Durham and Coventry could also be cited.

Gilbert was remembered as a bishop 'who conferred much good on the chapter of Hereford'.[1]

Gilbert's influence over his chapters appears in his frequent visits to the chapter-house, in his exercise of patronage, and in the personal relations between his household and the chapters; it does not appear that he tried to alter their constitutions or profoundly to affect their buildings.[2] Building was doubtless in progress both at Hereford and at London in his time; and at London he organised a fraternity to help pay for the work at St Paul's. But in neither case is there any evidence that the plan was modified under his patronage. The main design of Hereford cathedral belonged to an earlier generation, perhaps to the episcopate of Reinhelm (1107–15), while the nave of old St Paul's, if we may judge from Hollar's engravings, was of early twelfth-century design, even if partly executed in Gilbert's day.

To the same period belonged the pattern of both cathedral chapters. Hereford, as had many English cathedrals, had acquired a four-square constitution that lacked a 'chancellor'; all the other dignitaries were fully established before Gilbert's episcopate, probably very early in the twelfth century if not in the eleventh.[3] It may be that the chapter was directly modelled on that of Rouen. It was established, in a famous paper by Edmund Bishop, that the ritual for Holy Week in the Hereford use was derived from Rouen, and that both were quite distinct from the Sarum use.[4] It is indeed possible, as Bishop hinted, that the Sarum use was a novelty in the early thirteenth century, and that Hereford repre-

---

[1] R. Rawlinson, *History and Antiquities of…Hereford* (London, 1717), Appendix, p. (6). This was doubtless earned by Gilbert's care of the cathedral estates.

[2] On the architectural history of Hereford cathedral, see *Royal Comm. on Hist. Monuments, Herefordshire*, I (1931), 90 ff. There is no definite evidence of building in Gilbert's time, but the character of the nave in particular confirms A. W. Clapham, *English Romanesque Architecture after the Conquest*, p. 46, in suggesting that the cathedral was not completed till about the 1160's; on Old St Paul's see Clapham, pp. 31 f.; R. Graham in *Journal of Brit. Arch. Assn*, 3rd series, X (1945–7), 73–6 (on Gilbert's letter 235, setting up the confraternity).

[3] See Z. N. and C. N. L. Brooke in *CHJ*, VIII (1944–6), 5–6, 183, corrected below, p. 267.

[4] *Liturgica Historica* (Oxford, 1918), pp. 276–300.

sented in this respect the kind of ritual which was more wide-spread among English cathedrals in the twelfth century. It can be shown, for instance, that the version of the use of Rouen represented in the *De officiis ecclesiasticis* of Archbishop John of Avranches (1069–79) was known in England elsewhere than at Hereford, and it can be argued that it formed the main source of St Osmund's *Institutio*.[1] Edmund Bishop suggested that the link between Rouen and Hereford should be sought in Bishop Robert de Bethune, Gilbert's predecessor; Robert's old home at Lanthony is known, then or later, to have had a copy or at least extracts from the work of John of Avranches. But it is more likely that Hereford's link with Rouen was earlier, and part of a more general debt which English cathedrals owed to Rouen.[2] It is in any event clear that the constitution and the use of Hereford were established before Gilbert moved from Gloucester.

Of the use of St Paul's, then or later, we know singularly little. But on the constitution and the personnel of the chapter we are well informed. It would seem that Gilbert affected the latter pro-foundly, the former not at all. St Paul's was very slow to adopt the 'four-square' constitution. In Bishop Maurice's time (1086–1107) it had a dean and four archdeacons; it also had thirty pre-bends. These remained stable in number and dignity. In his day there may have been a *cantor*, a person who controlled the music and who would have been a senior dignitary in any other cathe-dral; but at St Paul's he held no dignity until the early thirteenth

---

[1] See above, p. 189 n. 1: this will be amplified elsewhere. The most import-ant passage from John's first recension was printed by R. Delamare in his edition of the *De offic. eccl.* (Paris, 1923) from a late-twelfth-century MS of English provenance (Bodl. 843). Delamare supposed this version to be a second, revised recension; but the indications are that this was really the original version of the book.

[2] Gerald of Wales indicates that the Lincoln chapter was founded by Remigius, its first Norman bishop, 'iuxta ritum Rotomagensis ecclesie...' (*Opera*, RS, VII, 19). A mid-twelfth-century charter for Lincoln refers to the customs of Salisbury (*Reg. Lincoln*, I, no. 287), and charters of the 1120's for St Mary's Warwick link it to London, Lincoln, Salisbury and York (*Mon.* VI, 1327). This list of connexions could be considerably extended: it indicates that there was a notion of an English norm, of which Salisbury and Lincoln were early and out-standing examples, which owed a good deal to Rouen; and the debt seems mainly to have been through the work of John of Avranches.

century. The institution of the precentorship on a formal basis in the early thirteenth century called forth a woebegone complaint to Pope Innocent III from Peter of Blois who, as archdeacon of London, held first place in chapter after the dean. A similar fuss had accompanied the establishment of a treasurer shortly before Gilbert's translation to the see.[1] These dignitaries, in fact, never achieved the standing held by their colleagues in other chapters: the archdeacons retained their precedence. The fourth dignity, that of chancellor, was established, like the precentorship, early in the thirteenth century. As at most English cathedrals, the chancellor replaced an official called the master of the schools. The cathedral chancellor held the chapter seal and ran its school; in practice the latter function was the more prominent, anyway in his title, until the late twelfth century.

Curiously enough, there is no official recorded even with the title 'master of the schools' at Hereford before the 1180's. It is clear, however, that Hereford, like St Paul's, had a school, and was even a centre of scholarship. *Magistri* are numerous among its dignitaries and canons; it was, anyway for a time, the home of the celebrated Roger of Hereford, the scientist.[2] Late in the century it achieved a certain scholastic celebrity.

Probably St Paul's had more to offer. The school had been organised in the opening years of the century under a certain Master Durand; and apart from the succession of *magistri* who held the post of master of the schools, the chapter included several men known to have been engaged in learned activities of one kind or another. Early in the century Quintilian, archdeacon of Colchester, passed on his office to his son Cyprian: the names suggest that Quintilian's father and Quintilian himself had more than a passing interest in antiquity but we know little about them besides. From 1128 to 1134 the most eminent of the pupils of Anselm of Laon, Gilbert the Universal, himself part-author of the *glossa ordinaria* to the Bible, held the see of London, and his

---

[1] Gibbs, pp. xxxv–xxxvi, and nos. 47, 187–8, 192–3, 231.
[2] See below, p. 291; C. H. Haskins, *Studies in the Hist. of Medieval Science* (Harvard, 1924), pp. 124–6. His compotus was dedicated to one Gilbert, who may have been Foliot.

protégés included his nephew, Arcoid, who wrote the *Life of St Erkenwald*, a composition, it must be admitted, of no great substance, and Master Alberic, author of the more considerable *Mythographus tertius Vaticanus*.[1] In Gilbert Foliot's time quite a number of the canons bore the title magister, and of these several were his protégés, including Master David, who studied at Bologna. Peter of Cornwall, whose *Pantheologus* was inspired by Gilbert, dedicated the first book to his teacher Master Henry of Northampton, a canon of St Paul's frequently in residence in the 1170's and 1180's; Peter dedicated the second and third books to Master Ralph of Hauterive, clerk to Gilbert and canon and master of the schools of St Paul's, and subsequently archdeacon of Colchester, and the fourth to Godfrey de Lucy, bishop of Winchester, who had been a fellow-student. Godfrey was also a canon of St Paul's before he was bishop; but he was a pluralist on a grand scale. It is possible that he had studied with Peter under Henry of Northampton; but we know that part of Godfrey's scholastic career was abroad.[2] Ralph of Hauterive's successor as master was Master Richard of Stortford, another of Gilbert's men—successively clerk, canon and master of the schools. The canons of Hereford in Gilbert's time included at least fifteen *magistri*; those at St Paul's while he was bishop at least sixteen.

Of the Hereford chapter little more can be said. The names of the canons seem to suggest that Gilbert's (and his predecessor's) patronage was often given to scions of local families. They include a Chandos, three Cliffords and a Clare; one cannot, however, assume that all of these were closely related to the barons of those names. The hereditary element is represented at Hereford only by the family of Erchemer, who had been dean early in the century: his son Ranulf and Ranulf's son Ranulf held canonries in the mid- and late-twelfth century. Two contemporaries of Ranulf son of

---

[1] Brooke in *A History of St Paul's Cathedral*, pp. 25 ff.; W. Dugdale, *History of St Paul's Cathedral* (ed. H. Ellis, London, 1818), pp. 289–91; E. Rathbone in *Med. and Renaissance Studies*, I (1941–3), 35–8; below, p. 287. Alberic also seems to have edited a version of the *Miracles of the Blessed Virgin*: see R. W. Southern in *Med. and Renaissance Studies*, IV (1958), 201–3.

[2] Godfrey de Lucy was overseas 'scolas frequentans' in 1176 (*Chron. de Bello*, ed. J. S. Brewer, London, 1846, p. 174).

Erchemer, Osbert and Master Richard, were brothers. Gilbert's links with the chapter did not start with his episcopate: his old friendship with Dean Ralph (see no. 1) and with Bishop Robert may help to account for his appointment to the see. In Gilbert's time one or two deans, a precentor and two or three treasurers were appointed; but we know nothing of them save their names. The archdeacon of Hereford, who had been appointed by Robert de Bethune's predecessor, survived until *c.* 1179; and so Gilbert appointed only one archdeacon, in the archdeaconry of Shropshire, his relative Walter Foliot, to whom he later dedicated his *Commentary* on the *Pater noster*. Among the canons appears one nephew, Hugh Foliot, but none of the other Foliots, Britos and Banastres who gathered round him at St Paul's—although one or two of them received prebends from the second Foliot bishop of Hereford. This may simply mean that Gilbert's nephews were too young in the 1150's for prebends; or it may be due to deficiencies in our evidence. The real invasion of Foliots into the cathedral dignities was to come in the last quarter of the century, after the consecration of Robert Foliot in 1174.

As at Gloucester, Gilbert as bishop of Hereford had to struggle to secure the properties of his see and of his cathedral. Robert de Bethune had lost nothing of his affection for Llanthony and the regular canons when he moved to Hereford in 1131. He had appointed one of the canons of Llanthony, Peter le Kauf, rector of Lydbury North and archdeacon of Shropshire; Peter retired to Llanthony before the bishop's death. Four prebends belonging to the see had been alienated to Llanthony, and a host of privileges secured for the house.[1] In a letter to Pope Eugenius III announcing his consecration Gilbert put forward a claim for the return of all these properties and ultimately a compromise was reached, which involved some restitution by the canons of Lanthony. It looks as if Robert, like many regulars of the generations following the papal reform, may have been out of sympathy with the secular canons, or at least reckoned that their abilities and virtues needed supplementing from a more congenial community. Gilbert was evidently acquainted with both sides of the case: he was friendly

[1] *PUE*, I, nos. 35, 39; Gilbert's nos. 80, 327.

with both bishop and chapter; and the promptitude with which he acted after his consecration shows that he was well aware of how Robert had acted, and also, no doubt, that the chapter of Hereford lost no time in briefing him as to his duties. It is interesting to observe that Gilbert, though himself a regular, took a more conventional view of a secular chapter's affairs than Robert. At Hereford he was the immediate successor of a man whose heart was with the regular canons, and at London he was next but one after another, Robert de Sigillo, who seems to have had a similar inclination.[1] Gilbert also had to handle the aftermath of Bishop Robert's difficulties with the great lords of the march. Robert had suffered from onslaughts of both the earls of Hereford. Once again, Gilbert knew both sides of the question, since the earls were his cousins, and on at least one occasion he felt moved to defend one of them against the bishop.[2] Waleran of Meulan and Hugh Mortimer had acquired possession of two towns (or fortresses: *castella*) of the bishopric of Hereford before 1148; the chapter had an old controversy on its hands with Robert de Chandos.[3] Gilbert attempted with vigour to recover these properties and settle the controversy. It seems likely that he was hampered in his early years by the political difficulties, and benefited from the restoration of order by Henry II. In any event, the controversy with Chandos was only ended in the last years of his episcopate at Hereford, when Robert closed the account by endowing the prebend of Wellington.

Gilbert, good canonist that he was, knew that a bishop should act in accord with his chapter, that its consent was necessary for major acts. This aspect of the law was to be much emphasised by later popes, especially by Innocent III, at the time when bishops and chapters were, *de facto*, drifting apart. Gilbert seems to have acted in accord with his chapter both from conviction and convenience. Several of the Hereford charters were issued by both Gilbert and his dean and chapter, while expressions such as *consensu et consilio capituli* appear several times. The settlement of

---

[1] Cf. Brooke in *A History of St Paul's Cathedral*, pp. 27–8.
[2] No. 22.
[3] Nos. 80, 313, 315–16.

a dispute about a prebend expressly states that the consent of both bishop and chapter was necessary for an arrangement affecting the disposal of a prebend after the holder's death.[1] When a church was appropriated to Gloucester abbey, the chapter supplied its *auctoritas*; the whole episcopal synod added its *decretum* to uphold the grant by threat of excommunication.[2] These phrases mark an interesting contrast both to the practice of Bishop Robert de Bethune, and to the phraseology of Gilbert's own acts as bishop of London. Bishop Robert had frequently promulgated his charters in gatherings of the clergy of his diocese in synod: his *acta* provide us with as much evidence about twelfth-century synods as almost any other bishop's.[3] But references to his cathedral chapter are comparatively rare. This may be chance; but it seems quite likely that Gilbert's emphasis on capitular consent was a deliberate attempt to efface the somewhat uneasy relations between his predecessor and the chapter. In the mid-twelfth century, however, a new uniformity appears in the acts of English bishops; certain conventions spread by a process of infection among the episcopal offices. These conventions, perhaps deliberately, perhaps by accident, made it unfashionable to mention synods and chapters in episcopal charters, although one can often infer, from the list of witnesses, that a document was in fact drawn up in chapter or synod. The majority of Gilbert's charters as bishop of London were witnessed by a group of dignitaries and canons, and also by a group of episcopal clerks. It seems probable that it was still his normal practice to consult his chapter on important issues, and to have his formal documents, when convenient, drawn up in the chapter-house of St Paul's.[4] These documents suggest that Gilbert was a frequent visitor in the chapter house. It is possible that they deceive us: there is nothing,

---

[1] No. 314.   [2] No. 305.

[3] See especially St Guthlac's Cart., Balliol MS. 271, fos. 88 r–v—two agreements (the second somewhat corrupt in text) dated in Robert's first year, made in his second synod.

[4] Assuming that the witnesses were all present when the document was drawn up, or at least when the arrangement recorded in it was formally made. This is a reasonable assumption, although one can never be entirely sure that witnesses to charters of this period were all present together on one occasion.

strictly speaking, to forbid the supposition that he visited the chapter-house once a quarter or even less frequently, and had his official documents drawn up on those solemn occasions. But such a suggestion is not very probable. It is hardly likely that the sort of business represented by many of his charters would have been kept waiting for months, or even for more than a few weeks. Gilbert travelled round his diocese, and we know that from time to time he went abroad, in attendance on the king or on his own affairs. But there are numerous indications that London was his normal place of residence; and while there, he no doubt lived in his palace adjacent to the west end of the cathedral—the palace which his successors in later centuries found it tactful increasingly to ignore. From the palace to the chapter-house was a short walk, and we may be tolerably sure it was often made, even when Gilbert, in advanced old age, needed a hand to guide 'blind Homer's' steps.

The prebends at St Paul's were never exceptionally valuable, and they never became such prizes for the voracious as the best at York and Lincoln. But the situation of the cathedral in London, its traditional distinction and the fact that every canon, whether resident or not, received a share in the distribution of the food farms, made it worth the attention of great men who would have spurned Hereford or Exeter. In the fourteenth century its dignitaries and canons included squadrons of royal clerks, and occasional papal chaplains and even a cardinal or two. In the twelfth century we find royal servants in far smaller numbers; partly because they were anyway fewer, partly because the king seems to have had less grip on patronage. Local families, holders of property in the city, descendants of former canons were represented on the chapter in the mid-twelfth century; but a bishop who ruled long, and kept his hand on affairs, could reckon to fill something like a majority of the prebends and offices with his family and his protégés, and still have something over to meet the insistent demands of king, pope and great magnates.

Gilbert's predecessor and cousin, Richard de Belmeis II, in spite of his family's stake in the chapter, had had an uneasy episcopate and had run into difficulties. From these, no doubt, Gilbert was able to learn. He certainly observed them closely; for it is from his letters, as well as from Diceto's chronicle, that we learn about Richard's troubles. Bishop Robert de Sigillo (1141-50), like Robert de Bethune at Hereford, seems to have made himself unpopular by his attempts at reform and his regular leanings; so much so that when he died it was said that he had been poisoned. On his death it seems that the reformers in the chapter, wishing to perpetuate his regime—or perhaps with some specific candidate in view—requested the pope, the Cistercian Eugenius III, to demand the succession of a regular; and the pope duly issued a bull demanding the election of a man of learning and good life, 'clothed in the habit of religion'. But the majority of the canons wished to elect one of their own number, and their leaders were the protégés and relations of Bishop Richard of Belmeis I. They made an inquiry of the pope whether his bull was meant to exclude a secular canon; and the pope, doubtless realising that he had been misinformed on the state of feeling in the chapter, replied that a secular canon or any tonsured clerk was included in the terms of the bull. This, as John of Salisbury observed, caused some comment at the Curia, where it was felt that the words had been superfluous or the interpretation inept—'unless, indeed, His Holiness was afraid the Londoners intended to choose a layman for their bishop'.[1] But the pope was not the only power to be reckoned with; and it was only after further argument with both pope and king that the majority candidate, Richard de Belmeis, archdeacon of Middlesex and nephew of his namesake, secured the episcopal throne.

Bishop Richard immediately began to distribute patronage to his associates, and his own archdeaconry he gave to Ralph de Diceto, later to be promoted dean. But the pope meanwhile had appointed or at least recommended another to this office. Once again, Richard de Belmeis found himself involved in litigation at the Curia. Eventually he was pardoned, and Ralph de Diceto allowed to enjoy his archdeaconry. John of Canterbury was granted a *quid pro quo*: the valuable office of treasurer of York fell

[1] *HP*, c. 45 (P, p. 91, C, p. 88). On these troubles, see nos. 101-3, 139-40, and notes; Stubbs in Diceto, I, pp. xxiv ff.

vacant at the papal Curia itself, by Pope Anastasius IV's consecration there of Hugh du Puiset to the bishopric of Durham on
20 December 1153. This time the papal 'provision'—for this is an
early example of the exercise of a papal right which was to be of
great importance in the history of provisions later on—took effect.[1]
Gradually Bishop Richard's troubles died away; but they left him
heavily in debt; and at the end of his life, still in debt and afflicted
with paralysis, he was unable to sort out his affairs, and they had
to be managed by his relation Hugh de Marigny, the dean, and by
Nicholas, archdeacon of London.[2] Gilbert, indeed, was himself
invited to take over shortly before his death, but refused;[3] he did
what he could, however, to alleviate the difficulties of his cousins.

Richard's episcopate had been overshadowed by faction in the
chapter, by difficulties between the powers who dominated an
episcopal election, and by debt. All these difficulties Gilbert
strove, in various ways, to avoid. He did not agree to his own
translation until king, pope, and archbishop—and, if we may
believe Thomas Becket (no. 142), the canons—were agreed. He
was related to the Belmeis and was himself a regular, and so a
natural person to help settle the old disputes if their memory still
lingered. Although this is not likely seriously to have affected
his appointment, it no doubt helped him to assume peaceful
control. The wider political reasons for his translation have already
been discussed. We may be sure, however, that he would not have
accepted the bishopric of London if he had not felt confident that
he could evade or overcome his predecessor's difficulties.

Of the thirty canons whom Gilbert found in the chapter at his
accession in 1163, at least five and perhaps eight or more were of
the Belmeis family; one was the son of another former bishop,
and at least four more were the sons of former canons or members
of families which held canonries for more than one generation.
The hereditary element was still strong, but it was on the wane.
Gilbert was as much a nepotist as his predecessor; but only one of

---

[1] No. 99 note; G. V. Scammell, *Hugh du Puiset* (Cambridge, 1956), pp. 12 ff.,
esp. p. 16.
[2] No. 140.
[3] No. 139.

the resident canons of his time is known to have had a child. It has been argued elsewhere that the marriage of higher clergy, a common practice still in the first third of the century, was rare and fast disappearing from 1150 onwards.[1]

The number of canons created in Gilbert's time cannot be exactly estimated, but it seems to have amounted to about twenty-eight. Of these at least eight were his relatives. This does not, however, give an adequate impression of his influence in the chapter. As has been said, he appointed four archdeacons, all of whom were his relations. He appointed one treasurer and two masters of the schools: two of the three were nephews or cousins, the third had been his clerk. During most of his episcopate the dean was Hugh de Marigny, who was related to the Belmeis, and so, even if perhaps somewhat distantly, to Gilbert too. In 1179 or 1180 Hugh died, and Gilbert had to face what (so far as the evidence goes) was the one serious crisis in his relations with the chapter. Gilbert's former protégé, Master David of London, with whom he had quarrelled about 1173 for some reason now obscure, made a bid for the deanery.[2] The grounds of this are far from clear. There seem, however, to be two possibilities. It may be that David was the ringleader among a group of canons who wished to vindicate the right of the chapter to elect its own dean. In later centuries the law became established that the canons elected the dean, although in practice the election was normally the acknowledgement of a *fait accompli*.[3] It may be that David, the canonist, trained at Bologna, was aware of the tendencies in this direction already in existence. It is possible that he remem-

[1] Brooke in *CHJ*, XII, i (1956), 1–21. Roger of Worcester had a son: below, p. 277. Mabel, relict of Richard Rufus, occ. 1222 (Hale, p. 29); but her husband may well not have been the canon of that name.

[2] On Master David see Z. N. Brooke in *Essays...presented to R. L. Poole*, ed. H. W. C. Davis (Oxford, 1927), pp. 227–45. Z. N. Brooke threw some doubts on the story of David's intrigue for the deanery, but Gilbert's phrase in no. 240—'iniecit oculos in precipuam ecclesie nostre dignitatem'—leaves little doubt that Gilbert believed him to be aiming for the deanery.

[3] The origin of this is obscure, but it was firmly established in the late-twelfth and early-thirteenth centuries. 'Among the last [chapters to obtain the right to elect the dean] were Wells by 1217, Lichfield by 1222, and Exeter, which had no dean until 1225' (Edwards, p. 122 n.; see references there cited).

bered the story of John of Canterbury's appointments in 1152–3. It is possible, though it cannot be proved, that Hugh de Marigny died on his way back from the Third Lateran Council in 1179.[1] If so, it could have been argued by an ingenious lawyer that the appointment of his successor lay with the pope, and David may have hoped to win the pope's nomination. If so, he was disappointed. As in 1152, Ralph de Diceto was successful. Stubbs conjectured that Ralph was related to the Belmeis; if he was, yet another dignity went to a relative of Gilbert. Ralph was clearly the leading figure in the chapter. He may have been promoted at Gilbert's behest as an available candidate to end a dispute; but there is nothing to forbid the notion that he was a faithful colleague to Gilbert. He was clearly a man of power, and as Gilbert declined Ralph took more and more effective control. He was something of a scholar, author of biblical commentaries as well as of the famous chronicle.[2] The copy of his chronicle now in the Lambeth library used to reside in the treasury at St Paul's. It was the only book of secular interest to do so; and its presence is an indication of the repute in which later generations regarded the man whom one of the cathedral necrologies described as 'the good dean'.[3] No one who has worked among the records of St Paul's can fail to realise how large a part in its life and traditions was played by the two great deans called Ralph: Ralph de Diceto and Ralph of Baldock, dean and bishop at the end of the thirteenth and beginning of the fourteenth centuries. Of the two it was Diceto who had the compliment of having a spurious statute of residence fathered on him in the fourteenth century. This was doubtless because he was indeed author of the genuine statute on residence; but it shows that his name was still remembered in the fourteenth century.

Diceto was a survivor from Gilbert's predecessor's regime.

---

[1] Other evidence shows that Dean Hugh died on 27 June 1179 or 1180 (*CHJ*, x, 129 and note (1951)); the Council was held in Rome in March 1179; unless post-conciliar business or illness caused Hugh to make a slow return, one would expect him to have been back in England by the end of June.

[2] On Diceto, see Stubbs, introd. to his edition; Brooke in *A History of St Paul's Cathedral*, pp. 28–9, 51–2, etc.

[3] BM Harl. MS 6956, fo. 110, from the lost Liber F.

Master David, so far as we can tell, was of Gilbert's own creation. Apart from the eight or more relatives of the bishop among the canons installed between 1163 and 1187, there were a number who had been one way or another his clerks. For these Gilbert seems to have established some approach to a *cursus honorum*. The young men of his *familia* did their apprenticeship as bishop's clerks, and so rose to be canons and dignitaries in the chapter. The evidence indeed suggests that this was the normal path to promotion. Some prebends were granted to outsiders: at least three royal clerks, one member of the archbishop's curia and a precentor of Rouen were so endowed in Gilbert's time.[1] But the majority were young men trained in his service. No doubt some or most of these received their early education at St Paul's itself. The more promising, and the more favoured, went on to other schools, at home or abroad, to finish their education. Early in his episcopate Gilbert made two of his nephews archdeacons and sent them to Bologna; with them, as a somewhat more senior student, was Master David, at this time on good terms with the bishop, receiving patronage (as he later received it from the bishops of Lisieux and Worcester) for his talents. In spite of his quarrel with Gilbert, David returned to St Paul's in later life, and died as a resident canon, about two years after Gilbert's death. The most famous of Gilbert's clerks and canons was Walter Map, a native, it seems, of the diocese of Hereford, who had in all probability attracted Gilbert's notice in Hereford days.[2] In the 1160's he was a clerk in Gilbert's service; in the 1170's and 1180's a royal clerk. But this did not dry up the flow of Gilbert's patronage. In or about 1173 Gilbert gave him the prebend still known as Mapesbury; and in the early 1180's Walter repaid the bishop's kindness by writing the respectful, indeed moving passages about him in his *De nugis curialium*. Map continued to hold his prebend after he had left the royal service, in his old age at Lincoln and Oxford.

Two canons gave up their stalls the year before Gilbert's translation, one, John of Canterbury, to be bishop of Poitiers and later archbishop of Lyons, the other, Thomas Becket, to be archbishop

---

[1] See below, pp. 278–88.
[2] On Map, see pp. 80 n. and ref., 283.

of Canterbury. In Gilbert's time there were seven future bishops in the chapter—three of them canons of his creation—an unusual number for a twelfth-century chapter, and an unusual proportion for St Paul's. Of these, only two were normally resident: William de Vere and William of Northolt, both of them at one time clerks of Archbishop Theobald. The latter never wholly lost touch with St Paul's before he became bishop of Worcester in 1186; but from *c.* 1174 he was normally absent in the service of the archbishop of Canterbury, and from 1177 he held the archdeaconry of Gloucester. His was a career characteristic of the age: archbishop's clerk, cathedral prebendary and archdeacon; for some years he held these offices in plurality and performed the duties of each in turn. It is characteristic of the twelfth century that canons and dignitaries normally non-resident will appear from time to time witnessing charters and visiting their cathedrals. The conditions of employment in the royal and archiepiscopal service are very far from clear to us; but it seems that clerks could often reckon to have a considerable amount of free time in which the more conscientious attended to the benefices from which they drew their regular incomes. In any event the service of king and archbishop often brought a man to London or Westminster; and other cathedrals were also visited by their non-resident or occcasionally resident brethren from time to time. William of Northolt and his like help us to understand the sense in Ralph de Diceto's apparently lax statute of residence.

William de Vere came from a family which had climbed even higher than the Foliots. He was the son of Aubrey de Vere, the Master Chamberlain, who rose 'from the ranks of the aristocracy' to be one of Henry I's leading servants, and whose son, William's brother, Aubrey II, became first earl of Oxford. Gilbert was much involved in the first earl's matrimonial tangles in the late 1160's and early 1170's;[1] the earl's brother meanwhile had left St Paul's. William in early life had been promised the royal chancellorship by the empress (1142); later he had been a clerk in Theobald's service, and was perhaps an old school friend of John of Salisbury and Ralph de Diceto. He moved to St Paul's after

---

[1] See nos. 162–4 and notes.

Theobald's death but retired, probably shortly after Gilbert's accession, to become a canon regular at St Osyth. While there he wrote an account of the life and miracles of the patron saint of the house. He was a personal friend of Henry II, and his retirement from St Paul's did not involve complete withdrawal from the world. He was successively clerk of the works at the royal foundation at Waltham, a house partly colonised from St Osyth, royal justice for one eyre, and finally bishop of Hereford, where he died in ripe old age, surrounded by Foliots and Veres, in 1198.

The five non-resident canons who obtained mitres were John Cumin, later archbishop of Dublin, John of Greenford, dean and later bishop of Chichester, Richard FitzNeal, royal treasurer and later Gilbert's successor as bishop of London, Godfrey de Lucy, royal clerk and justice and later bishop of Winchester, and Geoffrey 'Plantagenet',[1] Henry II's illegitimate son, able, vital and cantankerous like all his family, who probably gave up his prebend to Walter Map in 1173 when he was elected bishop of Lincoln, but was not in fact consecrated until 1191, as archbishop of York. In these men we see some of the variety of life among the twelfth-century upper, secular clergy: in the diversity of their social origin, in the routes by which they came to the episcopate, and in the different ways in which they treated their duties as canons of St Paul's, one resident, one occasionally resident, and the rest (so far as we know) not resident at all.

Apart from the chapter's function in relation to the bishop and the diocese, and its other role, of increasing importance, as a source of income for clerks possessioner in the growing bureaucracies of Church and kingdom, it was a body with some measure of coherence, with traditions and prestige of its own. As a religious community maintaining the liturgical rites of the cathedral, and as an economic unit administering the extensive properties of the dean and chapter, it worked independently of the bishop. If Gilbert had the decisive voice in the appointment of new members there was always a nucleus not of his creation;

---

[1] Called 'Plantagenet' by a modern convention: the use of the surname for the English royal family seems to have begun in the fifteenth century (cf. *CP*, I, 183 n., XII, ii, 905 n.).

M & B

and the care with which the prebendal catalogue was preserved in his time shows that the chapter had at least some members who cared for the continuity of its customs and traditions. Yet cathedral chapters were not sufficiently stable communities or sufficiently prosperous, nor could they offer sufficiently interesting employment, to command the undivided attention of their canons: many of them sought variety, learning and advancement in the schools, the service of pope, bishops or other chapters, or on the legal and administrative staff of the king. In the twelfth century residence may still have been normal in most chapters; the non-residents may commonly have been in a minority. This rapidly ceased to be true in the thirteenth and fourteenth centuries; and already in the twelfth the chapter of York was suffering from the value of its prebends and offices. At the death of Henry II three out of the four dignitaries and two out of the four archdeacons were royal clerks or justices.[1] At St Paul's the number of canons permanently non-resident remained more or less constant at about seven out of the thirty to the end of the century, or just under one quarter of the total. The frequency with which numbers from twelve to fifteen canons witnessed charters of the second half of the twelfth century suggests that it was then normal for about half the chapter to be in residence at one time.[2] In the early 1190's, shortly after Gilbert's death, Ralph de Diceto promulgated his statute on residence. Virtually all the canons ultimately gave their assent, but only fourteen out of thirty were actually present when the ordinance was drawn up.

In the fourteenth century the resident canons attempted to corner the perquisites of residence by savage taxation of canons entering residence. The non-resident community, largely royal clerks, retorted by a fierce onslaught on the efforts of the residents to close down the brewery and bake-house and put an end to the distributions of commons to non-resident prebendaries. The heroic age of conflict lay far in the future in Gilbert Foliot's time. But

[1] For the York dignitaries, see Sir Charles Clay, *York Minster Fasti*, I (Yorks. Arch. Soc., Record Series, 1958).

[2] See, e.g. nos. 403, 427; *Rep.* pp. 12 a, 50 b; Gibbs, nos. 164, 186, 220, 243 (19 canons), 285.

there was already some adumbration of the problem in the one dispute, apart from the obscure question of the deanship, between bishop and chapter which is recorded. It appears that he and the canons who were regular members of his *familia* claimed that residence on his staff was tantamount to residence in the cathedral, and that canons in his *familia* were entitled to their full share of the common fund. The dispute went to the pope, but the outcome is unknown.[1] It underlines the close links, in personnel, between *familia* and chapter, and reveals some of the tensions which lay behind a relationship which, so far as can be seen, was normally harmonious.

THE *FAMILIA*

It has been observed that there was something like a regular *cursus honorum* in Gilbert's household, from clerk to canon and above. Approximately twenty-eight canons were created in Gilbert's time. Of these twelve had been his clerks, and perhaps more. Of those who were evidently not drawn from the number of his clerks, one was a canon of Hereford, and a Foliot;[2] one was a Belmeis;[3] seven at least were in the royal service;[4] and, allowing for two Foliots not certainly his clerks, this leaves unaccounted for Master David, who may have been promoted by Gilbert's predecessor, and was certainly Gilbert's protégé; William of Northolt, who had been in Theobald's service; Richer, precentor of Rouen, whose claims on Gilbert's patronage are quite obscure; and only two others.[5] Twelve or more of Gilbert's clerks won

---

[1] BM Egerton MS 2819, fo. 65 v.

[2] Ralph Foliot (see p. 284). One should possibly add Robert Folet (occ. as canon of Hereford before 1198 and in 1205: Worcester Cathedral, Reg. A 4, fo. xxvii; Gloucester Cathedral, Reg. A, fo. 97 r–v). Folet was clearly a name distinct from Foliot.   [3] Richard Junior (p. 280).

[4] Richard FitzNeal (possibly canon before 1163), Godfrey de Lucy, John Cumin, Osbert de Camera, Geoffrey, the king's son; Walter de Insula (possibly made canon before 1163: below), and Ralph Foliot (see above). Walter Map was both royal clerk and clerk to Gilbert.

[5] But Gilbert may have had relations living in Rouen: see no. 261. The two others were Master Ralph (Holywell) and Robert Folet (Wenlocksbarn)—see above.

prebends. But this leaves at least twenty of his clerks as bishop of London unaccounted for. Most of these make rare appearances in Gilbert's documents. It is probable that many of them were birds of passage, who passed on elsewhere; of a few this is certain. Some were too young to be promoted before 1187: this no doubt applies to the four Foliots, the Banastre and the Brito. If we may judge from the evidence of later centuries, Gilbert had other preferment as valuable as many of the prebends in his hands, and may well have provided some of these men with rectories. We do not know on what terms a bishop's clerk stood to his patron; but the study of twelfth-century witness-lists strongly suggests that it could be a very stable, and also a very unstable relationship.

A glance at the list of Gilbert's clerks immediately suggests two things. The first is that they were exceedingly numerous, far beyond the number one can feel that a bishop needed for the administration of his diocese: it is clear that he frequently had as many as a dozen or twenty at a time. He may have been especially well provided, particularly generous in his patronage; but it is likely that these figures were not exceptional. Theobald, in a somewhat shorter episcopate, had at least twenty, and perhaps twice that number of clerks altogether.[1] This multiplicity is reflected in another way. Mr T. A. M. Bishop has shown that although in the heyday of Becket's chancellorship Henry II sometimes had as many as fifteen clerks regularly engaged in writing his writs and charters, in his later years he could make do with only two.[2] There were doubtless other clerks doing different kinds of work; but if it was possible for the main duties of the royal chancery to be performed by two scribes, we may be tolerably sure that one or two could have done all that a bishop needed.

---

[1] Saltman, pp. 214 ff.: twenty witness with sufficient regularity for us to be reasonably sure that they were in Theobald's employment; Saltman's list contains nearly fifty names, but there are some duplications (e.g. Ralph 'Bixon' and Ralph of Lisieux were probably the same man) and some ghosts (Masters David and Richard are recorded only in Saltman no. 281, which is spurious: see *Misc. D. M. Stenton*, pp. 48–9 and notes, 59).

[2] *Scriptores Regis* (Oxford, 1961), esp. pp. 9 ff. FitzStephen (*MB*, III, 29) tells us that Becket as chancellor employed 52 clerks in all.

Indeed, it is doubtful if English bishops of the early twelfth century commonly had an organised writing office, although they always had plenty of literate men about them, who could turn to and write a letter or charter when needed.[1] A few had an official called a chancellor; and in Theobald's later years his secretarial work seems to have been divided between Philip, his chancellor, who presumably organised the routine business, and John of Salisbury, who evidently drafted, though he apparently did not himself write, the more important letters.[2] But among Theobald's originals, as among those of many bishops whose *acta* survive in large quantities, we find a multiplicity of hands. Of this, Gilbert Foliot's charters and other documents offer a striking example. Among the originals which survive, at least a dozen different hands have been detected. In Bodleian MS E Musaeo 249, the collection which we have shown came from Gilbert's own *familia* in the late 1170's, the same diversity of hands is evident. We have detected four main hands in the manuscript; perhaps as many as a dozen more make an occasional appearance. Of the principal scribes, three wrote book-hand, and may have been professional scribes, hired for the occasion. But one of these hands[3] shows signs of having been influenced by the writing of papal bulls, as was common among scribes employed in episcopal households at this time, and one of the chief scribes of the MS wrote charter-hand. He can be identified as the scribe of at least two surviving original charters of Gilbert Foliot of the early 1170's, and it was this scribe who, after most of the book had been completed, went through filling up blank leaves with charters and such-like material, and even formulas. When he had finished this tedious work, he added a quire of his own for good measure. Although one other scribe carried on—to add *Multiplicem*—it is clear that the scribe who filled the blanks felt himself to be a man having authority over the book; one might even guess that he was the chief clerk of Gilbert's *familia*.

The second point which impresses itself on first reading of the

[1] See esp. C. R. Cheney, *English Bishops' Chanceries*, and Saltman, *passim*.
[2] Cheney, *op. cit.* pp. 28 ff.; Saltman, pp. 229 ff.; *JS Epp.* I, pp. xxviii ff.
[3] Hand I: see *GFL*, introduction.

list of Gilbert's clerks is the regularity with which one name appears in the lists, that of Richard of Salisbury. He is in thirty-six out of the total of sixty witness-lists in which he could reasonably appear,[1] and he appears very commonly first among the clerks. But he never ceased to be a clerk; he never rose to be a canon. One would guess from the witness lists that he was a permanent chief clerk, dedicated to his task, without wish for preferment; perhaps, rather, without need for preferment, for a chief clerk no doubt had valuable perquisites apart from any bene-fice he might hold. We know nothing about him but his name; and we have no means of checking the speculations aroused by Gilbert Foliot's chief clerk proving to be the namesake of John of Salisbury's brother.[2] Thus it remains a possibility, incapable of proof, that the 'chief clerk' of the charters and of the Bodleian manuscript was Richard of Salisbury.

Richard of Salisbury devoted his career to service as a clerk in Gilbert's household. Others of Gilbert's clerks also stayed with him to the end of his life, but usually in more exalted stations, as canons or as archdeacons. The *familia* was an administrative head-quarters, with a fair amount of business on its hands. It was the centre of a diocese and of an honour, of a legal and social and military complex, with several castles to garrison and a feudal levy to run. This side of Gilbert's business was no doubt in the hands of his seneschal; the domestic affairs of his large household were run by his chamberlain. These were lay officials. The other official who had in his hands the spending of sums of money, probably of large sums of money, and the dispensing of other kinds of goods, was the almoner, who was one of the clerks.[3] But however one multiplies the duties of a medieval bishop, it remains rather difficult to understand how Gilbert managed to find employment for all his clerks. It is clear, in fact, that his household was more than an administration in being: it was also a school in which the young Foliots and others who had attracted the bishop's attention

---

[1] 38 out of 62 if he is the Richard who witnessed nos. 359, 384.
[2] On John's brother Richard, see C. C. J. Webb, *John of Salisbury* (London, 1932), pp. 2–3; Morey, p. 21; *JS Epp.* I, 32 n., 244 n., etc.; Saltman, p. 215.
[3] See p. 291.

and won his patronage were brought up, and served an apprenticeship in the career of ecclesiastical law and administration
which was to provide the path to promotion for so many of the
clerks possessioner between the twelfth century and the end of the
Middle Ages. In the main we can only conjecture the way in
which their lives were organised. We may presume that they received their formal education in one of the London schools, in
part, at least, at St Paul's itself. Both Gilbert's nominees to the
post of master of the schools, Ralph de Hauterive and Richard of
Stortford, had been his clerks; so had Henry of Northampton,
the *magister* who taught Peter of Cornwall. There may have been
direct instruction in the household; there were certainly opportunities for secondment to schools elsewhere. The very favoured
went to Bologna; but of these the most favoured, the nephews,
had already acquired archdeaconries, and so incomes, of their own;
and Master David also had his prebend before he went to Bologna,
and both he and the archdeacons used their revenues to provide
credit for their debts. Thus we may be reasonably sure that from
among the young men of his household Gilbert chose the more
clerically minded to write his letters and charters, and to organise
his routine business, the more legally minded to run his courts
and cases, the more promising and ambitious to be recommended
for patronage or service elsewhere, or on occasion for higher
preferment in his own cathedral—and gave to his favoured relations the majority of the plums in his orchard.

The great man's household was the central institution of
medieval society. From time immemorial kings and nobles had
brought up the young men of colleagues and subordinates in their
halls, had them taught the profession and code of arms in return
for service of many different kinds. In a similar way the household
of a great ecclesiastical lord was the meeting place of his own
relations and of men from many different sources learning the
profession. Young men from London, Sawbridgeworth, Stortford—Bishop's Stortford, where the ruins of Gilbert's castle may
still be seen—Waltham and elsewhere mingled with men from
Witney, Northampton, Worcester, and Salisbury, and with men
from Herefordshire and the March, a Clifford and a Map, and

took their place beside the Banastres, Britos and Foliots, in the hope of picking up the crumbs which the nephews dropped from the great man's table.

ADMINISTRATION

Apart from the bishop's household clerks, a diocese was organised by a hierarchy of archdeacons, rural deans and parish clergy. This hierarchy was in full working order when Gilbert became bishop of Hereford. The early history of the offices of archdeacon and rural dean in England is somewhat obscure. It is clear that the archdeacon was not altogether unknown before the Conquest, yet one can name hardly any holders of the title in the tenth and early eleventh centuries.[1] The first generation of Norman bishops appointed archdeacons in every diocese; and very soon the larger sees were divided into territorial archdeaconries. It has been said that this process was slow; that archdeacons first began to multiply, and were then only gradually provided with precise territories to administer. No doubt the full organisation of territorial arch- deaconries took time; but the Norman bishops were used to territorial archdeaconries on the continent, and there is no evidence that they ever employed two or more archdeacons in one diocese without a territorial division of labour. It can be established that the diocese of Lincoln was divided into seven archdeaconries by Remigius, its Norman re-founder;[2] to these an eighth was added in the twelfth century. Hereford had an archdeacon at least before the end of the eleventh century; but the first evidence of a second

---

[1] The most recent discussion of this problem is by F. Barlow, *The English Church 1000–1066* (London, 1963), pp. 247 ff.; see also M. Deanesly, *Sidelights on the Anglo-Saxon Church* (London, 1962), pp. 145 ff.

[2] Henry of Huntingdon (ed. T. Arnold, RS, pp. 302–3) says of Bishop Remigius 'septem...archidiaconos septem prouinciis...imposuit', and pro- vides us with a complete succession back to *c.* 1090 or before for the Lincoln diocese; and in several other dioceses there is evidence of a rapid growth from one to something approaching the final number of archdeaconries. In no case can one prove a slow evolution, although the number of archdeaconries was sometimes increased later on—as at Lincoln, from seven to eight, in the twelfth century. On archdeacons and rural deans in general, see A. Hamilton Thomp- son in *Proc. British Academy*, XXIX (1943), 164 ff.

archdeacon comes in the pontificate of Robert de Bethune, who (characteristically) appointed a canon of Llanthony called Peter le Kauf archdeacon of Shropshire; from then on the diocese was divided between two archdeaconries, of which Hereford was held for at least half a century by another Peter, appointed in the 1120's, and Shropshire successively by Odo, another of Bishop Robert's nominees, and Walter Foliot. At London there is evidence of an archdeacon soon after the Conquest; and part of the reorganisation under Bishop Maurice (1086–1107) evidently took the form of the division of the diocese into four archdeaconries. Of these, the archdeacon of London was the senior. In eleventh- and twelfth-century witness-lists there were few very precise rules about the precedence of the witnesses. On the whole, ecclesiastics figure before laymen, and they are arranged in the order of seniority of their office. Within a diocese, the bishop will witness before his archdeacons, and they before canons. But the archdeacons may be in any order. The only clearly defined exceptions to this among archdeacons are in the sees of London and Salisbury: in Salisbury witness-lists the archdeacon of Dorset almost invariably comes before his colleagues, and in London witness-lists the archdeacon of London takes precedence. This corresponded to his precedence in the choir of St Paul's; but every English archdeacon had his special place in choir. Perhaps it also reflected the place which the archdeacon's master, the bishop of London, had vindicated in the 1070's as first of Canterbury's suffragans.[1] But it is somewhat surprising that the archdeacons of London and Dorset should have felt, and made others feel, so notable a precedence as to affect the normal laxity in the order of witness lists; and one may well suspect the inspiration of the continental *archidiaconus maior*, the senior archdeacon common in French sees.[2] In the case of the archdeacon of London this was made the more appropriate by his position as second dignitary in chapter, immediately after the dean, a position unique in English chapters.

But the archdeacon's primary function—and the chief source of

---

[1] See below, pp. 228–9.
[2] Cf. Hamilton Thompson, art. cit. pp. 159 ff.

his income—lay in his capacity as the bishop's deputy and *alter ego* in the administration of the diocese. This was a function potentially of great importance, but in the twelfth century, it seems, not at all clearly defined. Already the archdeacon could perform some of the bishop's duties in his own territory: he held courts and synods, and went on visitations.[1] The end of the twelfth century saw the emergence alongside the archdeacon of the bishop's officials, and the thirteenth century witnessed the formalisation of the offices of bishop's official and vicar general and of the officials of the archdeacon. In the twelfth century the hierarchy was apparently much more loosely defined. There is no trace of bishop's or archdeacon's officials in Gilbert's *acta*, nor is there even evidence, such as quite commonly appears in other dioceses, that his archdeacons delegated their functions to vice-archdeacons.[2] In part this may have been because none of Gilbert's archdeacons was a permanent absentee. His nephews, the archdeacons of Essex and Colchester, were indeed at Bologna for some length of time—yet they were there to study canon law and improve their qualification for their offices. It is impossible to give a precise picture of their activities, but the frequency with which they are referred to in Gilbert's charters shows that he expected them to act; and it would be possible to compile a small collection of their charters which do something to suggest that they did what Gilbert expected of them. The most important of an archdeacon's functions was the visitation. We know that the visitation of the archdeacon of Berkshire was a burden on his clergy, and Pope Alexander III had to limit his retinue to seven horse- and three foot-servants, and his stay in each parish to one day and night a year; we have a detailed account of a visitation undertaken by Gerald of Wales when he became archdeacon of Brecon—a livelier affair perhaps than was normal in English archdeaconries;[3] but we have no information on the visitations conducted by Gilbert's archdeacons.

[1] See Hamilton Thompson, art. cit.; C. R. Cheney, *From Becket to Langton*, pp. 145–6.
[2] On vice-archdeacons see *English Bishops' Chanceries*, pp. 143–6.
[3] JL 13170 (*PL*, CC, col. 1194); Giraldus, *Opera* (RS), I, 30 ff.

The archdeacons were the bishop's close friends, and several of them were his relations. But there is no indication that he had much personal contact with the rural deans or parish clergy. The line between upper and lower clergy, drawn firmly (with all allowances made for exceptions and borderline cases) between the archdeacon and the rural dean, was a fundamental social barrier in the mid- and late-Middle Ages. Gilbert's letters indicate that his relations with the rural deans were purely formal. They tell us, indeed, comparatively little about the deans' functions. But they show that the routine business of the diocese was done in a hierarchy of chapters: the ruridecanal chapter, the archdeacon's synod and the bishop's synod.[1] It seems clear that the deaneries were well established, although the process by which they had grown up in the preceding century is extremely obscure.[2]

The life and character of the ordinary parish priest at this time is shrouded by an almost impenetrable fog; to form a picture of the country parson we must turn to the brief sketch of St Wulfric of Haselbury's parish priest, to scattered references in the writings of Gerald of Wales, or to Roger of Wendover's story of Bartholomew of Exeter on visitation.[3] The bishop's chief means of control of his clergy lay in his check on their recruitment by ordination, and on their promotion by institution; here the canon law was a useful weapon to his hand. In the better dioceses no doubt, and under the influence of bishops who were spiritual men, the clergy received such rude formation as was possible before the cathedral

[1] Cf. Cheney, *From Becket to Langton*, pp. 145 ff. No. 264 shows that the rural dean could pass sentence of suspension on delinquent clergy, subject to confirmation by archdeacon or bishop; no. 154 shows that the rural dean was expected to execute the judgement in the case (one in which Gilbert acted as judge-delegate). The latter case belonged to his Hereford days: the deans are more prominent in London records. They are sometimes included in the addresses of charters; two Stoke-by-Clare documents show the ruridecanal chapter of Hedingham (Hinckford) at work under Gilbert its dean (Cotton MS Appendix xxi, fos. 108, 110).

[2] In this context W. Hudson's article on the Chichester deaneries (arguing that their boundaries were settled between 1066 and 1086) is of particular interest: *Sussex Arch. Collections*, LV (1912), 108–22.

[3] *Wulfric of Haselbury*, ed. M. Bell (Somerset Rec. Soc. 1933), esp. pp. 28–9, 30–1; cf. pp. xxvi ff.; Giraldus, *Opera*, II, *passim*; Wendover, ed. H. O. Coxe, II (London, 1841), pp. 290–1.

schools had come to their full development in the last part of the century. But neither then nor at any time in the Middle Ages was any systematic effort made to educate the clergy either by founding seminaries or diverting the education in the schools and incipient universities to provide pastoral instruction. The rising schools tended to enhance the difference between upper and lower clergy: those who passed through the rising schools generally became members of the higher clergy. Thus new movements affected the privileged far more rapidly than the rank and file, among whom old customs seem to have been far more tenacious than among the 'possessioners'.

This is not to say that the bishops were not concerned with their parochial clergy. Attempts were made to prevent illicit ordination: clergy who moved from diocese to diocese had to provide themselves with certificates of ordination or letters dimissory.[1] Two of Gilbert's letters show something more than a formal concern that men whom he had ordained deacon should be allowed to become priests in due course.[2] It is probable that Gilbert moved round each diocese more frequently than the fragmentary evidence proves: and we hear much, while he was at Hereford, of the dedication of cemeteries and chapels.[3] From his own documents we should know little of his diocesan synod. It is only the incidental reference by Peter of Cornwall which reveals to us how Gilbert could inspire his younger clergy by the sermons he preached there.[4]

Though we may be sure that Gilbert was concerned about his clergy, it is extremely doubtful whether he had any substantial success in altering their manner of life. It has been argued elsewhere that the campaign for clerical celibacy undertaken in the Church at large by the papal reformers, and instituted in England by Lanfranc and Anselm, had wrought a real change among the upper clergy by the second quarter of the twelfth century. Gilbert's St Paul's, unlike that of Richard de Belmeis I, was vir-

---

[1] Cf. nos. 280, 471–2.
[2] Nos. 471–2.
[3] Nos. 290, 301, 334–7.
[4] See above, p. 71.

tually free from married canons or the threat of hereditary prebends. But there is no reason to suppose that the campaign had had a comparable effect on the parish clergy.[1] Bartholomew of Exeter and Roger of Worcester were active in campaigning for celibacy; the evidence does not suggest that it was a special preoccupation of Gilbert's, although it is the most notable theme in the *Collectio Belverensis*. The province of Canterbury seems to have caused the pope particular disquiet in this respect. Three letters of Alexander III were addressed to Gilbert on this subject, which contain injunctions such as were sent to all the suffragans of Canterbury and to Archbishop Richard.[2]

In 1166 Gilbert was personally warned by Becket to deal with the married clergy of his diocese; this might lead us to suppose that Gilbert was lax in this respect.[3] There is, however, one stern letter to the rural dean of Ongar on the subject; and the evidence is quite inadequate for a final judgement. When the material for the history of clerical marriage throughout the later Middle Ages has been sifted, it may well appear that the bishops were compelled, or felt themselves compelled, for many generations after this, to accept married clergy and their sons to orders for want of more suitable recruits and under the powerful pressure of accepted custom.[4]

There is much evidence in Gilbert's letters and charters of the familiar processes by which the parish system was being modified in the middle and late twelfth century: of the attack on lay ownership, which led popes and bishops to encourage appropriation of parish churches to monasteries; of the establishment of vicars and vicarages; of the freezing of parish boundaries and the disputes to which the developing law on this subject gave rise. Gilbert was called in to give evidence in a case in which Gilbert de Muntfichet was trying to recover two churches on his fee: during the anarchy of Stephen's reign, while he was a minor, his guardian had granted

---

[1] Brooke in *CHJ*, XII, i (1956), 1 ff.
[2] See art. cit. pp. 5–6 and nn.; JL 14267, 14222–3 (from the *Belverensis*; ed. Giles, *Gilberti Foliot Epistolae*, nos. 360–2). On the *Belverensis*, see chap. XI.
[3] *MB Epp.* 223 (p. 504). On Bartholomew, see Morey, pp. 92–3.
[4] Cf. Brooke, art. cit.; Cheney, *From Becket to Langton*, pp. 137–8.

them away to Gloucester abbey. Gilbert not unnaturally responded to Gloucester's call to defend its acquisition.[1] The Hereford *acta* of Gilbert supply two instances of the appointment of vicars; the London *acta* a great number.[2] In one of these, precise details were given of how the vicar's rights were secured, when the church of Barkway in Hertfordshire was appropriated to Colchester abbey. The church is granted *in propriis usibus*, saving the rights for life of the existing vicar, and, for the future, of a priest serving the church who is to be responsible to the monks for the temporalities and to the bishop for the spiritualities; the provision for the vicar is to be perpetual and not annual.[3]

Documents concerning appropriation are one of a variety of kinds of document illustrating the bishop's relations with the religious houses of the dioceses. Since the bulk of his charters survive in monastic cartularies, it is natural that their concerns should be particularly well documented. To his former abbey of Gloucester Gilbert was a constant friend and benefactor; as bishop of Hereford, for example, he exempted the abbot from attendance at diocesan synods and from part of the episcopal taxation in respect of Gloucester churches in the diocese, and he also granted him freedom to appoint the vicars of Cowarne.[4] There were no great religious houses in the diocese of Hereford, and Gilbert was mainly concerned as bishop with the dependencies of Gloucester, the Reading dependency at Leominster, Battle's priory at Brecon, and the alien priory of Monmouth. The documents include general confirmations of churches, tithes and the like, and an early indulgence; also the settlement of several law-suits. These were the standard themes of his later acts as well. More remarkable were the confirmations of corrodies, unusual so early as this—Lanthony gave food and clothing to the mother of Ralph, son of Ernald, for life in return for a grant of land, Aubrey de Loges received the same benefits from Hereford priory in return for the grant of half her land, while her son was pro-

---

[1] No. 371.
[2] Nos. 306, 326; 361, 395, 400, 434, 443—and nos. 376, 392, 398, 402, 406, 457 deal with perpetual vicars (or vicarages).
[3] No. 361.   [4] Nos. 304-6.

vided with an annuity; also interesting was the establishment of Bromfield priory. Robert of Haseley, monk of Gloucester, was instituted as prior and parish priest—the priory church is still the parish church of Bromfield; and the priory was made a royal chapel, exempt from the bishop's control, by Henry II: 'nor does the lord king', writes Gilbert (c. 1155), 'permit me to have any jurisdiction over the prior'.[1]

As bishop of London, Gilbert was brought into contact with the great abbey of Westminster; but by persistence and forgery Westminster had established its exemption from his authority, and he seems for the most part to have maintained peace with his powerful neighbour. A controversy developed, however, over the legal position of St Margaret's church; Gilbert pointed out to Abbot Laurence that its subjection to the bishop of London had never previously been called in question, while during his own episcopate it had paid the customary *cathedraticum* to the archdeacon of London. Doubtless the archdeacon stiffened Gilbert's attitude by complaining—as Peter of Blois was to complain a generation later—of the poverty of his archdeaconry; but the letter seems to be characteristic of Gilbert's own view of how to handle such a case. He was firm but conciliatory, and expresses a strong desire to stamp out the quarrel in its early beginnings.[2] The abbey, however, won. At the very end of Bishop Roger of Worcester's life a dispute broke out between Roger and the abbot of Westminster over the bishop's right to institute the prior of Great Malvern. Gilbert wrote, perhaps at the abbot's request, on behalf of Prior Walter. But Roger did not take a tender view of Malvern's efforts to exert the exemption of the mother house, and Prior Walter did not secure institution from the bishop of Worcester until 1190.[3]

The cartularies of religious houses in the diocese of London, or of orders and communities with extensive property in the diocese,

[1] Nos. 329, 319, 303 (for Bromfield, cf. *MB Epp.* 202; and for earlier evidence, F. E. Harmer in *The Anglo-Saxons*, ed. P. Clemoes, London, 1959, pp. 90 ff.).

[2] No. 229. On Westminster's exemption, see D. Knowles, *Downside Rev.*, L (1932), 415 ff. After a dispute Gilbert acknowledged the exemption of Kilburn, a priory of nuns dependent on Westminster, in no. 463.

[3] See no. 239 and notes.

provide us with numerous general confirmations by Gilbert: for Colchester, Walden, Stoke-by-Clare; for the Hospitallers; for Holy Trinity, Aldgate, and for one or two of the smaller Augustinian houses. The scanty records of hospitals are supplemented from his letter-collection, which suggests that his indulgences were quite frequently granted to encourage alms to hospitals, including the new hospital dedicated to St Thomas Becket in Southwark.[1] He issued indulgences also to encourage support for bridge-building at London, Stratford and St Ives (outside his diocese); for church-building at St Ives and within his castle at Bishop's Stortford; above all, for the completion of his cathedral.[2] Of the scanty indications of his dealings with houses of religious women, the most interesting is no. 172, a letter written to Bishop Robert of Lincoln on behalf of the nuns of Haliwell in Middlesex; in it he gives a brief but vivid account of a small foundation of twenty sisters living on an inadequate site and supported mainly by the revenues of the church of Dunton in the diocese of Lincoln. The ownership of this church was now in dispute: Gilbert asks his uncle and brother-bishop not to decide against the nuns, since without the church's revenues the site of the convent is adequate for burial but not for sustenance.

Across the pages of Gilbert's *acta* pass some of the greatest names of the time: Earl Roger of Hereford, Bernard of Neufmarché, Gilbert de Lacy, Baderon of Monmouth, in the diocese of Hereford; Earl Richard of Clare, William de Mandeville, earl of Essex, Earl Robert of Leicester, at London. All of them were substantial benefactors of religious in their day; some of them had special need to atone for their career in the anarchy. Of Gilbert's relations as bishop with the laity we know little, and the evidence is not surprisingly restricted, in the main, to his relations with the baronial class. The letters of spiritual direction to the earl of Leicester and his countess give one aspect of that relationship; the ups and downs of his intimacy with his own relative, Earl Roger of Hereford, illustrate another.[3] The penal arm of the Church

[1] No. 452; cf. nos. 352, 363, 413-14, 424.
[2] Nos. 418, 448, 353, 235 and n.
[3] Nos. 120, 194-6; see above, pp. 73, 88.

would be extended to correct the earl's misdemeanours, the bishop would support his good deeds, and at one decisive moment would intervene to hold him back from open rebellion against the king.[1] There is evidence that Gilbert could take a forceful line with the mighty in the letters in which he deals with the attempt of Elias de Say to judge a cleric in his baronial court, and to Philip of Sarnesfield regarding the oath which had been falsely sworn in the court of the abbot of Reading.[2] There is evidence of his tact in the claim which he put to Josce de Dinan for the restitution of Church lands, and perhaps of his kindness in the letter of commendation written to Henry II on behalf of the orphaned son of Ralph of Worcester.[3] Occasionally one finds him concerned with lesser folk: with a former parishioner of the London diocese who had deserted his wife some seven years previously and was now, optimistically, invited to return, or with the convert from the Jewish faith for whose support Gilbert granted an indulgence.[4]

Of the administration of his estates, and of his personal wealth we know very little. The witness-lists to the *acta* give us the names of his lay officials—chamberlain, dispenser, steward, butler and others.[5] He gave land at Fulham for the support of one of his lesser serjeants, his cook; and after his translation he complained of the treatment meted out to four of his Hereford serjeants by his successor.[6] One of these was William Folet, who was granted a holding which he himself had bought in Hereford from Robert de Chandos, together with other properties, on conditions which included the performance of the duties of cupbearer on the greater feasts and attendance at the bishop's court.[7] In his early years at Hereford he made determined efforts to recover the lands of his see lost during the civil war; and as bishop of London he gave testimony about the service of two knights owed by the Lacys, which was one of the pieces of evidence from which Mr Colvin was able to piece together a fascinating case history of a feudal

[1] Gervase, I, 162.   [2] Nos. 117, 119.
[3] Nos. 114, 125.   [4] Nos. 268, 419.
[5] See below, p. 292.   [6] Nos. 397, 175–6.
[7] No. 312.

tenure of a somewhat unusual kind.[1] But his letters and charters tell us almost nothing of estate management: we have to wait till the thirteenth century before we can hope to have any circumstantial evidence on this. A slight exception is the charter which determined the conditions under which a supply of water was channelled through Bishopsgate to episcopal property over land belonging to the chapter of St Paul's.[2] But it is to a stray reference by the satirist Nigel Wireker that we owe the information that Gilbert employed a merchant on his business in Italy, in the hope, so Nigel tells us, of lengthening his nose.[3] No doubt this was a proverbial expression for gain; it may also be our one hint about his personal appearance. That Gilbert is signalled out for Wireker's attention certainly implies that he was known as an efficient administrator of his temporalities. All the indications, specific and circumstantial, suggest that he was a conscientious administrator also in spiritual things—capable, even admirable, according to the standards of his day, though not attracting the admiration of contemporaries as did Bartholomew of Exeter nor their reverence as did St Hugh.

OUTSIDE THE DIOCESE

Of the bishop's relations with the king and kingdom, sufficient has been said in the context of the Becket dispute; some indications of his relations with religious houses, with bishops and laymen outside his see have already been made; his activities as papal judge-delegate form the theme of the next chapter. In accordance with custom, Gilbert acted from time to time as vicar of vacant sees—that is, as episcopal caretaker, in charge of spiritual affairs, not as tenant or farmer of their temporalities.[4] In 1148 he was

[1] Nos. 80, 378; H. M. Colvin in *Medieval Studies presented to Rose Graham*, ed. V. Ruffer and A. J. Taylor (Oxford, 1950), pp. 15–40.

[2] No. 405. For the bishopric's income after his death, see *PR 35 Henry II*, p. 29, *34 Henry II*, pp. 11–12.

[3] Wireker, al. Nigel de Longchamps, *Speculum stultorum*, ed. J. H. Mozley and R. R. Raymo (Univ. of California, 1960), lines 755 ff. and notes. We also know that he owed William Cade £6 in 1165–6 (*EHR*, xxviii (1913), 226): but the debt was not large and the date was soon after his translation.

[4] But he did for a time act as farmer of the temporalities of some of the exiles in the 1160's (see no. 169 and notes).

vicar before becoming bishop of Hereford; in 1150–1 he had expected to be vicar of the diocese of Worcester, but he was ousted by the archdeacon of Worcester who claimed to have the old bishop's designation to this office;[1] in 1160–4 he did act as vicar of the same diocese, and made a vigorous attempt to secure liberty of election for the monks of Tewkesbury.[2] In Becket's absence Gilbert found himself in the embarrassing position of being the leading bishop in the southern province, obliged to perform certain functions on this account, expected by the king to be a kind of acting archbishop, denounced by the archbishop for making profit from his exile. Under these conditions Gilbert strove to do what had to be done, to see for instance that Peter's Pence was collected and delivered to the papal bankers;[3] but he tried to avoid accepting from the king commissions which would be too compromising.

The basis of his position as leading bishop of the province was partly his personal prestige, partly the tradition of his office. Traditionally the bishop of London was dean of the province: that is, he summoned his colleagues to provincial councils—one of Gilbert's letters issuing a summons to the council of Westminster of 1175 is the first clear evidence of this duty—and presided over their meetings in the archbishop's absence. In 1173–4 Gilbert was thus probably a somewhat uneasy chairman of the discussions about the election of the new archbishop of Canterbury.[4] The only rival to his precedence would have been the bishop of Winchester, traditionally precentor of the province; but in the 1160's Henry of Winchester was an old man in semi-retirement, and after his death in 1171 his see was vacant until 1173–4.

The origin of these titles, 'dean' and 'precentor', is somewhat

---

[1] Above, p. 97; no. 93.
[2] He wrote no. 135, urging them not to give up their right of free election.
[3] Nos. 155–6.
[4] Cf. Gervase, I, 244, 251, and nos. 220–1. On the deanship of the province, see I. J. Churchill, *Canterbury Administration* (London, 1933), I, 355–9. On the title, cf. M. Deanesly, *Sidelights on the Anglo-Saxon Church*, pp. 143–4, who suggests that it was related to the 'dean' of Roman Law, an official messenger. But the links with the 'precentor' and the election of an archbishop strongly suggest an ecclesiastical origin.

obscure. They indicate clearly that at some stage the bishops of the province regarded themselves as canons of a chapter, and it is clear that their prime function as a chapter, in their own eyes, was to elect the archbishop. The dispute between the bishops and the monks of Canterbury about who should elect the archbishop was a running sore in the twelfth and thirteenth centuries. Such a dispute could only have arisen in a situation in which the precise body of electors to the archbishopric was being discussed; and it is most unlikely that anyone thought of there being a defined body of electors before the eleventh century—indeed before the late eleventh century when the ideas of the papal reform were seeping in, however little they affected the practice of episcopal selection in that period. The titles 'dean' and 'precentor' belong to the north French capitular system introduced by the early Norman bishops: these offices could not be older than c. 1080-90.[1] The titles were not applied to the bishops of London and Winchester in any surviving document before the twelfth century, but Eadmer's account of St Anselm's consecration as archbishop in 1093 strongly suggests that London and Winchester had already achieved the status, and Eadmer actually gives London the title 'dean' in 1109. He tells us under 1093 that it was the bishop of London's function to read the formal record of election, and that in that year Bishop Maurice delegated it to Bishop Walkelin of Winchester.[2] Behind this lay the ardent discussions in the Councils of 1072 and 1075 about the precedence of the English bishops.[3] The canons of 1075 include a decision that London and Winchester have precedence after Canterbury and York, while the rest of the bishops have precedence according to seniority of consecration. The order of signatories to the council of 1075 conforms to this

[1] See above, p. 189 n.
[2] *Historia Novorum*, ed. M. Rule, RS, pp. 42, 211 (the events of 1109 were written down in the years 1119–22; those of 1093 between 1109 and 1115: Southern, *St Anselm and His Biographer*, pp. 298 ff.).
[3] D. Wilkins, *Concilia Magnae Brittaniae*, 1 (London, 1737), pp. 363–4 for 1075. The argument is reflected in the order of signatories, and a close comparison with the signatories of the council of 1072 (Wilkins, 1, 325) strongly suggests that the argument in 1075 had been anticipated in the former year (these councils will be the subject of a forthcoming study by Mrs H. Clover).

rule: that of 1072 shows that London had already achieved its position, but not Winchester, in that year. It looks as if London's claim to superiority—based perhaps on its ancient claim to primacy, or the antiquity of the see, or the importance of London —was established in Lanfranc's time. The titles 'dean' and 'precentor' were no doubt devised in the last quarter of the eleventh century, perhaps in the vacancy after Lanfranc's death, between 1089 and 1093—the first vacancy which would have given the suffragans of Canterbury leisure to reflect on their claims to be the body to elect the archbishop, though it gave them mighty little opportunity to exercise them. The deanship was certainly well established in Gilbert's time. It survived, and survives still, for certain formal purposes, even though, as the law of episcopal election was gradually defined, and the actual electors became less and less important and the bishops were ousted, the original claim implicit in the title 'dean'—to preside at and have the first voice in electing the archbishop of Canterbury—was rapidly forgotten.

Between 1164 and 1174, apart from the brief interlude in December 1170, there was no archbishop at Canterbury: for six years he was an exile; for four more the see was vacant. Becket's successor, Richard of Dover (1174–84), was a nonentity. Under these conditions Gilbert Foliot was for a number of years the leading figure in the southern province, both by virtue of his office and of his personal position. He was *primus inter pares*: he could hardly dominate a bench which also included Bartholomew of Exeter and Roger and Baldwin of Worcester; and his prestige was badly shaken by the disasters of 1169–70. But with his long experience, his ability, his connexions—in particular the family connexions which dominated the sees of Hereford and London, and included the precentor of the province, his cousin, Richard of Ilchester, bishop of Winchester from 1174—he remained to the end a power to be reckoned with; and in the last years, after Baldwin had been translated from Worcester to Canterbury and the province had once more a forceful head, Gilbert remained its doyen in another sense.

CHAPTER XI

JUDGE-DELEGATE

THE *COLLECTIO BELVERENSIS*

In the middle of the Bodleian manuscript of Gilbert's letters, E Musaeo 249 (B), is a group of three quires mainly given over to letters and decretals of Pope Alexander III. The first quire contains letters written in the course of the dispute with Becket. The second and third form the decretal collection known to modern students of canon law as the *Collectio Belverensis*—from Belvoir, the home of the manuscript in the late Middle Ages.[1] This is an exceptionally early decretal collection, and is of great interest in helping to determine the way in which decretals were collected. It was becoming increasingly common in this period for legal cases to go to Rome on appeal, and for the pope to delegate them to judges in their country of origin; in such cases he commonly (and in the long run invariably) laid down in a decretal letter a decision on the legal issue involved. Even in cases in which there was no appeal, it was common in the mid- and late-twelfth century for local judges to consult the pope. This meant that the papal chancery was issuing statements of legal principle on an unprecedented scale; it was natural that some attempt should be made to collect these statements—and it was only to be expected that in course of time collections of them should be promulgated as official reservoirs of papal decretal legislation. The process got under way

---

[1] There is in fact no doubt that these quires, like the rest of the MS, were written by Gilbert Foliot's clerks, or under their direction, *c.* 1175-80. Duggan, pp. 155 ff., gives a full analysis of the collection, and comparative tables; see pp. 71-3 for a discussion. The early decretal collections have been subjected to intensive study in recent years: in this Dr W. Holtzmann and Professor S. Kuttner have been the pioneers (see esp. Kuttner, *Repertorium der Kanonistik*, I, Rome, 1937, pp. 272 ff.; Holtzmann, 'Über einer Ausgabe der päpstlichen Dekretalen des 12. Jahrhunderts', *Nachrichten der Akad. der Wissenschaften in Göttingen, phil.-hist. Klasse* (1945), pp. 15 ff.; Kuttner in *Traditio*, VI (1948), 345 ff., and more recent articles; Holtzmann and E. W. Kemp, *Papal Decretals relating to the Diocese of Lincoln*, Lincoln Rec. Soc., 1954); studies on the English collections have been brought together and usefully supplemented in Duggan.

about 1170, and was completed by the publication of Gregory IX's *Decretals*, the *Liber Extra*, in 1234. The *Liber Extra* replaced all earlier collections of decretals and made them useless, and it would hardly be surprising if they had all disappeared. In fact a very large number have survived in whole or in part, and this reveals in a striking way how numerous the early decretal collections must have been: what survives can only be a small proportion of what once existed. Collecting decretals became something like a mania in late-twelfth-century Europe; English collectors were particularly active; and the *Collectio Belverensis* was written soon after collecting first began.

The materials in *Belverensis* fall into four groups. The first consists of eight canons of the Council of Tours of 1163 and ten decretal letters of Alexander III, four addressed to Roger, bishop of Worcester, the remainder to the archbishop of York, the bishop of Exeter, the bishop of Norwich, and the archdeacon of Lincoln. This section is very similar to what may be the earliest surviving English decretal collection, *Wigorniensis Altera*, which was clearly written at Worcester. The second section of *Belverensis* contains seven letters, four addressed to Gilbert Foliot, and one to all the English bishops. There is no distinction between these sections in the manuscript: both are written in the same hand, without a break between them. But the two parts clearly come from different sources: the first from a small collection of Worcester provenance, the second from Gilbert's own archives. All the decretals in the first section are known elsewhere—all but one of them occur in *Wigorniensis Altera*. Of the seven items in section II, five occur nowhere else in surviving collections, and none occurs in *Wigorniensis Altera*. It is clear that the scribe has put together two small collections, and it is possible that they had already been combined in his source. But if so, the combination was very recent. The early Worcester collection cannot be earlier than 1173 or 1174;[1] the *Belverensis* itself cannot be more than about four or five years later than 1175, and perhaps less. At the end of section II another hand has added the papal bulls of 1173 canonising Thomas Becket; then follow (in yet another hand) the

---

[1] Duggan, p. 70. On the date of *Belverensis*, see above, pp. 26, 28.

decrees of the council of Westminster of May 1175, the latest
certainly datable items in the whole manuscript, which comprise
section III; and finally section IV, nine decretals addressed to the
archbishop of Canterbury or groups of English monks, most of
which are known in other collections.

It has been estimated that out of the 713 known decretals of
Alexander III, 363 were addressed to England.[1] This figure signi-
fies, first and foremost, the influence of English canonists in collecting decretals. The large number of early collections shows that
many hands must have taken part in this enterprise in the last
thirty years of the twelfth century. But it is likely that the
English initiative was due to the inspiration of one or of a small
group of expert legal advisers in the circle of the leading English
bishops of this age. The chief contributions to the early collections
came from the archives of Exeter, Worcester and Canterbury.
The bishops most frequently addressed were Bartholomew of
Exeter, Roger of Worcester and Richard of Canterbury, but it is
clear that the development of the collections bears some relation
to the career of Baldwin, Bartholomew's archdeacon and successor to Roger at Worcester and Richard at Canterbury. Dr Mayr-
Harting has recently made the suggestion that the central figure
in the production of *Wigorniensis* (*c.* 1181), the Worcester collection slightly later than *Wigorniensis Altera* and *Belverensis*—in
which the first steps in the transition towards systematic collections were made—was one Master Silvester, clerk successively to
Roger and Baldwin at Worcester, then a member of Baldwin's
familia at Canterbury.[2] This seems very probable, and it may well
be that the *Belverensis* shows us the fruit of consultation between
Silvester and his colleagues in the households of other bishops at
the council of 1175.

The canons of the council of 1175 were based on earlier
authorities. All but three were to be found in Gratian; the three
exceptions were from decretals of Alexander III, two from a
single decretal which can be found both in *Wigorniensis Altera*

---

[1] By W. Holtzmann, *Papal Decretals relating to the Diocese of Lincoln*, p. xvii.
[2] In a paper read to the Ecclesiastical History Society in Cambridge in July
1963 (to be published in *Studies in Eccl. History*, II).

and *Belverensis*, and the other, if it can be identified at all, is also in these collections.[1] Thus we can see in *Belverensis* both the canons of this council and one of its major sources. We can also see the beginnings of the council's later career. *Belverensis* also contains the canons of the general council of Tours of 1163. Soon after, probably at Worcester, a copy was made of *Wigorniensis Altera* (or something very similar), in which Tours and Westminster were set side by side, and Westminster, as in *Belverensis*, had no heading. Later scribes wrongly deduced from this arrangement that the canons of Westminster were additional canons from Tours, and so they came to be treated as canons of a general council and as legislation of the Church at large.[2] In this disguise they flourished in later decretal collections, and six of them found a place in the *Liber Extra*. Thus sections I and III of *Belverensis* indicate collaboration between the households of Roger of Worcester and Gilbert Foliot during and perhaps after the council of Westminster; and section IV perhaps shows evidence of an exchange with Canterbury at about the same time.[3] It may be that Master David of London, Gilbert's old protégé, known to be working for Bartholomew and Roger in the 1170's, acted as a go-between among the bishops' households. In any case, the *Belverensis* is a valuable early witness to the collaboration between different households in collecting decretals. But it is evidence of the influence of Worcester rather than of London in this respect; for most of the local material, represented by section II, is

---

[1] Cf. Duggan, p. 73; Brooke in *Traditio*, XIII (1957), 476, 478, where it is pointed out that the decretal to the bishop of Norwich which is cited in the canons of the council as the source of canon 12 cannot be identified. But the canons of the council often differ substantially from the sources cited, and since the decretal to the bishop of Norwich which occurs in *Wigorniensis Altera* and *Belverensis* (no. 14: JL, nos. 12253, 14146) contains a section dealing with a vicar who tries to act as rector in a vacancy, and canon 12 deals with vicars who arrogate rectorships to themselves (not, apparently, in vacancies), it is possible that the reference was to this decretal.

[2] Brooke in *Traditio*, XIII (1957), 471–80 (corrected in detail, by S. Kuttner, *Traditio*, XVII (1961), 536–7).

[3] Three of the items in section IV were addressed to the archbishop of Canterbury (one or two to Becket, one or two to Richard); one to all regulars in the province of Canterbury; the others to monastic houses or congregations. All but two are also in the primitive collections *Cantuariensis* or *Roffensis*.

otherwise unknown, and the *Belverensis* itself, close as it was to the fountain-head of English decretal collecting, had no direct influence on later collections.[1]

Thus the real interest of the *Belverensis* lies not in its relation to Gilbert himself, but to the development of canonist studies in English bishops' households at large. The manuscript as a whole, and the other sources from which Gilbert's *acta* can be reconstructed, provide rich materials for the study of papal appeals and the growth of the courts of judges-delegate. These, too, are best seen in a wider context.

THE GROWTH OF APPEALS

The development of papal jurisdiction in England in the second half of the twelfth century has been carefully studied in the last forty years.[2] We know that appeals to Rome were growing in the middle of the century, and grew steadily as the century advanced; we know how this development is reflected in the development of the system of papal delegation, how a group of leading bishops acted very frequently as delegates in the days of Roger of Worcester, Bartholomew of Exeter and Gilbert Foliot;

---

[1] Cf. Duggan, p. 123. In section II, four items are addressed to Gilbert, of which only one occurs in other collections; one to the archbishop of Rouen, which is not otherwise known; one to the abbot of St Albans, which occurs elsewhere. The other three items concern the Becket dispute, and occur in other MSS of the correspondence. The section is not meant to contain items of legal interest alone, and if we reflect that five of the nine items were available in Canterbury circles in this period, Dr Duggan's statement that this part of the *Belverensis* 'was entirely without influence on later canonical works' seems somewhat to beg the question. It is, however, probably true that the other copyists of these five items only depended on Gilbert's archives for one of them at most. The letters in Liverani, pp. 608 (1), 757, 593, 641 (1), show that Master David worked for Roger of Worcester and apparently Bartholomew of Exeter in the 1170's, and Liverani, p. 608, shows that he visited Canterbury (on Master David, see above, p. 205).

[2] Z. N. Brooke in *CHJ*, II, iii (1928), 213–28; *The English Church and the Papacy from the Conquest to the Reign of John* (Cambridge, 1931), pp. 211 ff.; Morey, chap. IV; Mary Cheney, *EHR*, LVI (1941), 177–97; W. Ullmann, *Yorks. Arch. Journ.* XXXVI (1948–51), 456–73; S. Kuttner and E. Rathbone, *Traditio*, VII (1949–51), 279–80; Duggan; W. J. La Due, *Papal Rescripts of Justice and English Royal Procedural Writs, 1150–1250* (Rome, 1960).

how the law and procedure of the courts in which papal delegates tried these cases was increasingly defined. Z. N. Brooke, the pioneer in these studies in England, attributed this growth partly to local causes: notably to the relaxation of royal control in Stephen's reign and the effect of Becket's murder and Henry II's surrender of the right to restrict appeals in the Compromise of Avranches. But it has since been shown that the evidence does not establish that appeals were much commoner in the 1170's than the 1160's, certainly not that there was any noticeable change in and after 1172; and we now know that the chronology of the growth of appeals from England is very much the same as for many parts of Europe.[1] The development was more even than was originally supposed, and that in England was hardly exceptional. The activities of Bartholomew and Roger as judges-delegate have been examined in detail; so has the legal attitude of Hilary of Chichester. Very recently the numerous investigations of the English contribution to the early collections of decretals have been brought together by Dr Duggan. The contribution of English canonists to the formation of the first collections of decretals stands out more clearly than ever; but he has argued that the very high percentage of the surviving decretals which were addressed to England is a reflexion of the origin of the early decretalists, not of the exceptionally papalist or exceptionally criminous nature of the English church. This may not be the whole truth: England may have played a particularly conspicuous part in the story of appeals and decretals; the local causes must surely have counted for something. But the chief interest of the English evidence is that it helps to bring the general movement of the day into sharper focus and clearer light.

Gilbert's letters and *acta* provide a body of material as great as for any English judge-delegate of the century. The records of his career also provide two glimpses of special interest of the development of canon law. It is very doubtful whether Becket's murder opened the floodgate to appeals, because it is doubtful if there was a gate to open. The Constitutions of Clarendon were the ostensible *casus belli* on which Henry and Becket finally broke,

[1] On the evidence, cf. *JS Epp.* I, pp. xxxi ff., esp. pp. xxxi–xxxii n.

and Henry was doubtless determined to enforce them, in the long run, if he could. But between 1164 and 1170 he seems to have been much more determined to defeat and depose Becket than to stand on his rights. There were moments when he threatened to go over to the anti-pope, when he issued supplementary decrees, when even Gilbert was amerced for breaking the rules.[1] But by and large he allowed Gilbert to take such steps as he felt were absolutely necessary to fight Becket. The outstanding example of this was the king's apparently meek acquiescence in Gilbert's continual appeals to the pope against Becket. This was a very special kind of appeal; but it was special among other things because it was notorious. Gilbert's appeals may well have accustomed men naturally antagonistic to the idea to the usefulness of the papal Curia; and the mere existence of Becket must have encouraged royal supporters to appeal to Rome. The alternative laid down in the Constitutions was that appeals should go to Canterbury and no further (anyway without the king's special consent). But appeals to Canterbury were obnoxious and unthinkable between 1164 and 1170. If we may take Hilary of Chichester as a representative of the expert lawyer-bishop of the age who was none the less inclined in cases of conflict to support king against pope[2]—whether from conviction, tradition or expediency—we can understand that in the circumstances of the 1160's appeal to the pope would seem a natural and proper corollary to conflict with Becket. There is no doubt that this is how Gilbert viewed the matter, and his numerous appeals, discussed in chapter IX, may well have helped to keep the gate open. Whatever the explanation, there is no evidence that it was seriously more difficult to take an appeal to Rome in the 1160's than in the 1170's.

This does not mean that the path to Rome was smooth or easy in the 1160's. The Constitutions of Clarendon also laid it down that a tenant-in-chief should not be excommunicated without the king's permission, and Gilbert seems to have been little inclined to a breach of this decree. Aubrey de Vere, earl of Oxford,

[1] MB Epp. 599.
[2] See H. Mayr-Harting in EHR, LXXVIII (1963), 209–24.

repudiated the lady to whom he was married on trumped-up grounds. Already in 1166 Gilbert was writing to the pope about this case; but he evidently shrank from stern action: a letter to the earl makes no mention of the papal sentence, and the pope had to rebuke Gilbert for refusing his counsel to the countess when she applied to his diocesan court.[1] The case hung fire until after Becket's murder: in 1172 the pope issued his final mandate to the earl to take back his wife; after years of degradation, even involving imprisonment, the countess won her case and the outcome of this singularly inauspicious opening was apparently a successful marriage. In this case Gilbert seems to have succeeded in keeping pope, king and earl at bay for some time; in the case of the canons of Pentney he was less successful. Once again he tried to evade responsibility for offending the king by excommunicating a tenant-in-chief—this time the earl of Norfolk, with whom the obscure canons of Pentney were (as Gilbert complained) obstinately disputing.[2] His attitude is hardly admirable; but he had reason to feel aggrieved at being ground between pope and king in a dispute on a small piece of property. In the end he obeyed the pope. Thus Gilbert's letters reveal with some clarity the ambivalent effect of the archbishop's exile on relations between England and Rome: it made the king prepared to allow a ceaseless flow of appeals in what he regarded as a good cause, but strengthened Henry's determination not to allow interference with the lives of his barons.

GILBERT FOLIOT'S LEGAL VIEWS

The *Belverensis* represents in part Gilbert's concern as a busy judge-delegate; but even more, in all probability, the concern of his legally minded clerks. In Gilbert's early letters, as we have seen,[3] there is much evidence of his personal interest in Roman and canon law and legal problems. In his decisions as judge-delegate

---

[1] Nos. 162–4. In no. 164, written early in 1172, the pope instructed Gilbert to excommunicate the earl and lay an interdict on his lands if he did not submit. But see p. 184.　　[2] Nos. 159–61; cf. *MB Epp.* 599, 644, 700, 725–8.

[3] See above, pp. 59–69.

it is impossible to tell how much is his own work, how much that of the advocates employed by the parties in the cases, how much the work of Gilbert's own legal advisers. The judge-delegate material is interesting more as the record of an institution than of a person; none the less there is a general presumption that Gilbert's own views and concerns are reflected in his decisions.

There are some cases in which we can be tolerably sure that Gilbert's own views are being presented, especially when he is being consulted by other bishops on points of law. He was regarded as an authority on procedure; but even so it is somewhat surprising to find him in no. 243 administering a strongly worded lecture on the subject to Bishop Roger of Worcester, one of the best known judges-delegate of the time. A case had gone from Gilbert's jurisdiction, presumably after appeal to the pope, to Bishop Roger: Gilbert asserts that Roger has treated him technically as if he were the defendant, when he was the judge from whose court the appeal came. Gilbert evidently reckoned that the appellant had misled Roger and was causing bad blood between the bishops—hence the warmth of his complaint. On an earlier occasion the bishop of Chester-Coventry had consulted him as to whether he could appeal in a case in which he was the defendant and had received a mandate from Archbishop Theobald, acting as papal legate, containing the clause *appellatione remota*.[1] In his reply Gilbert urged the bishop to scrutinise the papal mandate carefully to see whether an *exceptio* might be raised on the ground of false evidence, and he buttressed his opinion that the prohibition of appeal could not be sustained against such an exception by no less than six quotations from the *Code*. The clause *appellatione remota* was coming into common use at this time: it first appears under Innocent II, and under Alexander III (1159–81) the first serious steps were taken towards a solution of the many technical difficulties to which this reasonable measure intended to limit frivolous appeals none the less inevitably led.[2] Alexander III settled that a third party retained the right of appeal when a sentence affected his interests even if the papal mandate contained the clause *appellatione remota*; its use was further defined by his

[1] No. 110.   [2] Cf. *JS Epp.* I, p. xxxv.

successors; and Innocent III finally decided (in effect) that both parties retained their right to raise recognised exceptions.[1] Alexander III on one occasion refused to quash a judgement by Gilbert and referred to the fact that the appellant had himself applied for the clause to be inserted in the mandate.[2] But Gilbert's cases provide instances where the clause had little effect in restricting litigation, and during the lengthy case between Osney abbey and St Frideswide's priory the pope rebuked Gilbert and Roger of Worcester for their inaction, complaining with some irritation that appeals had been made in spite of the clause.[3]

In no. 113 Gilbert expressed some criticism of the way in which his cousin of London had handled a difficult case, and he advised the bishop to postpone execution of the papal mandate which, as seems likely, might have been obtained by fraud—in which case it was open to the defendant to claim an exception. The possibility that mandates were forged, or obtained under false pretences—*tacita ueritate*—and difficulty in interpreting the mandate were major problems in the courts of judges-delegate. In a case before Gilbert and the bishop of Norwich a second mandate was obtained, the details of the first—including the fact that it had the words *appellatione remota*—being suppressed; this led to one of the earliest definitions by Alexander III as to the genuineness of a papal rescript which was incorporated into the decretal collections and subsequently confirmed and amplified by Innocent III.[4] The defendant in the case was a nephew of Gilbert, Ralph de Hauterive, subsequently master of the schools at St Paul's and archdeacon of Colchester, and the plaintiff successfully appealed against the two judges as friends of his opponent. Gilbert did not try the case, but it is ironical that he should have been associated with the first important papal decretal on forgery. No. 185 (1167–8) concerns

---

[1] *Extra*, i, 29, 15; ii, 4, 2; ii, 13, 10–11; ii, 28, 36, 28, 41; ii, 28, 53.

[2] No. 186; cf. Arnulf of Lisieux, *Ep.* 78 (ed. F. Barlow), where the judge urged that the clause should not operate to the plaintiff's detriment since it had been inserted at his request; also *Ep.* 64, where the defendant noticed the clause in the mandate and objected 'quia malebat apud delegantem quam coram delegato iudice litigare'.

[3] No. 427. For the use of the clause, see *GFL*, index.

[4] *Extra*, ii, 22, 3 (JL 14142), cf. v, 20, esp. c. 9.

a case in which he and the bishop of Winchester had delayed a hearing beyond the term laid down in the mandate, a critical matter in the interpretation of mandates. Gilbert's defence is extremely interesting. The case had to be postponed because the bishop of Winchester was detained by urgent business in the king's court, and a later date was fixed with the consent of both parties. The authorities, Gilbert observed, were not agreed: some held that under these conditions the commission expired, and he supported this from the *Code*; others held that on the principle *a similibus ad similia* the chapter of the *Digest* which allowed a judge to exceed the sum fixed for his judgement could be extended to apply to the case in question. Gilbert took the latter view, which he stated was also the custom of the English church, and claimed to be able to extend the term if necessary. Gilbert based his view on civil law, and the pope confirmed his decision; the principle involved was in fact assumed some years later in a decretal of Alexander III which appears in the *Belverensis* itself.[1] In this he stated that a judge cannot prolong the term of a case without the assent of both parties, which implies that with their consent postponement was permissible.

In this case, characteristically, Gilbert bases an argument on procedure on citations from Roman Law. In a similar way, early in his career, in defending a layman's advowson against Jocelin of Salisbury he cites the *Code* in support of custom against the letter of the law. It would, indeed, Gilbert argues, be better if laymen had neither the gift of churches nor the right of presentation, but we should not enforce on humble people a strict law which is not in fact enforced against the great. He appeals to the *Code* for the force of custom, but he breaks off his quotation at the point where the *Code* goes on to state that custom cannot override the law; it is surprising that he did not quote the passage from the *Digest* which equates custom and *lex*.[2] The issue was

---

[1] JL 12636 (1173–6); *Gilberti Foliot Epistolae*, II, no. 372 (from *Belverensis*): 'sine assensu utriusque partis non licet iudici terminum a delegatore prefixum aliquatenus prorogare.' Cf. *Extra*, i, 29, 4, 32.

[2] Nos. 17, 18; *Code*, 8, 52 (53), 2; *Digest*, 1, 3, 32, 1. Cf. Rogerius: 'In Digestis enim legi, legum interpretem optimam esse consuetudinem', *Enodationes quaestionum super Codice*, ed. H. Kantorowicz and W. W. Buckland,

much in dispute among the glossators, but we have no later or fuller discussion of it from Gilbert's pen.

In one of his later consultations, however, we find Gilbert ignoring Roman Law and citing canonical evidence alone. The question put to him, by the archdeacon of Gloucester, was whether a woman accused of adultery could clear herself simply by oath, or should be put to the ordeal as the husband desired. The influence of Roman Law, which punished a husband who did not repudiate a wife guilty of adultery, led to a doubt among the canonists whether a husband might pardon this offence. In his answer (no. 237) Gilbert says nothing of this: he is content to emphasise the mercy of the Church and the necessity for confession where the woman is guilty; a good man will be satisfied with his wife's repentance. Where the woman is only suspected her oath will suffice. Gilbert's wording follows a view which became the accepted official teaching.[1] There can be no doubt that in the 1160's (and possibly earlier) Gilbert reckoned to use Gratian's *Decretum* as the basis for his citation of canonical texts— the dispute made him a student of Gratian as it did the archbishop himself—although he or his legal advisers could depart from the views of the master when they felt moved to.[2]

Of exceptional interest are Gilbert's letters 157–8, on the treatment of heresy. The English church had hitherto been remarkably free from this problem. The heresies of the early eleventh century, so far as the evidence goes, touched it not at all; nor did the Petrobrusian and other movements of the early twelfth. In the second half of the twelfth century, when the Cathar churches were flourishing and multiplying in many parts of the continent and establishing a regular hierarchy of heretical bishops in France

---

Studies in the Glossators of the Roman Law, p. 282; for the views of the glossators see S. Brie, *Die Lehre vom Gewohnheitsrecht*, I (Breslau, 1899), chap. III; *Dissensiones dominorum*, ed. G. Haenel (Leipzig, 1834), pp. 151–3. Vacarius appears to follow the view that custom cannot abrogate law (F. de Zulueta, *Liber Pauperum of Vacarius*, Selden Soc. 1927, p. lxxvii).

[1] See Gratian, C. 2, q. 5, c. 21 and *dictum post*; c. 7 forbids the use of the ordeal (cf. C. 20).

[2] Nos. 201, 203 give a clear indication that Gilbert was using Gratian; as also the *Causa* (cf. above, p. 163), esp. *MB*, IV, 218. See p. 165 n.

M & B

and Italy, only one invasion of heretics into England is known. About 1160 a small group of Flemish Cathars landed in the country. In due course the bishops became anxious about them; Roger of Worcester consulted Gilbert; a council was held under the direction of the king, and the Cathars were whipped and expelled by the lay power after condemnation by the Church, early in 1166.[1] Between the Council of Oxford in 1166 and the days of Wyclif outbreaks of heresy were very infrequent in England, and very small affairs compared with the successes of the Cathars and the Waldensians on the continent.

It is interesting to observe that Henry II, who was no doubt well acquainted with the Cathars in his French possessions, seems to have taken a sterner view of them than Gilbert. Although Gilbert had been a protégé of Peter the Venerable, whose work against the Petrobrusians was the chief contribution to the controversies with heretics of the early twelfth century, Gilbert writes as a man who has not had to face this problem before. The dramatic growth in heresy had led French councils to urge repression; the secular power, which had commonly burned heretics out of hand in the eleventh century as if they were witches,[2] was being looked to once again to assist in the work. At the general council of Tours in 1163 the problem of heresy was ardently canvassed: confiscation and imprisonment were reckoned fitting treatment for heretics, and from then on the Church reckoned increasingly on the assistance of the lay power, although it was not formally defined that this was the correct procedure until the decree *Ad abolendam* of 1184; and even after *Ad abolendam* Pope Innocent III could prefer to kill heresy by kindness rather than by violence. But even he was brought in the end to accept the view of his lieutenants that the Church had a violent crisis on its hands and must settle it by violent means, and so to the preaching of the Albigensian Crusade. This development was very much in the

---

[1] See notes to letters; A. Borst, *Die Katharen* (Stuttgart, 1953), p. 94 and n.; Walter Daniel's *Life of Ailred of Rievaulx*, ed. Powicke, NMT, pp. ci–cii.

[2] On the legal development in the treatment of heretics, see H. Maisonneuve, *Etudes sur les origines de l'Inquisition* (2nd edn, Paris, 1960; but on the burning of heretics, cf. Brooke in *EHR*, LXXVII (1962), 137–8).

wind among the panic-stricken Catholic leaders in the south of France and in parts of Italy in the 1160's, but there is no trace of it in Gilbert's letters. He recommended solitary confinement and an attempt at conversion by suitable visitors.[1] But these were interim measures: judgement and punishment should be reserved for a meeting of the bishops. He then outlines the diversity of opinions on the subject. What he says appears to be an academic exercise based on Gratian, and, more remotely, on the changing views of St Augustine, and it is, for the age of the Cathar triumphs, notable for its restraint and moderation. Some have urged clemency, others imprisonment, others have claimed that heresy is an offence against the *Lex Julia* and therefore equivalent to *lèse-majesté*, while yet others have recommended that heretics should be burnt, or scourged as Augustine had advised against the Donatists. He comes to no decision, and seems unaware of the Tours decree: his letter is dramatic confirmation of the contrast between the situation in England and on the continent at this time.

Apart from these cases in which the legal issue or method of proceeding is of special significance, the interest of Gilbert's cases lies in their bulk. About forty of his letters and *acta* deal with delegated cases and twenty surviving papal decretals were addressed to him. In many cases Gilbert was sole judge, but he was frequently appointed to act with Bishop Roger of Worcester, and other colleagues included Richard, archbishop of Canterbury, Henry of Winchester, the bishops of Chichester and Norwich, the abbots of St Albans, Evesham and Peterborough, and the prior of Kenilworth. He was involved in two notable *causes célèbres*; the struggle of the monks of Ely to recover the manor of Stetchworth in the 1150's and the controversy between Osney and St Frideswide's in the 1170's; both were long drawn out and in the second Gilbert was blamed for being dilatory, but the massive accounts of each case which he sent to the pope illustrate with particular clarity how easily obstructive litigants

---

[1] No. 158; in no. 157 he advocates moderate flogging and does not discuss the general principles; in both he reserves judgement for a council. What follows is based on no. 158.

could prolong difficult cases. The letter on the Ely case, with its long and lucid statement of the arguments put forward by the litigants, gives a vivid account of legal proceedings in a delegates' court: it is a fit companion to the pleadings in the chronicle of Battle abbey and John of Salisbury's letter on the Anstey case as a major source for the understanding of ecclesiastical litigation in the 1150's.

Thus Gilbert's letters and *acta* reveal to us a trained lawyer already, in the 1140's, with a coherent idea of canonical procedure based on Roman Law, an idea into which the developing notions of popes and decretists slowly penetrated in the 1150's, 1160's and 1170's. They also illustrate the growth in the bulk and sophistication of the cases which went to the pope on appeal and were returned to judges-delegate in their country of origin. They help to confirm the picture of the development of appeals in England as, in the main, a reflexion of conditions which prevailed throughout the western Church; but they show too, with special clarity, the effect of local conditions, and in particular the way in which the Becket dispute both discouraged and encouraged appeals to Rome, without, however, seriously deflecting the trends of the age. They show, finally, the way in which the bishops were helping to shape the papal courts in this period: Gilbert, the jurist turned monk, belonged to precisely that generation of bishops whose work was most crucial for the growth of papal jurisdiction. In the generation before he became bishop, appeals were rare and delegation rarer; at the time of his death they were becoming so common that lesser dignitaries came more and more commonly to fill the role of judge-delegate which bishops had performed at the height of his career. Gilbert was one of a group of active and energetic bishops who played a leading part in making this transition possible.

CHAPTER XII

EPILOGUE

The Reverend Doctor Folliott...[Peacock tells us in *Crotchet Castle*] claimed to be descended lineally from the illustrious Gilbert Folliott, the eminent theologian, who was a bishop of London in the twelfth century, whose studies were interrupted in the dead of night by the devil; when a couple of epigrams passed between them; and the devil, of course, proved the smaller wit of the two.

The devil began: (he had caught the bishop musing on politics):

> Oh Gilberte Folliott!
> Dum revolvis tot et tot,
> Deus tuus est Astarot.

> Oh Gilbert Folliott!
> While thus you muse and plot,
> Your God is Astarot.

The bishop answered:

> Tace, daemon: qui est deus
> Sabbaot, est ille meus.

> Peace, fiend; the power I own
> Is Sabbaoth's Lord alone.

It must be confessed, the devil was easily posed in the twelfth century.[1]

It was noticed already in Gilbert Foliot's lifetime that his name rhymed with Astaroth; and out of this coincidence grew the most famous story about him. To Thomas Becket's closest disciples the bishop of London had been Doeg, Achitophel, the servant of Astaroth, the scheming pharisee. To his own disciples he was the flower of monks, ascetic, learned, the inspiring preacher, the old, blind scholar whose last years were 'tuneful as...those

---

[1] Peacock, *Crotchet Castle*, chap. 1 (text and footnote), presumably from Fuller's *Worthies* (see p. 43 n.) or Godwin's *De Praesulibus*. The earliest source to give the rhyme (though not this answer) is Roger of Wendover (ed. H. O. Coxe, Eng. Hist. Soc. 1841–2, II, 323). But the reference in Guernes de Pont-S.-Maxence's *Life* of Becket (1172–4)—'Des lettres sout asez, et servi Astarot' —strongly suggests that in some form it went back to his own lifetime (Guernes, ed. E. Walberg, Paris, 1936, line 2172).

of dim-eyed Homer'. Further study has added to the catalogue of his attributes: has shown more evidence of his zeal as monk and abbot, his capacity to absorb new theological fashions, his interest in many aspects of the work of his diocese—and also has shown how he condoned forgery and practised nepotism. The sources reveal a diverse and interesting personality; it may be that they do not give us the material to make a single, coherent portrait of the man, still less to trace in detail the development or deterioration of his character through a long and varied career. Yet there seems to us to be a certain consistency visible in the most diverse of his activities, sufficient to give the portrait a sense of construction, though hardly sufficient to make it intimately revealing. Gilbert's rapid rise, and the impression he still made in his old age on Peter of Cornwall and Walter Map, show that he could impress his fellows, had the capacity to guide, to give a lead, even to inspire others. He could be impressive and eloquent, and a few of his letters come near to brilliance. But on the whole his writings give the impression of competence rather than of mastery, both as a writer and as a man. Yet his record surely suggests that the letters (with a few exceptions) lead us to underestimate him; he was one of the very numerous eminent men whose power is lost, or partly lost, in cold print.

The writings prove that he was not a man of original mind; nor was he a mere traditionalist. It was Gilbert's capacity to absorb and expound new fashions which inspired Peter of Cornwall, his intellectual energy even on the verge of eighty which struck Walter Map. He was *par excellence* a man of his age—able on occasion to absorb and interpret new ideas all the more successfully, perhaps, because his own outlook was in so many ways conventional and traditional. What saves him from dullness is the extraordinary way in which he reflects the assumptions and interests of his contemporaries. He was a trained lawyer and theologian in the heyday of Bologna and Paris; a fervent monk and a Cluniac while it was still possible, and conventional, to be both; a skilled controversialist in an age of bitter pamphlet wars; a generous patron in the first golden age of patronage and nepotism; a revered bishop who condoned forgery in one of the

very few ages in the Church's history when the combination
(though always singular) was not impossible. There are also
copious hints in his letters that he was a supple diplomat, and this
did not escape notice at the time: William FitzStephen tells how
he modified his prayers according to the political situation—
mentioning the archbishop when peace seemed near, omitting
him when Henry and Becket were at variance; praying for two
kings between 1170 and 1173, for one when the younger re-
belled.[1] FitzStephen clearly regarded the story as a sample of
time-serving; in view of the circumstances—and of Gilbert's
doubts about Becket's status—it seems today ordinary diplomatic
prudence. But it was not combined with Laodicean calculation.
Gilbert could wax hot—when Roger of York accused Gloucester
of forgery, when Becket appeared at Northampton carrying his
cross, when he learned that his excommunication had been published in St Paul's. Yet the final impression of his letters is neither
of excessive prudence nor of violent temper, but of a man aware
of his own notable talents, not unself-critical, but without the
imagination ever wholly to avoid the conflicting prejudices of
his age: of a man, neither great nor bad, conscientiously striving
in a practical way to set in operation what he thought was right
in many difficult and complex situations.

Perhaps the most striking of all the testimonials Gilbert Foliot
received in his lifetime was the letter in which the king urged him
to accept translation to London. Henry expressed admiration for
the bishop's virtues and good name, and observed that he had
always had sound and helpful advice on all matters affecting
Gilbert himself, or the kingdom at large, or any other business,
from him. And so he wished to have him near at hand, and urged
Gilbert to accept the pope's mandate for his translation. London
was the city where royal councils were most commonly held,
where the barons gathered to give the king counsel; there the
bishop's 'immeasurable goodness and virtue' could have wider
influence. Finally, with a characteristic touch of impatience,
Henry tells him to translate himself without delay. 'Witness
Thomas archbishop at Windsor.' The irony of this brief witness-

[1] *MB*, III, 83–4.

list is enhanced by the accompanying letter in which Thomas Becket himself, writing as a Londoner, tells how the church of London had looked for a man whose manner of life, learning and prudence in secular affairs were appropriate to the excellence of the city, and how the unanimous choice of clergy, king, archbishop and pope, had found the man they sought in Gilbert.[1] Soon after, Becket wrote again,[2] to apologise that he could not be in London when Gilbert arrived. He was expansive on the grounds for Gilbert's translation: 'your character, your noted religious life, your wisdom given from above, the good work you have accomplished in the church of Hereford' dictated that it be said to him 'Friend go up higher: you were faithful over few things, you are fittingly set over many'; Gilbert was no novice sailor, but an expert helmsman. Furthermore, the pope had made Gilbert the king's confessor, and so made London a more appropriate home for him. The archbishop believed that this transference was God's work, so that Canterbury could lean more heavily on Gilbert's help 'and that our imperfection which we observe in many ways may be made up by your blessedness'. The letter makes strange reading; we cannot forget that Clarendon was eight months away, Northampton eighteen, *Multiplicem* only three and a half years. It was a bouquet to a defeated rival; but Becket was no hypocrite, and he had been acquainted with Gilbert and had ample opportunity to observe him for fifteen or twenty years. When we weigh the harsh words of Becket's supporters about Achitophel, the product of two or three years of strife, we do well to remember the generous phrases of their David, Archbishop Thomas Becket himself.

[1] Nos. 143, 142. Becket's letter is formal; this may need no explanation, but it is possible to imagine that behind its reserve lay the embarrassment of the successful rival. It is less easy to believe that Becket's compliments were insincere.

[2] No. 144.

KEY TO THE NUMBERS OF LETTERS AND CHARTERS

The number in the first column is that of our forthcoming edition (used in this book throughout for reference); that in the second refers to the edition of J. A. Giles (2 vols., London, Oxford, 1846, reprinted in *PL*, cxc) unless otherwise stated. We have noted all the letters which occur in Giles and *MB Epp.*; for other letters and charters we have given a single reference to the most available edition or the best MS. Full references will be given in our edition.

A. LETTERS

Letters as abbot of Gloucester

1	*81*	23	*5*
2	*2*	24	*6*
3	*66*	25	*7*
4	*27*	26	*79*
5	*4*	27	*34*
6	*9*	28	*10*
7	*12*	29	*58*
8	*24*	30	*59*
9	*26*	31	*11*
10	*29*	32	*14*
11	*49*	33	*31*
12	*60*	34	*18*
13	*64*	35	*41*
14	*8*	36	*25*
15	*57*	37	*36*
16	*71*	38	*13*
17	*51*	39	*15*
18	*53*	40	*30*
19	*62*	41	*37*
20	*54*	42	*45*
21	*35*	43	*19*
22	*3*	44	*21*

45	*16*	62	*72*
46	*20*	63	*52*
47	*28*	64	*1*
48	*33*	65	*22*
49	*32*	66	*23*
50	*67*	67	*17*
51	*38*	68	*63*
52	*44*	69	*74*
53	*92*	70	*56*
54	*50*	71	*61*
55	*43*	72	*68*
56	*39*	73	*55*
57	*42*	74	*75*
58	*46*	75	*76*
59	*47*	76	*77*
60	*48*	77	*78*
61	*69*	78	*73*

Letters as bishop of Hereford

79	*83*	100	*140*
80	*87*	101	*130*
81	*88*	102	*94*
82	*82*	103	*133*
83	*84*	104	*106*
84	*93*	105	*143*
85	*96*	106	*90*
86	*99*	107	*136*
87	*40*	108	*112*
88	*134*	109	*137*
89	*107*	110	*144*
90	*103*	111	*141*
91	*108*	112	*113*
92	*91*	113	*222*
93	*135*	114	*85*
94	*131*	115	*86*
95	*138*	116	*80*
96	*142*	117	*100*
97	*104*	118	*101*
98	*105*	119	*102*
99	*95*	120	*118*

121	*139*	129	*110*
122	*132*	130	*111*
123	*121*	131	*124*
124	*117*	132	*128*
125	*115*	133	*148*;
126	*116*		*MB Epp.* 11
127	*114*	134	*254*
128	*109*	135	*126*
		136	*291*

137	*127*
138	E. Martène and U. Durand, *Veterum Scriptorum...amplissima collectio*, VI (Paris, 1729), col. 240
139	*119*; *MB Epp.* 10
140	*120*; *MB Epp.* 15
141	*146*; *MB Epp.* 18
142	*145*; *MB Epp.* 17
143	*147*; *MB Epp.* 16

Letters as bishop of London

144	*412*; *MB Epp.* 19
145	*215*
146	*149*; *MB Epp.* 28
147	*257*
148	*193*; *MB Epp.* 40
149	*151*
150	*161*
151	*278*
152	*265*
153	*181*
154	*205*
155	*174*; *MB Epp.* 108 (extract in 168)
156	*172*; *MB Epp.* 110
157	*249*
158	*250*
159	*285*; *MB Epp.* 481
160	*176*; *MB Epp.* 482
161	*162*; *MB Epp.* 483
162	*164*
163	*282*
164	*363*

165	MS Bodl. Rawlinson Q. f. 8, fo. 25 v.
166	*437; MB Epp.* 204
167	*436; MB Epp.* 205
168	*275; MB Epp.* 208
169	*274; MB Epp.* 167
170	*194; MB Epp.* 225
171	*273; MB Epp.* 236
172	*220*
173	*221*
174	*286*
175	*267*
176	*213*
177	*271; MB Epp.* 107
178	*272; MB Epp.* 111
179	*150; MB Epp.* 109
180	*242; MB Epp.* 346
181	*438; MB Epp.* 344
182	*441; MB Epp.* 345
183	*173; MB Epp.* 569
184	*184*
185	*165*
186	*375*
187	*256*
188	*216*
189	*217*
190	*283*
191	*258*
192	*240*
193	*167*
194	*279*
195	*281*
196	*280*
197	*199; MB Epp.* 433
198	*195; MB Epp.* 474
199	*243; MB Epp.* 477
200	*175; MB Epp.* 475
201	*268, 276; MB Epp.* 503
202	Liverani, p. 644 (1); *MB Epp.* 513
203	*277; MB Epp.* 504
204	*209; MB Epp.* 509

205	*262*
206	*245*; MB *Epp.* 336
207	*471*; MB *Epp.* 337
208	*247*; MB *Epp.* 338
209	*223*
210	Liverani, p. 642; MB *Epp.* 621
211	Liverani, p. 644 (2); MB *Epp.* 657
212	*154*; MB *Epp.* 667
213	*159*
214	*156*; MB *Epp.* 562
215	*177*
216	Liverani, p. 641 (2); MB *Epp.* 512
217	*241*; MB *Epp.* 761
218	*155*; MB *Epp.* 762
219	*179*; MB *Epp.* 511
220	*269*; MB *Epp.* 792
221	*158*
222	*160*
223	*168*
224	*169*
225	*170*
226	*178*
227	*211*
228	*171*
229	*266*
230	*197, 292*; MB *Epp.* 393
231	*208*
232	*263*
233	*157*; MB *Epp.* 347
234	*244*
235	*238*
236	*313*
237	*261*
238	*251*
239	*248*
240	Liverani, p. 641 (1)
241	*260*
242	*252*
243	*253*
244	*270*

Letters of uncertain date

B.   CHARTERS

Charters as abbot of Gloucester

284   Cart. Gloucester, I, 311; II, 246–7
285   Cart. Gloucester, II, 138
286   Gloucester Cathedral, Dean and Chapter, Reg. B, p. 56
287   Ibid.
288   MS cit. p. 500

Charters as bishop of Hereford

289   (Profession) Canterbury, Dean and Chapter, C 115; noted in
       St Paul's Ecclesiological Soc., Trans. VII (1911–15), 168
290   Cart. Brecon, Archaeologia Cambrensis, 4th series, XIV (1883),
       20–1.
291   Art. cit. p. 21
292   Ibid.
293   Gervase, I, 164–5
294   129
295   Liber Eliensis, ed. E. O. Blake (Camden 3rd series, XCII,
       1962), pp. 355–8
296   Op. cit. pp. 361
297   Op. cit. p. 361–2
298   BM Cotton MS Vesp. B. xxiv, fo. 17v (Cart. Evesham)
299   Cart. Eynsham, I, 62–3
300   Cart. Gloucester, I, 176–7
301   Op. cit. I, 375–6
302   Gloucester Cathedral, Reg. A, fo. 72v
303   Reg. Swinfield, p. 426
304   Gloucester Cathedral, Reg. B, pp. 20–1
305   Cart. Gloucester, I, 252–3; III, 6
306   Op. cit. III, 5
307   Gloucester Cathedral, Reg. B, p. 55
308   MS cit. p. 75
309   Cart. Gloucester, II, 4
310   R. W. Eyton, Antiquities of Shropshire (London, 1854–60),
       XI, 208 (abbreviated)
311   Capes, pp. 11–12
312   Bodl. MS Rawlinson B 329, fo. 121r–v (Cart. Hereford)
313   MS cit. fos. 11, 160
314   122

315   *Reg. Swinfield*, p. 55
316   Capes, p. 18
317   Balliol College, Oxford, MS 271, fos. 97, 103 v, 104 v (Cart. St Guthlac's, Hereford)
318   MS cit. fo. 101
319   MS cit. fo. 65
320   MS cit. fo. 88 v
321   *125*; MS cit. fo. 103
322   MS cit. fo. 53
323   MS cit. fo. 69
324   MS cit. fos. 82 v–83
325   MS cit. fo. 103 v
326   *186*
327   PRO Chancery Masters' Exhibits, A 1, sec. VI, no. 38 (Cart. Lanthony)
328   MS cit. sec. VI, no. 15
329   Cart. Lanthony A 9, fo. 113
330   MS cit. fo. 113 r–v
331   *Mon.* VI, 1093
332   *Bibliothèque de l'École des Chartes*, XL (1879), 183–5; calendared in *CDF*, no. 1143
333   *Bibliothèque*, XL (1879), 185; calendared in *CDF*, no. 1144
334   BM Egerton MS 3031, fo. 56 (Cart. Reading)
335   MS cit. fo. 55 r–v
336   MS cit. fos. 55 v–56
337   MS cit. fo. 55 v
338   MS cit. fo. 55
339   BM Additional Charter 19587
340   BM Cotton MS Domit. A. iii, fo. 72 r–v (Cart. Leominster)
341   BM Egerton MS 3031, fo. 56
342   MS cit. fo. 56 r–v
343   MS cit. fo. 55
344   Nat. Library of Wales, MS 7851 D, pp. 296–7 (Cart. Shrewsbury)
345   PRO Exch. K.R. Misc. Books (E 164), 22, fos. 18–19 (Cart. Warwick)
346   MS cit. fo. 19 v
347   MS cit. fo. 20 r–v
348   Worcester, Dean and Chapter, Reg. A 4 ('Reg. I'), fo. xxvii
349   *89*

Charters as bishop of London

350	*231*
351	Essex Record Office, D/DP T1/692
352	*236*
353	*224*
354	*Reg. Sudbury* (London), I, ed. R. C. Fowler (Cant. and York Soc. 1927), p. 211
355	*259*
356	PRO Transcripts, 31/8/140ᴮ, Pt. 3, fo. 205; calendared in *CDF*, no. 433
357	BM Cotton MS Claud. D. x, fos. 258v–9 (Cart. St Augustine's, Canterbury)
358	MS cit. fo. 184
359	*Cart. Colchester*, I, 86–8
360	*Op. cit.* II, 525–7
361	*Op. cit.* I, 83–4
362	*Op. cit.* I, 83
363	*327*
364	*Cart. Colne*, ed. J. L. Fisher (Essex Arch. Soc. 1946), no. 27
365	*Op. cit.* no. 17
366	*229*
367	London, Guildhall Library, Reg. Gilbert, fo. 180v
368	MS cit. fo. 180
369	Essex Rec. Office, D/DBy Q 19 (Audley End Estate Archives), fo. 26 (Cart. Eye)
370	*Cart. Eynsham*, I, 64
371	*Cart. Gloucester*, II, 168–9
372	*Op. cit.* I, pp. lxxvi–lxxvii
373	*Op. cit.* II, 11–12
374	King's College, Cambridge, Muniment Room, B17–19 (Great Bricett)
375	*210*
376	*Facsimiles of...Charters in the BM*, I, ed. G. F. Warner and H. J. Ellis (1903), no. 58
377	*192*
378	*Reg. Swinfield*, p. 477
379	Balliol College, Oxford, MS 271, fos. 96, 97
380	BM Harl. MS 4015, fos. 157, 211v (Cart. St Giles in the Fields, London)
381	*Mon.* v, 157

382	*226*
383	*185*
384	BM Cotton MS Nero E. vi, fo. 85 (Cart. Hospitallers)
385	MS cit. fo. 124 v (wrongly attributed to Bishop Robert)
386	*237*
387	BM MS Cotton Nero E. vi, fos. 124, 204 (wrongly attributed to Bishop Richard)
388	MS cit. fo. 218
389	MS cit. fo. 305
390	*235*
391	PRO Exch. T.R., Anc. Deeds (E 40), A 14395 (Lewes)
392	BM Cotton MS Vesp. F. xv. fo. 310, calendared in *Cart. Lewes*, ed. L. F. Salzman (Sussex Rec. Soc. 1933–43), II, 126
393	PRO Exch. T.R., Anc. Deeds (E 40), A 13876 (Lewes)
394	*Ibid.* A 13879
395	*Ibid.* A 13877 (2), calendared in *Cart. Lewes*, III, no. 58
396	*187*
397	*296*
398	Gibbs, no. 215
399	Gibbs, no. 66
400	St Paul's Cathedral, Box A 8/970; calendared in *Rep.* p. 8a
401	Gibbs, no. 92
402	Gibbs, no. 158
403	Gibbs, no. 72
404	Gibbs, no. 57
405	Gibbs, no. 65
406	Gibbs, no. 71
407	St Paul's Cathedral, Box A 78/3015, calendared in *Rep.* p. 58b
408	Gibbs, no. 67
409	St Paul's A 30/431, calendared in *Rep.* p. 33a
410	*Ancient Charters*, ed. J. H. Round (Pipe Roll Soc., 1888), no. 46, pp. 74–5
411	PRO Exch. K.R., Eccl. Docts., E 135/19/48
412	PRO Exch. T.R., Anc. Deeds (E 40), A 10845
413	*234*
414	*323*
415	N. Moore, *Hist. of St Bartholomew's Hospital* (London, 1918), I, 198 n.
416	*Op. cit.* I, 147 n.

417	*Op. cit.* I, 199 n.
418	*183, 188*
419	*309*
420	*Cart. Missenden*, ed. J. G. Jenkins, I (Bucks Archaeol. Soc. 1938), no. 247
420A–C	BM Stowe MS 935, fos. 24–5
421	*Sarum Charters*, pp. 31–2 (wrongly attributed to Bishop Richard)
422	New College, Oxford, Archives, Hornchurch deeds, no. 399, calendared in H. F. Westlake, *Hornchurch Priory* (London, 1923), no. 399
423	*230*
424	*305*
425	*191*
426	*Cart. Oseney*, II, 224–5
427	*Op. cit.* II, 219–23
428	*228*
429	*Chron. Ramsey*, pp. 309–10; *Cart. Ramsey*, II, 192–3
430	BM Egerton MS 3031, fo. 58
431	BM Cotton MS Domit. A. x, fo. 148 r–v (Cart. Rochester)
432	BM Cotton MS Domit. A. x, fo. 148 v; St Paul's A 28/284, calendared in *Rep.* p. 32 a
433	BM Cotton MS Domit. A. x, fo. 148 v–149
434	MS cit. fos. 149 v–150
435	*PUE*, II, no. 239
436	*326*
437	*227*
438	BM Harl. MS 3697, fo. 38 (Cart. Saffron Walden)
439	MS cit. fos. 38 r–v, 39
440	MS cit. fo. 39
441	MS cit. fo. 38
442	MS cit. fo. 38 v
443	MS cit. fo. 45
444	MS cit. fo. 38 v
445	MS cit. fo. 39
446	MS cit. fo. 38 v
447	MS cit. fo. 38
448	*314*
449	*233*
450	*312*

451   New College, Oxford, Birchanger Deeds, no. 49
452   *225; MB Epp.* 803
453   BM Cotton MS Appendix xxi, fos. 58v–59 (Cart. Stoke-by-
        Clare)
454   MS cit. fos. 56v–57
455   MS cit. fo. 56
456   MS cit. fos. 57–58
457   MS cit. fo. 52
458   MS cit. fo. 56
459   *239*
460   PRO Exch. K.R. Misc. Books (E164), 22, fo. 21v
461   Wells Cathedral, Liber Albus I, fos. 47v, 49; calendared in
        HMC, Wells, I, 56
462   Westminster Abbey Muniment Room, Domesday Cart.,
        fo. 627
463   MS cit. fos. 636v–637
464   MS cit. fo. 131r–v
465   Westminster Abbey Muniments, no. 1045
466   *Ibid.* no. 1044; facs. in *New Palaeographical Soc.* I, 98b
467   Westminster Abbey, Domesday Cart. fo. 501r–v
468   MS cit. fo. 131
469   *325*
470   Worcester, Dean and Chapter, Reg. A4 ('Reg. I'), fo. xxvi
471   *182*
472   *189*
473   *190*
474   *232*

Charters of uncertain date

475   *306*
476   *307*

FOLIOT FAMILIES
IN TWELFTH-CENTURY
ENGLAND
(excluding those on Chart 2, p. 51)

I. CHILTON (WILTS) AND FRITWELL (OXFORDSHIRE)

See above, p. 42; *HKF*, III, 234 ff.; *Sir C. Hatton's Book of Seals*, ed.
L. C. Loyd and D. M. Stenton (Oxford, 1950), p. 157. There is no
evidence of precise relationships before the late twelfth century, but
the holders of these properties fall into the following generations: (1)
Rainald, tenant in 1086 of the fees of William FitzOsbern, the bishop
of Bayeux and Milo Crispin; (2) Ralph Foliot and Roger Foliot (cf.
nos. 29–30), tenants and knights of Milo's successor, Brian FitzCount;
also Robert, Roger's brother (no. 312; *Chron. Abingdon*, ed. J. Stevenson,
RS, II, 109; BM Cotton MS Vesp. B. xxiv, fo. 17; above, p. 42; *Cart.
Oseney*, I, 51 f.); (3) Walter Foliot and Robert Foliot (occur before 1147—
Select Docts. of the English lands of...Bec, ed. M. Chibnall, Camden 3rd
series, 1951, pp. 24–5—and 1166–7);[1] (4) Ralph Foliot and his brothers
Henry, Roger, Richard (they may have been sons of another Ralph,
intermediate between (3) and (4)). Ralph died c. 1204 and was succeeded by Henry, who died c. 1233, and was succeeded by his son
Sampson (for his descendants, see *EYC*, X, 105). Farrer also gives notes
of other Foliots called Ralph, Bartholomew and Walter (see p. 42) in
the late twelfth century. Farrer was probably right to see in Rainald
the founder of this family, but wrong to identify him with Rainald son
of Croc the huntsman (Croc's descendants were still living in a small
way in Hants in the thirteenth century: *VCH Hants*, IV, 391, 393–4).

2. NORTH TAWTON, ETC. (DEVON)

In or before 1106 Robert Foliot granted the church of North Tawton
in Devon to St Nicholas' Exeter (*Reg. Regum Anglo-Normannorum*, II,
ed. C. Johnson and H. A. Cronne, Oxford, 1956, no. 779 (XL), of
doubtful authenticity). According to thirteenth-century evidence,

---

[1] Among the Oxfordshire Foliots presumably belong the Foliots listed
above, p. 45 and n. For Gilbert, cf. p. 292.

Robert Foliot received 'Madishawe' from Henry I for service of serjeanty, and also (the same Robert or more probably his successor) Hemyock from Earl Richard de Reviers (either 1155–62 or 1188–93: *Book of Fees*, II, 1368; I, 98). Another of his properties (see below) was Dunchideock, of which the Peverels were dispossessed by Henry II (cf. *VCH Devon*, I, 553 and n.): this may have been the occasion of his obtaining it. There are several other references to Robert Foliot; also to Payne (1130: *PR, 31 Henry I*, p. 154);[1] also to Gilbert, his daughter Agnes (wife of Adam de 'Lanual') and a much later Robert (BM Cotton MS Tib. D. vi, pt. i, fos. 106r–v, 29), tenants of the Reviers earls in the Isle of Wight and Hampshire.

In 1187–8 Robert Foliot was amerced ten marks for a fine against Joel de *Valle Torta* for Butterleigh, Washford Pyne (?), Dunchideock and Cadbury; the money was paid off in 1193–4 (*PR, 34 Henry II*, p. 170; *6 Richard I*, p. 168). Two years later (1195–6: *PR, 8 Richard I*, p. 148) Thomas Foliot, Richard de Hidon', Emma de Boterell' and Geoffrey de Barinton' owed 80 marks for receiving the inheritance of Robert Foliot their grandfather in the King's court. A few years later again (*PR, 1 John*, p. 198) the inheritance was specified as lands in Hemyock, Dunchideock, 'Maddeshamele', 'Almadeston' (? Almiston in Woolfardisworthy), 'Luuinecot' (? Limescote in Bradworthy or Luffincott), and North Tawton. All the properties identified were in Devon. By 1200 a new claimant had appeared: Roger de Rames owed 3 marks 'ut baronia que fuit Roberti Foliot participetur inter ipsum et conpartices suos...' (*ibid.*).

In 1141–4 Sampson Foliot witnessed Earl Baldwin's foundation charter of Quarr abbey, and *c*. 1196 another Sampson Foliot witnessed Earl William's charter to Montebourg confirming them land in Berkshire (V. H. Galbraith in *CHJ*, IV, iii (1934), 298; *CDF*, no. 904). Of these, the second is probably to be identified with Sampson Foliot, lord of Montfarville (see above, p. 42).

The earls of Devon, then, suggest a link between Devon and Normandy; and they also suggest a link between the Foliots of Devon and those of Oxfordshire, one of whose tenants-in-chief the earl was. The possibility that Gilbert studied in the school at Exeter suggests a further connexion (and see p. 55).

---

[1] Payne was Robert's successor. To the same branch may belong Geoffrey Foliot, who occ. manumitting a villein in Exeter *c*. 1135–40 (*The Exeter Book of Old English Poetry*, ed. R. W. Chambers, M. Förster and R. Flower (London, 1933), p. 48; cf. *Trans. Devonshire Assoc.* LXIX (1937), 428).

3. FENWICK AND NORTON (YORKS)

The following pedigree is based on *EYC*, III, 214–21, esp. 219–20 (Farrer); cf. also *HKF*, III, 399; *CP*, v, 538 ff.; *EYC*, IX, 37 (Sir C. Clay).

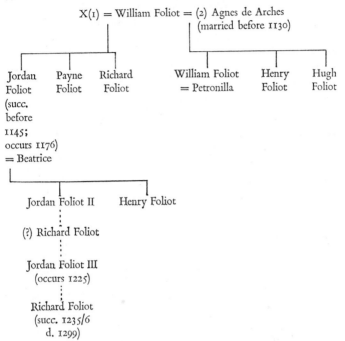

X(1) = William Foliot = (2) Agnes de Arches (married before 1130)

Jordan Foliot (succ. before 1145; occurs 1176) = Beatrice

Payne Foliot

Richard Foliot

William Foliot = Petronilla

Henry Foliot

Hugh Foliot

Jordan Foliot II

Henry Foliot

(?) Richard Foliot

Jordan Foliot III (occurs 1225)

Richard Foliot (succ. 1235/6 d. 1299)

4. HACKTHORN (LINCS)

A group of Sir Frank Stenton's *Danelaw Charters* (London, Brit. Academy, 1920, pp. 22 ff.) exhibit the Foliots of Hackthorn (Lincs)— William (*c.* 1150), Ralph and Eda his wife (late Henry II), Gilbert and Alexander his son (late Henry II and late-twelfth century). Alexander married Alice of Hackthorn and the property passed to an heiress (? their daughter), Juliana, who married Robert of Wendover.

It is interesting to note that one Richard of Hackthorn witnesses three charters of the Yorkshire Foliots in the mid- and late-twelfth century (*EYC*, III, nos. 1527–40); in the 1150's Jordan and William Foliot appear in Lincs charters (*Transcripts of Charters relating to... Gilbertine houses*, ed. F. M. Stenton (Lincoln Rec. Soc. 1922), pp. 41, 84).

This by no means exhausts references we have found to twelfth-century Foliots; but gives, we think, the essential evidence to make some sort of sense of the known branches. Most other references either probably or certainly relate to one or other of the branches given above. Probable exceptions are Richard Foliot,[1] his wife Beatrice of London (perhaps connected with the Londons of Kidwelly), Robert their son and Hawise his wife (mid-late twelfth century) (Cart. Lanthony, PRO, C115/A1, sec. xvii, nos. 1, 3, 4), and Geoffrey Foliot, who held a knight's fee of the abbot of Glastonbury in 1189—the tenure was said to go back to the eleventh century (*Liber Henrici de Soliaco*, ed. J. E. Jackson, Roxburghe Club, London, 1882, pp. 1, 116, 120; cf. pp. 56–7 for a Robert Foliot holding ½ virgate and 2 acres with peasant services in Ashcott (Somerset)).

[1] Possibly of the same line as the Richard Foliot who witnessed the foundation charter of Kidwelly priory by Roger, bishop of Salisbury, before 1115 (*Monasticon*, IV, 65).

GROUPS OF FORGERIES

(see pp. 127–45)

A full bibliography would require a volume in itself, and much work remains to be done: what follows is a very selective and provisional list of recent work on the early charters of houses or cathedrals known to have produced a substantial amount of forgery (i.e. more than two or three spurious documents). Unless otherwise stated the forgery is presumed to be of the eleventh or twelfth centuries (before *c.* 1160). Several houses, such as Reading and Tewkesbury, known to have produced forgeries, have been omitted because in the present state of knowledge the number of forgeries, etc., seems trivial. But it is likely that this list ought in fact to be considerably longer than it is.[1]

Abingdon. F. E. Harmer, *Anglo-Saxon Writs* (Manchester, 1952), pp. 122–9; F. M. Stenton, *Early History of the abbey of Abingdon* (Reading, 1913).

Battle. T. A. M. Bishop and P. Chaplais, *Facsimiles of English royal writs to A.D. 1100* (Oxford, 1957), pp. xxi ff.; D. Knowles, *Downside Rev.* L (1932), 218 ff.

Bury. Harmer, pp. 140 ff.; above, p. 140 n.

Canterbury, Christ Church. R. W. Southern, *EHR*, LXXIII (1958), 193–226; Harmer, pp. 166 ff. (for a thirteenth-century forgery, C. R. Cheney, *BIHR*, XXXVI, 1963, 1–26).

Canterbury, St Augustine's. W. Levison, *England and the Continent in the 8th Century* (Oxford, 1946), Appendix I; Harmer, pp. 190 ff.

Chertsey. Harmer, pp. 201 ff., esp. 204 n.; Levison, p. 26 n.

Colchester. J. H. Round, *EHR*, XVI (1902), 721–30; J. Armitage Robinson, *Gilbert Crispin abbot of Westminster* (Cambridge, 1911), pp. 158 ff.

Coventry. J. Lancaster in *BIHR*, XXVII (1954), 113 ff.; Bishop and Chaplais, p. xxii; Harmer, pp. 214 ff.

Crowland. See above, p. 137 (fourteenth century).

Durham. G. V. Scammell, *Hugh du Puiset bishop of Durham* (Cambridge, 1956), Appendix IV (mainly of the 1180's).

[1] On the problems of establishing the authenticity of pre-Conquest documents, see especially F. E. Harmer, *Anglo-Saxon Writs*, and D. Whitelock in *English Hist. Documents*, I (London, 1955), 337 ff.

Ely. See *Liber Eliensis,* ed. E. O. Blake, p. l.

Evesham. Knowles, art. cit. pp. 396 ff.; cf. Levison, p. 26 n.

Glastonbury. Cf. J. A. Robinson, *Somerset Hist. Essays* (London, 1921), pp. 29 ff. (a fair number of revised and rewritten charters, though the number of total forgeries may be small).

Gloucester. CS, pp. 268 ff.

Lewes. H. Mayr-Harting, *Acta of the Bishops of Chichester* (Cant. and York Soc. 1964), pp. 62–70 (early thirteenth century).

Llandaff. SEBC, pp. 218 ff.; cf. CS, pp. 312, 322 for criticisms of this.

Malmesbury. Cf. Dom A. Watkin, *VCH Wilts,* III, 211 ff., 228 ff., esp. p. 211 nn. 19–21, 25, p. 212 n. 34, p. 213 nn. 71–2, 80, 82.

Peterborough. Levison, pp. 219 ff.

Ramsey. Bishop and Chaplais, pp. xxi, xxii; Harmer, pp. 248–56.

Westminster. Harmer, pp. 286–339; Bishop and Chaplais, pp. xx ff.; Chaplais in *Misc. D. M. Stenton,* pp. 89 ff.

Winchester. W. H. Stevenson, *EHR,* XXVII (1912), 5 and n. (but cf. Harmer, pp. 378 ff.: Stevenson may have been too sweeping in his condemnation of Winchester charters).

Wix. Brooke in *Misc. D. M. Stenton,* pp. 45–63 (1190's).

Worcester. J. A. Robinson, *St Oswald and the Church of Worcester* (London, 1919); E. John, *Bull. John Rylands Lib.* XLI (1958–9), 54 ff.; *Land Tenure in early England* (Leicester, 1961), pp. 90–112.

GILBERT FOLIOT'S CHAPTERS AND HOUSEHOLD[1]

1. HEREFORD CATHEDRAL CHAPTER, 1148–63

(The lists of dignitaries are based on articles by Z. N. and C. N. L. Brooke in *CHJ*, VIII (1944–6), 1–21, 179–85, supplemented in particular by the St Guthlac's cart., Oxford, Balliol MS 271, cited as Guth.)

DEANS

Ralph c. 1135 (or before)[2]*–c.* 1158 (alive 1158: *CHJ*, VIII, 7–8, 182). Occ. in nos. 313, 317–19, 326, 333.
? *W. c.* 1158: occ. only in no. 305 (cf. *CHJ*, VIII, 8); but the initial must have stood in the original—perhaps by mistake, but there may well have been a Dean W. between Ralph and Geoffrey.
Geoffrey c. 1158–*c.* 1181 (*CHJ*, VIII, 8, 182). Occ. in no. 315.

PRECENTORS

Robert occ. 1132, 1131–9 (Guth. fos. 88 v, 56 v).
William occ. prob. Dec. 1139.[3]
Gilbert c. 1140–*c.* 1155 (*CHJ*, VIII, 10). Obit, 5 May. Occ. in nos. 82, 317–19.
Reginald c. 1155–? Occ. 2 Oct. 1172 (Guth. fo. 16) and in nos. 312–13, 315.

---

[1] References given for dignitaries and canons are to establish outside dates only: in most cases intermediate references are in fact fairly numerous. It is not practicable to give detailed evidence for the dates assigned to all the documents used here; for those in Capes, see *CHJ*, VIII, 19–21, 183–4; for Gilbert's *acta*, *GFL*; where vital, evidence is given below. Hereford obits are from R. Rawlinson, *The History and Antiquities of...Hereford*, Appendix, pp. (3)–(31); London obits (unless otherwise stated) are from obituaries listed in *BIHR*, XXIX (1956), 231 n., especially from St Paul's MS W.D. 12, fos. 10–15 v (early thirteenth century) and BM Harl. MS 6956, fos. 107–10 (transcript of lost MS of 1279).

[2] His only known predecessor was Erchemer, occ. 1107–15 (Guth. fo. 93 v); obit, 15 May.

[3] *Records of the Templars in England...*, ed. B. A. Lees (British Academy, London, 1935), pp. 181–2. This is possibly a scribal error for Gilbert.

TREASURERS

Brian occ. 1132, 1144 (Guth. fo. 88; *CDF*, no. 1142); he seems to have been a monk (BM Harl. MS 6976, fo. 14v).

Walter occ. 1148–55, no. 318.

Reginald occ. *c.* 1154–5; probably became precentor *c.* 1155 (*CHJ*, VIII, 12). Obit, 23 February.

Ivo c. 1155–1181 or later (*CHJ*, VIII, 182; called sacrist in 1172, Guth. fo. 108). Obit, 28 August. Occ. in nos. 312–13, 315, 326.

ARCHDEACONS OF HEREFORD

Peter c. 1127–*c.* 1179 (*CHJ*, VIII, 15; he last occ. in a document of 1179, Gloucester Cathedral Reg. A, fos. 152v–3, and his successor, Ralph Foliot, became archdeacon between December 1178 and June 1182, *CHJ*, VIII, 15–16). Obit, 15 March. Occ. in nos. 310, 312–13, 315, 317–19, 326, 333.

ARCHDEACONS OF SHROPSHIRE

Peter le Kauf, canon of Lanthony, was made rector of Lydbury North and archdeacon of Shropshire by Bishop Robert de Bethune, and would appear to have resigned his archdeaconry some time before his death, which occurred during Gilbert's episcopate (*Mon.* VI, 346); but it is possible that he succeeded Odo, and died in office *c.* 1148–50.

Odo occ. 1144–8 (*CHJ*, VIII, 17).

Walter Foliot c. 1150–*c.* 1178 (*CHJ*, VIII, 17–18). Resigned *c.* 1178 (no. 271); obit, 13 August. Occ. in nos. 307, 310–12, 315, 317, 320, 326, 329, 334–6, 344; see p. 70.

CANONS
(in alphabetical order)

Master Aldred occ. 1158–63, 1173–82 (Capes, pp. 16–17, 26). For dating of documents in Capes, see *CHJ*, arts. cit.).

Master David occ. 1154–60, 1163–81 (Capes, p. 16; Guth. fos. 53, 97v–98) and in no. 313.

David de Aqua, prebendary of Moreton, occ. 1154–60, 1173; apparently dead by 1182 (Capes, pp. 16, 23, 26). Occ. in nos. 313, 344.

Master Edward occ. in no. 344.

Master Eustace occ. 1131–9, 1144 (Guth. fo. 56v); *CDF*, no. 1142; obit, 31 December. A Eustace canon occ. 1107–15 (Guth. fo. 93v), and it is possible that he is to be identified with the Master Eustace of the 1130's and 1140's.

Master Geoffrey of Clifford occ. *c.* 1150–55, Dec. 1157 (no. 333; *Cart. Gloucester*, II, 106). Occ. in nos. 312, 317, 326, 333; perhaps the Master Geoffrey of no. 344. Cf. Hugh and Robert, and p. 285.

? *Gilbert of Walford* occ. in no. 333.

Gilbert of York occ. 1132, 1145 (Guth. fos. 88, 76v).

Herbert, also bishop's chaplain, occ. 1151–5 (Capes, p. 12) and in no. 314.

? *Hugh de Caples* occ. in no. 333.

Master Hugh of Clifford occ. 1143 and before, Dec. 1157 (Giles, no. 123— cf. *CS*, pp. 264 n., 280; Guth. fo. 18; *Cart. Gloucester*, II, 106); obit, 6 February. He may be the Hugh who occ. 1132 (Guth. fo. 88); he may also have been bishop's chaplain. Occ. in nos. 311, 318–20, 331.

Hugh Foliot occ. *c.* 1154–5, 1180–2 (Capes, pp. 13–14, 24–5); obit, 25 November. Occ. in nos. 312, 331, and probably to be identified with Hugh, nephew of the bishop, nos. 334–6.

Master Hugh of Hungary occ. 1158–63 (Capes, pp. 16–17).

N. de Chandos held the prebend of Wellington in Gilbert's time (Capes, p. 16: for 'H.' read 'N.'). He was doubtless related to Robert de Chandos, founder of the prebend (Capes, pp. 16–17).

Master Nicholas occ. *c.* 1160, 1174–80, 1179–82 (charter cited *CHJ*, VIII, 183, under no. 27; Capes, p. 24; BM Harl. MS 6976, fos. 14v–15); obit, prob. 23 January. Occ. in no. 344.

Odo occ. 1158–63, *c.* 1160 (Capes, pp. 16–17; see Master Nicholas).

Osbert occ. 1144 (*CDF*, no. 1142); probably the Osbert brother of Master Richard, occ. *c.* 1154–5 (Capes, pp. 13–14).

Ralph of Ledbury occ. *c.* 1154–5 and resigned his prebend 1163–7 or in or soon after 1174 (Capes, pp. 13–14; no. 259); obit, 28 August. Occ. in nos. 259, 312, 326.

Master Ran(d)ulf occ. probably 1132, before 1139 and after 1163 (Guth. fos. 88, 56v, 53); and in nos. 313, 318, 320, 326.

Master Ranulf son of Erchemer occ. 1144 and after *c.* 1150 (*CDF*, no. 1142; no. 311); he was dead by 1182 (Capes, p. 24). His father Erchemer had been dean of Hereford (occ. 1107–15, Guth. fo. 93v); Ranulf's son Ranulf was later also a canon (occ. 1172, Guth. fo. 16; cf. Capes, pp. 24, 32). For another benefice held by him, see no. 254.

Master Richard, brother of Osbert (q.v.) occ. *c.* 1154–5 (Capes, pp. 13–14).

Richard son of the chancellor occ. 1151–5 and *c.* 1150–63 (Capes, p. 12; no. 310). A man of the same name was canon of St Paul's (Newcourt, I, 165).

Richard Foliot occ. *c.* 1155 (no. 312).

? *Richard of Westbury* occ. 1148–55 (no. 333).

Master Robert de Clare occ. 1163–7 (Cart. Lanthony, PRO C115/A1, pt. vi, no. 28); cf. no. 116.

Robert of Clifford, probably also canon of St Paul's (q.v., under Portpool) occ. *c.* 1160, 1154–80, 1188–9, *c.* 1185–*c.* 1205 (see Master Nicholas; Capes, pp. 19, 33–4, 37–8). Obit of his mother, Matilda, 12 November.

Robert Foliot, archdeacon of Oxford and later bishop of Hereford, occ. 1173 (John of Salisbury, *Epp.* ed. Giles, no. 317).

Roger occ. *c.* 1155 (no. 312).

? *Roger de Burkell'* occ. *c.* 1155–*c.* 1158 (no. 326).

Master Simon occ. 1158–63, 1173, 1186–98 (Capes, pp. 16–17, 23; Guth. fo. 21v).

Stephen occ. *c.* 1158–81 (Cart. Hereford, Bodl. MS Rawlinson B 329, fos. 17v–18).

Thomas occ. *c.* 1158–81 (*ibid.*).

Master Walter occ. in no. 307, perhaps the same as:

Master Walter de Ardep' (?=Hardeperier, see under St Paul's, canons, Wenlocksbarn) occ. *c.* 1155–*c.* 1158 (no. 326).

? *Walter de Beauchamp* occ. 1151–5 (Capes, p. 12).

Walter of Bromyard occ. *c.* 1150–55 (no. 317) and in nos. 319, 331; dead by 1163 (no. 145).

? *Walter of Clun*, bishop's chaplain, occ. 1148–54/5 (nos. 333–5; Guth. fo. 76v).

Walter de Fresne occ. 1148–55, *c.* 1160 (no. 333; see Master Nicholas).

Walter of Humber occ. *c.* 1158–81 (Guth. fo. 21).

Walter scriptor occ. 1163–81 (Guth. fos. 53, 97v–98).

William (possibly one of the following) occ. *c.* 1158–81 (Guth. fo. 21).

William Parvus occ. 1151–5 (Capes, p. 12); obit probably 11 August.

Master William of Salisbury occ. 1154–60, 1163–7 (Capes, p. 16; see Master Robert de Clare) and in no. 313. Obit, 27 February.

The following canons of Hereford witness charters of Gilbert Foliot as bishop of London:

Henry Banastre, treasurer of St Paul's (cf. no. 259; Capes, pp. 20–1; obit recorded on 11 August).

Ralph Foliot, clerk of Bishop Robert Foliot, canon of Hereford, archdeacon of Hereford, clerk in the royal chancery and royal justice (*CHJ*, VIII, 15–16).

Richard Foliot, archdeacon of Colchester, and possibly *Robert Banastre*, archdeacon of Essex (nos. 188–9).

Roger FitzMaurice, clerk of Gilbert Foliot (possibly already in no. 326); occ. as canon in 1181–6, 1201–4 (Capes, pp. 25–6, 38); obit, 13 July.

Walter Map, also canon of London (see Mapesbury); obit, 1 April.

2. ST PAUL'S CATHEDRAL CHAPTER, 1163–87

DEANS

(See C. N. L. Brooke in *BIHR*, xxix (1957), 233; *CHJ*, x, ii (1951), 129.)

Hugh de Marigny, probably related to William de Marigny, dean *c*. 1111–38, who was a nephew of Bishop Richard de Belmeis I. Hugh was archdeacon of London 1154/5–*c*. 1157/8; dean *c*. 1157/8 to 1179 or 1180 (see *JS Epp.* I, 113 n.; below, archds. London, above, p. 206); obit, 27 June.[1] Occ. in nos. 382, 399, 400, 410, 427 (1), 442.

Master Ralph de Diceto, archdeacon of Middlesex 1152–80, dean 1180–1202, died 22 November 1202 (see Stubbs, *Diceto*, I, introduction, *passim*; above, p. 206). Occ. in nos. 387, 403–7, 440, 446.

ARCHDEACONS OF LONDON

Nicholas (cf. canons, Oxgate) *c*. 1157/8–1189/90. Hugh de Marigny was archdeacon in 1157 (*JS Epp.* I, 113 n.); Nicholas by *c*. 1160 (Gibbs, no. 245; *Rep.* pp. 31b–32a, 39b; 1162 in Gibbs, nos. 192, 217), and probably by 1158, since he was restored to Henry II's favour by Becket as chancellor (*MB*, III, 26), and Becket was not in England between August 1158 and his election as archbishop. He last occ. 1189 (*PR*, *1 Richard I*, p. 11) and his successor was in office well before April 1192;[2] since Nicholas's obit was 3 November, he

---

[1] For obits, see above, p. 267 n.

[2] Archdeacon Peter occ. 1191–2 (*Cart. Colchester*, I, 88: cf. below) and he was present when Ralph de Diceto's Statute of Residence was drawn up. This was printed by Stubbs (*Diceto*, II, pp. lxix ff.) from St Paul's Liber L (MS W.D. 4), fo. 61 r–v, with the date 1192. There is some doubt, however, whether this date should not be attached to the document immediately preceding the statute in the MS. In MS W.D. 19, fo. 1, the statute is undated. But in any case there can be little doubt that it was drawn up in 1192. Fourteen canons were present when it was drawn up; eighteen subsequently gave their assent (including William of Ely, omitted from Stubbs's edition; cf. H. G. Richardson in *EHR*, LVII (1942), 132 n.). Since there were thirty prebends, at least two must have changed hands before the list was closed; and it is almost certain that we have no canon representing Wildland, and that three of the names on the second list replaced three men on the first—Richard of Ely, archdeacon of Colchester, succeeded Henry of Northampton in Kentish Town, Roger the chaplain succeeded Richard of Windsor in Oxgate, and Henry de Civitate (if he be the

probably died in 1189 or 1190. Occ. in nos. 351, 358, 379, 383–4, 391–3, 403, 405, 422, 433–4.

ARCHDEACONS OF ESSEX

Richard Rufus I before 1127–67. Brother of Richard de Belmeis II (*Rep.* p. 63 a; etc.), and therefore son of Robert de Belmeis and nephew of Bishop Richard I. Clearly related to Richard Rufus II and Richard Junior, who were brothers (see canons, Twyford, Holborn). The former succeeded him in the farm of four chapter manors and the latter, probably, in the prebend of Holborn, and it is likely that they were his sons—one of them is very likely Richard son of Richard archdeacon, occ. 1138–52 (*Rep.* p. 62a). Richard Rufus I was probably appointed by his uncle, i.e. before 1127; occ. 1132 (*Rep.* p. 67b); died between Easter and Michaelmas 1167 (*PR, 13 Henry II,* p. 154; cf. H. G. Richardson in *EHR,* LVII (1942), 128).

Robert Banastre c. 1167–after 1196. Nephew to Gilbert Foliot, studied at Bologna *c.* 1167–9 (above, pp. 48–9), occ. 1174, 1196 (no. 427; Gibbs, no. 186);[1] his successor first occ. 1204 (Gibbs, no. 58); obit,

Henry son of James of the statute, who cannot otherwise be identified) succeeded Hugh of Reculver in Reculversland. Several names in both lists establish a date later than 1190; Roger was not yet a canon in or after 1191 (*Cart. Colchester,* I, 88); Henry of Northampton was alive in August 1191; his obit was 2 April (see below), so he died in or after 1192. But Richard of Ely (two obituaries under 4 April give his full name) succeeded, as archdeacon, Ralph de Hauterive, who died in 1190–1 on crusade. Richard must have been appointed archdeacon in 1190–1 or 1192 at latest, and under the conditions then operating would normally have been given the first available vacant prebend—and since his name indicates that he was related to the bishop of the time, a long gap between his promotion to the archdeaconry and to his prebend is hardly likely. Thus a date later than 1192 for the statute is unacceptable; we may assume that Henry of Northampton died on 2 April 1192, that the statute had been drawn up a few days or weeks previously, and that the list was completed in the months which followed. We have used the list for evidence of the composition of the chapter in 1192, although it is possible that some at least of the names were added in a later year.

Archdeacon Peter is sometimes identified with Peter of Blois (archdeacon in the early thirteenth century). But there is copious circumstantial evidence against this identification and in favour of Peter of Waltham; the specific evidence of a story in one of the *Miracula* of the Blessed Virgin (cited *CHJ,* XII, ii (1956), 188) that his father was called John of Waltham establishes this identification.

[1] This is one of a group of documents (cf. below, Moorfields) which Mr H. G. Richardson has dated to 1196 (*TRHS,* 4th series, XV (1932), 79–80; *EHR,* LVII (1942), 132).

20 May. Occ. in nos. 360, 368, 381, 391, 407–9, 417, 420 A, 427 (1), 440, 444, 456, 461, 464.

ARCHDEACONS OF MIDDLESEX

Master Ralph de Diceto 1152–1180. See under deans; occ. in nos. 351, 385, 391–4, 410, 427 (1), 429, 454, 456, 461.

? *Richard Foliot* 1180–c. 1181. See under Colchester.

Gilbert Foliot c. 1181–1196/8. Presumably related to Bishop Gilbert; clerk to the bishop, canon of St Paul's (see Newington); occ. as archdeacon 1181–3, ? *c.* 1181, 1196 (no. 365; Gibbs, no. 186); his successor in his prebend, John de Garland, occ. 1196–8 (PRO Anc. Deeds, D.L. 25/220). Occ. in nos. 365, 407, 440, 451, 458, 468.

ARCHDEACONS OF COLCHESTER

William occ. only once, in 1162 (*MB Epp.* 14), and may never have existed; but there is otherwise a gap in the list of archdeacons between Ailward, died *c.* 1154 (see *JS Epp.* I, 7 n.) and Richard Foliot.

Richard Foliot 1163/7–c. 1180. Nephew of Gilbert, and so presumably appointed archdeacon after 1163; studied at Bologna (when already archdeacon) *c.* 1167–9 (see p. 48). He last occ. 2 Dec. 1178 (no. 410), and had certainly been succeeded by 1183 (see below). A Richard Foliot occ. as archdeacon of Middlesex in the prebendal catalogue under Wenlocksbarn; a note in the *Liber I* (St Paul's MS W.D. 16, fo. 32) says that Richard Foliot, archdeacon of Middlesex, was *firmarius* of the manor of Sutton; and in a thirteenth-century St Paul's obituary (known from copy in BM Harl. MS 6956, fo. 107) Richard Foliot, archdeacon of Middlesex, is noted under 26 January.[1] These documents suggest that 'Middlesex' is not a mere mistake for 'Colchester'; and the coincidence of dates and the fact that there is no entry in the obituaries or prebendal catalogue for Richard Foliot, archdeacon of *Colchester*, combine to suggest that Richard Foliot transferred from the archdeaconry of Colchester to Middlesex when Ralph de Diceto became dean in 1180. It is possible, however, that all but the first of these pieces of evidence relate to another Richard Foliot, who seems to have been archdeacon of Middlesex in the mid-thirteenth century, and who was almost certainly farmer of Sutton (MS W.D. 16, fo. 32 v). It is even possible that the catalogue has

---

[1] In *CDF* no. 434 occ. Richard Foliot, archdeacon of Middlesex; but the MS read G., clearly for Gilbert Foliot. This confusion is unlikely to have occurred in the other documents.

'Middlesex' for 'Colchester' by confusion with the later Richard Foliot, and that the earlier Richard died archdeacon of Colchester. Richard Foliot was one of the most constant witnesses of Gilbert's charters, and it is striking that he never witnesses them with the title archdeacon of Middlesex;[1] and this, combined with the evidence of no. 365 that Gilbert Foliot was archdeacon of Middlesex soon after 1180 (see p. 276 n. 1), suggests that Richard's tenure of the second archdeaconry—if he held it at all—was very short. It may be conjectured that he died on 26 January 1181,[2] and in any event he must have ceased to be archdeacon of Colchester c. 1180. Occ. in nos. 359–60, 367, 381–4, 387, 391, 394, 401, 410, 427 (1), 429, 439, 442, 444–5, 453–4, 456–7, 461, 464.

Master Ralph de Hauterive c. 1180–1190/1. Previously clerk to Gilbert Foliot, canon of St Paul's (see Caddington Major) and Master of the Schools. There is other evidence that he ceased to be Master of the Schools in 1180 or 1181 (certainly by 1183). Occ. as royal clerk and justice from 1187 to 1189,[3] went on the Third Crusade in 1189 and died at the siege of Acre in 1190 or 1191.[4] Occ. in nos. 365, 370, 440, 441, 451. For other benefices, see nos. 410–11 and above, p. 239 n.

[1] But he sometimes witnesses without the title of his archdeaconry, and in one or two of these he may have been archdeacon of Middlesex. For other evidence on the changes of 1180–1 see Broomesbury, Rugmere. These changes evidently took some months to complete, and if it is true that Ralph de Diceto held the prebend of Rugmere before transferring to Tottenham in 1180, it is interesting to note that in no. 365 Ralph of Chilton witnesses still among the clerks, with Ralph de Diceto's successor Gilbert Foliot, archdeacon of Middlesex. It is just possible that the unidentified R., archdeacon of Middlesex in 1203–4 (Gibbs, no. 137) was Richard Foliot; if so, the prebendal catalogue is in error.

[2] By 30 January 1181 Nicholas, archdeacon of London, was farmer of Sutton (Hale, p. 112).

[3] E.g. D. C. Douglas, Feudal Docts. from...Bury St Edmunds (Brit. Academy, 1932), p. 187 (1186); Feet of Fines, Pipe Roll Soc. XVII (1894), p. 3 (1189). He occ. in a document dated 1177 (Cart. Lewes, ed. L. F. Salzman, Sussex Rec. Soc. 1933–5, II, 82); but the list of judges suggests that this really belongs to a date about ten years later.

[4] Gesta Henrici II et Ricardi I, ed. Stubbs, RS, II, 147 (under 1190, but some of the men listed died in 1191); cf. Itinerarium regis Ricardi, ed. Stubbs, RS, pp. 91, 93; Diceto, II, 84—Ralph was alive on 25 July 1190. He was Gilbert's nepos: see above, p. 45 n.

TREASURERS

Godfrey 1162/3–*c.* 1170/4. Canon (see Harlesden); first treasurer of St Paul's; given the office by Bishop Richard de Belmeis II, who established it as a regular dignity in 1162–3 (Gibbs, introduction, pp. xxxv–xxxvi and refs.). Last occ. *c.* 1170 (*Rep.* p. 24a–b).

Henry Banastre occ. 1174, 1196, 1197–1202 (no. 427 (1); Gibbs, nos. 186, 285; *Rep.* p. 49a—after Richard Rufus's death: see Twyford); previously clerk to Gilbert and canon (see Willesden), also canon of Hereford and presumably related to Gilbert. His successor as treasurer (Robert du Val) occ. 1196–1212 (*EYC*, IV, 103). Obit, 12 August.[1] Occ. in nos. 358, 374, 387, 408, 427 (1), 442, 444, 461, 464.

MASTERS OF THE SCHOOLS

Master Henry ? *c.* 1160–*c.* 1179. Masters of the Schools sometimes witnessed without title, and this makes it difficult to reconstruct their careers with precision. This is made even more difficult in Master Henry's case, since there may well have been at least two Masters of the Schools of this name. Master Henry occ. as such before 1127, 1134–9, 1162–74, 1163–80, *c.* 1170–80 (Gibbs, nos. 274, 275; *Rep.* pp. 12a and 50b, 21b, 5b–6a, 13b, 24b, 25b); over the same period a Master Henry witnesses without title frequently—e.g. in nos. 354 (? canon), 391, 427 (1) (1174), 429 (cf. no. 100) (and see Hoxton). If all the references with title are to one man, he was in office at least 50 years; it seems likely therefore that there were two, and that the second held office from *c.* 1160 or before.

Master Ralph de Hauterive c. 1179–1180. Clerk of Gilbert Foliot, canon (see p. 239 and Caddington Major), Master of the Schools and archdeacon of Colchester 1180–90/1. Occ. without title 1176 or later and 2 December 1178 (nos. 358, 410);[2] it is possible that he was already Master of the Schools (see above), but as he carries the title in six episcopal documents (nos. 360, 374, 401, 411, 445, 461) and is called chancellor in one (no. 457) it is probable that he normally used it.

[1] 11 August at Hereford: see above.

[2] In neither case does position in a witness list help us to establish his status (nor is this a safe criterion: Master Henry occ. with title several times in the middle of the canons, not among the dignitaries; in one charter, *Rep.* p. 63a, he is 'Henry master' in the original, 'Master Henry' in a cart. copy). Richard of Stortford occ. twice without title when certainly in office, against about twenty references with title (Gibbs, no. 70—an original; *Cart. Clerkenwell*, ed. W. O. Hassall, Camden, 3rd series, LXXI, 1949, no. 29).

It is therefore unlikely that he was already in office in December 1178, even more unlikely that he was in office in 1176. He occ. 11 June 1180 (no. 374) and he probably became archdeacon in 1180. *Master Richard of Stortford c.* 1181[1]–1203. Clerk of Gilbert Foliot, canon (see Harlesden); occ. as Master of the Schools *c.* 1181, 1183, after 22 Nov. 1202 (nos. 388, 403; Gibbs, no. 79, *Rep.* pp. 14a, 17a, 26a–b). His successor in his office, Master John of Kent, and in his prebend, Master Gilbert, both occ. in March 1204 (Gibbs, no. 58). Richard's obit was on 20 June, so he presumably died 20 June 1203. Occ. in nos. 380, 388, 403, 405, 440, 446, 451, 458.

CANONS OF ST PAUL'S

(Arranged under prebends, and based on the prebendal catalogue, for which see Brooke in *CHJ*, x, ii (1951), 113 ff.[2] The relevant extract from the catalogue is given under each prebend, from the seventeenth-century transcript of the thirteenth-century copy in BM Harl. MS 6956, fos. 91–6; significant variants only from the (independent) fourteenth-century copy in St Paul's Cathedral archives MS W.D. 2, fos. 110–12. Our list contains only names of men likely to have held their prebends under Gilbert Foliot. Occurrences in 1192 without references are from Ralph de Diceto's Statute of Residence.)[3]

BROOMESBURY (Newcourt, I, 116–17; Harl. MS, fo. 95: Rogerus Brun, Laurentius Belesmeins, Rogerus de Wyrecestria).

Roger Brun: see *JS Epp.* I, 7 and n.

Laurence Belesmeins (? Belmeis), not otherwise known.

Master Roger of Worcester previously clerk of Gilbert Foliot, occ. (clerk) after 11 June 1180 (no. 370),[4] (either clerk or canon) 1163–76, *c.* 1179–80, *c.* 1181 (nos. 440–1), (as canon) *c.* 1181, 1222 (no. 446; also in nos. 389, 407, 468; Hale, pp. 99–100). Obit 23 March, and since

---

[1] Not before 1181 if, as seems probable, he was not yet in office in no. 365.

[2] Where, however, for Liber *B* read Liber *F*. The names of the prebends are usually given in the modern form of the place-name from which they derived, where such exists; where the official modern name is different, it is given in brackets. For the history of the names, see the relevant volumes of the English Place-Name Soc., esp. P. H. Reaney, *Place-Names of Essex* (Cambridge, 1935), pp. 229–30 (p. 230 for Reculversland); J. E. B. Gover, A. Mawer and F. M. Stenton, *Place-Names of Middlesex* (Cambridge, 1942), pp. 140–3, 146–7, 160–3 (p. 162 for Mapesbury).   [3] See above, pp. 193, 271–2 n.

[4] In deciding whether a man was clerk or canon in witness-lists where the distinction is not specified, one has to assume (where the order is not otherwise confused) that canons regularly witnessed before clerks. In no. 370 it is assumed

his successor was appointed on 25 March 1229[1] (*Cal. Patent Rolls, 1225-32*, p. 243), he probably died 23 March 1229. He seems also to have been canon of Lincoln (*Linc. Cathedral Statutes*, ed. H. Bradshaw and C. Wordsworth, II, Cambridge, 1897, p. 793). *Rep.* p. 11b, has a grant to Roger and his son Philip (cf. p. 290).

BROWNSWOOD (Newcourt, I, 116–17; Harl. MS, fo. 93v: Willelmus de Costentin, Dauid).[2]
William de Coutances (?), perhaps the William de 'Costentin' who occ. as rector of Edmonton in the mid-twelfth century in the Walden chronicle (*Essex Review*, XLV (1936), 84).
Master David of London before 1167–1189. Born in London, studied in Bologna, protégé of Gilbert Foliot, also of Roger, bishop of Worcester (see above, p. 205 and reference to article by Z. N. Brooke). Obit 31 March, and the evidence that he died in 1189 (Z. N. Brooke, *loc. cit.*) is confirmed by the fact that his successor, Brand, occ. in 1192. Occ. in nos. 360, 391–3, 427 (1), 461, 464–6.

CADDINGTON (CADINGTON) MAJOR (Newcourt, I, 124–5; Harl. MS, fo. 92v: Alexander Saccauil, Radulfus de Alta ripa).
Alexander de Saccavilla occ. 1155, after *c.* 1170 (Hale, p. 134; *Rep.* pp. 5b–6a); probably also canon of Lincoln (occ. 1147–8, *EHR*, XXXV (1920), 213 f.).
Master Ralph de Hauterive, Master of the Schools *c.* 1179–80, archdeacon of Colchester *c.* 1180–1190/1. Previously clerk of Gilbert Foliot: occ. without title (either clerk or canon) in nos. 351, 358, 376, 410, 443, 465–6.

CADDINGTON MINOR (see *CHJ*, X, ii (1951), 131–2; Newcourt, I, 129–30; Harl. MS, fo. 93: Parisius nepos Roberti Pulli).
Paris, nephew of Robert Pullen, archdeacon of Rochester, *c.* 1145–1190/2. His predecessor in the prebend occ. 1145; Paris witnesses London charters in 1145–50 and 1183 (no. 403) and apparently held his prebend till his death between 1190 and 1192 (*CHJ*, ut sup.).

that Roger of Worcester was a clerk because he follows master Nicholas of Lewknor who was never, so far as our evidence goes, a canon. The nature of the London witness-lists make such assumptions reasonable; but in many cases the distinction is probable, not certain.
[1] By the king during the vacancy of the see—in a hurry, because the vacancy was nearly over.
[2] Followed by 'Brand regis clericus'; in St Paul's MS W.D. 2, fo. 111, David follows Brand; this is certainly wrong.

CHAMBERLAINWOOD (Newcourt, I, 133; Harl. MS, fo. 94: Nicholaus).

Master Nicholas son of Clement[1] occ. before 1152, 1183 (*Rep.* p. 62a; no. 403); but as his predecessor in this prebend, Geoffrey Constable, also witnesses the former document, Nicholas may have held another prebend before Chamberlainwood. Geoffrey last occ. 1148 (*Rep.* p. 63a); Nicholas's successor, Richard de Humframville, first occ. 1192. He is very probably the Master Nicholas of nos. 359, 382–4. Obit, 13 or 14 February.

CHISWICK (Newcourt, I, 137; Harl. MS, fo. 93: Ricardus thesaurarius).

Richard FitzNeal, royal treasurer *c.* 1158–95, bishop of London, 1189–98. A reference to domain 'scotlande thesaurarii' ('of the treasurer's prebend') in Sutton, from which the prebend of Chiswick drew its income, early in 1181, seems to show that he held the prebend by then (Hale, p. 151, cf. p. 93). He may have held it many years before, since his predecessor, Richard de Amanville, occ. *c.* 1140 or a little later (*Rep.* pp. 63a, 64b; Hale, pp. 124–5). But a name may have fallen out of the list, and the gap *c.* 1140–1180 would fit Ralph de Diceto's tenure of a prebend before he became dean (see Tottenham: the alternative is Rugmere). Occ. in no. 404 (with other royal clerks).

CONSUMPTA PER MARE (Newcourt, I, 141; Harl. MS, fo. 94v: Ranulfus Patin, Ricardus archiepiscopus, Ailebertus Banastre).[2]

Ranulf Patin occ. 1138–52, 1148 (*Rep.* pp. 62a, 63a), and may be identified in some or all the references to a Canon Ran(d)ulf *c.* 1128–1145 (H. W. C. Davis in *Essays...presented to T. F. Tout*, ed. A. G. Little and F. M. Powicke, Manchester, 1925, pp. 56–7; Gibbs, no. 154); he had probably been a clerk of Richard de Belmeis I (*Vita S. Osithe* in Leland, *Itinerary*, ed. L. T. Smith, v, 169; cf. *Mod. Lang. Rev.* VI (1911), 499).

? *Richard Foliot*, archdeacon of Colchester, 1163/7–*c.* 1180 and Middlesex, 1180–*c.* 1181. Richard the arch(deacon) is almost certainly

---

[1] This identification seems highly probable, in spite of the difficulty noted in the text. All the other canons called Nicholas are satisfactorily identified, and it would be very hard to find another prebend to suit the long career of Nicholas, son of Clement, even as well as this.

[2] 'Ricardus archiepiscopus' (so both copies) is evidently a corruption for 'Ricardus archidiaconus' (perhaps due to infection from 'Turstinus archiepiscopus' above; cf. Wildland); for 'Ailebertus' read 'Gilebertus'—initial A for G occurs elsewhere in the lists.

either Richard Rufus, archdeacon of Essex, or Richard Foliot; but the former was more probably prebendary of Holborn. Richard Foliot was also prebendary of Wenlocksbarn, but there is evidence that he had previously held another prebend. Richard presumably received this prebend from Gilbert between 1163 and 1167.

Gilbert Banastre occ. 1183, 1213–16 (no. 403; Gibbs, nos. 145, 254); previously clerk of Gilbert Foliot; succeeded by Alexander of Swereford, archdeacon of Shropshire (first occ. 1217–*c.* 1221, *Rep.* p. 11 b). Occ. in nos. 361, 380, 407 (clerk or canon), 356, 403–4, 408–9, 415, 451 (canon).

EALDLAND (Newcourt, I, 144–5; Harl. MS, fo. 94: Hugo de London).
Master Hugh of London ? 1154/60–1191. His predecessor, Ailward archdeacon of Colchester, died in or soon after 1154; his successor, Laurence nephew of Pope Celestine III (1191–8), occ. 1192 (i.e. well before April 1192), and if appointed after his uncle became pope, must have received his prebend in 1191. He occ. as canon in nos. 403 (1183), 405 (1181–7), 407, 417 (1175–*c.* 1181), 464 (1175–9, prob. before 1177) and in 1183–92 (Gibbs, no. 167),[1] probably as canon also in nos. 365, 387, 420 c, 453, 461; and is most probably to be identified as the Hugh or Master Hugh who occ. *c.* 1160, 1162, 1183 (*Rep.* pp. 23 b, 39 b; Gibbs, nos. 217, 68) and in nos. 391 (1170–2), 427 (1), 429, 446 (*c.* 1181–3).

EALDSTREET (Newcourt, I, 148; Harl. MS, fo. 94v: Theodoricus iunior, Godefridus de Luci).
Theodoric Junior occ. 1128–38, 1162 (*Rep.* p. 67a: 'iuuenis'; Gibbs, no. 217; possibly earlier too, but earlier references may be to the elder Theodoric); dead by 1177 (*Rep.* p. 50b).[2]
Godfrey de Lucy: this and no. 251 (which is not, however, quite specific) are the only evidence that this curial official, son of the justiciar Richard de Lucy and bishop of Winchester, 1189–1204, was a canon (but see p. 198); but he was. certainly a pluralist, and there is no reason to doubt the catalogue. His successor, Peter of Waltham, occ.

[1] In this document Hugh of Reculver, who died in 1192, is alive; Ralph *divinus*, probably alive in 1183 (Gibbs, no. 72: Ralph *theologus*), is dead.
[2] Dated by William of Northolt, not yet archdeacon of Gloucester. The elder Theodoric occ. 1111, 1115 (*Rep.* pp. 67 b–68 a, 61 b)—in the latter year as brother of Hamo, i.e. Hamo of Rheims, predecessor of Theodoric junior at Ealdstreet. This coincidence suggests the possibility that Theodoric junior, like several other canons of his generation, was his predecessor's son.

soon after 1189, when Godfrey became bishop, and was later archdeacon of London (see above, p. 272 n.).

HARLESDEN (HARLESTON) (Newcourt, I, 151–2; Harl. MS, fo. 94:
Godefridus thesaurarius, Ricardus de Storteford).
Godfrey, treasurer of St Paul's 1162/3–*c.* 1170–4.
Master Richard of Stortford, previously clerk of Gilbert Foliot (occ. 1174),
    canon from *c.* 1174—certainly by 1176 (no. 427 (2))—Master of the
    Schools *c.* 1181–1203. Occ. as clerk or canon in nos. 351, 358, 365,
    368, 370, 381, 417, 420 c, 438, 461–2, as canon in nos. 360, 387, 393,
    410, 427 (2), 442, 444, 464 (in some of these he may already have
    been Master of the Schools, q.v.). For his prebend cf. Gibbs, no. 103.

HOLBORN (HOLBOURN) (Newcourt, I, 156; Harl. MS, fo. 91v:
Ricardus nepos ⟨episcopi⟩ archid(iaconus?) [arch': St Paul's MS
W.D. 2, fo. 110], Ricardus iunior).
Richard Rufus I, archdeacon of Essex, before 1127–67. This identi-
    fication seems almost certain: it places Richard Rufus between his
    predecessor as archdeacon of Essex and Richard Junior, who may well
    have been his son (see above, p. 272) and succeeded a few years
    before 1171; if it is rejected, Richard Rufus I's career has to be spread
    over three prebends. If we emend the catalogue as suggested above,
    the identification presents no difficulties: his brother Richard de
    Belmeis II appears in Caddington Major as 'Ricardus nepos episcopi
    frater Ricardi'.
Richard Junior (see above) occ. 1164–71,[1] 1212–13 (Gibbs, nos. 169,
    255, 263); obit, 22 (or 23) April, presumably in 1213 or 1214, since
    he is referred to as dead in 1214 (*Curia Regis Rolls*, VII, 138). Brother
    of Richard Rufus II (Twyford), held office of chamberlain (*Rep.*
    p. 17a; Gibbs, no. 168). Occ. in nos. 392, 403.

HOLYWELL (FINSBURY) (Newcourt, I, 159; Harl. MS, fo. 96: Robertus
filius Generanni, magister Radulfus, Walterus precentor).
Robert son of Generannus, brother of Hugh (see Willesden; Gibbs, no.
    245), occ. 1114, *c.* 1160, 1162 (Hale, pp. 127–8, *Rep.* pp. 31b–32a,
    64b; Gibbs, no. 217).
Master Ralph occ. 1174, 1170–6, 1183 (nos. 427 (1), 392; Gibbs, no. 69—
    but the two former could be for Ralph de Hauterive); he is probably
    to be identified with Master Ralph Theologus, who occ. 1183 (no.

---

[1] Peter, abbot of Quarr, had been succeeded by 1171 (L. Voss, *Heinrich von Blois*, 1932, p. 175).

403), obit, 13 or 14 (or 15) February, and possibly with Master Ralph Divinus, occ. 1162–74, dead by 1192 (*Rep.* p. 12a; Gibbs, no. 167).

Walter FitzWalter, precentor of St Paul's.[1] Clerk of Gilbert Foliot at least as late as 1183–4 (no. 404); occ. as canon and precentor 1192, late 1198 (Diceto, II, 165); died 21 September (BM Cotton MS Nero C. ix, fo. 12), probably in 1203 (since his successor as precentor, Master Benedict of Sawston, took office between November 1202 and March 1204: Gibbs, nos. 79, 137, 58, cf. 49).

HOXTON (Newcourt, I, 162–3; Harl. MS, fo. 95: Hugo archidiaconus, Henricus filius eius, Iohannes Cumin, Robertus de Camera).

Henry son of Archdeacon Hugh (of Middlesex)[2] is probably to be identified with the Master Henry who was Master of the Schools ? *c.* 1160–*c.* 1179, who cannot otherwise be identified in the catalogue, and possibly with the Henry of London of *JS Epp.* 5.

John Cumin is presumably to be identified with the royal clerk and pluralist who was elected archbishop of Dublin in September 1181 and consecrated in 1182 (on him see J. Armitage Robinson, *Somerset Hist. Essays* (London, 1921), pp. 90–9, esp. p. 98).

Master Osbert de Camera occ. 1184,[3] after November 1202 (Gibbs, no. 79; *Rep.* p. 26a), and it is almost certain that 'Robertus de Camera' in the catalogue is a corruption for 'Osbertus'. Obit, 14 May, probably in 1203.[4] Occ., possibly not yet canon, *c.* 1181, in no. 387; and a

---

[1] The precentorship does not seem to have become a properly endowed dignity until *c.* 1204 (cf. Gibbs, no. 58; Brooke in *A History of St Paul's Cathedral*, pp. 71–2, 362). A canon called Leofgar occ. called *cantor* in 1104 (*Rep.* p. 61 b); clerks of Gilbert called Nicholas and Ralph occ. called *cantor* (see below). It is not certain in all these cases that the word is a title rather than a nickname; but Ralph is three times called precentor, and doubtless performed the functions of precentor. He seems never to have become a canon. He was doubtless succeeded in his functions by Walter FitzWalter; but there is no evidence of a normally constituted office before 1204 (cf. the similar story of the treasurership, above, p. 275; the mastership of the schools also grew into the chancellorship in this period). Cf. Gibbs, pp. xxxi ff. Walter was son of Walter FitzRobert (BM Harl. MS 662, fos. 11 v–12).

[2] Hugh (a protégé of Bishop Gilbert the Universal) took the archdeaconry to which Richard de Belmeis II had been presented as a boy, and was finally ousted by Richard in 1138 (Diceto, I, 251 f.).   [3] BM Harl. MS 6956, fo. 84.

[4] Since he was succeeded by Peter of Blois, who became archdeacon of London in that year, when Archdeacon Alard of Burnham succeeded Ralph de Diceto as dean (Ralph died 22 November 1202). The Osbert de Camera said to have died on 3 May 1201 (cf. *Bull. John Rylands Library*, XXXIX (1956–7), 400) was presumably a different man, unless the date is wrongly given in Thorne's chronicle (but cf. art. cit. pp. 401–2 n.).

man of the same name witnessed a charter of Bishop Richard Peche of Coventry in 1181–2 (*Facs. of Early Cheshire Charters*, ed. G. Barraclough, Lancs and Ches. Rec. Soc. 1957, p. 22).

ISLINGTON (Newcourt, I, 165; Harl. MS, fo. 95 v: Iohannes episcopus Cicestr(ensis), Richerus [Nitherus, St Paul's MS W.D. 2, fo. 111 v] de Andeli, Robertus Banastr' archidiaconus).

John of Greenford, dean of Chichester 1147/50–1173, bishop-elect 1173–4, bishop 1174–80 (see H. Mayr-Harting, *Acta of the bishops of Chichester*, Cant. and York Soc. 1964, pp. 12 f., 85 f.; idem, *The Bishops of Chichester, 1075–1207* (Chichester, 1963), pp. 12–14). The catalogue is the only evidence for his connexion with St Paul's, but there is no reason to doubt it, and he presumably held the prebend from the promotion of his predecessor, Robert II, to be bishop of Exeter in 1155 to his own promotion, i.e. to 1173 or 1174.[1]

Richer de Andelys is clearly to be identified with Richer, precentor of Rouen, who occ. as canon of St Paul's in no. 417 (1175–*c.* 1181). He became precentor in 1175 or 1176 and occ. as such in 1177 (*Cartulaire de...Pontoise*, ed. J. Depoin, Pontoise, 1895, pp. 139, 145–6; L. de Glanville, *Hist. du prieuré de Saint-Lô de Rouen*, II, Rouen, 1891, p. 326). For his name, cf. J. F. Pommeraye, *Hist. de l'abbaye de S. Amand de Rouen* (Rouen, 1662), p. 84. Obit, 22 February (*Recueil des historiens des Gaules et de la France*, XXIII (Paris, 1876), 360).

Robert Banastre was archdeacon of Essex *c.* 1167–after 1196, and so presumably held another prebend (which cannot be identified) before succeeding to Islington on Richer's death or resignation.

KENTISH TOWN (CANTLERS) (Newcourt, I, 169; Harl. MS, fo. 92: Hubertus Vacca, Henricus de Norhamton).

Hubert Vacca is presumably to be identified with the Hubert who occ. 1115, *c.* 1160 (*Rep.* pp. 61 b, 23 b, 31 b–32 a, etc.; his predecessor Audoen became bishop of Evreux in 1113).

Master Henry of Northampton (al. *Pium*, cf. Gibbs, no. 138) occ. 1178 and later (no. 410; also in nos. 379, 387, 393, 403, 405, 415, 417; and as either clerk of Gilbert Foliot or canon in nos. 351, 370, 385, 420 & c, 465–6). Alive August 1191 (*Epistolae Cantuarienses*, ed. W. Stubbs, RS, p. 343); obit, 2 April; since he and his successor (Richard of Ely)

---

[1] In the later Middle Ages a bishop surrendered his former benefices on consecration, but it is clear that this was not the invariable, perhaps not the normal practice in the twelfth century: cf. Geoffrey, son of King Henry II, at Mapesbury.

both occ. in the Statute of Residence, he presumably died 2 April 1192.[1] Apparently taught in the school at St Paul's (above, p. 198); founded the almonry hospital (Gibbs, nos. 131, 308). Probably to be identified with the H. of N. who was an envoy of Henry II in 1168 (*MB Epp.* 395) and witnessed charters of Roger bishop of Worcester and Baldwin archbishop of Canterbury (H. Mayr-Harting in *Studies in Eccl. History*, II, forthcoming); but not with the man who witnessed a charter of Archbishop Hubert Walter and was a royal justice in 1203 (*Hist. Collections for Staffs*, William Salt Soc. III, 79); or the H. son of P. of Northampton who took over the care of the Hospital of St Thomas, Northampton, *c.* 1200 (BM Addit. Charter, 22, 380).

MAPESBURY (Newcourt, I, 173; Harl. MS, fo. 95 v: Baldewynus, Gaufredus filius regis, Walterus Map).

Baldwin occ. 1138–42, 1163–8 (*Rep.* p. 68 a; no. 196).

Geoffrey, illegitimate son of King Henry II, seems to have resigned his prebend when he became bishop-elect of Lincoln in 1173 (Map, *De nugis curialium*, ed. M. R. James, Oxford, 1914, p. 248; cf. revised edn., NMT, forthcoming, introd.). He resigned Lincoln in 1181, was elected archbishop of York in 1189 and died in 1212 (on him see esp. Stubbs's introd. to Roger of Hoveden, *Cronica*, RS, IV).

Master Walter Map ? 1173–1208/10 (see above: he still held the pre-bend, to which he apparently gave his name, in 1192, and presumably held it to his death between 1208 and 1210; obit, 1 April—see Hereford). Previously clerk of Gilbert Foliot; royal clerk and justice; canon, chancellor and precentor of Lincoln; archdeacon of Oxford from 1197; canon of Hereford; etc.; famous as author of *De nugis curialium* (see introd. to revised edn.). Occ. in no. 439 as clerk or canon.

MOORFIELDS (MORA) (Newcourt, I, 176–7; Harl. MS, fo. 96: Henricus filius Roberti episcopi).

Henry son of Bishop Robert 1142/50–*c.* 1196. His predecessor, William of Calne, occ. 1142; Henry was presumably appointed by his father before 1150, and occ. *c.* 1160, 1192, 1192–6; his successor, Alan the Chaplain of Bishop Richard FitzNeal, apparently became a canon in 1196 (*Rep.* p. 67 b; Gibbs, no. 245; *Rep.* p. 15 a; cf. *Rep.* p. 33 a, Gibbs, nos. 103, 183, 186—Alan, chaplain, not canon—and Gibbs, no. 285; *Trans. Royal Hist. Soc.* 4th series, XV, 79—chaplain *and* canon).

[1] See above, pp. 271–2 n.

NEASDEN (NESDEN) (Newcourt, I, 183; Harl. MS, fo. 91 v: Willelmus de Ver episcopus Herfordensis, Willelmus de Norhale episcopus Wigorniensis, Radulfus Foliot archidiaconus Herfordiensis).

William de Vere, son of Aubrey de Vere, Master Chamberlain, and brother of the first earl of Oxford, clerk of Archbishop Theobald; occ. as canon 26 May 1162 (Gibbs, no. 217), and apparently became a canon regular at St Osyth shortly afterwards; later bishop of Hereford (1189–98: on him see *JS Epp.* I, 217 n.; *CP*, X, Appendix J, pp. 114–15; Saltman, p. 216; Leland, *Itinerary*, ed. L. T. Smith, V, 167 ff., giving extracts from his *Life of St Osyth*; cf. A. T. Baker in *Mod. Lang. Rev.* VI (1911), 476 ff.; cf. no. 382 n.).

Master William of Northolt (*Northall*), clerk of Archbishop Theobald (Saltman, p. 216), and later (1175–86) of Archbishops Richard and Baldwin (whose charters he frequently witnesses); archdeacon of Gloucester, 1177–86 (ann. Tewkesbury and Worcester, *Ann. Mon.* I, 52–3; IV, 384–5); bishop of Worcester, 1186–90. Occ. as canon in nos. 382 (1163–73), 420 (1173–7), 403 (1183) (also *c.* 1160–70 in Hale, pp. 138–9; *Rep.* pp. 12a, 39b, 50b; he retained his interest in St Paul's after returning to the archbishop's service, witnessing no. 403 and Gibbs, no. 243, 1180–6, and farming the chapter manor of Drayton—occ. as farmer in 1181, Hales, p. 112).

Ralph Foliot, archdeacon of Hereford *c.* 1180–1198 (see above, pp. 268, 270); presumably canon of St Paul's, *c.* 1186–98; occ. 1192, and in nos. 410 (as canon of Hereford in 1178) and 404 (as royal *sigillarius* in 1183–4).

NEWINGTON (i.e. Stoke Newington) (Newcourt, I, 186–7; Harl. MS, fo. 95: Walterus filius Ricardi episcopi, Gilebertus Foliot).

Walter de Belmeis, son of Bishop Richard de Belmeis I, before 1127–after 1148 (occ. frequently as Walter brother of Archdeacon William, who was certainly son of Richard de Belmeis I—e.g. *Rep.* p. 24a; no doubt collated by his father, and occ. ? before 1127, Hale, p. 124; last occ. 1148–55, *Rep.* p. 68a). He may well have survived into Gilbert Foliot's episcopate; but there are no references to him later than 1152, and a name may have fallen out of the list.

Gilbert Foliot, clerk of his namesake, occ. as canon 1174–80, 1175–9, 1178, 11 June 1180 (nos. 442, 464, 410, 374; also in nos. 360, 393; and —clerk or canon—in nos. 351, 376, 385, 401, 417); archdeacon of Middlesex *c.* 1181–1197/8.

OXGATE (Newcourt, I, 189–90; Harl. MS, fo. 94v: Nicholaus Croce-mannus, Nicolaus filius eius archidiaconus London.).
Nicholas archdeacon of London *c.* 1156/8–1189/90. The catalogue helps to establish the following pedigree:

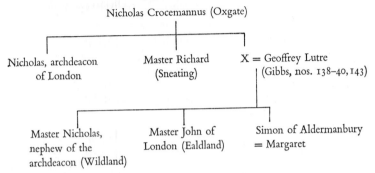

PORTPOOL (Newcourt, I, 198; Harl. MS, fo. 93: Gilebertus nepos archidiaconi, Robertus de Clifford).
Gilbert nephew of the archdeacon is otherwise unknown—possibly related to Theobald, archdeacon of Essex, who heads the Portpool list. He may be the Master Gilbert of nos. 383–4, 391 (1163–72, 1170–2), but his successor also witnesses no. 391; his predecessor, Robert brother of Geoffrey son of Wulfred, occ. 1145 (Gibbs, no. 154).
Robert of Clifford, previously clerk of Gilbert Foliot, occ. 1170–2, 1183, 1184, 1204–15 (nos. 391, 403, 379; Gibbs, no. 168; also occ., clerk or canon, in nos. 354, 417, 438, 440); probably also canon of Hereford; possibly related to the marcher lord Walter of Clifford.

RECULVERSLAND (Newcourt, I, 202; Harl. MS, fo. 92: Hugo Rac').
Hugh of Reculver (who apparently gave his name to the prebend) *c.* 1162–1192. Succeeded Thomas Becket ('Sanctus Thomas de Lond''), presumably on his consecration to Canterbury; occ. 1182, ? 1180–1, 1192 (Gibbs, no. 220; *Cart. Clerkenwell,* ed. W. O. Hassall, Camden 3rd series, LXXI, 1949, no. 319); apparently both he and his successor occ. in 1192.[1] Occ. in no. 405 (*c.* 1181–7).

RUGMERE (Newcourt, I, 206; Harl. MS, fo. 95v: Radulfus de Chilton, Iohannes Wyting).

[1] See above, pp. 271–2 n.; the document in *Cart. Clerkenwell* is not later than 1181 if Richard of Stortford (who occ. without title) was not yet Master of the Schools.

There seems to be a gap between William son of Ralph son of Algod (? occ. 1138–55, *Rep.* p. 64a–b) and Ralph of Chilton, who became canon *c.* 1180. This would neatly fit Ralph de Diceto's career before he became dean (see Tottenham).[1]

Ralph of Chilton (possibly from Chilton Foliat; see p. 45), previously clerk of Gilbert Foliot, occ. as such in or after 1180, i.e. *c.* 1181 (nos. 365, 440–1, 446); occ. as canon 1183, 1186–7 (nos. 403, 408; also in nos. 356, 362, 379, 389, 404–5, 415, 451, 468; and as clerk or canon in nos. 351, 361, 380, 407, 420 c, 465–6).

Master John Witing, previously clerk of Gilbert Foliot, occ. 1192, after 1218, 1222–3 (Gibbs, nos. 81, etc.; Newcourt, II, 675); obits of his father, William, and his mother, Pollicia, on 1 September and 23 August. He was still a clerk in or after 1189 (C. R. Cheney, *English Bishops' Chanceries*, p. 156) and so was evidently collated by Gilbert's successor.

ST PANCRAS (ST PANCRATIUS) (Newcourt, I, 193–4; Harl. MS, fo. 93 v: Willelmus de Belemeis).

William de Belmeis c. 1162–1183/92. Son of Robert de Belmeis and nephew of Bishop Richard II (Gibbs, no. 69); his predecessor, John of Canterbury, became bishop of Poitiers in 1162 (above, p. 207); William was probably collated before his uncle's death in the same year. He occ. 1163–72, 1183 (nos. 383–4, 403; also in nos. 392, 402, 405, 427 (1)). His successor, John of St Lawrence, occ. 1192. For his prebend, see no. 403.

SNEATING (Newcourt, I, 209; Harl. MS, fo. 92: Ricardus filius Nicholai).

Master Richard son of Nicholas occ. *c.* 1160, 1180–90 (Gibbs, no. 245; *Rep.* p. 13 a); his successor, Master Edmund (of Southwell) occ. 1192. He may be the Master Richard who occ. in nos. 383–4, 427 (1) (but this is possibly Richard of Stortford). He was brother of Nicholas, archdeacon of London (*Rep.* pp. 12a, 13a; etc.), and so was evidently son of Nicholas Crocemannus (see Oxgate).

TOTTENHAM (i.e. Tottenham Court) (TOTENHALL) (Newcourt, I, 212–13; Harl. MS, fo. 91: Hugo de Mareni, Radulfus de Diceto).

---

[1] Another 'Radulfus' could easily have fallen out of the list; but it is odd that this should happen to the celebrated Ralph de Diceto, and it is perhaps more probable that it was common practice to enter a canon on his death or departure; hence any other prebend he had held would easily be overlooked.

The list of prebendaries of Tottenham in this period is a list of the deans: see *CHJ*, x, 129 ff.; it is not known which prebends Hugh de Marigny and Ralph de Diceto held before they became dean—cf. Chiswick, Ealdland and Rugmere for suggestions.

TWYFORD (East Twyford in Willesden) (TWIFORD) (Newcourt, I, 216; Harl. MS, fo. 93 v: Ricardus pa⟨r⟩uus Rufus—'pauus' *in both MSS*).

Richard Rufus II, brother of Richard Junior (Holborn), probably son of Richard Rufus I, archdeacon of Essex; his predecessor, Robert of Caen, last occ. 1145; he was very likely appointed by his uncle (?) Bishop Richard II, i.e. between 1152 and 1162; occ. *c.* 1162–74, 1196 (Gibbs, no. 154; *Rep.* pp. 12a, 50b; Gibbs, nos. 103, 186). Obit, 18 January; died in or before 1202 (*Rep.* p. 49a). He succeeded Richard Rufus I as farmer of the chapter manors of Barling, 'Adulvesnasa' (The Sokens), Belchamp and Runwell, and also farmed Thorpe, Navestock and Sandon (Hale, pp. 14–15, 40–1, 65–6, 70–1, 79, 111, 129). Occ. in nos. 392, 417, and may possibly be the Richard de Belmeis, canon, of no. 427 (1) (otherwise unidentified and possibly due to corruption).

WENLOCKSBARN (Newcourt, I, 219; Harl. MS, fo. 92 v: Walterus Berdeperier (*sic both MSS*), Ricardus Foliot archidiaconus Midd., Robertus Folet).

Master Walter of Hartpury (Glos.) (Hardeperier, Hardepirer: in spite of corruption in the catalogue, the identification seems reasonably certain), probably clerk of Gilbert Foliot as bishop of Hereford, occ. as clerk or canon 1163–72 (no. 439) and may be the Master Walter of nos. 241 (who was dead by 1179), 382 (1163–73) and of no. 241 (1163–79). His predecessor, Master Alberic, last occ. 1162 (Gibbs, no. 217: see above, p. 198).

Richard Foliot, archdeacon of Colchester 1163/7–c. 1180 and Middlesex 1180–c. 1181 (?) (see under Colchester). Since he occ. in no. 439 with Walter of Hartpury he presumably held another prebend before Wenlocksbarn: see Consumpta per Mare.

Robert Folet occ. 1183–4 (no. 404), 1192; also in nos. 356, 389, 404, 407–9, 468 (in 1192 he is called 'Foliot'—*sic* MS: there is no doubt that the names were distinct and that this is a scribal error). His successor, Ralph of Neville, became bishop of Chichester in 1222–4. See p. 211 n.

WILDLAND (WELDLAND) (Newcourt, I, 224; Harl. MS, fo. 91 v: Walterus de Dunstanuill. (dunfranuile, St Paul's MS W.D. 2, fo. 110), Valterus de Insul(a), Nicolaus nepos archiepiscopi—*sic both MSS*).

Walter de Dunstanuil (or d'Unfranuile: cf. Chamberlainwood) is not otherwise known; his predecessor, Geoffrey brother of Robert son of Wulfred, last occ. 1145 (Gibbs, no. 145).

Walter de Insula is possibly to be identified with the royal clerk and justice of that name, who occ. *c.* 1163–*c.* 1176 (R. W. Eyton, *Court, Household and Itinerary of King Henry II*, index, *s.v.* Insula; L. Delisle, *Recueil des actes de Henri II*..., Introduction, Paris, 1909, p. 468). His successor, Nicholas, nephew of the archdeacon,[1] before he became canon, occ. in 1169 (?), 1183 (Gibbs, nos. 134, 69; also in no. 398), and as canon (probably) in 1202–3 (Gibbs, no. 135). See below.

WILLESDEN (WILSDEN) (Newcourt, I, 227–8; Harl. MS, fo. 92 v: Hugo filius Generanni, Henricus thesaurarius).

Hugh son of Generannus occ. 1115, *c.* 1160 (*Rep.* p. 61 b; Gibbs, no. 245); brother of Robert son of G. (Holywell), father of Richard son of Hugh son of G. (Hale, p. 135).

Henry Banastre, doubtless collated by his relative, Gilbert Foliot; occ., clerk or canon, 1163–74 (no. 385), treasurer of St Paul's, occ. 1174, after 1197. Also canon of Hereford.

UNIDENTIFIED (the following canons cannot be assigned to their prebends).

John de Marigny occ. *c.* 1169–76 (no. 442; cf. *Rep.* p. 33 b).

Master Walter of Witney, previously clerk of Gilbert Foliot; rector of St Leonard, Shoreditch (no. 404); occ. as clerk in 1186–7 (no. 389); as canon 1186–7 (nos. 408–9) and *c.* 1191–2 (Westminster Abbey, Domesday Cart. fo. 617v).[2] Obit, 5 December.

William archdeacon of Colchester (q.v.).

3. CLERKS AND CHAPLAINS[3]

AS BISHOP OF HEREFORD

Ambrose, no. 317 (? canon); no doubt Ambrose the glossator, of no. 106 —who was also very likely Master Ambrose the Roman lawyer,

---

[1] Cf. Consumpta per Mare; on him see Oxgate.

[2] Unless he was prebendary of Wildland, he was presumably dead by 1192 (cf. pp. 271–2 n.).

[3] It is far from clear that there was any distinction between a clerk and a chaplain in Gilbert's household. On the whole, the title chaplain seems to have died out in his later years. In contrast, chaplains and clerks seem to be clearly

later clerk of the abbot of St Albans and adviser to Richard of Anstey (*JS Epp.* I, 269).

Master Geoffrey, nos. 320, 325.

Gilbert, nos. 311–12, 320 (? also canon).

? *Gilbert* the monk, no. 307.

Herbert, canon and chaplain, Capes, p. 12.

Hugh, nos. 299, 307, 312; possibly Hugh of Clifford, who may be chaplain in no. 311 (see canons).

Ivo, no. 320.

? *Louis,* no. 307 (see London).

? *Ralph,* no. 332; possibly Ralph scriptor (no. 326) and/or Ralph de Wycherch' (no. 329).

Roger, nos. 307, 317, 320, 325; possibly Roger FitzMaurice (no. 326; see London; canons of Hereford).

Walter, chaplain, no. 313; possibly Walter of Clun or of Hartpury (no. 299; see canons of Hereford, London, Wenlocksbarn).

Walter of Clun, see canons.

William, chaplain, no. 319.

AS BISHOP OF LONDON

(references in which it is uncertain whether a man was clerk or canon are collected under canons)

? *Benjamin,* nos. 360, 381, 401.

David, chaplain, nos. 356, 398, 455.

? *Master Eraclius,* 360, 381.

Fulk, no. 383.

Gilbert Banastre, nos. 395, 432, 462; possibly the Gilbert of nos. 362, 422 (canon, Consumpta per Mare).

Gilbert Foliot I (canon, Newington, and archdeacon of Middlesex).

Gilbert Foliot II, nos. 408–9 (1186–7).

? *Helias,* no. 420.

Henry Banastre, nos. 412, 420 A (canon, Willesden, and treasurer).

Henry Foliot, nos. 359, 408–9.

Master Henry of Northampton, nos. 359, 383–4 (canon, Kentish Town).

Hugh, nos. 384, 439; possibly Hugh of London (canon, Ealdland).

distinguished grades in the witness lists to the charters of his successor at London, Richard FitzNeal. There are numerous doubtful cases in this list; we only accept a group of witness lists, or some other evidence, as unambiguous testimony that a 'clerk' was a member of the *familia*. Dates are not given unless they have some special significance.

?John, nos. 361, 383–4, 401, 465–6.
? Master John Hierteshorn, chaplain, no. 359.
?John de Hospitali, no. 412.
?John Storcestr', no. 356.
?John of Tilbury, nos. 394–5, 444.
Master John Witing, nos. 356, 360–2, 365, 370, 374, 380, 389, 395, 398, 403–4, 408–9, 411, 415, 420 C, 440–1, 445–6, 461, 468 (all *c.* 1179–87 except 395, 420 C, 1163– *c.* 1180, 398, 1163–87) (canon, Rugmere).
Louis of Landon, no. 394; probably the same as Louis (cf. nos. 394–5), nos. 351, 375, 384, 395, 412, 438–9, 444, 468 (see Hereford).
? Master Maurice, no. 358; possibly Maurice of Sawbridgeworth, nos. 375, 439.
Milo Folet, nos. 393, 410, 438, 442.
Nicholas, chaplain, no. 398; cantor,[1] no. 462; Master Nicholas, no. 374.
? Master Osbert, no. 358; Master Osbert of St Albans, no. 360.
? Master Payne, no. 362.
? Master Peter of Waltham, no. 387 (later canon, Ealdstreet, and archdeacon of London).
? Philip of Worcester, no. 445 (cf. p. 277).
? Ralph Brito (? layman), no. 398.
Master Ralph cantor, nos. 361–2, 374 (precentor), 380–1, 395, 403, 408–9, 411 (precentor), 415, 432, 438, 440–1, 445–6, 461, 465–6, 468 (precentor).
Ralph of Chilton, nos. 358, 360, 365, 376, 385, 393, 401, 410, 412, 420 A, 432, 438, 440–4, 446, 461 (canon, Rugmere).
Master Ralph de Hauterive, nos. 427 (1, 2), 442 (1174, 1176, 1174–80) (canon, Caddington Major, Master of the Schools and archdeacon of Colchester).
? Ralph of London, no. 462.
? Reginald Folet, no. 445.
Richard, chaplain, nos. 359, 384 (clerk).
? Richard Aguillun, nos. 442, 465–6.
Richard Banastre, nos. 360–1, 370, 380, 398, 401, 403, 411, 440–1, 445–6 (all possibly later than *c.* 1179).
? Richard of Barking, no. 462.
Richard Foliot (not the same as the archdeacon of Colchester and Middlesex), nos. 361, 380, 398.
Richard of Salisbury (see p. 214), nos. 351, 354, 358, 360–1, 365, 374–5, 380–1, 383, 385, 393–5, 398, 401, 403, 410–12, 415, 420 C, 427 (1, 2),

---

[1] Presumably meaning 'precentor': but see above, p. 281 n.

432, 438–43, 445–6, 461–2 (none can be proved earlier than 1172 or later than 1183).

Master Richard of Stortford, nos. 392, 412, 417 (?), 420 A, 427 (1) (1174) (canon, Harlesden, Master of the Schools).

Robert, chaplain, no. 356.

? *Brother Robert de Broi, Broy* (? Cluniac monk and prior of Lenton, see no. 147), 375, 394–5.

Robert of Clifford, nos. 383–4, 439 (canon, Portpool).

Robert Foliot, nos. 395, 404, 408, 468.

? *Master Robert of Kent,* no. 360.

Robert Uscarl, Huscarl, nos. 382, 391 n.; *MB,* III, 82.[1]

? *Roger,* no. 383; Master Roger, no. 427 (1).

? *Roger the chamberlain* occ. among clerks in no. 395; but probably a layman.

Roger FitzMaurice, nos. 376, 385, 392, 410, 412, 438, 442, ? 443–4 (see Hereford; canon Hereford).

Roger of Hereford, nos. 375, 394–5 (see p. 197).

Master Roger of Worcester, nos. 360, 370, 381, 395, 401, 411, 445, 461–2 (canon, Broomesbury).

? *Master Sampson,* nos. 427 (2), 462.

? *Simon,* no. 361.

Stephen Walensis, nos. 362, 409, 468.

Thomas Bartholde, no. 415 (? error for Brito).

Thomas Brito, nos. 389, 395, 404, 432, 468.

Walter, chaplain, nos. 356, 359; ? clerk, no. 422; ? scriptor, no. 410.

? *Walter son of Robert,* no. 411.

Walter the almoner, nos. 351, 360, 375, 381, 401, 411–12, 438, 440–1, 443–6, 461, 465–6 (none later than *c.* 1181).

Walter FitzWalter, nos. 362, 404, 432 (canon, Holywell, and precentor).

? *Master Walter of Hartpury* (canon, Wenlocksbarn).

Master Walter Map, no. 439 (canon, Mapesbury).

Master Walter of Witney (Oxon., or Whitney, Herefs.), nos. 356, 389, 404, 468 (canon, unidentified).

? *William,* no. 361.

? *William of Barnes,* no. 375.

? *William de Carnamuilla,* no. 415.

? *William of Ely,* no. 417.

? *Zacharias* scriptor, 395, 468.

[1] Given by FitzStephen as Gilbert's agent in managing the churches of exiled clerks.

4. SECULAR OFFICIALS

HEREFORD

It is possible that some of the following may have been Gilbert's officials: Ralph the butler (no. 330), William the constable (no. 318), Ilbert *dapifer* (no. 318), Walclin *dapifer* (no. 334). William Folet was one of his serjeants (nos. 312, 320); no. 312 has a group of his 'mancipia', including Robert the dispenser, Robert the butler and Reginald the chamberlain; no. 309 relates to the son of Robert, his vine-dresser at Ledbury, who was a villein.

LONDON

SENESCHALS (OR STEWARDS)

Gilbert[1] *Foliot*, occ. 1171–2 (*MB*, II, 149–50: cf. p. 41).
William Foliot, occ. 1167–74, 1181–7 (nos. 420 A, 376, 405, 451).
? *Osbert*, occ. *c.* 1179–80, ? 1180–7 (nos. 360–1).
William of Pontefract (Punfret), occ. 1186–7 (no. 409; cf. no. 245); 'constable' in *PR 33 Henry II*, p. 29.

MARSHAL

? *William*, occ. ? *c.* 1181–7 (no. 361).

CHAMBERLAINS

Reginald occ. in nos. 375 (1173–4), 376, 403, 408 (1186–7), 415, 432, 440–2, 446, 451.
Roger occ. in nos. 361 (probably after 1180), 394 (1163–80), 395 (before *c.* 1180).
Although they do not witness together, it looks as if Reginald and Roger may have held office together.

BUTLER

Robert Parage occ. in nos. 409, 415 (1186–7, *c.* 1181–7), and without title in nos. 408 (1186–7), 432 (before *c.* 1180).

DISPENSERS

Ralph, nos. 394–5 (1163–80, before *c.* 1180).
Reginald, nos. 409, 415 (1186–7, *c.* 1181–7).

[1] But he is called William in one MS, according to Robertson, and so may well be identical with William Foliot.

OTHER OFFICIALS

Cook: William, no. 397.
Forester: Thurstan, no. 409.
Hostiarius: Gilbert, no. 442; Roger, no. 441.
Piscator: Jocelin, no. 417.
For other serjeants and vassals, see *GFL*, index.

INDEX

The following abbreviations are used: abb. = abbot, abbey; abp. = archbishop; archd. = archdeacon; bp. = bishop; can. = canon; card. = cardinal; chanc. = chancellor; clk. = clerk (i.e. clerk or chaplain of Gilbert Foliot); d. = dean; H. = Hereford; k. = king; L. = London (St Paul's); pr. = prior, priory; prec. = precentor; treas. = treasurer.

Office-holders are indexed under their names, but cross-references are given for bishops, abbots, etc., under the name of their church; this is not normally done for cathedral dignitaries, since it would involve extensive repetition of lists in Appendix IV. Prebends of St Paul's are collected under London.

Page-references alone are given for entries in both text and notes on the same page.